Date Due

MAR 2 8 1986			
AUG 3 1 1986			
APR 2 0 1993			
MAY 1 1 1993			
AUG 2 0 '93			
DEC 1 0 1996			
9/4/97			
JUN 2 9 2004			
OCT 0 5 2004			

BRODART, INC.   Cat. No. 23 233   Printed in U.S.A.

GRANT PROPOSALS
THAT SUCCEEDED

Nonprofit Management and Finance

Series Editor: **VIRGINIA WHITE**

GRANT PROPOSALS THAT SUCCEEDED
Edited by Virginia White

A Continuation Order Plan is available for this series. A continuation order will bring delivery of each new volume immediately upon publication. Volumes are billed only upon actual shipment. For further information please contact the publisher.

GRANT PROPOSALS THAT SUCCEEDED

Edited by
VIRGINIA WHITE

PLENUM PRESS • NEW YORK AND LONDON

Library of Congress Cataloging in Publication Data

Main entry under title:

Grant proposals that succeeded.

(Nonprofit management and finance)
Includes bibliographical references and index.
1. Fund raising—Case studies. 2. Research grants—Case studies. 3. Proposal writing in research—Case studies. I. White, Virginia P. II. Series.
HG177.G69   1982   001.4'4   82-22262
ISBN 0-306-40873-2

© 1983 Plenum Press, New York
A Division of Plenum Publishing Corporation
233 Spring Street, New York, N.Y. 10013

Printed in the United States of America

LIST OF CONTRIBUTORS

Larry Adams, Department of Sociology, Texas Christian University, Fort Worth, Texas.

Robert Alexander, Director of the Living Stage Theatre Company, Washington, D.C.

Steven C. Bernard, Office of the Director, National Institutes of Health, Bethesda, Maryland.

Elizabeth Brunazzi, Writer-in-Residence and Instructor of Creative Writing for the D. C. Commission on the Arts and Humanities.

David Caplovitz, Sociology Professor, Graduate School and University Center of the City University of New York.

George N. Eaves, Deputy Director, Division of Blood Diseases and Resources, National Heart, Lung and Blood Institute of the National Institutes of Health.

Myra Ficklen, Senior Research Assistant, Education Policy Research Institute, Educational Testing Service, Washington, D.C.

John F. Fleischauer, Chairman of the Humanities Division of Columbus College, Columbus, Georgia.

Albert Flores, Assistant Professor of Philosophy, Rensselaer Polytechnic Institute, Troy, New York.

Susan Hellweg, Assistant Dean for Academic Affairs for the College of Professional Studies and Fine Arts and Assistant Professor of Speech Communications, San Diego State University, California.

Paul Hennessey, Program Coordinator at the University of California, Berkeley.

Terry Lawler, Acting Director of the Film Fund, Inc., New York.

John Lippincott, Public Affairs Specialists, National Endowment for the Humanities.

Joan Marks, Director of the Human Genetics Program and Co-Director of the Health Advocacy Program at Sarah Lawrence College, Bronxville, New York.

James M. Pike, National Heart, Lung, and Blood Institute, National Institutes of Health, Bethesda, Maryland.

Donna Bonem Rich, Assistant Executive Director, Lennox Hill Neighborhood Association, New York.

Ray Ring, Director of Exhibitions, City University of the New York Graduate Center Mall, New York.

David R. Schubert, The Salk Institute, La Jolla, California.

The Talent Bank, San Francisco, California.

Gerald V. Teague, Director, Bureau of Educational Research, The College of Education, University of Maryland.

Barry Tuchfeld, Department of Sociology, Texas Christian University, Fort Worth, Texas.

Harriet L. Warm, Executive Director of the Florence V. Burden Foundation, New York.

Lucy Winer, Independent Filmmaker, New York.

CONTENTS

INTRODUCTION

No fund-raising technique is as effective as a personal presentation, a detailed discussion between the applicant and the potential funder of the proposed activity held before the written request is submitted. If, during the discussion, the presentation is made effectively, the chance of success is immeasurably greater and the final preparation of the application is comparatively easier.

It is not, unfortunately, always possible to make a personal presentation. In many, actually most, cases the only form of contact the applicant has with the funding organization is the written request. And even in those cases where there has been extensive discussion, *there always comes a time when a request must be presented in writing in some form.* And every applicant who expects to succeed must know how to do that in a professional style.

When GRANTS MAGAZINE began publication in 1978, a feature called *Grants Clinic* was put into the format. In each issue a sample of a grant application that was approved and funded was presented. In addition to the application itself, a short history, explanation, or critique of the application was given describing the research techniques, pre-application negotiations with the granting agency, and the strong features of the written application that contributed to its success.

Examples that have appeared and continue to appear in GRANTS MAGAZINE were suggested or contributed by many people, among them the magazine's editors, editorial board members, and their colleagues, friends, and associates many of whom are successful grantees or administrators of grant programs. It became clear from the number of reprint requests for the *Grant Clinic* feature that a compendium of some examples that had appeared there would make a useful reference volume containing exemplary applications.

It must not be assumed that grant writing can be reduced to a formula or that what worked for one organization dealing with a certain agency will also work for another at a different time or with a different funder. Nor should it be assumed that a beautifully prepared application will always be successful—they can and do fail to find support from time to time. Less often, but occasionally, a poor application will be successful, primarily because some need of the funder will be met by the accomplishment of the proposed activity.

Grant applications differ greatly in form, style, and content depending upon such factors as the granting agency requirements, the type of project for which support is requested, the size and type of the organization that will administer the funds, and many others. Some granting organizations use application forms; many do not. The forms provided may be lengthy, especially those of government agencies, but others may be one or two pages long. Foundations and corporations rarely use forms, and while some prefer one- or two-page letter requests, others have detailed guides for the preparation of the application and require numerous supporting documents.

Programs supported by every funding organization are unique to the particular organization and moreover they are not static. In every sector and in every field, change is constant; programs are discontinued and new ones launched; popular ideas and trends die out as social changes occur; and new information may render invalid a previously favored research approach or the need for a particular service. The numbers of fund requests grow larger steadily and funding agencies must revise their requirements and reviewing procedures to accomodate to the increase.

In arriving at funding decisions, government agencies must consider the national priorities that have been established by the current administration, or geographic distribution, or the state of the art in a particular field. Private foundations nearly always reflect the partialities and biases of the donors, and it is not unusual for foundation grants to be made to friends of the trustees of greatest influence. This happens in small foundations more often than in larger ones where the review and selection process is more sophisticated. Corporations are known to favor applications that come from localities where their headquarters or operational units are situated. The examples selected for this compendium

are: three research proposals; three training grant requests; four arts applications; one humanities proposal with a supplement which outlines the grantmaking process of the National Endowment for the Humanities; and one response to a Request for Proposal (RFP) which is, strictly speaking, not a grant application but a bid on a contract. Many projects that are funded by contracts are the same kinds of activities that may also be funded through the grant mechanism.

Several of these applications are accompanied by short histories of the negotiations that led to the final preparation of the application; others include statements by objective critics about the strengths of both the negotiation and the written request which contributed to its success. One is preceded by a statement from the executive director of the funding organization stating why the foundation found that particular application acceptable.

There is one entry containing examples of effective letters that may be written to foundation or corporation officials in order to open negotiations about a request for support. This feature also reprints instructions of one community foundation and of one private foundation for the preparation of applications. They are useful models that may serve as guides for requests to other similar organizations.

The proposals presented here are exactly as they appeared in the magazine, with minor editorial changes, the addition of headings, a Table of Contents, and an Index.

I want to express my appreciation to Paul Hennessey who, as editor of the *Grants Clinic* feature for the first two years, assisted in locating successful grants and provided critiques for a number of them. I would also like to thank the current editors of GRANTS MAGAZINE, Frea E. Sladek and Eugene Stein, for their cooperation in the preparation of this compendium.

Virginia White
Editor

RESEARCH GRANTS

This section contains three research grants: one each in the biomedical sciences, the social sciences, and engineering. They were funded by different agencies of the federal government, the largest source of funds for scientific research, although private and community foundations also make research grants.

The first application in this group, that of Dr. David R. Schubert of The Salk Institute, La Jolla, California, is in the field of molecular biology: *A Proposal to Study the Differentiation and Physiology of a Neuroblastoma.* It was funded by the National Institute of Neurological and Communicative Disorders and Stroke of the National Institutes of Health. Dr. George N. Eaves, now Deputy Director, Division of Blood Diseases and Resources, National Heart, Lung, and Blood Institute, was Executive Secretary of the NIH Molecular Biology Study Section to which the Schubert application was first referred for review. Dr. Eaves, then a member of the editorial board of GRANTS MAGAZINE, recognized it as an outstanding basic research grant proposal and arranged for it to be published as a *Grants Clinic*

feature. He added his own critique of the proposal entitled "A Successful Grant Application to the National Institutes of Health: Case History," and an article on the preparation of budgets for such research studies written by James M. Pike and Steven C. Bernard.

In his article, Dr. Eaves describes the NIH review process, discusses the questions raised by the reviewers, and the subsequent application for continuation of the work, which was approved. His comments on the written proposal are particularly noteworthy: "The proposal was selected without special consideration of its literary merits. Had the principal investigator's writing skills been seriously deficient, his scientific achievements probably would not have been as significant as they were at the time he wrote the proposal, and, consequently, this application would not have been among the successful."

Although the Reagan administration has spared the National Institutes of Health in its waves of budget cutting, inflation has raised the average cost of research grants meaning that fewer grants can be made with the same levels of funding. Inflation has also forced up indirect costs to such an extent that funds in each grant available for program activities have decreased. And, to make the picture even darker, the number of applications continues to grow, making the competition keener than ever. There is never enough money to support all the meritorious applications submitted; researchers in the biomedical fields must therefore be persuasive, thorough, and articulate in preparing applications to the National Institutes of Health.

Social science research has not fared well at all in the current administration—in fact, it has been singled out for particularly drastic reduction, except for those programs under the aegis of the National Institutes of Health. Not only have funds for alcohol and drug abuse research and treatment and other mental health needs been reduced, but activities that were formerly funded through grants-in-aid have been lumped into the block grants administered by state and regional officials. This makes it necessary for applicants to learn to deal with a new bureaucratic echelon which has its own priorities and its own procedures as well as its own regional biases.

The second research proposal included here, *The Impact of Inflation-Recession on Families in Cities,* a study conducted by Prof. David Caplovitz of The City University of New York Graduate Center, was funded the National Institute of Mental Health (NIMH) of the Alcohol, Drug Abuse, and Mental Health Administration (ADAMHA). This is a study of national scope dealing with two subjects—the economy and the family—that are of deep concern to people in every part of the country. It would have difficulty in being funded in today's Washington climate, as would other studies of this type which are designed to yield basic information vital to the formulation of public policies that best serve the needs of the nation.

While funds for studies of human behavior are being slashed, some programs are being maintained or even increased—national defense, for example, and a few programs dealing with problems of the elderly. The imaginative human behavior researcher may have to emphasize the importance of his proposed study as it relates to those areas where funds are available. All of the military services have a need for more knowledge on which to base training programs, and more information about human problems in dealing with new technology, human stress in both combat and non-combat situations, the abuse of alcohol and other drugs, and about crime prevention. Some of the most important work on human behavior has been supported by the Office of Naval Research. The research branches of the Army, Navy, and Air Force are predominantly concerned with technology and material, but there is no reason why they should not—in fact, every reason why they should—support studies of human behavior.

Some programs for the benefit of older people continue to receive support, especially those that are concerned with biomedical studies of the aging process, but services to the elderly are not being entirely abolished. Every agency that has responsibility for providing such services—including Social Security—has a need for more basic knowledge about mental as well as physical well being. The social science application should indicate the relevance of the proposed work for special populations, the elderly, the physically handicapped, and disadvantaged ethnic groups. This is not to suggest that research objectives be distorted in order to obtain funding, but information about human behavior has no restrictive constituency and to emphasize the importance of a project for one particular group does not diminish its value to all.

The third research proposal, *Engineering Ethic Study,* by Prof. Albert Flores of Rensselaer Polytechnic Institute, was funded by the National Science Foundation's program called Ethics and Values in Science and Technology (EVIST). It is both an engineering and a humanities study and in another example of work that would have difficulty in being funded today.

In spite of the austerity of the times, the public has become actively concerned about the deleterious effects technology may have on our lives even as it serves to improve our overall standard of living. The ethical aspects of science and society began to be a concern of some foundations in the early 1960s and the federal government will not likely abolish all studies in this area. It is anticipated, and hoped, that the Departments of Energy, Agriculture, and Health and Human Services, as well as some of the specialized agencies like the National Science Foundation, the National Transportation Safety Board, the Nuclear Regulatory Commission, the Environmental Protection Agency and others will continue to consider support of projects dealing with the ethical aspects of technological progress.

The Differentiation and Physiology of a Neuroblastoma

Funded by: National Institute of Neurological and Communicative Disorders and Stroke

of the National Institutes of Health

Principal Investigator: David R. Schubert, Research Scientist, The Salk Institute, La Jolla, California

Proposal prepared by: David R. Schubert

A SUCCESSFUL GRANT APPLICATION TO THE NATIONAL INSTITUTES OF HEALTH: CASE HISTORY*

by George N. Eaves

The peer review system used by the National Institutes of Health (NIH) and related variations used by a few other federal agencies have been described,[1-4] studied,[5,6] discussed,[7-10] investigated,[11] analyzed,[12-16] debated,[17] criticized,[18] ridiculed,[19] threatened,[20, 21] attacked,[22] defended,[23] encouraged,[24] praised,[25] endorsed,[26-28] codified,[29] and legalized.[30] Although apparently nothing about the peer review system has been left unsaid, the preparation of a research-grant application still arouses uncertainty or apprehension in neophyte[31] and Nobelist scientist alike.[32] A few concerned people have tried to help by giving reasons for disapproval of applications,[2, 33, 34] by explaining the variables that influence approval or disapproval,[35] and by offering advice about preparation.[36-48] Nevertheless, as one of my astute colleagues† observed in relation to my own discussion of reasons for disapproval of applications,[2] it is easier to identify the weaknesses in a proposal than to offer *specific* suggestions about how to write a successful application.

Having accepted the challenge from that observation, I soon concluded that it is probably not feasible to offer more specific practical guidance than already appears in the "Information and Instructions for Application for

*Address correspondence concerning the following three papers to: Public Inquiries and Reports Branch,NHLBI, National Institutes of Health, Bethesda, Maryland 20014.

George N. Eaves is Deputy Director, Division of Blood Diseases and Resources, National Heart, Lung, and Blood Institute of the National Institutes of Health. Dr. Eaves was a member of the Editorial Board of *Grants Magazine*.

†The late Dr. Ilse Bry, who founded the *Mental Health Book Review Index*, which was published from 1956 to 1972, and who also served as Chairman of the Editorial Committee of that journal.

Research Grant, Form NIH (PHS) 398."* The alternative selected is to publish the text of a successful research grant application submitted to the NIH and allow those who read the proposal to draw their own conclusions about its merit.

In presenting only the narrative portion of the proposal, I have not meant to diminish the importance of other sections of a grant application, such as the budget, the facilities, and the biographical sketches. I have condensed into a footnote essentially all the information contained in the principal investigator's biographical sketch, except, of course, his publications, most of which are cited throughout the text of the proposal. The requested budget (not reprinted here) would now seem unrealistically modest in view of the inflation that has pervaded the national economy since 1970. I have therefore left the consideration of budgets, which also involves facilities, to the experts in grants management, two of whom have discussed this subject in the accompanying article.[49]

Criteria for Selection

The application published here fulfilled six criteria. First, I wanted the application to be the first submitted by an investigator who was initiating independent studies. Second, the text was not to exceed twenty pages, in keeping with a proposed restriction being considered currently by the NIH.[50] Third, the application had to have a priority score in the top 10 percent of all research grant applications reviewed at that meeting of the study section. Fourth, the primary factors used to judge the scientific and technical merit of the application had to be the same as those used currently.[29] Fifth, so that the proprietary rights of the principal investigator to his

original ideas would be protected, the work proposed in the application had now to be completed. Sixth, the investigator had to have fulfilled the study section's expectations by successfully competing for renewal of the grant.

The application thus selected as a *case* of a successful, first application — not necessarily a model — was submitted to the NIH in 1970 by Dr. David R. Schubert* of The Salk Institute. The application, entitled "Differentiation and Physiology of a Neuroblastoma," resulted in the award of a three-year grant (NS-09658) from the National Institute of Neurological and Communicative Disorders and Stroke.

Modifications in the Application

In presenting the text of this application as a case history, I have refrained from imposing my own stylistic and organizational preferences on the application. In some instances, however, abbreviations that the author used only occasionally or that are now obsolete, such as BUdR for BrdU (5-bromodeoxyuridine), have been abandoned in favor of the terms they represent. No words within sentences, sentences within paragraphs, or paragraphs within sections have been rearranged; the content and order of the proposal are exactly as originally submitted to the NIH. In three areas, however, I have introduced some modifications — mostly mechanical and nonverbal — that would either enhance the readability or increase the usefulness of the proposal. First, the introductory statement of

---

*The Instruction Sheet for NIH 398 (Revised 2-73) is included in the well-known package, "Application for Public Health Service Grant or Award," which is available in the business offices of institutions eligible for grants from the Public Health Service.

*Dr. Schubert, who was 26 years old when he wrote this proposal, was born in Indianapolis, Indiana. He received his B.A. degree in 1965 from Indiana University and his Ph.D. degree in 1969 from the University of California, San Diego, where he was a graduate student of Dr. Melvin Cohn. Dr. Schubert's postdoctoral research on neuroblastoma tissue culture was with Dr. Francois Jacob at the Institut Pasteur, in Paris, during the academic year 1969-1970, since when he has been a Member of The Salk Institute.

the general objectives and the later statement of specific aims have been listed to give those who read the proposal[2] a readily comprehensible definition of the proposed work. Second, I have changed punctuation where necessary to effect editorial consistency and thus enhance readability. Since Dr. Schubert had already demonstrated his knowledge of the function of the series comma, which is not widely understood, even by many "editors" and teachers of English(!), this task required little effort. Third, I have modified the reference section so that it includes complete citations with titles of the articles and inclusive pagination, as recommended for scholarly publications,[51] for the benefit of the reader who may wish to know the precise subject of a cited paper or who may wish to request a photostatic copy from a library. In addition, Dr. Schubert has provided references to those papers that were either in press or in manuscript form at the time the proposal was submitted. Each of these references has been signaled with an asterisk that refers to an explanatory footnote. The intent in providing a complete reference section is to enhance the archival value of this proposal, which is an interesting account of the status of a specific aspect of cell and molecular biology eight years ago.

The proposal was selected without special consideration of its literary merits. Had the principal investigator's writing skills been seriously deficient, his scientific achievements probably would not have been as significant as they were at the time he wrote this proposal, and, consequently, this application would not have been among the successful.

The writing of most of us is not without flaws, and the successful applicant has not necessarily mastered the art of efficacious exposition. In some cases, the scientific originality and technical proficiency may be so meritorious as to be evident despite syntactical and grammatical improprieties and other weaknesses, but dependence on such good fortune is a frightfully risky situation and certainly incompatible with the attributes and goals of the scholar. As part of

our professional growth and maturity, we must therefore continually try to improve our writing skills as well as all other aspects of our scholarship. Who is not dissatisfied with what he wrote eight years ago — or last week? Those who wish to concentrate on the grammatical and syntactical aspects of this proposal can profit from an analysis of the text in relation to the excellent advice recently offered by renowned experts.[47, 48]

In pointing out some of the features responsible for the success of the proposal, I have purposefully, and appropriately, restricted my comments to the opinions of the reviewing study section, since these are the only ones that count. A responsibility of the executive secretary of a study section is to obtain all the materials needed for the review of the application. For Dr. Schubert's proposal, no additional information was needed; his application was complete as submitted, and there was consequently no delay in processing it.

Review by Study Sections

The proposal to study the "Differentiation and Physiology of a Neuroblastoma" was reviewed by the Molecular Biology Study Section in September 1970, when I was the Executive Secretary of that Study Section. The proposed research was concerned with the differentiation of nerve cells and the chemical and electrophysiological properties of differentiating cells. The experimental system that was to be employed, as developed largely by Dr. Schubert, was unique: cells derived from a neuroblastoma that would grow in culture and differentiate when in serum-free media or when treated with 5-bromodeoxyuridine. From their preliminary investigations, the principal investigator and his colleagues had reported that these cells developed neuronal extensions with associated tubular and filament structures, nerve-specific enzymes, and electrophysiological properties similar to intact nervous tissue, including responsiveness to acetylcholine. Dr. Schubert proposed to continue his analysis of this interesting system by using the parent cell line in attempts to isolate mutants that affect developmental properties and electrophysiological behavior. Although the members of the Study Section readily recognized the overly ambitious scope of the project, they were favorably impressed. The résumé of the summary statement reads as follows:

> The proposed approach has great promise for advancing information about the regulation of animal cells. In fact, it may be the only way to obtain definitive answers. The system is one with great potential; it provides a ready means of invoking differentiation; and it would permit the correlation of biochemical, structural, and physiological parameters. In general, the experimental design is good, and the investigator appears to have a facile use of all techniques available. Although it is questionable whether "true" synapses could be developed in this system, there are so many questions that could be answered by the use of this system that the inability to obtain the formation of a true synapse would be inconsequential.

The detailed criticism included questions about the starting cell — a neoplastic neuroblast — not being a truly "wild-type" cell but a mutant with no guarantee for differentiation into a neuron. The reviewers also had doubts about formation in culture of clearly recognizable interneuronal synapses when the neuroblasts differentiated. The Study Section concluded, however, that:

> . . . this . . . interesting and ingenious proposal . . . describes the applicant as a skilled emigrant from molecular biology to the underdeveloped areas and their problems, although he may not know the terrain in sufficient detail to avoid illusions and misplaced effort. Nevertheless, the proposal represents a very interesting departure that definitely deserves the support necessary to insure its launching. Contact with reality, once the project is going, would take care of the rest.

Indeed when the continuation application was reviewed in April 1973, the Molecular Biology Study Section, which by then had changed significantly in membership, remarked that the confidence shown in the investigator almost three years before had been justified; he had been so productive as to warrant the accolades of "bright

and imaginative" and "outstanding investigator." Continued support for four years was recommended with the same enthusiasm expressed earlier, even though the proposed approach remained questionable, since by then it was apparent that the tumors definitely did *not* form organized nervous tissue. Nevertheless, as in many research projects, the skills of the investigator and the other projects he proposed concurrently — in this instance, especially the prospects of new lines of nerve, muscle, and glial cells in clonal cell culture — offered the promise of a rewarding investment.

The next, and most recent, renewal application was reviewed in June 1977 by the Neurological Sciences Study Section because the research was now concerned primarily with the differentiation, physiology, and interactions of nerve, muscle, and glia. In reviewing progress during the previous period of support, the Study Section was pleased to note the large collection of cell lines from nerve, glia, smooth muscle, heart muscle, and skeletal muscle that had been isolated and subsequently characterized biochemically and electrophysiologically.

The report of this latest review clearly indicates one of the primary reasons for the investigator's success in the laboratory and in competing for later research grant funds: his ability to design original, imaginative, and useful experiments within the context of what he clearly and accurately recognized to be the strengths and limitations of the experimental system that he used. In the words of the reviewers:

> The most serious question that can be raised about this proposal is whether cell lines derived from neoplasms can generate useful information about mechanisms underlying cell-cell interactions. Certainly, if experiments are not carefully thought out and designed, this can be a problem. The refreshing aspect concerning Dr. Schubert's proposal is that he is constantly aware of the limitations of the system and designs his experiments accordingly.

As an interesting commentary on the objectivity of a system of peer review that involves collective judgment of merit, all of Dr. Schubert's research grant applications have been awarded about the same priority score[2] by each of the three reviewing Study Sections.

Acknowledgments

I wish to express my sincere appreciation to Dr. Schubert for permitting me to present his proposal as a case history. I would also commend him for his courage in doing so, because this application is likely to be reviewed critically by more people than have ever read any other proposal in the history of NIH granting!

I am also grateful for the gracious and generous help of Lois and Selma DeBakey, whose suggestions not only improved this article but also provided valuable instruction to their devoted student and friend.

References

1. Lore, J. I., and Gutter, F. J. The embryogeny of an NIH research grant. *Asha (Journal of the American Speech and Hearing Association)* 10:7-9, 1968.
2. Eaves, G. N. Who reads your project-grant application to the National Institutes of Health? *Federation Proceedings* 31:2-9, 1972.
3. Lipkin, B. S. The role of the study section in the NIH peer review system. *Behavior Research Methods and Instrumentation* 8:61-64, 1976.
4. Merritt, D. H., and Eaves, G. N. Site visits for the review of grant applications to the National Institutes of Health; views of an applicant and a scientist administrator. *Federation Proceedings* 34:131-136, 1975.
5. Barish, N. H. A study of the priority system for reviewing Public Health Service research proposals. A doctoral dissertation presented to the faculty of the graduate school of The American University. May 1967.
6. United States, Department of Health, Education, and Welfare, National Institutes of Health, Grants Peer Review Study Team. *Grants Peer Review. Report to the Director, NIH, Phase I. Volume I.* December 1976. (No DHEW publication number.)
7. Carey, W. D. Peer review revisited. *Science* 189:331, 1975.
8. Wade, N. Peer review system: how to hand out money fairly. *Science* 179:158-161, 1973.
9. Lawrence, S. V. Grants: fuel that feeds research. *The Bulletin of the American College of Physicians* 19:18-26, 1978.
10. United States, Department of Health, Education, and Welfare. *Report of the President's Biomedical Research Panel. Appendix D: Selected Staff Papers.* 30 April 1976. [DHEW Publication Number (OS) 76-504.]
11. Conlan, J. B. Introduction of bill H.R. 9892. *Congressional Record — House,* pages H 9266-H 9267, 29 September 1975.
12. Westhead, E. W. Peer review: distribution of reviewers. *Science* 188:204-205, 1975.
13. Carter, G. M. Peer review, citations, and biomedical research policy: NIH grants to medical school faculty. R-1583-HEW. The Rand Corporation, Santa Monica, California, 1974.
14. Bondurant, S. Peer review of research project grants by NIH study sections. Report of the Committee on National Medical Policy, American Society for Clinical Investigation. *Clinical Research* 25:297-305, 1977.
15. Gustafson, T. The controversy over peer review. *Science* 190:1060-1066, 1975.
16. Cole, S., Rubin, L., and Cole, J. R. Peer review and the support of science. *Scientific American* 237:34-41, 1977.
17. Symington, J. W., and Kramer, T. R. Does peer review work? *American Scientist* 65:17-20, 1977.
18. United States, Department of Health, Education, and Welfare, National Institutes of Health, Grants Peer Review Study Team. *Grants Peer Review. Report to the Director, NIH, Phase I. Volume II: Appendices* (Appendix F-3: Grassetti v. Weinberger *et al.*). December 1976. (No DHEW publication number.)
19. Cohn, V. How does NIH parcel out cash? *The Washington Post,* page A14, 13 September 1972.
20. Cullinton, B. J. Peer review: OMB may dismantle NIH study sections. *Science* 180:843-844, 1973.
21. Norman, C. The threat to peer review. *Nature* 260:740, 1976.
22. Helms, J. A. Introduction of bill S. 2427. *Congressional Record — Senate,* pages S 17003-S 17005, 29 September 1975.
23. Cochrane, C. G. Parceling out NIH cash. *The Washington Post,* page A22, 28 September 1972.
24. United States, Department of Health, Education, and Welfare, Office of the Secretary. *The Advancement of Medical Research and Education Through the Department of Health, Education, and Welfare.* Final Report of the Secretary's Consultants on Medical Research and Education. Washington, D.C.: U.S. Government Printing Office, 27 June 1958.
25. United States, The White House, The President's NIH Study Committee. *Biomedical Science and Its Administration: A Study of the National Institutes of Health.* Report to the President. Washington, D.C.: U.S. Government Printing Office, February 1965.
26. The Presdient's Commission on Heart Disease, Cancer, and Stroke. *Report to the President: A National Program to Conquer Heart Disease, Cancer, and Stroke.* Volume I. Washington, D.C.: U.S. Government Printing Office, December 1964.
27. United States, Department of Health, Education, and Welfare, Office of the Secretary, Office of the Assistant Secretary of Health and Scientific Affairs. *Report of the Secretary's Advisory Committee on the Management of National Institutes of Health Research Contracts and Grants.* Washington, D.C.: U.S. Government Printing Office, 29 March 1966.

28. United States, Department of Health, Education and Welfare. *Report of the President's Biomedical Research Panel.* 30 April 1976. [DHEW Publication Number (OS) 76-500.]

29. United States, Department of Health, Education, and Welfare, Public Health Service. Title 42 — Public Health, Part 52h — Scientific peer review of research grant applications and research and development contract projects [sic]. *Federal Register* 43:7862-7866, 1978.

30. 42 United States Code (U.S.C.) 289*l*-4. Peer review of grant applications and contract projects.

31. Rifkin, D. B. A beginning scientist's first project-grant application. *Federation Proceedings* 32:1543, 1973.

32. Szent-Gyorgyi, A. Looking back. *Perspectives in Biology and Medicine* 15:1-5, 1971.

33. Allen, E. M. Why are research grant applications disapproved? *Science* 132:1532-1534, 1960.

34. Lisk, D. J. Why research grant applications are turned down. *BioScience* 21:1025-1026, 1971.

35. Berthold, J. S. Nursing research grant proposals: what influenced their approval or disapproval in two national granting agencies. *Nursing Research* 22:292-299, 1973.

36. Merritt, D. H. Grantsmanship: an exercise in lucid presentation. *Clinical Research* 11:375-377, 1963.

37. Woodford, F. P. Writing a research project proposal. Pages 142-149. *In* F. P. Woodford (editor), *Scientific writing for graduate students.* The Rockefeller University Press, New York, 1968.

38. Gortner, S. R. Research grant applications: what they are not and should be. *Nursing Research* 20:292-295, 1971.

39. Eaves, G. N. The project-grant application of the National Institutes of Health: introduction. *Federation Proceedings* 32:1541, 1973.

40. Eaves, G. N. The grant application: an exercise in scientific writing. *Federation Proceedings* 32:1541-1543, 1973.

41. Gee, H. H. Preparation of the project-grant application: assistance from the administrator in charge of a study section. *Federation Proceedings* 32:1544-1545, 1973.

42. Malone, T. E. Preparation of the project-grant application: assistance from the institutes and other awarding units. *Federation Proceedings* 32:1546-1547, 1973.

43. Ross, R. Participation of the administration of the grantee institution in the preparation and transmission of a project-grant application. *Federation Proceedings* 32:1547-1548, 1973.

44. Schimke, R. T. Preparation of the project-grant application: assistance from the grantee institution's experienced investigators. *Federation Proceedings* 32:1548-1550, 1973.

45. Lee, F., and Jacquette, B. L. What makes a good proposal? *Foundation News,* January-February:18-21, 1973.

46. Stallones, R. A. Research grants: advice to applicants. *The Yale Journal of Biology and Medicine* 48:451-458, 1975.

47. DeBakey, L. The persuasive proposal. *Journal of Technical Writing and Communication* 6:5-25, 1976.

48. DeBakey, L., and DeBakey, S. The art of persuasion: logic and language in proposal writing. *Grants Magazine* 1:43-60, 1978.

49. Pike, J. M., and Bernard, S. C. The research grant budget: preparation and justification in relation to the proposed research. *Grants Magazine* 1:283-286, 1978.

50. *The Blue Sheet (Drug Research Reports).* 'Flexible study sections' proposal first sign of change in NIH peer review; appeals system, release of priority scores mulled by in-house work groups. Volume 21 (Number 14), page 6, 15 April 1978.

51. DeBakey, L. *The Scientific Journal: Editorial policies and practices.* The C. V. Mosby Company, St. Louis, 129 pages, 1976.

* * *

A PROPOSAL TO STUDY THE DIFFERENTIATION AND PHYSIOLOGY OF A NEUROBLASTOMA: A SUCCESSFUL RESEARCH GRANT APPLICATION SUBMITTED TO THE NATIONAL INSTITUTES OF HEALTH

by David R. Schubert, Ph.D.[1]

Abstract[2]

The differentiation and physiology of nervous tissue will be studied in vitro using cloned tissue culture lines of a mouse neuroblastoma as a model system. The parameters of the differentiation process will be defined with emphasis on control mechanisms and the induction of specific cytoplasmic and membrane proteins. Mutants which are blocked at the various steps in the differentiation process will be isolated. Similarly, the molecular biology of the cholinergic receptor and catecholamine uptake, storage, and release will be defined by studying the wild-type functions in relation to a series of mutants blocked in these functions. Finally, the nature of synaptic specificity will be studied with respect to membrane structure in electrical and, perhaps, chemical synapses in the neuroblastoma and other cloned tissue culture lines.

[1] The Salk Institute, La Jolla, California.
[2] Page 2 of Form PHS-398.

Research Plan

A. Introduction

1. Objectives

The objectives are:

- to define, at the molecular level, the control processes involved in the differentiation of a neuroblast to a mature neuron;
- to understand the molecular biology of the coupling between cellular depolarization by acetylcholine resulting in the generation of an action potential and the subsequent release of catecholamine neurotransmitter in a sympathetic neuron; and
- to define the basis of neuronal and other intercellular specificities at the level of the membrane subunits involved in the contact.

2. Background

The analysis of differentiated function is hampered by the fact that the end cell usually does not divide. In the case of extremely heterogeneous cell populations such as those found in the endocrine, nervous, immune, and hepatic tissues, further advances require a way of establishing, in tissue culture, clones of end cells which express their differentiated phenotype. Such cells are most easily derived from neoplasms and have been successfully used in the study of endocrine (Sato and Yasumura, 1966), hepatic (Thompson, Tomkins, and Curran, 1966), and endoreticular (Cohn, 1967) cell function. In addition to using cloned, tissue-culture-adapted neoplasms to study a differentiated *function* such as antibody biosynthesis (Schubert, 1968), it has recently been possible to examine the *process* of differentiation in a mouse neuroblastoma (Schubert, Humphreys, Baroni, and Cohn, 1969; Schubert, Humphreys, de Vitry, and Jacob, 1971; Schubert and Jacob, 1970).

The experimental approach that was used during our investigation of antibody biosynthesis and assembly in mouse plasma cell tumors was somewhat novel in the field of animal cell research, but classical in the methodology of molecular biology. The wild-type function of immunoglobulin synthesis was defined (Schubert, 1968; Schubert, 1970), and a series of mutants defective in this function was isolated (Schubert, Munro, and Ohno, 1968; Schubert and Horibata, 1968). An analysis of these mutants revealed that they were blocked at various stages of immunoglobulin biosynthesis and assembly (Schubert and Cohn, 1968).

The characterization of the mutant cell lines shed a great deal of light on the wild-type synthetic mechanisms and generated a number of facts and concepts which would have been missed if only the wild-type cell lines were studied (Schubert and Cohn, 1968; Schubert, 1970; Schubert and Cohn, 1970). It is evident that this approach to the study of mammalian cell function should be extended to other types of differentiated end cells and also to the process of differentiation itself. Such studies would not only extend our present knowledge and verify our predictions; they could also define new concepts which are not readily deduced from investigations of the normal function. If coupled with somatic cell genetics, an enormous amount of information could be gained about regulatory mechanisms in higher organisms.

It has recently been possible to induce a cloned neuroblastoma tissue culture line to differentiate into a population of cells which has the morphological and functional characteristics of mature neurons (Schubert, Humphreys, Baroni, and Cohn, 1969). The process of differentiation is defined in the following manner. When grown in suspension culture in bacteriological Petri dishes, the cells have a primitive round cell morphology — high nuclear cytoplasmic ratio and no morphological specialization; however, when given a surface on which to attach, such as glass or collagen, cells send out processes (neurites) up to 3 mm in length and assume the morphology of mature neurons. Whereas the cells grown in suspension are not, the attached cells are stained by the Bodian silver procedure for neurons. Electron microscopy reveals that the attached cells contain neurofilaments, neurotubules, and dense-core vesicles indicative of nerve fibers. Both free floating and attached cells have tyrosine hydroxylase activity characteristic of sympathetic nervous tissue (Schubert, Humphreys, Baroni, and Cohn, 1969).

By recording from single cells, it has been shown that there is a sequential development of resting potential and acetylcholine sensitivity concomitant with morphological differentiation (Harris and Dennis, 1970). The highly differentiated end cells (attached cells with long cytoplasmic processes and well developed neurotubules) have resting potentials of about -60 mV and are induced to generate 85 mV action potentials by current depolarization or the extracellular (iontophoretic) application of acetylcholine. The undifferentiated round cells growing in suspension culture have much lower resting potentials but are also depolarized by acetylcholine. The spread of acetylcholine sensitivity over the cell surface during maturation was shown to be similar to that of naturally developing nervous tissue, and the existence of electrical synapses between cells via cell processes has been demonstrated. Electron microscopy has revealed process endings containing high concentrations of mitochondria and dense-core vesicles which are embedded in soma and processes of other cells (Schubert, Humphreys, Baroni, and Cohn, 1969). Such nerve endings are usually associated with chemical synapses, but the physiological demonstration of chemical transmission is still lacking.

In a continuation of the above work, conditions have been defined in which *quantitative* differentiation of neuroblast to neurons can be *induced* within 24 hours (Schubert, Humphreys, de Vitry, and Jacob, 1971). This process is completely reversible, and it has been shown that the synthesis of a limited number of proteins can be either induced or repressed, depending on the growth conditions of the cells and their state of differentiation (Schubert, Humphreys, de Vitry, and Jacob, 1971). We feel that this experimental situation offers a unique opportunity to examine the control mechanisms at the molecular

level in a reversible differentiation process which is quite analogous to in vivo neuronal development and regeneration (Harris and Dennis, 1970).

Since this tissue culture line can be depolarized to generate an action potential by acetylcholine, and since it contains the catecholamine neurotransmitters (Schubert, Humphreys, Baroni, and Cohn, 1969; Agusti-Tocco and Sato, 1969) characteristic of postganglionic sympathetic neurons, it follows that this neuroblastoma cell line is ideally suited for both the study of the acetylcholine receptor and the interaction between receptor and membrane which leads to depolarization, propagation of the action potential, and the subsequent release of transmitter from pre-synaptic cells. At present, virtually nothing is known about the chemistry of this linkage.

In addition, it has been shown that the neuroblastoma cell line can form electrical synapses in vitro (Harris and Dennis, 1970) through contacts which have some morphological semblance to chemical synapses (Schubert, Humphreys, Baroni, and Cohn, 1969). The neuroblastoma also formed similar contacts with a muscle tissue culture line (Schubert, unpublished observation). It should thus be possible to study the nature of the specificity involved in these synaptic contacts and the effect of the innervated end cell on nerve development, and, conversely, the effect of innervation on muscle development.

3. Rationale

Wild-type function will be studied in detail, and mutants will be isolated which are blocked in these functions. An analysis of the sites of the mutational blocks will help define the wild-type function. This is clearly the classical approach to complex biochemical mechanisms, and perhaps the *only* approach which can lead to clear answers. Surprisingly, however, this approach has not until recently been used to study a differentiated function in animal cell tissue culture lines (Schubert, Munro, and Ohno, 1968; Schubert and Horibata, 1968; Schubert and Cohn, 1968; Schubert and Cohn, 1970).

B. Specific Aims

The first aim is to define the molecular control processes involved in the differentiation of a neuroblast to neuron in terms of the induction and repression of specific proteins, the level at which these control mechanisms act, and the process by which the cell manipulates what appears to be a surface stimulus that induces differentiation. This study will be supplemented by the isolation of mutants which are unable to differentiate.

The second aim is to determine the physical-chemical nature of the acetylcholine receptor and the mechanism by which acetylcholine depolarization is coupled to the release of catecholamine neurotransmitters. Again, these mechanisms will be studied through the use of mutants blocked at the receptor site, the sodium-potassium-adenosine-triphosphatase-linked pump, and catecholamine uptake and storage.

The third aim is to isolate, purify, and characterize the membrane components involved in the specificity of cell-cell interactions — both in the nervous system and between cells of different tissue origin.

C. Methods

I. Differentiation

Since differentiation of the neuroblastoma can be induced by transferring cells grown in suspension culture to culture dishes where they can attach to a surface, it follows that the stimulus leading to induction is associated with the interaction between that surface and the limiting membrane of the cell. Analogous membrane-mediated cell-cell and cell-effector interactions are possibly the most important, yet least understood, group of reactions involved in cellular and tissue differentiation. By looking at the induced differentiation of the neuroblast, it should be possible to define the role of the cytoplasmic membrane in these processes.

The induction process has been clearly defined as an interaction (presumably electrostatic) between the cell and the surface of the tissue culture dish (Schubert, Humphreys, de Vitry, and Jacob, 1971). Morphological differentiation can be quantitatively induced within one day by placing cells in tissue culture dishes in the absence of serum. This process can be reversed by compounds which buffer the cell-surface interaction, such as nonspecific proteins and serum. In the presence of serum, *partial* differentiation of the culture takes about five days, and it has been shown that this process is controlled by a low-molecular-weight metabolite secreted from the cells, which enhances the electrostatic interaction between the cell and surface, thus leading to induction. Treating the cells with 5-bromodeoxyuridine (10^{-4} to 10^{-7} M) will mimic the effect of the low-molecular-weight fraction (Schubert and Jacob, 1970).

Differentiation is not coupled to cell division, for cell division can be inhibited without the concomitant induction of differentiation, and, conversely, differentiation can be induced in an exponentially growing culture (Schubert, Humphreys, de Vitry, and Jacob, 1971).

The induced differentiation of the neuroblastoma also *appears* to be an example of translational control in animal cells, for differentiation can be blocked with protein synthesis inhibitors such as puromycin and cycloheximide, but not with concentrations of actinomycin D which inhibit RNA synthesis greater than 90 percent (Schubert, Humphreys, de Vitry, and Jacob, 1971). The chemistry of this process remains to be defined.

(a) Isolation of Mutants. Since the differentiation of the neuroblastoma requires a surface on which the cells can attach, it follows that a surface-mediated stimulus may be necessary, but perhaps not sufficient, to induce differentiation. Two distinct processes, one leading to cell attachment and the other to differentiation, could be dissociated by the selection of mutants blocked in the ability to attach to a surface and those which attach but do not differentiate. Both types of cells could easily be selected following muta-

genesis and expression for several generations by plating cell suspensions under conditions where there is 100 percent attachment and differentiation (Schubert, Humphreys, de Vitry, and Jacob, 1971). The cells unable to attach are selected by removing the culture fluid, allowing the decanted, unattached cells to grow up in suspension, and then repeating the selection procedure against attached cells. After several cycles of selection, the resultant cells would be cloned in agar (Schubert, Humphreys, Baroni, and Cohn, 1969). Each clone would then be individually tested for its ability to attach and differentiate.

The second class of differentiation-defective mutants would be those cells which attach but do not differentiate in the sense that neurite formation is lacking. The isolation of these mutants would require the picking of individual cells by micromanipulation (Horibata and Harris, 1970) or by trypsinization of isolated cells. Clones of these cells would be grown up and again tested for their ability to attach and differentiate.

(b) Characterization of Mutants. Mutants which do not attach, or those which attach and do not differentiate, will be initially screened on different substrates which normally lead to attachment. For example, mutants isolated on tissue culture plates will be screened for attachment and differentiation on collagen and glass. If there are differences, the nature of the stimulus leading to induction of differentiation could be studied. In any case, the mutational defects could be defined in the following terms.

There are three groups of mutants which one would expect to find. The first would be cells defective in some substance required for attachment. This function is not *necessarily* related to induction but is only a prerequisite. Examples of this class could be more carefully characterized by looking for differences between them and the wild type in the various cytoplasmic membrane components.

A second class would be those cells which can attach but have lost the specific function — presumably defined in terms of a membrane protein — which serves as a transducer between the extracellular phenomenon of attachment and the intracellular control of differentiation. Again, differences in membrane structure could be examined, the study being greatly facilitated by comparison with the wild-type cell line.

The third class of mutants, which are phenotypically similar to the second, is that which attaches but is defective in some cytoplasmic process required for differentiation. For example, it is known that the undifferentiated round cells lack neurotubules, while the differentiated attached cells contain large quantities of these organelles (Schubert, Humphreys, Baroni, and Cohn, 1969). It has also been shown that the spectrum of proteins synthesized by the round and differentiated cells is quite different as defined by acrylamide electrophoresis (Schubert, Humphreys, de Vitry, and Jacob, 1971). It follows that a structural defect in one of these proteins may inhibit differentiation.

One such defect may be the inability to synthesize or assemble the neurotubule protein which probably is responsible for the structural stability of neuronal processes. The purification of the neurotubule protein is quite easy (Marantz, Ventilla, and Shelanski, 1969). Once the protein is purified, antisera could be prepared against it and the serum used as an assay for the neurotubule synthesis in a manner analogous to the use of antisera to detect immunoglobulin biosynthesis (Schubert, 1968). In addition, antisera could be used to study the assembly of the neurotubule organelle as with immunoglobulin assembly (Schubert, 1968). Since the synthesis and assembly of the microtubule organelle is inducible with differentiation (Schubert, Humphreys, Baroni, and Cohn, 1969; Schubert, Humphreys, de Vitry, and Jacob, 1971), this type of investigation is of particular interest for three reasons. First, the control mechanisms involved in microtubule synthesis could be studied in relation to the process of differentiation. For example, what is the relationship between cell attachment and induction of specific protein synthesis? Secondly, it could be asked how the microtubule is assembled in the cell. The fact that there may be de novo protein synthesis makes this question easier to answer than with other systems. Thirdly, mutant cell lines which attach and do not differentiate will be available. It is possible that some of these cells will be blocked at a step in microtubule synthesis. By using antisera selection techniques (to be discussed later) it may be possible to select differentiated cell lines which lack microtubules. Information of the above type cannot help but lead to the definition of a function for the cellular microtubules.

A number of other types of experiments may also lead to a better understanding of neuroblast differentiation. For instance, it is known that mitotic inhibitors such as colchicine also inhibit microtubule formation (Adelman, Borisy, Shelanski, Weisenberg, and Taylor, 1968) and axonal flow (Kreutzberg, 1969). In addition, by the use of such inhibitors of microtubule formation it may be possible to define the function of the microtubules in the following way. It is known that during the development of axons, the axoplasm at first lacks microtubules, which then appear to develop as the cell matures (Schubert, Humphreys, Baroni, and Cohn, 1969). If cells were allowed to attach and initiate differentiation, followed by the addition of colchicine, then cells may develop without microtubules. Correlated electrophysiology and electron microscopy could then answer questions relative to microtubular function, such as: what is the effect on resting and action potentials, are mitochondria and synaptic vesicles localized in axoplasm as before, and are the cells lacking microtubules able to form functional synapses as untreated cells? By the use of isotopically labeled cells and antisera directed against microtubule protein, it should also be possible to define the mode of action of colchicine: where in the synthesis and assembly of microtubules does this compound act?

As mentioned previously, it has been shown that micromolar amounts of 5-bromodeoxyuridine can rapidly *induce* differentiation of the neuroblastoma under conditions which normally inhibit this process (Schubert, Humphreys, de Vitry, and Jacob, 1971; Schubert

and Jacob, 1970). Although of doubtful physiological significance, this observation is of some interest since, in all other systems examined, 5-bromodeoxyuridine *inhibits* the expression of the differentiated trait. (See, for example, Bischoff and Holtzer, 1970.) It has repeatedly been argued that this inhibition of differentiation effects specifically the transcription of genes involved in differentiation (Bischoff and Holtzer, 1970). In light of the above results, however, this is an unlikely proposal, for the primary site of action of 5-bromodeoxyuridine is probably the membrane, which, in turn, alters the metabolism of the cell *through* its increased affinity for the surface of the tissue culture dish. If this hypothesis is true, it should be possible to induce differentiation with 5-bromodeoxyuridine under conditions where cell division and DNA replication are inhibited — with cytosine arabinoside or ultraviolet light. It may also be possible to detect surface antigens which are unique to the 5-bromodeoxyuridine-induced cells and different from the normal differentiated and undifferentiated cells. The electrophysiological properties and distribution of acetylcholine sensitivity on the cells will also be examined for the possibility of finding a unique state of membrane development which can be analyzed chemically and which will shed some light on the natural process.

It has also been observed that the chromosome ploidy of the neuroblastoma varies as a function of its differentiated state. The undifferentiated cell line is tetraploid, while the majority of the differentiated cells are octaploid or greater (Schubert, Humphreys, Baroni, and Cohn, 1969). Since the differentiation of these cells is reversible (Schubert, Humphreys, de Vitry, and Jacob, 1971), this poses an interesting problem in the control of mitosis and its relationship to cell division. Although it has been shown that cessation of mitosis does not *induce* differentiation and that the differentiated cell can dedifferentiate and divide, the detailed relationship between the increase in ploidy and differentiation has not been examined. This could be readily accomplished by a combination of karyotyping,

DNA trace labeling with thymidine, radioautography, and pulse-chase experiments. (See, for example, Bischoff and Holtzer, 1970.) Another approach will be to look at surface antigens unique to differentiated cells, the precursor round cell, and the 5-bromodeoxyuridine-induced differentiated cells. Does attachment induce the synthesis on new surface antigens, and are there unique antigens which define two states? Once surface antigens are defined with antisera, it should be possible to isolate these structures and characterize their role in the differentiation process. For example, if the formation of an antigen unique to the differentiated cell is blocked under normal condition of differentiation, are the cells able to attach to the surface, or attach but not differentiate? It may be possible to select against a given surface antigen and find mutants which are blocked at some stage in the differentiation process. The pertinent technology for these experiments will be discussed later (Sections II and IV).

II. Junctional Specificity

(a) Nervous Tissue. Although electrophysiological evidence for chemical synapses is still lacking, morphological evidence indicates that this type of cell contact may be present (Schubert, Humphreys, Baroni, and Cohn, 1969). Electrical contacts via cell processes, which may be functional precursors to chemical synapses, have been observed (Harris and Dennis, 1970). In addition, there is morphological evidence for synapses between the neuroblastoma and a myoblast tissue culture line (Schubert, unpublished observation). It thus appears that the neuroblastoma tissue culture line has the potential for forming functional contacts with a variety of target cells, although sympathetic neurons usually do not, in vivo, form cholinergic-like synapses where direct cell-cell contact is involved (Iverson, 1967). These results may be analogous to the specification of axons by their motor and sensory end organs (reviewed by Edds, 1967).

Since the specificity of nervous contacts is probably defined in terms of complementary membrane proteins at the synaptic site, and since the amount of membrane surface area involved in the synapse is quite small relative to the total area of the membrane, it follows that the characterization of the proteins involved in specificity is technically impossible unless these proteins are amplified in some manner. There are two experimental approaches to this problem. One involves the purification of presynaptic nerve terminals or synaptosomes (Whittaker and Sheridan, 1965) and the other involves the use of antisera directed against *unique* surface components. Perhaps the combined use of these techniques could help characterize the proteins involved in synapse formation — a somewhat hopeless task when whole animal tissue is used. The following paragraphs outline one of several possible experimental approaches.

Cells would be allowed to differentiate either on different surfaces, such as glass, collagen, and sponge, or in the presence of different types of cells, such as embryonic smooth- and skeletal-muscle tissue culture lines. Once contacts are made and demonstrated morphologically and electrophysiologically, synaptosomes would be prepared, the synaptic vesicles, limiting membranes, and mitochondria separated by lysis in hypotonic buffer and differential centrifugation (Whittaker and Sheridan, 1965), and antisera prepared against each preparation. In the case of cells which were grown on different surfaces, synapses would be formed between like cells, as would be some of the contacts in the mixed populations. Once made, the antisera would be absorbed with membrane preparations from heterologous cell types and also synaptosome membranes of the neuroblastoma-neuroblastoma type. The resulting antisera should be specific for any unique proteins found in each preparation, which presumably would define the specificity of the synapse. Once this assay for these membrane proteins is available, it would be possible to purify and characterize them from large quantities of cells. By labeling cells during the differentiation process with amino acids, it could be shown when in the maturation process (Harris and Dennis, 1970) these proteins are synthesized. A great deal of information could be collected about their structure simply through the use of isotopic labeling, serological precipitation, and examination of the labeled proteins dissociated from the precipitate (Schubert, 1968), without having to prepare large numbers of cells. Similarly, by preparing antisera against cells at different stages of differentiation, it may be possible to define these stages in terms of cell-surface structure which, in turn, may be related to specificity.

It is not known whether the cloned neuroblastoma round-cell stem line is generating round cells which, when induced to differentiate, give rise to cells with different potential specificities, or whether all of the cells derived from this clone are equipotential with regard to junctional specificity. There is, however, good evidence that different clones derived from the same mouse tumor, and also individual cells derived from the same clone, differ in their electrical properties (A. J. Harris, personal communication).

In addition, a number of different clones from the round-cell population and the original tumor will be isolated and characterized with respect to surface antigens, electrical properties, and the potentiality for differentiation and synapse formation. Similarly, it would be most interesting to clone the attached, differentiated cells and ask how their morphological, electrical, and antigenic properties differ from other cells derived from the same clone.

(b) Tight Junctions in Other Tissue Culture Lines. Electrical or "tight" junctions have been demonstrated both in the central nervous system (Bennett, Nokajima, and Pappas, 1967) and between cells of most other tissues (Loewenstein, 1967), including embryonic (Potter, Furshpan, and Lennox, 1966). It has been strongly argued that these permeability junctions play an essential role in development and nervous function (Loewenstein, 1967), yet little is known about their genesis and mechanism of specificity. Since

similar electrical junctions have been demonstrated in fibroblast tissue culture lines (E. S. Lennox, personal communication), it follows that the study of tight junctions in various cloned tissue culture lines could lead to an understanding of the mechanism of tissue-tissue interactions and also serve as a model system for nervous specification. This is particularly true since tight junctions have both functional (Politoff, Socolar, and Loewenstein, 1967) and structural (Brightman and Reese, 1969) similarities to chemical synapses. In addition, it is relatively easy to isolate pure sheets of tight junctional membrane (Benedetti and Emmelot, 1968), and it has been demonstrated that this material is made up of *hexagonal arrays of subunits* (Benedetti and Emmelot, 1968). That such a repeating subunit structure is involved in specific cell-cell interactions is predictable from our knowledge of enzyme structure but has not been studied at the molecular level. The following paragraphs outline an experimental approach to the mechanisms involved in the specificity and also the development of cell-cell contacts.

To define the mechanism of specificity, the limiting membranes of a large quantity of cloned contact-inhibited cells such as 3T3 fibroblasts, where electrical coupling has been demonstrated (Section III), will be isolated. Tight junctional membranes will be isolated according to Benedetti and Emmelot (1968) and checked for purity by electron microscopy.

Once purified, the complex will be dissociated under as mild conditions as possible, such as high salt and low pH (Cook and Koshland, 1969), until a subunit of the approximate size of that observed by electron microscopy is generated and characterized by density centrifugation and electron microscopy. Then, conditions will be defined where specific reaggregation can be demonstrated, again using the technique of density gradient centrifugation.

Reaggregation could be quantified in a manner analogous to that used to study the complementation between immunoglobulin subunits (Mannik, 1967; Schubert and Cohn, 1968). By isolating tight-junction subunits from several cloned tissue culture lines and assaying the relative competition between homologous and heterologous subunits, the basis of tissue specificity may be elucidated. The physico-chemical nature of the individual subunits would then be determined and the structural proteins isolated. Specific questions could be asked regarding the structure-function relationship between the proteins (or glycoproteins) making up the subunit. For example, are there a number of proteins shared by all of the mouse cells, while a few are different? What is the relationship between the tight-junction proteins and those involved in nerve specificity? [See Section II(a).]

To examine the natural distribution of the tight-junction determinants and to establish when in the growth of tissue culture cells these determinants are expressed, antisera will be prepared against the purified tight-junction membrane sheets and also against the subunits and component molecules at each stage of purification. By adsorption of the sera with membranes from cells functionally lacking tight junctions, specific antisera could be prepared against the junctional determinants. These antisera could then be used to define the time of induction of these surface proteins — is it before or after cell-cell contact? — by the use of radioactive labeling and indirect immune precipitation (Schubert, 1968) and the cytotoxic assay for surface antigens. As with synaptosomal proteins [Section II(a)], specific antisera could be prepared against tight junctions from several mouse tissue culture lines and used to define the molecular determinants of tissue specificity. In addition, the role of the tight junction in the establishment and release from contact inhibition could be studied once some insight has been gained into the structure and specificity of the synapse. Clearly, the problems surrounding cell-cell interactions such as contact inhibition and tissue specification are central to cancer research, but as yet these problems have, for the most part, remained unsolved.

III. Electrophysiology and an Alternative Assay for Membrane Depolarization

The development of the electrical properties of the neuroblastoma has been studied in some detail, particularly with respect to the spread of acetylcholine sensitivity during cytodifferentiation (Harris and Dennis, 1970). Harris will continue the work that he originally initiated at The Salk Institute. This will include more work on the development of acetylcholine sensitivity in the neuroblastoma (to be correlated with the biochemistry of the receptor), examination of cells for evidence of chemical and electrical synapses, and the characterization of mutant cell lines with respect to their electrophysiological properties.

Since electrophysiological recording from single cells is a rather difficult and tedious procedure, attemps will be made to develop an alternative procedure for the measurement of membrane permeability changes. Clearly, the most promising of these is the measurement of radioactive potassium or sodium uptake and release with whole cells or closed membrane fragments. The techniques using whole cells have been worked out for the red cell system (Villamil and Kleeman, 1969) and could easily be adapted to the neuroblastoma system. Several modifications, such as the collection of cells on Millipore filters instead of by centrifugation, would be introduced. It may also be necessary to inactivate the adenosine triphosphatase-linked sodium-potassium pump with ouabain before the technique is sensitive enough to detect acetylcholine-induced permeability changes. In addition, it has recently been demonstrated that isolated fragments of the *Electroplax* electric organ can be used to quantitatively study acetylcholine-induced ion transport (J. P. Changeux, personal communication). This technique could be adapted to purified animal-cell membranes. Once the assay for depolarization is functional, the detailed pharmacology and kinetics of chemically induced depolarization could be studied. Then, similar techniques could be used to study catecholamine uptake and release and, finally, the coupling between acetylcholine depolarization and neurotransmitter release. (See below.)

IV. Acetylcholine Receptor

Since the neuroblastoma tissue culture line can be induced to generate an action potential by the extracellular iontophoretic application of acetylcholine, it necessarily has the acetylcholine receptor. The molecular mechanism which is responsible for acetylcholine-induced depolarization remains obscure; the neuroblastoma could clarify matters in at least two ways. These are the possible isolation of the acetylcholine receptor and, of more interest to the understanding of excitable membrane function, the selection and characterization of mutant cell lines blocked in their ability to respond to acetylcholine and others lacking the (or having an altered) active sodium-potassium pump.

There appear to be two philosophies regarding the characterization and isolation of the acetylcholine receptor. Several investigators have attempted to affinity-label the receptor protein (Changeux, Podleski, and Wofsy, 1967; Silman and Karlin, 1969), with relatively little success. Part of the difficulty is due to the heterogeneity of the cell population being labeled, which can be overcome by the use of cloned tissue culture lines. The other major difficulty, the relative lack of specificity of the highly reactive labeling reagent, is present in both systems. On the other hand, few investigators have tried directly to isolate the receptor using a binding assay for acetylcholine (O'Brien and Gilmour, 1969). This method has the distinct advantage of being able to work with a functional protein as opposed to an inactive affinity-labeled molecule. The techniques of equilibrium dialysis, and particularly the membrane filter assay (Jones and Berg, 1966; Riggs, Bourgeois, Newby, and Cohn, 1968; Schubert, Roman, and Cohn, 1970), would be most applicable. Cytoplasmic membranes are readily prepared, and these could be gently taken apart by a unique nonionic detergent, Nonidet P40 (Particle Data Laboratory Limited, Elmhurst, Illinois). This detergent has been shown to enhance the activity of several membrane-bound enzymes (Y. S. Choi, personal communication), and it is possible to do immune precipitations and hapten-antibody equilibrium dialysis in the presence of 1 percent detergent (Schubert, unpublished observation). Thus, by controlled lysis with detergent, followed by the fractionation of acetylcholine-binding activity in the presence of esterase inhibitors, it may be possible to isolate the pharmacological receptor. Reconstitution of the dissociated membrane may lead to a better understanding of both structure and function.

The isolation of the receptor could be facilitated by a comparison with cells which lack a functional receptor — by looking for a structural difference between mutant and wild type. The receptor-negative mutants may be isolated in the following manner. Acetylcholine or one of its functional analogues would be coupled to bovine serum albumin or any other suitable carrier. A population of mutagenized cells would be grown up and various concentrations of the conjugated acetylcholine added to the suspension. Antiserum prepared against the carrier would be added, followed by the addition of complement. In this manner, cells having the acetylcholine receptor would bind the hormone-protein conjugate and be lysed when anti-protein and complement were added. The survivors would be grown up and the selection procedure repeated many times until the survival was sufficiently high to indicate the existence of mutants. The cells would then be cloned and individual clones tested both electrophysiologically and directly for the binding activity.

A similar selection procedure may be used to select mutants effecting active sodium-potassium transport. Ouabain specifically blocks active transport at an apparently external membrane site in nervous tissue (reviewed by Whittam, 1967). The same selection procedure as above may be functional, this time coupling ouabain to the carrier. Acetylcholine esterase mutants would similarly be selected by coupling esterase-specific reagents, such as eserine, to the carrier molecules.

It should be pointed out, however, that the above selection procedure depends on the ability of the conjugated hormone or blocking agent to function normally. If the initial protein conjugates are not functional, it is relatively easy to couple the pharmacological agents on less conformationally rigid antigenic carriers such as polyamino acids or polysaccharides.

An alternative possibility for selecting both acetylcholine-receptor-negative mutants and ouabain-insensitive mutants is the following. It has been shown that cells grown in certain levels of ouabain are lysed by this reagent, presumably due to an alteration in their active transport mechanism (Schubert, unpublished observation). If cells were mutagenized and grown in a concentration of ouabain which limits growth 80 percent to 90 percent until the inhibition is partially overcome, followed by increasing the concentration of ouabain, mutants resistant to the drug may eventually be selected. A similar procedure has been successfully used to select hydrocortisone-resistant lines of a mouse lymphoma (Baxter, Harris, Tomkins, and Cohn, 1971).

The same technique may also be used to select against cells with the acetylcholine receptor. If cells were grown under conditions of *partial* growth inhibition — a 10 percent decrease in growth rate — by ouabain, it follows that any alteration in the delicately balanced active-transport-mediated permeability could be lethal or growth-inhibitory to the cells. Thus, if cells were grown under these conditions in the presence of a cholinergic agonist such as decamethonium, the cells which respond (those with an active acetylcholine receptor) would be selectively killed, selecting for uneffected receptor-negative mutants. This effect should be blocked by antagonists, such as *d*-turbocurarine and flaxedil, thus defining the specificity of the selection procedure. Since the pharmacology of the receptor on this neuroblastoma has not yet been

studied in detail, a large number of different agonists and antagonists will be tested.

Once mutants of the acetylcholine receptor, the acetylcholine esterase, and the ouabain-sensitive adenosine triphosphatase-activated sodium-potassium pump are isolated, the functional relationships between these processes could be studied and a number of *specific models* of nervous function tested. For example, it has been proposed that the acetylcholine receptor and the acetylcholine esterase are necessary for the conduction of an action potential (Nachmansohn, 1966) and that the acetylcholine receptor and the acetylcholine esterase may be the same molecule (Changeux, Leuzinger, and Huchet, 1968). Both models require that the receptor be coupled to an ion transport mechanism. Thus, if a mutant were isolated which lacked the acetylcholine receptor, but were still able to conduct an action potential, Nachmansohn's argument would be weakened; similarly, a mutant lacking the esterase but still able to be depolarized by acetylcholine would rule out Changeux's model. By scoring for the pleotropic loss of several unique functions following selection against one, a great deal of insight could be gained into both membrane structure and function in nervous tissue. It is doubtful that physical and chemical characterization of membranes alone can generate this kind of information any more than the details of macromolecule biosynthesis and regulation in bacteria could be understood without the aid of mutants.

Finally, it should be pointed out again that this neuroblastoma cell line is tetraploid, a fact which makes the selection of mutants more difficult, but far from impossible. Mutants derived from tetraploid plasmacytoma cell lines have been described and studied in detail (Schubert, Munro, and Ohno, 1968; Schubert and Horibata, 1968; Schubert and Cohn, 1968; Schubert and Cohn, 1970). Furthermore, it has been possible to select large numbers of mutants from tetraploid cells which are defective in surface antigens by a cytotoxic selection procedure similar to that described above (R. Hyman and M. Cohn, personal communications). It is, however, likely that any selection on polyploid cell lines may generate a disproportionally high number of trans-dominant regulatory-type mutations, a possibility which makes their study *no* less interesting.

V. Storage, Release, and Uptake of Catecholamines

It is known that the catecholamine neurotransmitters are stored in dense-core vesicles localized in the presynaptic nerve endings of the sympathetic nervous system (reviewed by Iverson, 1967). It is also known that, following release, the adrenergic transmitter is inactivated by uptake into the presynaptic nerve ending from which it originated. The molecular mechanisms of catecholamine uptake, storage, and release are for the most part unknown, primarily because of the complexity of the tissues studied (Iverson, 1967). The neuroblastoma tissue culture line synthesizes and accumulates catecholamines, and the cells also contain dense-core vesicles which are morphologically similar to those thought to contain norepinephrine. In addition, these vesicles are frequently found concentrated in regions of cell-cell contact which are suggestive of chemical synapses (Schubert, Humphreys, Baroni, and Cohn, 1969). It follows that this tissue culture line may be an ideal system to investigate transmitter release and its integration with axonal depolarization.

To establish that depolarization leads to neurotransmitter release, a Millipore chamber would be built which would contain the cells and a pair of electrodes and, at the same time, allow a steady stream of medium to pass around the cells. The outflow of this system would then be attached to a fraction collector. Since it is possible to induce cell depolarization and norepinephrine release in tissue slices by passing a low-frequency 5 V ac potential across a tissue culture dish (Baldessarini and Kopin, 1966), by using a similar mechanism catecholamine release should be demonstrable in these cells. In addition, if an assay for chemical depolarization is

successfully developed (Section III), it should be possible to devise a membrane assay for both catecholamine uptake and release. For example, cells would be "loaded" with ^{14}C-norepinephrine or a radioactive nondegradable false transmitter, depolarized with an agonist, and the rate of release of transmitter studied by stopping the reaction by collecting the cells on a Millipore filter. Similar experiments could be used to study catecholamine uptake. The numerous pharmacological agents which affect storage and release could then be studied initially at this macroscopic level, followed by a more rigorous definition of their modes of action. Perhaps some of these results would prove relevant to the natural mode of release.

Probably a more direct approach would be the isolation and characterization of the synaptic vesicles (Whittaker and Sheridan, 1965). Once purified, questions could be asked relative to the effect of membrane depolarization on the release of transmitter from isolated vesicles and whether or not individual vesicles are capable of catecholamine synthesis and uptake.

The derivation of the limiting membrane of the vesicles and possibly the mechanism of transmitter release could be investigated if it were possible to prepare antisera which recognize only vesicle membrane or the unique protein of unknown function which is found associated with adenosine triphosphate inside purified norepinephrine-containing vesicles (Iverson, 1967). There are two models which can be used to explain transmitter release; by the use of specific anti-vesicle sera one of these models could be ruled out. Either the vesicles internally release their contents which are then channeled to the outside, or the vesicles fuse directly with the presynaptic membrane, releasing their contents directly into the synaptic cleft, and the vesicle membrane becomes incorporated into the limiting cellular membrane. The latter may make sense if vesicle membranes could contribute to specificity, for it has frequently been suggested that repeated firing stabilizes nerve networks (Cohn, 1970). A necessary consequence of firing is the release of transmitter (and perhaps the vesicle protein) into the cleft. The vesicle-membrane fusion may reinforce the connection, as may the protein of unknown function contained in the vesicle. In this context, it may be of interest to see if synapses (electrical or chemical) are formed more rapidly in cultures which are frequently depolarized by alternating current.

One type of experiment would be the following. Two groups of ^{3}H-leucine-labeled cells would be prepared, and one would be electrically depolarized for 30 minutes. At the end of this time, antiserum directed against synaptic vesicle membrane, and another antiserum against vesicle protein, would be added to separate aliquots of washed cells and cell supernatants. A cytotoxic test would be done with the cells, looking for killing by the two types of anti-vesicle sera. If the depolarized cells are killed by the antisera and not the control, it would indicate that vesicle or vesicle contents are extracellularly bound after repeated firing of the cell, thus supporting the vesicle-membrane-fusion model. Similarly, the release of vesicle protein into the cell supernatant would be assayed by serological precipitation and acrylamide electrophoresis (Schubert, 1968). It would also be worth looking for other release proteins by running the entire cell supernatant on gel electrophoresis and comparing the two types of cells. This type of experimental approach could also be used to look at other cell functions following repeated firing.

In addition to looking at normal function, it should be possible to select mutants which lack synaptic vesicles and possibly the ability to synthesize catecholamines. It has been shown that 5- and 6-hydroxydopamine selectively destroy sympathetic nerve endings in vitro (Tranzer and Thoenen, 1968; Thoenen and Tranzer, 1968), with the concomitant loss of tyrosine hydroxylase activity (Mueller, Thoenen, and Axelrod, 1969). The effect of these two compounds on cell viability will be tested with respect to dosage and time required for killing. After a suitable concentration of the dopamine derivatives is determined, resistant cells will be selected in suspension, and possibly on agar plates containing the catecholamine. Clones of resistant lines

will then be characterized with respect to catecholamine synthesis, uptake, and release, and also synaptic vesicle synthesis. If it were possible to isolate lines lacking vesicles but still able to synthesize and release catecholamines, the controversies relative to the role of synaptic vesicles would be partially solved.

VI. Cyclic AMP

After reviewing the current literature, it appears that no grant request would be complete without a section on adenosine 3',5'-cyclic monophosphate (cAMP), so in this light we will make the following proposals. It is clear that cAMP plays a central role in the regulation of a large number of membrane-mediated, hormone-dependent processes (reviewed by Butcher, Robinson, and Sutherland, 1970). In addition, increasing evidence indicates that cAMP may promote nervous transmission by facilitating the release of neurotransmitters (Goldberg and Singer, 1969). There are thus two points in the neuroblastoma system where cAMP may be involved.

The first of these is the membrane-mediated induced differentiation of the neuroblast to neuron. Since cAMP mediates many hormone-dependent membrane phenomena, it is a good candidate to be involved in the induction of differentiation. This could be tested by examining the effects of cAMP, dibutyl cAMP, and the methyl xanthines on the process of differentiation and also by looking for changes in the levels of intracellular cAMP and the specific activity of adenyl cyclase under conditions leading to differentiation. If differentiation can be induced or enhanced by mimicing the adenyl cyclase system, then the cAMP effect will be examined in detail, particularly with respect to several proteins which appear to be induced by conditions leading to differentiation. The microtubule protein appears to be the most accessible in this group, and the control of its synthesis could be examined in a cell-free system. If mutants are found which are unable to differentiate (Section I), the possibility of a genetic lesion at the cAMP step will be examined. In this manner, some insight into the mechanism by which a cell handles a surface (tactile) stimulus (a process which is clearly of great importance to tissue formation and differentiation) may be gained.

The second area of interest is the role of cAMP in neurotransmitter release, for the neuroblastoma offers a unique opportunity to study this process. To determine whether or not cAMP is involved in release, cells would be "loaded" with radioactive norepinephrine or a nonmetabolizable false transmitter and the rate of transmitter release (both spontaneous and induced) studied in the presence of cAMP, dibutyl cAMP, and the methyl xanthines by methods described in Section III. If cAMP is involved, the rate of release should be facilitated by these compounds (Goldberg and Singer, 1969). Once facilitation is observed in the whole-cell system, then it should be possible to take apart the cell and ask specific questions regarding the integration or coupling of acetylcholine depolarization and transmitter release. For example, do acetylcholine and other agonists directly affect the specific activity of adenyl cyclase? Does cAMP induce the release of catecholamines from purified synaptic vesicles or membrane fragments?

VII. Complementation

The observation that the mouse neuroblastoma can undergo *reversible* differentiation (Schubert, Humphreys, de Vitry, and Jacob, 1971), along with the possibility of inducing somatic cell hybrids (Harris and Watkins, 1965), offers the opportunity to study the complementation between cells at various stages of phenotypic expression. For example, attached cells at various stages of differentiation could be fused by Sendai virus with rapidly dividing undifferentiated cells whose nuclei are marked with ^{3}H-thymidine. After fusion, the unattached, undifferentiated cells would be washed away and the attached cells

placed under conditions where mitosis is inhibited — low serum, 5-fluorodeoxyuridine, or cytosine arabinoside (Schubert, Humphreys, de Vitry, and Jacob, 1971); then, specific questions could be asked regarding the complementation of functions at the level of a *single cell*. For example, are the electrophysiological properties and acetylcholine sensitivity of the fused cell similar to the undifferentiated or differentiated parent? This could be answered by recording from a large number or cells and marking them by the iontophoretic injection of dye, followed by radioautography to score for the fused cells. In addition, if a number of mutants are selected which lack a given function (the acetylcholine receptor), complementation groups could be defined in the manner described above, without the need for growing out clones from fused cells, which is, in most cases, a very difficult task.

VIII. Other Cell Lines

It is planned that, during the tenure of this research proposal, the types of investigations outlined above can be extended to several other tissue culture lines, including those of muscle, adrenal chromaffin cells (which share many properties of the mouse neuroblastoma), and other cells of nervous tissue origin. In conjunction with Dr. M. Cohn (The Salk Institute), attempts are being made to induce brain tumors in a large number of mice by means of a wide spectrum of carcinogens. (See, for example, Ivankovic and Druckrey, 1968.) If successful, the induced tumors will be adapted to tissue culture by the methods used for the initial mouse neuroblastoma and characterized as described above. In addition, attempts will be made to establish embryonic cell lines in culture by transforming *specific* embryonic tissues in vitro, either with viruses (Dulbecco, 1969) or chemically (Heidelberger, 1964). This approach was successful with embryonic skeletal muscle (Yaffe, 1968), and there is no reason why it could not be extended to the nervous system.

IX. Tentative Time Schedule

The following[3] time schedule is based on the assumption that three postdoctoral fellows, a research technician, and the principal investigator are involved full time in the research the first year and that an additional postdoctoral fellow and an additional research technician are added during the second year.

References[4]

Adelman, M. R., Borisy, G. G., Shelanski, M. L., Weisenberg, R. C., and Taylor, E. W. 1968. Cytoplasmic filaments and tubules. *Federation Proceedings* 27:1186-1193.

Agusti-Tocco, G., and Sato, G. 1969. Establishment of functional clonal lines of neurons from mouse neuroblastoma. *Proceedings of the National Academy of Sciences* 64:311-315.

Baldessarini, R. J., and Kopin, I. J. 1966. Tritiated norepinephrine: release from brain slices by electrical stimulation. *Science* 152:1630-1631.

*Baxter, J. D., Harris, A. W., Tomkins, G. M., and Cohn, M. 1971. Glucocorticoid receptors in lymphoma cells in culture. *Science* 171:189-192.

Benedetti, E. L., and Emmelot, P. 1968. Hexagonal array of subunits in tight junctions separated from isolated rat liver plasma membranes. *Journal of Cell Biology* 38:15-24.

Bennett, M. V., Nokajima, Y., and Pappas, G. D. 1967. Physiology and ultrastructure of electronic junctions. *Journal of Neurophysiology* 30:161-179.

Bischoff, R., and Holtzer, H. 1970. Inhibition of myoblast fusion after one round of DNA synthesis in 5-bromodeoxyuridine. *Journal of Cell Biology* 44:134-150.

Brightman, M. W., and Reese, T. S. 1969. Junction between intimately apposed cell membranes in the vertebrate brain. *Journal of Cell Biology* 40:648-677.

Butcher, R. W., Robinson, G. A., and Sutherland, E. W. 1970. The role of cyclic AMP in certain biological control systems. Pages 64-67. *In* G. E. W. Wolstenholme and J. Knight (editors), *Control processes in multicellular organisms.* J. A. Churchill, London.

Changeux, J. P., Leuzinger, W., and Huchet, M. 1968. Specific binding of acetylcholine to acetylcholinesterase in the presence of eserine. *FEBS Letters* (Federation of European Biomedical Societies) 2:77-80.

Changeux, J. P., Podleski, T. R., and Wofsy, L. 1967. Affinity labeling of the acetylcholine-receptor. *Proceedings of the National Academy of Sciences* 58:2063-2070.

Cohn, M. 1967. Natural history of the myeloma. *Cold Spring Harbor Symposia on Quantitative Biology* 32:211-221.

Cohn, M. 1970. Anticipatory mechanisms of individuals. Pages 255-297. *In* G. E. W. Wolstenholme and J. Knight (editors), *Control processes in multicellular organisms.* J. A. Churchill, London.

Cook, A. C., and Koshland, D. E. 1969. Specificity in the assembly of multisubunit proteins. *Proceedings of the National Academy of Sciences* 64:247-254.

Dulbecco, R. 1969. Cell transformation of viruses. *Science* 166:962-968.

Edds, M. V. 1967. Neuronal specificity in neuronogenesis. Pages 230-240. *In* G. C. Quarton, T. Melnechuk, and F. O. Schmitt (editors), *The neurosciences: a study program.* The Rockefeller University Press, New York.

Goldberg, A. L., and Singer, J. J. 1969. Evidence for a role of cyclic AMP in neuromuscular transmission. *Proceedings of the National Academy of Sciences* 64:134-141.

*Harris, A. J., and Dennis, M. 1970. Acetylcholine sensitivity and distribution on mouse neuroblastoma cells. *Science* 167:1253-1255.

Harris, H., and Watkins, J. F. 1965. Hybrid cells derived from mouse and man: artificial heterokaryons of mammalian cells from different species. *Nature* 205:640-646.

Heidelberger, C. 1964. Studies on the molecular mechanism of hydrocarbon carcinogenesis. *Journal of Cellular and Comparative Physiology* 64(Supplement I):129-148.

*Horibata, K., and Harris, A. 1970. Mouse myelomas and lymphomas in culture. *Experimental Cell Research* 60:61-77.

Ivankovic, S., and Druckrey, H. 1968. Transplazentare Erzeugung maligner Tumoren des Nervensystems. I. Athyl-nitrosoharnstoff (ANH) und BD IX-Ratten. *Zeitschrift für Krebsforschung und Klinische Onkologie* 71:320-360.

Iverson, L. L. 1967. *The uptake and storage of noradrenaline in sympathetic nerves.* Cambridge University Press, Cambridge, England, 293 pages.

Jones, O. W., and Berg, P. 1966. Studies on the binding of RNA polymerase to polynucleotides. *Journal of Molecular Biology* 22:199-209.

Kreutzberg, G. W. 1969. Neuronal dynamics and axonal flow. IV. Blockage of intra-axonal enzyme transport by colchicine. *Proceedings of the National Academy of Sciences* 62:722-728.

Loewenstein, W. R. 1967. On the genesis of cellular communication. *Developmental Biology* 15:503-520.

Mannik, M. 1967. Variability in the specific interaction of H and L chains of gamma-G-globulins. *Biochemistry* 6:134-142.

Marantz, R., Ventilla, M., and Shelanski, M. 1969. Vinblastine-induced precipitation of microtubule protein. *Science* 165:498-499.

Mueller, R. A., Thoenen, H., and Axelrod, J. 1969. Adrenal tyrosine hydroxylase: compensatory increase in activity after chemical sympathectomy. *Science* 163:468-469.

Nachmansohn, D. 1966. Chemical control of the permeability cycle in excitable membranes during electrical activity. *Annals of the New York Academy of Sciences* 137:877-900.

O'Brien, R. D., and Gimour, L. P. 1969. A musarone-binding material in electroplax and its relation to the acetylcholine receptor. I. Centrifugal assay. *Proceedings of the National Academy of Sciences* 63:496-503.

Politoff, A., Socolar, S. J., and Loewenstein, W. R. 1967. Metabolism and the permeability of cell membrane junctions. *Biochimica et Biophysica Acta* 135:791-793.

---

[3] The time schedule that followed this paragraph in the original proposal is not reprinted here.

[4] Throughout this References section, an asterisk preceding an entry denotes the reference was in press or submitted for publication when the application was written.

Potter, D. D., Furshpan, E. J., and Lennox, E. S. 1966. Connections between cells of the developing squid as revealed by electrophysiological methods. *Proceedings of the National Academy of Sciences* 55:328-336.

Riggs, A., Bourgeois, S., Newby, R., and Cohn, M. 1968. DNA binding of the *lac* repressor. *Journal of Molecular Biology* 34:365-368.

Sato, G. H., and Yasumura, Y. 1966. Retention of differentiated function in dispersed cell culture. *Transactions of the New York Academy of Sciences* 28:1063-1079.

Schubert, D. 1968. Immunoglobulin assembly in a mouse myeloma. *Proceedings of the National Academy of Sciences* 60:683-690.

*Schubert, D. 1970. Immunoglobulin biosynthesis. IV. Carbohydrate attachment to immunoglobulin subunits. *Journal of Molecular Biology* 51:287-301.

Schubert, D., and Cohn, M. 1968. Immunoglobulin biosynthesis. III. Blocks in defective synthesis. *Journal of Molecular Biology* 38:273-300.

*Schubert, D., and Cohn, M. 1970. Immunoglobin biosynthesis. V. Light chain assembly. *Journal of Molecular Biology* 53:305-320.

Schubert, D., and Horibata, K. 1968. Immunoglobulin biosynthesis. II. Four independently isolated myeloma variants. *Journal of Molecular Biology* 38:263-273.

*Schubert, D., and Jacob, F. 1970. 5-Bromodeoxyuridine-induced differentiation of a neuroblastoma. *Proceedings of the National Academy of Sciences* 67:247-254.

Schubert, D., Humpreys, S., Baroni, C., and Cohn, M. 1969. In vitro differentiation of a mouse neuroblastoma. *Proceedings of the National Academy of Sciences* 64:316-323.

*Schubert, D., Humphreys, S., de Vitry, F., and Jacob, F. 1971. Induced differentiation of a neuroblastoma. *Developmental Biology* 25:514-546.

Schubert, D., Munro, A., and Ohno, S. 1968. Immunoglobin biosynthesis. I. A myeloma variant secreting light chain only. *Journal of Molecular Biology* 38:253-262.

Schubert, D., Roman, A., and Cohn, M. 1970. Anti-nucleic acid specificities of mouse myeloma immunoglobins. *Nature* 225:154-158.

Silman, I., and Karlin, A. 1969. Acetylcholine receptor: covalent attachment of depolarizing groups at the active site. *Science* 164:1420-1421.

Thoenen, H., and Tranzer, J. P. 1968. Möglichkeit der chemischen Sympathektomie durch selektive Zerstörung adrenerger Nervenendigugen mit 6-Hydroxydopamin (6—OH—DA). *Naunyn-Schmiedebergs Archiv für Pharmakologie und Experimentelle Pathologie* 261:271-288.

Thompson, E. B., Tomkins, G. M., and Curran, J. F. 1966. Induction of tyrosine alpha-ketoglutarate transaminase by steroid hormones in a newly established tissue culture cell line. *Proceedings of the National Academy of Sciences* 56:296-303.

Tranzer, J. P., and Thoenen, H. 1968. An electron microscopic study of selective, acute degeneration of sympathetic nerve terminals after administration of 6-hydroxydopamine. *Experientia* 24:155-156.

Villamil, M. F., and Kleeman, C. R. 1969. The effect of ouabain and external potassium on the ion transport of rabbit red cells. *Journal of General Physiology* 54:576-588.

Whittaker, V. P., and Sheridan, M. N. 1965. The morphology and acetylcholine content of isolated cerebral cortical synaptic vesicles. *Journal of Neurochemistry* 12:363-372.

Whittam, R. 1967. The molecular mechanism of active transport. Pages 305-312. *In* G. C. Quarton, T. Melnechuk, and F. O. Schmitt (editors), *The neurosciences: a study program.* The Rockefeller University Press, New York.

Yaffe, D. 1968. Retention of differentiation potentialities during prolonged cultivation of myogenic cells. *Proceedings of the National Academy of Sciences* 61:477-483.

* * *

THE RESEARCH GRANT BUDGET: PREPARATION AND JUSTIFICATION IN RELATION TO THE PROPOSED RESEARCH

by James M. Pike* and Steven C. Bernard†

Although the research grant budget is usually prepared after the text of a proposal has been completed, it is nonetheless an integral part of a research grant application and must clearly reflect resources needed for the proposed project. Experienced grant applicants know that the members of the staff of the granting agency and the reviewers expect to find a clear and justifiable relation between the proposed project and the requested budget. Without such a total presentation, there is little chance that the budget will be approved as requested.

The preparation of the budget should be approached as a two-part exercise. First, funds

*National Heart, Lung, and Blood Institute, National Institutes of Health, Bethesda, Maryland.

†Office of the Director, National Institutes of Health, Bethesda, Maryland.

are listed for specified categories. For the application used by the National Institutes of Health (NIH), the applicant fills in descriptors and dollar amounts on a printed budget form with specified categories.* Secondly, detailed and concise justification or explanation is provided for each category of funds requested. The need for a carefully considered justification for the budget cannot be emphasized too strongly. Those who have observed or participated in the review of research grant applications have repeatedly heard the reviewers state such criticisms as: "the need for that item of equipment is not clear," "there is no justification for that number of animals," or "this project would not seem to require that much participation of technical staff." Such statements are usually the result of an inadequate justification for the requested budget. The applicant should know best what the budgetary needs are for the project proposed and, if asked, could usually explain the reason for each amount requested. The review of most research grant applications, however, does not include an on-site visit.[1] Consequently, the merit of a research grant application must be evaluated almost solely on the basis of the application, without any opportunity for discussions between the applicant and the reviewers.[2,3] While a well-written presentation of the scientific protocol may serve indirectly to justify the requested budget, the need for a separate, complete, and concise explanation of the requested budget facilitates the review and enhances the likelihood that the budget will be recommended for funding in the amount requested.

The extent of clarification that accompanies the budget is best judged by the applicant. The detail that might be included as part of the wirtten clarification, however, depends on a number of considerations, such as the clarity and completeness of the text of the application,

the kinds and quantity of equipment and supplies already available, and the prospective judgment of future needs as the research progresses. The content of the clarification of the budget should also be developed with a constant awareness of the time the reviewers have to read each application. Since a large number of applications have to be reviewed at a meeting of the review group, the considerate — and wise — applicant will provide readily accessible, concise, and clear justification for the budget.

Justification for the First Year

The explanation of the budget should be prominently entitled "Justification for the Budget," or "Explanation of the Budget," and it should have the same sequence of items or budgetary categories as on the printed budget page. A simple and direct format enhances the usefulness and impact of this section. Each cost category, such as personnel, equipment, supplies, and travel, should clearly stand out as subsections so that the reviewers may quickly and easily find the needed information. In an example of such a format, we have presented below examples of typical questions that reviewers ask themselves as they assess the appropriateness of the requested budget. Categories for which funds are requested only rarely, such as for alterations and renovations and for patient care, usually require specific guidance from the anticipated awarding component of the NIH and have therefore not been included in the following list.

Personnel

- Are the number of professional and non-professional staff consistent with the effort required by the research protocol?
- Does the amount requested for personnel to be appointed reflect anticipated beginning dates for such appointments?

---

*The printed "Detailed Budget for First 12-Month Period" is provided as page 3 of the "Application for Public Health Service Grant or Award" (Form NIH 398). An example of this page of the NIH application form was presented in *Grants Magazine*, Vol. 1, No. 2, p. 175.

- Are the requirements for some portions of the research protocol so extensive that they justify what might otherwise be considered an inflated request for personnel?
- Is the time or effort allocated for each person consistent with other concurrent or pending efforts with which each may be involved?
- Does the budget reflect the time or effort for those who would be working on the project but who would receive total or partial remuneration from other sources of support?
- Does the budget reflect an appropriate request for fringe benefits?
- Does the institution allocate fringe benefits to indirect costs or to direct costs?
- Does the request reflect midyear salary increases that could be anticipated when the application was prepared?

Consultant Costs

- Who are the consultants?
- With what institutions are the consultants affiliated?
- Are the consultants so well known that biographical sketches are not needed?
- What portions of the project require advice from consultants?

Equipment

- Has it been determined whether these items are already available in the institution's inventory of unused equipment?
- Has it been determined whether these items are available in nearby laboratories and could be shared?
- Would it be more economical to rent any of the items rather than purchase them?

Supplies

- Are the major subcategories of supplies identified, such as animals, chemicals, and glassware?

- Where applicable, are unit prices shown?
- How has the rate of usage been determined?

Travel

- Is the amount of and reason for the anticipated travel consistent with the goals of the research project and with the amount of effort that the investigator will devote to the project?
- Has special justification been provided for any foreign travel requested?

Other Expenses

- Have maintenance costs for laboratory animals been included? Have these costs been estimated on the basis of the guidelines for the care of laboratory animals?
- Does the project require purchased services from third parties or other institutions? If so, has the need for third-party indirect costs been anticipated?

The Future Years

The application used by the NIH provides the opportunity to request up to seven years of support.* Development of the budget for future years of research support requires considerable foresight in predicting research results and probably a certain amount of clairvoyance. While many granting agencies have the authority to adjust budgets upwards to accommodate unforeseen needs, fiscal constraints often preclude the provision of exigency funds. For this reason, carefully and thoughtfully developed budgets

---

*The printed "Budget Estimates for All Years of Support Requested from Public Health Service" is provided as page 4 of the "Application for Public Health Service Grant or Award" (Form NIH 398). An example of this page of the NIH application form was presented in *Grants Magazine,* Vol. 1, No. 2, p. 176.

for future years are clearly advantageous to the applicant. The budgets for future years should also be accompanied, where appropriate, by written justification or explanation.

For the assessment of financial needs in future years, the simple percentage-based extrapolation of inflation-prone categories such as personnel or supplies will only partially suffice. When it is possible to do so, the investigator should estimate as accurately as possible the actual resources needed in future years. These budgets should reflect not only a reasonable and appropriate extension of the request for the first year but also the changing needs of the research project. For example, justification for the budgets for future years should reveal the rationale for increased or decreased amounts in the different categories. How have cost-of-living adjustments or promotions as mandated by institutional policy been reflected? Will the need for personnel increase or decrease in future years, and are the reasons clear? In relation to anticipated progress in the research, is there a need for a new and specific item of equipment in a future year, and has that been justified?

In summary, the judicious preparation of a budget for a research grant proposal should include an accompanying section that clearly and concisely justifies the funds requested for each category. Even though an applicant may feel that the text of the proposal provides adequate justification for the budget requested, the relation between the budget and the proposed project may not be readily apparent to the reviewers. Since the success of the proposed research project is dependent on adequate resources, the applicant should make certain that all information needed for the most advantageous review is readily available and that nothing is left to chance.

Acknowledgment

We wish to thank Dr. George N. Eaves for his editorial and literary advice and for his suggestions regarding the content of this article.

References

1. Merritt, D. H., and Eaves, G. N. Site visits for the review of grant applications to the National Institutes of Health: views of an applicant and a scientist administrator. *Federation Proceedings* 34:131-136, 1975.
2. Eaves, G. N. Who reads your project-grant application to the National Institutes of Health? *Federation Proceedings* 31:2-9, 1972.
3. Eaves, G. N. The grant application: an exercise in scientific writing. *Federation Proceedings* 32:1541-1543, 1973.

The Impact of Inflation-Recession on Families in Cities

Funded by: Center for the Study of Metropolitan Problems, National Institute of Mental Health (NIMH)

Principal Investigator: David Caplovitz, Professor, Sociology Department, Graduate School and University Center, City University of New York

Proposal prepared by: David Caplovitz

THE HISTORY OF THE INFLATION—RECESSION PROPOSAL

by David Caplovitz

The idea of studying inflation occurred to me in April of 1974. At that time, the inflation rate was soaring to over 10 percent and unemployment was also climbing sharply, a state of affairs that economists had long insisted could not happen. Conventional economic wisdom held that, when inflation was high, unemployment would be low and vice-versa. The anomaly of high unemployment and high inflation was shaking not only economics but also the political establishment as well.

David Caplovitz is a Professor of Sociology at the Graduate School and University Center of the City University of New York. At this writing, he is on leave, having been awarded a Guggenheim Fellowship to write a book based on the research made possible by the grant application presented here. The book, which will appear in 1979, is titled *Making Ends Meet: How Families Cope with Inflation and Recession.*

The idea for doing research came to me from reading an article in the *Wall Street Journal* on unemployment. I had naively assumed that the unemployed were people who had lost their jobs, but from the *Wall Street Journal* article I learned that a significant portion of the unemployed consists of people who are looking for their first job. The unemployed are defined as people who want to work but do not have a job, and of course this group includes new workers who have entered the labor market. I became quite excited for I felt I had an important clue to the enigma of high unemployment and high inflation. Trying to cope with rising prices was forcing new family members into the labor market. Many housewives, I assumed, were looking for work in order to make ends meet and were being counted as unemployed. A few days later, I told an economist friend that I was going to apply for a grant to find out how many of the unemployed were people who had been forced into the labor market because of inflation. My friend promptly discouraged me, explaining that there is an enormous body of economic literature on inflation and unemployment and, unless I was familiar with that literature, no one would take me seriously. This was discouraging because I could not see myself spending months getting familiar with this literature. I asked my friend if she did not think it important to know how many of the unemployed were new workers suffering from inflation? She persisted in her criticism and I tried to develop a new tack. Forget the economics literature, I said. Suppose I do a sociological study of the impact of inflation on families, how they are coping with inflation and who is hurting the most. She had no objection to this approach and so it was through this dialogue that the idea of a study of the impact of inflation on families was born.

A few days later I telephoned the director of the Center for the Study of Metropolitan Problems of the National Institute of Mental Health (NIMH) to find out whether the Center would be interested in funding such a study. He thought it was a pretty good idea and toward the end of April I sent him an eight-page memorandum spelling out the specific themes of the proposed study. In early May he called me and told me that he liked the memo and encouraged me to write a proposal; he reminded me that his was a center for the study of *metropolitan* problems. We agreed that, instead of doing a national survey, the research would focus on five large cities.

By the June 1 deadline, I submitted a proposal entitled "The Impact of Inflation on Families in American Cities," the phrase, "American Cities," being my homage to the Metro Center. This proposal was nineteen pages long, and ten of them consisted of various required forms such as budget pages and biographical sketches of the principal participants. I had decided to ask two colleagues to collaborate on the study, one a fellow sociology professor at CUNY's graduate school and the other an economics professor, with the result that six of the opening pages were biographical sketches. The entire research plan, its objectives and methods, was described in nine single-spaced pages. This description of the research plan followed the outline provided by NIMH: (1) a statement of Objectives; (2) Background, meaning a review of relevant literature; (3) Specific Aims; and (4) Methods of Procedure. The content of the final proposal follows, but I would like to provide some idea of the content as it appeared in the first proposal submitted in June 1974.

The original proposal began by identifying the problems of rampant inflation in a time of high unemployment. It argued that the current inflation was a relatively new phenomenon because, unlike past inflationary cycles which were relatively brief, this inflation seemed to be part of a long-term process — that inflation was becoming part of our way of life. It then argued that this long-range inflation should have a profound impact on the American way of life and that dramatic changes in that way of life were beginning to develop. Under "Objectives," I stated that the purpose of the proposed research was to document systematically the various ways in which the current era of inflation has affected the way of life of families in American cities. I added that the "ultimate purpose of the research is to provide information that will be useful to policy makers who must weigh the costs and benefits of the current inflationary pressures."

Under "Background" I pointed out that there was very little sociological literature on inflation and that perhaps the most relevant literature for such a study was the literature on poverty that had emerged in the sixties in connection with the "war on poverty." As I pointed out in the proposal, "the more well-to-do families of the middle class have in the past few years found themselves confronting a problem that the poor have always faced." The poor have long since learned to feed themselves on inexpensive foods, e.g., the various ingredients that constitute "soul food" in the black culture, and the middle class, in this period of hyperinflation, would appear to be following in the footsteps of the perennially poor. The proposed research would examine the ways in which the middle class is learning lifestyles formerly associated with the poor, a process that might be called the "proletarianization" of the middle class. This concept did not appear in the final proposal because in that proposal the recession element was equal in importance to inflation and there was an enormous body of recession literature to be summarized for background. In short, the final proposal made no reference to poverty research for I no longer had to struggle with the "Background" section. Not only was the interesting idea of the proletarianization of the middle class dropped from the final proposal, but also it was omitted in the final report, although the report did document the ways in which middle class families curtailed consumption. I am currently revising that report for publication and, when I reread the original proposal in order to prepare this paper, I fortunately rediscovered this idea in time to work it into the final manuscript. (I am, of course, taking advantage of this assignment to indulge myself in a tiny piece of intellectual history.)

Under "Specific Aims," I listed six topics that would be examined in the research: (1) changes in labor force participation, e.g., the extent to which housewives were being forced to seek work; (2) changes in providing for necessities, e.g., food, clothing, and household repairs; (3) changes in expenditures for nonessentials, e.g., leisure and recreational activities; (4) changes in family relations; (5) changes in mental health of family members; and (6) changes in social organization — the development of communal responses to inflation. It is perhaps useful to compare these themes with those listed under "Specific Aims" in the final proposal that follows.

Under the heading "Methods of Procedure" I enumerated the three types of studies that were planned in much the same way that they are described in the final proposal. These three types of study were closely connected to the research team I had assembled. The basic study was to be a large household survey of which I, an old hand at survey research, was to be in charge.

The second kind of study I built into the proposal was one based on field work, consisting of a series of depth interviews with people in different social strata to find out how they were coping with inflation. Building this kind of field work, which would generate qualitative data within the study, was done for two reasons. First, these data would undoubtedly enrich the survey, but the main reason was political. I was convinced that this would increase the likelihood that the proposal would be funded. Members of review committees that act on proposals typically come from a wide range of backgrounds. Some are experienced in survey research and feel comfortable with it; others are likely to be qualitative researchers who do field work. It was to appeal to this latter faction that I made certain to include qualitative research in the proposal. This turned out to be the correct decision. The qualitative data enrich the revised report and greatly improve its overall quality. My colleague, William Kornblum, an expert in field work, supervised the depth interviews that were carried out by research assistants during the early months of the study while the questionnaire was being formulated.

The third type of research proposed under "Methods of Procedure" called for econometric studies of inflation and unemployment to be carried out by an economist working with the kinds of data collected by the Bureau of Labor Statistics. An economist at the City University, Roger Alcaly, agreed to fill this role.

The initial proposal submitted to NIMH asked for $258,582 in direct costs for a two-year study. By far the biggest item in this budget was the cost of the envisioned 2500 interviews in five cities, for which $137,000 was requested.

Several months after the proposal was submitted, I was notified by NIMH (the Metro Center) that I was to be site visited in mid-August. The visitors raised a number of questions and suggested that they be answered in an addendum to the proposal.

The first question had to do with the sampling plan for the household survey. The original proposal talked about sampling five cities with populations of 200,000 or more. The five sampled cities were to represent differing degrees of inflation. By late August 1974, when the addendum was prepared, unemployment was vying with inflation as the major problem and in the addendum I said we would sample two high unemployment cities, probably Detroit and Seattle, two low unemployment cities, Chicago and Atlanta, and one city representing the middle range of unemployment, New York.

A second question raised by the site visitors dealt with our conceptual orientation and the logic of the analysis. The addendum pointed out that the various topics for investigation listed in the proposal dealt with two themes: strategies for coping with inflation, and the impact of inflation on the well-being of the individual and the family. I then developed a new idea in the addendum. The proposal as written focused on *responses* to inflationary pressures. As such, it made the unwitting and erroneous assumption that all families to be surveyed would experience the same degree of inflationary pressure. But of course some families would be harder hit by rising prices than others. Therefore, I pointed out that a central concept to be measured in the research "is the impact of inflation on the family, a variable that might be called 'inflation crunch'." This idea would be developed by both objective and subjective measures of the effect of inflation. "Objective crunch" was defined as the extent to which family income fell behind rising prices. "Subjective crunch" referred to the degree to which the family is hurting from inflation. These ideas which were developed in the addendum to the first proposal became central in the final proposal and in the research report.

One site visitor wanted more detail about the methods and functions of the field work. The addendum explained that fifty or so working class and middle class families would be periodically interviewed over the life of the project. These depth interviews would serve two functions: they would provide input for the questionnaire by alerting us to lines of inquiry that were not anticipated, and they would greatly increase our understanding of the impact of inflation.

Still another question had to do with the costs of the survey. In the proposal, the estimated cost of each interview was fifty-five dollars. To satisfy this site visitor, I called up several interviewing agencies and got estimates ranging from forty-two dollars to sixty dollars, suggesting that my original estimate was a good one.

One site visitor had suggested that the survey inquire about perceived causes of inflation and in the addendum we agreed to do this.

The review committee met in September of 1974 and I learned from the director of the Metro Center that there was considerable dissension about the merits of our proposal. Some review committee members thought we were asking for too much money for such a short (nineteen pages) proposal. By an extremely narrow vote the reviewers decided to reject the proposal as it was, but recommended that we be encouraged to submit a new proposal for the next round, by February 1, 1975, which I agreed to do.

By October 1974, unemployment had replaced inflation as the number one problem and I took this into account in revising the proposal. The title of the proposal was changed from "The Impact of Inflation on Families in American Cities" to "The Impact of Inflation—Recession on Families in Cities." If there was virtually no sociological literature on inflation, there was an abundance of literature on the Great Depression. I discovered, by chance, that the Social Science Research Council (SSRC) had, in the thirties, sponsored thirteen studies of the impact of the Depression on American institutions, and I spent the next two weeks at the SSRC reading these studies. This background was reflected in the revised proposal which had five single-spaced pages devoted to a review of the literature, mainly these SSRC Depression studies. The revised proposal, unlike the original one, talked about objective and subjective inflation crunch, the impact of inflation on basic values and attitudes, and interpretations of the causes of inflation and recession held by the respondents to be sampled. Once the review of the

Depression literature was completed, it took about three days to draft the revised and final proposal. Although it was completed in November, it was not submitted until January of 1975 for the proposal deadline of February 1.

The revised proposal was thirty-one pages long compared with nineteen pages for the original proposal; personnel costs were increased by about $45,000 over the two-year period bringing the total of direct costs to $303,062.

The review committee met in April and approved the proposal in principle. I was told that, although they liked the proposal, they thought it was too expensive and should be cut in half. They also felt that the econometric analysis I had proposed was unnecessary and should be eliminated. I was ready to acquiesce to the decision to eliminate the econometric study, which meant eliminating the economist, and thus reducing the personnel budget by $29,000 over the two-year period. But I was not prepared to settle for only half of the amount of money I asked for. I proposed reducing the sample size, doing the research in four cities instead of five, and reducing the household sample from 2500 cases to 2000. This meant a saving of another $28,000 or so, for a total saving of about $57,000. This brought the budget down to $246,000 in direct costs and I insisted that we needed this much, that a good study could not be done for the $150,000 the review committee had recommended. We finally agreed on $215,000 in direct costs over the two-year period.

So much for the history of the inflation—recession proposal. I have one closing comment. The research began in September of 1975 and was to be terminated in August of 1977. I asked for a three-month extension, without additional funds, to December 1977 which the funding agency readily granted. At the end of the grant period, the funding agency received a 268-page final report. They were extremely happy for it had been their experience to receive final reports many months, and even years, late and in some instances never to receive a report at all. One sure way to win friends and obtain influence with funding agencies is to deliver final reports on time. Knowing how to write a winning proposal is, of course, extremely important. But it is just as important to deliver the final goods and, unfortunately, many academic researchers fail to do so.

* * *

THE UNIQUE OPPORTUNITY

by Paul Hennessey

> UNIQUE (u-nek), adj. 1. one and only; single; sole. 2. different from all others; having no like or equal. 3. singular; unusual; extraordinary; rare.
>
> *Webster's New World Dictionary of the American Language*

At its most basic level, proposal writing is an attempt to convince a funder that your project is more deserving than others sitting on his desk. Perhaps the most powerful argument in favor of your case is that your proposed work is *unique,* as Webster says, "singular; unusual; extraordinary; rare."

Surprisingly, many grant writers do not deal with this important issue. They supply the vita of their principal investigator, but do not say why that person is best suited to lead this particular project. They point out the need, but do not emphasize the particular urgency of the need today. In short, they look on their proposal as a mere explanation of what they hope to do — and not as a description of the unique opportunity it offers the funder.

This important shift in emphasis — from "our project" to "your opportunity" — can make a world of difference to your fundability. The proposal reproduced in this issue, "The Impact of Inflation—Recession on Families in Cities," is a fine example of the right way to present your case. In readable, jargon-free language, David Caplovitz's grant winning application offers the National Institute of Mental Health (NIMH) a unique opportunity to solve a pressing problem.

Caplovitz accomplishes this by pointing out four important facts:

1. The problem he addresses is particularly pressing now.
2. Past attempts to deal with similar problems suggest this study will uncover important new findings.
3. Each staff member of the research team is uniquely qualified to work on his part of the project; in addition, the combination of these people represents a unique opportunity to tackle the task at hand.
4. There will be important, concrete, and practical applications as a result of this study.

By emphasizing these aspects of his project, he makes it appear more than a good investment — it also offers the opportunity to put a unique group of people to work on a problem that will never be more important.

Let's take a closer look at the application and see how this is done.

Throughout "The Impact of Inflation—Recession on Families in Cities," the problem of inflation—recession is described as a two-part issue:

● as an important social threat.
● as a particularly difficult fact of life for both individuals and families.

Caplovitz doesn't treat inflation as an abstract academic subject. On the contrary, he describes it as a problem threatening the American way of life. As the quoted editorial from *Skeptic* points out, "Unless we check inflation, it will cost us our freedom." He never loses track of inflation as a problem faced by *people*. The emphasis throughout is on families: "Families in all walks of life will have been touched by these economic conditions, and, for some, the pres-

sures will be so great that their very survival will be threatened." His emphasis on the family, and especially his interest in doing in-depth case studies on selected families, reflects his deep interest in the human side of this economic problem.

Emphasizing both the societal *and* individual dimensions of inflation makes all the difference. Funders are certainly interested in solving large problems, but they are also motivated by the desire to help individual people.

After the problem is outlined, Caplovitz goes on to describe the next unique aspect of his project: its potential to produce important findings. Interestingly, this is done in the "Background" section of the application. Rather than merely cataloging other works in the field, Caplovitz describes key work done in the past. The best example of this is the listing of "nuggets of information" from studies done on the Great Depression of the 1930s. The effect is striking: The reviewer senses the possibility that *this* study may produce similar or better information on important issues of today, such as crime, education, marriage, and mental health.

The effective focus on uniqueness is perhaps most clear in the proposal's description of project staffing and significance.

When the investigators (Caplovitz, Kornblum, and Alcaly) are introduced, they are described as more than competent researchers. Caplovitz's background is outlined as it directly relates to the proposed project: "It is widely assumed that rampant inflation is pushing people deeper and deeper into debt and the principal investigator's knowledge of this problem area will strengthen the proposed research in this respect."

Professor Kornblum's participation in the project is described as a unique opportunity to tie past research findings (of Dr. Sam Sieber, who we find is the only sociologist to have done a study of inflation) to the proposed project. "In short, by taking advantage of Professor Kornblum's close ties with the steelworkers of Union District #31, we will be able to tie our research more closely to the earlier work of Sieber." To make this opportunity seem even more attractive, we later find that Dr. Sieber himself will be part of the project, thus lending the credibility of an important earlier study to the proposed project.

The overall sense of the proposal is thus that an unusually qualified group is coming together to work as a team on an important contemporary problem.

The fourth unique aspect of the project that is emphasized is its potential for practical application. This becomes evident in both the "Objectives" and the "Significance" sections of the application.

Like many scholars, Caplovitz and his researchers are interested in "making a contribution to knowledge" (their own words). But the main thrust of their project is on two important practical applications of that knowledge: an improved understanding of the perplexing relationship between inflation and recession; and an improved ability of policymakers to act to help those most affected by that inflation–recession.

Applications

What can we learn from "The Impact of Inflation–Recession on Families in Cities"? Simply this: Each time you write a grant proposal, ask yourself "What makes this project a unique opportunity for the funder?"

Do you have particularly good facilities? A unique team of investigators? The potential to produce practically applicable results? A problem that is particularly important right now? The answers to these questions should become the key foci of your application.

Notable Features of This Proposal

ATTENTION TO DETAIL

Careful attention to details indicates that you have thought through your project. David Caplovitz's application demonstrates this, especially in the completion of the standard Application for Public Health Service Grant or Award (NIH 398). All appropriate boxes are completed. Social security numbers and the institutional IRS number are supplied. Note particularly box number 7, "Research Involving Human Subjects." All government funded projects involving people as subjects of research must be approved by an appropriate institutional committee, and that approval transmitted to the Office for Protection of Research Risks at the National Institutes of Health (NIH) before an award can be made. This application was submitted for institutional review concurrent with its mailing to the Division of Research Grants at NIH. Note also that the budget is broken down into detail, including professional time to be invested, salaries (actual figures deleted for confidentiality), and the cost of the interviews.

THROUGH DESCRIPTION OF METHODOLOGY

Under the heading "Methods of Procedure" Caplovitz begins an in-depth discussion of his methodology. Note the care with which he describes each phase of the study. Details are given about the selection of interviewees, timing, costs, and even about attempts to find the lowest reasonable cost for the interviews. Caplovitz has also spent a good deal of time scheduling his project.

AWARENESS OF THE FUNDER'S "AGENDA"

The project was tailored to reflect the funder's interests. As you read the history of the negotiations for the project, you note two important tailoring elements. First, Caplovitz acquainted himself with the proposal structure required by the National Institute of Mental Health (NIMH): *Objectives, Background, Specific Aims,* and *Methods of Procedure.* A quick glance through the final proposal shows how closely he adhered to that format. Second, and more important, Caplovitz was flexible enough to alter his project to give NIMH exactly what it wanted. Because he was applying to the Center for the Study of Metropolitan Problems at NIMH, for example, he focused his study on major American cities. Further, he designed the project with negotiable items. Aspects of his study could be deleted or altered without destroying the viability of the project. This turned out to be very important. At NIMH's request, Caplovitz reduced the number of household surveys from 2500 to 2000 to reduce project costs, and the econometric analysis described in the proposal was deleted. The project design was flexible enough to withstand these changes, and still remain fundable.

SECTION I

Form Approved
O.M.B. 68-R0249

DEPARTMENT OF
HEALTH, EDUCATION, AND WELFARE
PUBLIC HEALTH SERVICE

GRANT APPLICATION

TO BE COMPLETED BY PRINCIPAL INVESTIGATOR (Items 1 through 7 and 15A)

1. TITLE OF PROPOSAL (Do not exceed 53 typewriter spaces)

The Impact of Inflation-Recession on Families in Cities

2. PRINCIPAL INVESTIGATOR

3. DATES OF ENTIRE PROPOSED PROJECT PERIOD (This application.

2A. NAME (Last, First, Initial)

Caplovitz, David

| FROM | THROUGH |
| September 1, 1975 | August 31, 1977 |

2B. TITLE OF POSITION

Professor of Sociology

4. TOTAL DIRECT COSTS RE-QUESTED FOR PERIOD IN ITEM 3
$303,062

5. DIRECT COSTS REQUESTED FOR FIRST 12-MONTH PERIOD
$151,077

2C. MAILING ADDRESS (Street, City, State, Zip Code)

Graduate School and University Center
of the City University of New York
33 West 42nd Street
New York, New York   10036

6. PERFORMANCE SITE(S) (See Instructions)

Graduate School and University Center
of the City University of New York
33 West 42nd Street
New York, New York   10036

2D. DEGREE

Ph.D.

2E. SOCIAL SECURITY NO.

xxx-xx-xxxx

2F. TELEPHONE DATA | Area Code **TELEPHONE NUMBER AND EXTENSION**

212 | 790-4635

2G. DEPARTMENT, SERVICE, LABORATORY OR EQUIVALENT (See Instructions)

Ph.D. Program in Sociology

2H. MAJOR SUBDIVISION (See Instructions)

Graduate School of City University of N.Y.

7. Research Involving Human Subjects (See Instructions)

A.☐ NO B.☐ YES Approved: _____

C.☒ YES – Pending Review   Date

8. Inventions (Renewal Applicants Only - See Instructions)

A.☐ NO B.☐ YES – Not previously reported

C.☐ YES – Previously reported

TO BE COMPLETED BY RESPONSIBLE ADMINISTRATIVE AUTHORITY (Items 8 through 13 and 15B)

9. APPLICANT ORGANIZATION(S) (See Instructions)

Graduate School and University Center
of the City University of New York
33 West 42nd Street
New York, New York 10036   Jointly with
The Research Foundation of the City
University of New York IRS#13-1988190 N.
1411 Broadway
New York, New York 10018

11. TYPE OF ORGANIZATION (Check applicable item)

☐ FEDERAL   ☐ STATE   ☒ LOCAL   ☐ OTHER (Specify)

_____

12. NAME, TITLE, ADDRESS, AND TELEPHONE NUMBER OF OFFICIAL IN BUSINESS OFFICE WHO SHOULD ALSO BE NOTIFIED IF AN AWARD IS MADE

Controller
Research Foundation of the City University
of New York
1411 Broadway, New York, N.Y. 10018
Telephone Number (212) 354-2228

10. NAME, TITLE, AND TELEPHONE NUMBER OF OFFICIAL(S) SIGNING FOR APPLICANT ORGANIZATION(S)

(Authorizing Official)
Graduate School and University Center
The City University of New York
33 West 42nd Street, New York, N.Y. 10036

Telephone Number (s) (212) 790-4683

13. IDENTIFY ORGANIZATIONAL COMPONENT TO RECEIVE CREDIT FOR INSTITUTIONAL GRANT PURPOSES (See Instructions)

The Graduate School and University Center
of the City University of New York

14. ENTITY NUMBER (Formerly PHS Account Number)

73-2337

15. CERTIFICATION AND ACCEPTANCE. We, the undersigned, certify that the statements herein are true and complete to the best of our knowledge and accept, as to any grant awarded, the obligation to comply with Public Health Service terms and conditions in effect at the time of the award.

| SIGNATURES (Signatures required on original copy only. Use ink, "Per" signatures not acceptable) | A. SIGNATURE OF PERSON NAMED IN ITEM 2A | DATE |
| | B. SIGNATURE(S) OF PERSON(S) NAMED IN ITEM 10 | DATE Jan. 20, 1975 |

NIH 398 (FORMERLY PHS 398)
Rev. 1/73

DEPARTMENT OF HEALTH, EDUCATION, AND WELFARE
PUBLIC HEALTH SERVICE

RESEARCH OBJECTIVES

NAME AND ADDRESS OF APPLICANT ORGANIZATION

Graduate School and University Center of the City University of New York
33 West 42nd Street, New York, New York 10036

NAME, SOCIAL SECURITY NUMBER, OFFICIAL TITLE, AND DEPARTMENT OF **ALL PROFESSIONAL PERSONNEL ENGAGED ON PROJECT**, BEGINNING WITH PRINCIPAL INVESTIGATOR

David Caplovitz, Principal Investigator, Professor of Sociology, Graduate School
    and University Center of the City University of New York, S.S. No. xxx-xx-xxxx
William Kornblum, Assistant Professor of Sociology, Graduate School and University
    Center of the City University of New York, S.S. No. xxx-xx-xxxx
Roger Alcaly, Assistant Professor of Economics, John Jay College of Criminal Justice
    of the City of New York, S.S. No. xxx-xx-xxxx
Sam D. Sieber, Senior Research Associate, Columbia University, S.S. No. xxx-xx-xxxx

TITLE OF PROJECT
The Impact of Inflation-Recession on Families in Cities

USE THIS SPACE TO ABSTRACT YOUR PROPOSED RESEARCH. OUTLINE OBJECTIVES AND METHODS. UNDERSCORE THE KEY WORDS (NOT TO EXCEED 10) IN YOUR ABSTRACT.

The proposed research will investigate the impact of stagflation (inflation-recession) on American families. Through a detailed survey of 2500 households sampled from five American cities with varying unemployment rates, through repeated depth interviews with 100 families and through econometric analyses of official statistics on inflation and unemployment in major cities and the economy as a whole, we plan to find out the types of families that are suffering most from stagflation and how families are adjusting to these severe economic conditions. Specifically, we shall examine the strategies families employ in their efforts to maintain a balance between their income and their standard of living. The various ways in which families attempt to raise their income (e.g. having a secondary wage earner enter the labor force) and the various ways in which families attempt to reduce their standard of living will be systematically studied. We shall also examine the impact of inflation on the structure of families, the relationship between husband and wife, the mental health of family members and the basic value-orientations of the chief wage earner, such as commitment to materialism and the work ethic.

NIH 398 (FORMERLY PHS 398)
Rev. 1/73

DETAILED BUDGET FOR FIRST 12-MONTH PERIOD

FROM	THROUGH
Sept. 1, 1975	Aug. 31, 1976

DESCRIPTION (Itemize)		TIME OR EFFORT %/HRS.	AMOUNT REQUESTED (Omit cents)		
PERSONNEL			SALARY	FRINGE BENEFITS	TOTAL
NAME	TITLE OF POSITION				
David Caplovitz	PRINCIPAL INVESTIGATOR	20%			
2/9 Summer		100%			
William Kornblum	Project Director	33%			
2/9 Summer		100%			
Roger Alcaly	Project Director	33%			
2/9 Summer		100%			
Two and ½ Full-time Graduate					
Research Assistants at $10,000 per year each ...		100%			
Secretary		50%			
Fringe Benefit Rate					
27% during academic year					
20% summer and non-faculty personnel					
	Total		$65,576	$14,501	$80,077

CONSULTANT COSTS Dr. Sam Sieber days		3,000
EQUIPMENT		
SUPPLIES		1,000
TRAVEL — DOMESTIC		2,000
TRAVEL — FOREIGN		
PATIENT COSTS (See instructions)		
ALTERATIONS AND RENOVATIONS		
OTHER EXPENSES (Itemize) 2500 interviews at $52 per interview		
First year share of this cost		65,000
TOTAL DIRECT COST (Enter on Page 1, Item 5) ——————————————————>		$ 151,077

INDIRECT COST (See Instructions)	53% % S&W*	DATE OF DHEW AGREEMENT:	☐ WAIVED
	___ % TDC*	October 17, 1972	☐ UNDER NEGOTIATION WITH:
	*IF THIS IS A SPECIAL RATE (e.g. off-site), SO INDICATE.		

NIH 398 (FORMERLY PHS 398)
Rev. 1/73

BUDGET ESTIMATES FOR ALL YEARS OF SUPPORT REQUESTED FROM PUBLIC HEALTH SERVICE
DIRECT COSTS ONLY (Omit Cents)

DESCRIPTION		1ST PERIOD (SAME AS DE-TAILED BUDGET)	ADDITIONAL YEARS SUPPORT REQUESTED (This application only)					
			2ND YEAR	3RD YEAR	4TH YEAR	5TH YEAR	6TH YEAR	7TH YEAR
PERSONNEL COSTS		$80,077	$82,985					
CONSULTANT COSTS (Include fees, travel, etc.)		3,000	2,000					
EQUIPMENT		---	---					
SUPPLIES		1,000	1,000					
TRAVEL	DOMESTIC	2,000	1,000					
	FOREIGN							
PATIENT COSTS		---	---					
ALTERATIONS AND RENOVATIONS		---	---					
OTHER EXPENSES*		65,000	65,000					
TOTAL DIRECT COSTS		$ 151,077	$ 151,985					

TOTAL FOR ENTIRE PROPOSED PROJECT PERIOD (Enter on Page 1, Item 4) ⟶ $ 303,062

REMARKS: *Justify all costs for the first year for which the need may not be obvious. For future years, justify equipment costs, as well as any significant increases in any other category. If a recurring annual increase in personnel costs is requested, give percentage. (Use continuation page if needed.)*

*Since the interviewing for the household survey will be done toward the end of the first year, the total cost of these interviews, $130,000, has been divided equally between the first and second years.

THE IMPACT OF INFLATION–RECESSION ON FAMILIES IN CITIES

Introduction

The United States is now undergoing its most severe economic crisis since the Great Depression of the thirties. We are currently experiencing a staggering rate of inflation, well up into the double digits (at this writing, pressing 15 percent a year). At the same time, contrary to all economic theory, we are experiencing a severe recession, as the unemployment rate has risen above 7 percent and the Gross National Product has steadily declined, sure symptoms of a recession that might well mushroom into a full-scale depression. This double bind of rampant inflation and recession has given rise to a new coinage by economists, "stagflation," or even more dramatically, "slumpflation."

Just as the Great Depression was a worldwide phenomenon, so the current rampant inflation is devastating all the major countries of the world. In Britain the rate of inflation has risen beyond 16 percent; in Japan, inflation is beyond 25 percent a year, an inflationary rate comparable to that of Italy; in Brazil, inflation is running better than 15 percent a year and, of all the Western nations, Greece is hardest hit with an inflation rate of 34 percent, although Israel is not far behind. Canada, Sweden, and West Germany have managed to keep their inflation rates well below 15 percent.

Economists have diagnosed the current inflation as both "demand-pull" inflation in which consumer demand far exceeds the supply of goods and services (too much money pursuing too few goods) and as "cost-push" inflation in which rising costs of labor push prices ever higher. The general consensus is that both of these forces are now at work, reinforcing each other in an ever upward spiral of prices. Underlying these inflationary pressures are decidedly new features of the world economy, such as the energy crisis and the general scarcity of essential resources. The consensus of most scholars is

that the current inflation, with or without recession, is a long-range phenomenon not likely to recede in the near future. In fact, we may be on the verge of a new society, one in which inflation is endemic to our way of life. In a variety of circles, the alarm has been raised that hyperinflation can lead to the downfall of our democratic society. Thus President Ford has identified inflation as "public enemy number 1" and the conservative Arthus Burns, Chairman of the Federal Reserve, recently observed, "if long continued, inflation at anything like the present rate would threaten the very foundations of our society." The highly prestigious journal, *Skeptic*, published by the Forum of Contemporary History, recently devoted a special issue to inflation. The lead editorial of this issue warns that inflation can sap our freedom and bring down our democratic society, in much the way that Uruguay in the past decade has been transformed from a thriving democracy into a bankrupt dictatorship under the pressure of inflation. To quote from this editorial,

> As stiff as inflation's toll has been up to now, it is nothing compared to the cost which confronts us at the end of the road. Unless we check inflation, it will cost us our freedom. And if that sounds too apocalyptic, consider the ways in which inflation already has chipped away at freedoms we have taken for granted. Our options in the marketplace are more limited than they used to be . . . Our freedom of movement is circumscribed by the rising costs of operating a car . . . Our freedom to locate where we choose is limited by soaring rents and real estate prices . . . Our freedom to make plans of every imaginable sort, from having a baby to taking a vacation, has been diminished by inflation . . . Inflation has narrowed our choices and options. In the end it threatens to eliminate them entirely.[1]

Hovering over this period of rampant inflation is the specter of Weimar Germany in which the finances of whole classes of the population were wiped out by hyperinflation and the way was paved for the rise of Naziism.

Whether these apocalyptic events ever come to pass, it is clear that rampant inflation now

---

[1] *Skeptic* Special Issue Number 3, October 1974, p. 5.

joined by a dangerous recession has already had a dramatic impact on the way of life of many Americans.

Whether rampant inflation or widespread unemployment is the major problem at the time the proposed study is carried out remains to be seen. In either event, families in all walks of life will have been touched by these economic conditions, and, for some, the pressures will be so great that their very survival will be threatened. A basic thesis of this proposal is that stagflation has caused and will continue to cause considerable hardship for many American families and poses a serious threat to the mental health of a substantial proportion of the population.

Objectives

The proposed research has two fundamental objectives. First, through a household survey, we plan to identify those segments of the population which have been most hurt by inflation and, conversely, those which have managed to escape the ravages of inflation. A critical concept in the proposed research is what we call "inflation crunch," meaning the degree to which a family has been hurt by inflation. We plan to measure "inflation crunch" in both objective and subjective terms. This distinction is spelled out below in the section dealing with specific aims. As the sampling plan described in Section C indicates, particular attention will be paid to the two groups widely assumed to suffer most from inflation, the retired who live on fixed incomes and the poor. The sampling plan that has been devised insures that ample numbers of these groups will be included in the household survey for statistical analysis.

The second major objective of this research is to document in a systematic way how families that have experienced varying degrees of "inflation crunch" have adjusted to or tried to adapt to this pressure. We will examine the way in which their lifestyles have changed, the coping strategies they have evolved, and the impact that inflation has had on family structure, marriages, mental health, and basic value orientations.

The ultimate purpose of the proposed research is to provide information that will be useful to policymakers who must weigh the costs and benefits of the current inflationary pressures in contrast to a severe recession. We are convinced that this objective will be realized by research that documents the trends that are developing in the American way of life in response to hyperinflation. These trends are likely to have repercussions for all the major institutions of our society, from the occupational world, to higher education, to leisure time activities, to the functioning of local government, to the organization of the family.[2] In short, a careful study of the impact of inflation on American families will provide valuable insights into the future directions of American society which, in turn, will be of value to policymakers.

Background

Surprisingly enough, there have been virtually no sociological studies of the impact of inflation on American society or, for that matter, on any society.[3] The mass media have been flooded with anecdotal materials on how one or another typical family has been trying to cope with inflation. For example, last Spring the *Wall Street Journal* had a series of such articles and more recently the major networks have been presenting profiles of families coping with inflation.

---

[2] Focusing on the impact of inflation on American families as we propose is only one way of studying the impact of inflation on American society. As is described below, during the Depression, the Social Science Research Council sponsored a series of monographs which examined the impact of the Depression on various phases of American life, e.g., education, the family, recreation, health, the church, etc. A similar series of studies of the impact of inflation on various institutional spheres of society would be highly desirable. We are proposing a study of the impact on a single highly strategic institution, the family, but, of course, inflation's impact on other institutions is deserving of study as well.

[3] To be sure there is a vast literature dealing with inflation in economics but this deals exclusively with the causes of inflation and its impact on the economy rather than its impact on people.

A careful search of the sociological literature has uncovered only one study of inflation by a sociologist and that is a doctoral dissertation at Columbia in 1962 by Sam Sieber, entitled, *Union Members, the Public and Inflation.* Much of the Sieber analysis is based on a survey of 400 steel union members and 400 members of unions other than steel in Pittsburgh that was carried out in 1959. In addition to this survey, Sieber culls the various public opinion polls conducted since World War II to find out what the public attitude toward inflation and its causes has been over this period. Sieber's analysis of these polls indicates that inflation has been a major worry of the American people through much of the postwar period up through 1960. Sieber notes that most Americans considered inflation a serious problem even though the rate of inflation during these years was quite low (with the exception of the Korean war period) and even though income more than kept pace with inflationary pressures. To account for this public concern over a pseudo-problem, Sieber advances the interesting thesis that people were concerned not so much with making ends meet as they were with the threat of inflation to their realizing the American dream of steadily improving their lifestyles. This idea will be pursued in the proposed research as a possible explanation of why some people feel hurt by inflation (subjective inflation crunch) even though their incomes have kept pace with the rising cost of living (objective inflation crunch).

The Sieber analysis is primarily concerned with the reasons that the public at large and union members, particularly the steelworkers, gave for inflation. There was considerable debate at the time about the causes of inflation and the mass media, mouthing the propaganda of management, tended to place the cause on the unreasonable demands of the unions for salary boosts. The survey analyzed by Sieber took place during the long contract negotiations that eventually broke down and resulted in the longest steel strike in the history of the country in 1959. A major finding of the Sieber study was that many workers, even steelworkers, tended to buy the management line and blamed their union officials for causing inflation. Contrary to the assumptions of many labor economists who take it for granted that workers have an insatiable demand for higher wages, Sieber found that many workers were prepared to forego wage increases if this would check inflation. This question of whom the public blames for inflation will be pursued in the proposed study. It will be interesting to see whether the distribution of blame by the public among business, labor, and government is the same today as it was in 1959 and, if not, the ways in which it has changed.

If inflation has been largely ignored by sociologists, the same is not true for the opposite catastrophic economic event, depression. The Great Depression of the thirties gave rise to an untold number of studies by social scientists dealing with the impact of the Depression on various institutions of society. Although diametrically opposite phenomena, depressions and inflations have a number of similarities with respect to their impacts on individuals and families. Both involve adjusting to lowered standards of living, in the one case because the dollar won't buy as much and in the other because the opportunity to earn dollars has declined. But, of course, of the two, depression, meaning unemployment, is the much more severe problem — at least in the short run. If rampant inflation means, for many people, a reduction in living standards by 10 or 15 percent, unemployment means a reduction on the order of 50 percent or more (assuming that there are relief programs and insurance programs that prevent the reduction from going all the way to zero). In light of these similarities between depression and inflation, the proposed research has much to gain from a review of the vast body of Depression literature, and a more thorough review of that literature than is reported here will be one of the first tasks of the proposed research. Unfortunately, the research technology of the thirties was not nearly as advanced as it is today; hardly any of the Depression studies were on the scale of the proposed study. Whereas we plan to survey some 2500 households, these Depression studies are based largely on case studies of between fifty and one hundred or so families. One of the earliest of these ethnographic accounts of the impact of the Depression was carried out by Lazarsfeld and his colleagues who studied unemployment in a small town in Austria.[4] Other classic studies of the impact of the Depression were carried out by Komarovsky, Bakke, and Angell.[5] These Depression studies document the devastating effects of unemployment on the self-esteem of the breadwinner and the strains that developed within the family. A major theme of this research was the extent to which the unemployed male lost moral authority within his family. The Angell study is particularly interesting in light of the proposed research. Angell was concerned with the strengths and weaknesses of families that allowed some to withstand the pressures of the Depression while others succumbed to these pressures and became disorganized. He attempted to study the impact of two properties of families on their adjustment to the Depression, the degree to which they were integrated, that is, the degree to which the family members assisted and respected each other and helped each other grow, and what he called adaptability or flexibility, that is, the readiness of the family to adjust in good spirits to radically changed circumstances. Angell makes the very telling point that rigid, inflexible families are likely to be the ones deeply committed to material possessions and a lifestyle based on such possessions. Such families are likely to fall apart if they experience only a moderate reduction of income, in contrast with more flexible families that experience much larger reductions in income. This idea of Angell's

is directly applicable to the proposed research and is at the core of the distinction between objective and subjective inflation crunch.

By far the most ambitious project to assess the impact of the Depression on American society was carried out in 1936 and 1937 by the Social Science Research Council. The SSRC sponsored a series of 13 studies assessing the impact of the Depression on various facets of American society and institutions. This overall project was supervised by Samuel Stouffer and the various volumes were authored by experts in the various fields who culled a vast array of secondary sources for information. The title for the overall series was *Studies in the Social Aspects of the Depression* and each volume was entitled *A Research Memorandum on_____ and the Depression.* The topics that filled the blank included crime, recreation, the family, consumption, minority groups, reading, education, religion, health, rural life, etc.

These volumes are filled with nuggets of information — findings and hypotheses relevant to the proposed research on stagflation/inflation—recession. A cursory sample of the findings and hypotheses include the following:

1. Crimes against property (theft) increased during the Depression.
2. People became more tolerant, less morally indignant, of such crimes.
3. Attendance of high school increased sharply during the Depression even though college attendance declined.
4. "Depression colleges," i.e., junior colleges and adult education programs, came into being to absorb the energies of the unemployed.
5. There was a sharp expansion in leisure time and a sharp growth in recreational facilities. Use of inexpensive recreational facilities, such as parks and beaches, increased greatly. Automobile tours were very popular.
6. There was sharp curtailment of consumption of major durables. Many found relief in escape from conspicuous consumption, especially those who were having diffi-

---

[4] Maria Jahoda, Paul F. Lazarsfeld, and Hans Zeisel, *The Unemployed of Marienthal,* Allensback und Bonn: Verlag Fur Demoskopie, 1960. Reprinted by Aldine Press, Chicago, 1974.

[5] Mirra Komarovsky, *The Unemployed Man and His Family,* New York: Dryden Press, 1940. W. Wight Bakke, *The Unemployed Worker: A Study of the Task of Making a Living without a Job,* New Haven: Yale University Press, 1940. Robert Cooley Angell, *The Family Encounters the Depression,* New York: Charles Scribner Sons, 1936.

culty realizing their high consumer aspirations.

7. Marriage rates, birth rates, and divorce rates declined, but illegitimacy rates increased, findings stemming from economic considerations.

8. Youth were particularly hard hit by unemployment with the result that many of the young postponed leaving home and many who left home returned.

9. Reliance of youth on parents was part of a general lengthening of the period of child dependency.

10. The quality of housing decreased sharply as: few new homes were built and people moved to cheaper quarters often without electricity and hot water.

11. There was a sharp increase in doubled up families, i.e., two or more families living in the same residence.

12. Mutual aid among relatives, leading to a revival of the extended kinship unit, increased sharply.

13. Mixed marriages and impulsive marriages (e.g., marriages not performed by a minister) increased during the Depression, suggesting breakdown of traditional restraints.

14. There was a sharp increase in symptoms of "war neuroses" as previously stable men "went to pieces," had "nervous breakdowns," and developed neurotic traits.

15. Those in poor health, the handicapped, etc. were most likely to be laid off, in a revival of the survival of the fittest.

16. There was a sharp decline in public expenditures for sanitation and cleanliness, e.g., sewage disposal, street cleaning, etc.

17. There was a sharp decline in occupied hospital beds as people postponed needed operations.

18. Reliance on home entertainment increased sharply, e.g., radio listening, card playing, jigsaw puzzles, board games, like Monopoly.

19. The Depression stimulated the co-op movement.

20. The *Readers Digest* thrived during the Depression as did pulp magazines of the *True Story* variety at the expense of serious magazines and humor magazines.

21. Employed women, because of the industries they were in, were not as likely to lose their jobs as men, with the result that women assumed more of a responsibility relative to men for support of the family.

22. Unemployed men were likely to have their parental authority undermined.

23. Suicide rates increased sharply during the Depression.

24. Racial tensions among workers tended to increase during the Depression, as a result of the competition for scarce jobs.

As these findings indicate, the Depression had a profound impact on the mental health of the unemployed, on family structure, on style of life, on moral attitudes, and on social relations between families. These themes will be studied in the proposed research to see the ways in which the consequences of inflation are similar to and different from those of the Depression. The findings listed above and many more can be found in the following volumes:

Thorstein Sellin, *Crime in the Depression*, SSRC Bulletin 27, 1937.

Educational Policies Commission, *Education and the Depression*, SSRC Bulletin 28.

Samuel A. Stouffer and Paul F. Lazarsfeld, *The Family in the Depression*, SSRC Bulletin 29.

Warren S. Thompson, *Internal Migration in the Depression*, SSRC Bulletin 30.

Donald Young, *Minority Peoples in the Depression*, SSRC Bulletin 31.

Jessie Steiner, *Recreation in the Depression*, SSRC Bulletin 32.

Samuel C. Kineheloe, *Religion in the Depression*, SSRC Bulletin 33.

Dwight Anderson, *Rural Life in the Depression*, SSRC Bulletin 34.

Ronald S. Vaile, *Consumption in the Depression*, SSRC Bulletin 35.

Selwyn D. Collins and Clark Tibbitts, *Health in the Depression*, SSRC Bulletin 36.

Douglas Waples, *Reading in the Depression,* SSRC Bulletin 37.

R. Clyde White and Mary K. White, *Relief Policies in the Depression,* SSRC Bulletin 38.

F. Stuart Chapin and Stuart A. Queen, *Social Work in the Depression,* SSRC Bulletin 39.

Apart from the literature relevant to the proposed study, one facet of the principal investigator's experience should be mentioned as part of the background for this proposal. As is noted below, one theme that will be explored in the household survey is the extent to which families try to cope with inflationary pressures by making use of credit. The principal investigator recently completed a study of people deeply entangled in installment debt.[6] This research disclosed that debt troubles result in a series of debilitating consequences for the debtor and his family. It is widely assumed that rampant inflation is pushing people deeper and deeper into debt and the principal investigator's knowledge of this problem area will strengthen the proposed research in this respect. For example, the problem of measuring debt entanglement has been solved and we will apply it to families under study to test the hypothesis that one result of inflation crunch is debt entanglement.

Earlier in his career, the principal investigator was associated with another study that is quite relevant to the present research, a study of subjective feeling states, known as the happiness study. A major effort in the proposed research will be to measure the impact of inflation on the psychological well-being of the respondents and the principal investigator has considerable experience with questionnaire indicators that measure feeling states.[7]

Specific Aims

The proposed study encompasses three research strategies enumerated in the next section:

[6] David Caplovitz, *Consumers in Trouble: A Study of Debtors in Default,* New York: The Free Press, 1974.

[7] See Norman Bradburn and David Caplovitz, *Reports on Happiness,* Chicago: Aldine Press, 1965.

a household survey of 2500 families, field work involving case studies of 100 families, and an econometric analysis of inflation—unemployment data for the country as a whole and for a sample of large cities. Of these, the household survey is perhaps most critical and almost all the specific aims of the research can be described by identifying the goals of the household survey.

The household survey has four major objectives: (1) identifying the kinds of families that are suffering most from stagflation, i.e., rampant inflation and unemployment; (2) examining the strategies that families have employed in their efforts to cope with inflation—unemployment, strategies that for the most part involve radical changes in lifestyles; (3) identifying the impact of inflation—recession on the well-being of families, on the mental health of family members, and on basic value orientations of family members; and (4) learning how the public interprets the causes of inflation and which critical groups it blames for our economic troubles.

Measuring the Impact of Hyperinflation and Identifying Its Victims

It is extremely misleading to assume that people in all walks of life are equally affected by the sharp rise in the cost of living over the past several years. Even during the most traumatic economic crisis in our history, the Depression of the thirties, a majority of wage earners were able to escape the ravages of unemployment. The overall unemployment rate during the height of the Depression did not exceed 25 percent. Similarly, not all Americans are currently suffering because of hyperinflation. Partly as a result of cost of living clauses in union contracts and partly because many professional classes are free to raise the cost of their services, large segments of the population have been able to keep abreast of rampant inflation by raising their incomes, and their styles of life have not suffered in any material way. But, by the same token, equally large, if not larger, segments of the population have suffered because of the hyperinflation and stagflation we are now experiencing. For these families, hyperinflation has posed a series of difficult choices ranging from finding new sources of income to keep abreast of rising prices to deciding how to lower one's standard of living so as to make ends meet. The notion of the impact of inflation on families gives rise to a concept like inflation crunch. A major task of the proposed research will be to measure inflation crunch and identify the families who are experiencing inflation crunch and the families who are managing to avoid it. The concept of inflation crunch will be measured in two ways: objectively and subjectively. By *objective inflation crunch* we mean the degree to which the family's *normal* sources of income have failed to keep up with the rise in the cost of living. We will know how much the cost of living has risen in each of the sample cities included in the household survey over the two- or three-year period prior to the survey. We will then find out how much the earnings of the chief wage earners have risen during this period. The ratio of these numbers will serve as our measure of objective inflation crunch. In measuring objective inflation crunch we shall be careful to take into account new sources of income stimulated by the inflation, such as the chief wage earner taking on a second job or a secondary wage earner entering the labor force during this period. Expansions in family income due to such measures will be treated as consequences of inflation crunch and will not be included in the measure of objective inflation crunch.[8] In addition to objective inflation crunch the proposed research will measure the degree to which the family feels that it is hurting because of inflation. This will yield a measure of *subjective inflation crunch*. Presumably these two measures will be highly correlated but, as the Angell study of families dur-

ing the Depression makes clear, a critical intervening variable is the degree of adaptability or flexibility of the family. Families deeply committed to materialism, to "keeping up with the Joneses," will experience more subjective deprivation than families less committed to such values who experience the same degree of objective inflation crunch. These measures of inflation crunch will then be related to the various demographic characteristics of the respondents. In this fashion we shall be able to identify the social groups suffering most from inflation. As noted in the methodological section, the research plan will insure that the poor and the retired, two groups widely assumed to be hurt hardest by inflation, will be included in the study. Thus the first major objective of the study will be to identify the social groups that are being hurt by inflation and the groups that for whatever reasons are not being hurt.

Responses to the Imbalance Between Income and Standard of Living

Rampant inflation and unemployment represent for many families a sudden imbalance between their income and their standard of living. They find themselves unable to maintain the standard of living that their income previously permitted. Confronted with such a problem, two possible solutions emerge: either income can be raised to keep up with inflation or standard of living can be lowered.

Raising Income. Should families find that normal increments in the salary of the chief wage earner are insufficient to keep up with inflation, they have several options for increasing family income. The chief wage earner can work harder by doing more overtime work or by taking a second job. Also, a second potential wage earner, typically a spouse but also a teenage child, can enter the labor market. A major objective of the proposed research will be to document the extent to which efforts to raise the family income have occurred. It should be noted that pressures that lead additional family members to enter the labor force pro-

[8] Measuring objective inflation crunch is more complicated than this discussion indicates. Some housewives may have mixed motives for entering the labor force. For example, their children may be grown, they may be bored, and at the same time they may want to help make ends meet. Considerable care will be given to measuring this concept.

vide one link between inflation and unemployment. During the period that new entrants to the labor force are looking for work but have not found it, they are counted as unemployed and it may well be that one way that hyperinflation contributes to unemployment is by forcing secondary wage earners into the labor force. To the extent that these adjustments have been made by family members to raise family income, the structure of the family is likely to change and strains may develop within the families. These potential impacts of rampant inflation are discussed below in the section dealing with inflation and family well-being.

Reducing Standard of Living. The anecdotal material that has appeared in the mass media has pointed to sharp reductions in standards of living on the part of families who are experiencing inflation crunch. In family menus, steaks have given way to hamburger and casseroles. A shocking discovery has been that many of the poor and the retired have been forced to eat pet food. According to the issue of *Skeptic* cited above, there has been a sharp increase in the sales of pet food even though the number of pets in America has not increased. This can only mean that pet food is being used for human consumption.[9]   Families have learned to postpone the purchase of new merchandise, especially major durables, as is now being witnessed by the sharp slump in the automobile industry. Home repairs are either being neglected or are being made by the family members themselves, perhaps with the help of neighbors. Women who never consulted cook books before are now doing so in large numbers as they try to learn to prepare tasty but inexpensive meals. Shopping trips are more and more infused with bargain-hunting and many housewives are shopping around and learning the habits of the "good consumer." Similarly, when it comes to cloth-

ing, many housewives are learning to make clothes for themselves and other family members. In these ways, husbands and wives are being forced to develop new competencies which in turn may have implications for mental health (discussed below).

Apart from efforts to scrimp on the necessities of life, families confronted with inflation crunch are no doubt making drastic changes in their ways of life regarding leisure time activities. Rampant inflation has caused a sharp restriction in the geographic scope of vacations. Not only are fewer people vacationing abroad but domestic pleasure spots such as Miami Beach are experiencing hard times because many of their traditional clientele can no longer afford the journey.

Just as the Depression saw a marked increase in home-centered leisure time activities, such as card playing, puzzle solving, and Monopoly games, so the current inflation in conjunction with the energy crunch has led to a sharp rise in home entertainment. Parker Brothers, the manufacturers of the most popular board game, Monopoly, and numerous other board games, has experienced a dramatic increase in sales over the past year.

A major theme of the household survey will be to document in a systematic way the degree to which standards of living have been lowered and the ways in which lifestyles have been altered because of inflation—recession. Most importantly, the research will measure the family's response to such reductions in standard of living, ranging from acceptance with equanimity to severe stress, in much the way that Angell tried to measure the degree of adaptability of families to the deprivations of the Depression.

Reliance on Credit as an Adaptive Mechanism

Inflationary pressures are forcing more and more families to rely on credit as a mechanism for bridging the gap between their needs and wants and their ability to pay. Long before rampant inflation struck America, consumer credit grew by leaps and bounds. Between 1966 and

[9] A recent article in the *Wall Street Journal* called attention to a serious health hazard stemming from the consumption of pet food. Apparently fuel pollution has resulted in a sharp increase in the lead content of the grass eaten by cattle. This lead tends to concentrate in the livers of animals and livers constitute the chief meat in pet food. Thus the poor who eat pet food run the risk of lead poisoning.

1970, outstanding installment debt increased from $66 billion to $100 billion, a growth of $34 billion in the four-year period. But in the next four-year period, 1970 to 1974, characterized by rampant inflation, outstanding consumer debt climbed from $100 billion to $150 billion, a growth of $50 billion. At first glance, going into debt seems to be a sensible way of coping with inflation because the debtor can pay back his loan with cheaper dollars. But this is true only to a certain point. The debtor heavily in debt has committed a considerable portion of his future income to debt payments and he runs the risk of getting into debt over his head. A recent study by the Morgan Guaranty bank has shown that consumer debt has increased by 42 percent between the end of 1970 and the middle of 1974, but, after taxes, personal income in this period rose by only 37 percent. As a result "a bigger share than in the past of people's incomes is already committed just to make payments on past purchases." The imbalance in family finances caused by inflation is evident in the sharply increasing numbers of people deeply entangled in debt. Lenders and creditors are experiencing record default rates, and personal bankruptcy, one of the few remedies available to overextended debtors, has risen sharply in the past several years. (In fiscal 1974 personal bankruptcies increased by 8.4 percent over fiscal 1973, from 155,643 cases to 168,657. Only a tiny fraction of the families eligible for bankruptcy utilize this drastic remedy.) Debt entanglements induced by rampant inflation may well be wreaking havoc with many families in the patterns identified in *Consumers in Trouble* (see footnote 6).

Changes in the use of credit and the impact of credit use on families will be carefully measured in the household survey.

The Emergence of Communal Responses to Inflation

The Depression literature, as noted, documents a sharp rise in mutual aid among members of the extended kinship group and among neighbors, as people joined together to help fight the common enemy, the Depression. Neighboring, i.e., neighborly visits, increased sharply in rural communities and the number of multiple families sharing the same dwelling unit increased sharply during the Depression. Also, the co-op movement flourished. Similarly, communal responses to the current pressures of rampant inflation can be detected. Food-buying clubs, car pools, and babysitting pools have become increasingly popular as neighbors turn to mutual aid to cut down costs. There has even been an increase in doubled up households just as there was in the Depression. Numerous news stories have documented instances of families on Long Island and in other residential areas sharing large houses to cut down costs.

The development of community has been a surprisingly consistent response to adversity. The sharp rise in the crime rate in New York has resulted in the emergence of block associations, organizations whose main task is to raise funds to hire a private guard for the block. These block associations have turned the cold, anonymous big city of New York into a myriad of small neighborhoods in which people on the block have come to know each other. Similarly, the adversity of rampant inflation is having similar effects. These communal responses are quite different from the spirit of communality that thrived among the hippies and flower children of the sixties, who turned their backs on "straight" society. But it is of some interest whether rampant inflation is contributing to a new more communal lifestyle that in some strange way is bringing "straight people" closer to the values of the hippies of yesterday.

Impact of Inflation–Recession on Family Structure, Mental Health, and Values

In the previous section we reviewed the various strategies that families might employ to maintain the balance between income and standard of living. But these strategies have their consequences for families and family members. Some no doubt exact a heavy psychic toll, ranging from undermining the self-confidence of the chief wage earner to increasing marital strains. But diametrically opposite psychological effects might result. Breadwinners may feel proud that they have been able to keep their heads above water through self-help activities and they may develop new bases for self-esteem. To the extent that wives and teenagers are forced to work, major changes are likely to result in the the family structure. And finally, just as in the Depression, the drastic changes forced upon families as a result of rampant inflation—recession may lead to major changes in value orientations. Some families may become radicalized by the hard times they are experiencing, others may abandon their blind pursuit of material wealth, and still others may have their faith in major institutions, especially government, seriously undermined. These ramifications of inflation—recession for the well-being of families and individual family members will be carefully studied in the household survey and the case study.

Modifications in Family Structure

The Depression literature demonstrates that unemployment results in considerable strain in the marital relationship as husbands become less capable of fulfilling their responsibilities. Do comparable strains and changes in marital relationships occur as a result of rampant inflation? To the extent that changes in labor force participation occur on the part of either or both spouses, then changes in the marriage are likely to occur. Wives may learn to be more independent; husbands may feel less in command. A potential for strain exists with respect to expenditures made by one or the other spouse. A husband's drinking habits may be more or less tolerated in times of prosperity, but, in times of rampant inflation, money squandered in this

fashion may be a source of considerable strain. Similarly, the housewife who fails to economize on the household budget or who insists on indulging her vanity with expenditures on cosmetics risks the wrath of her husband. In short, rampant inflation reduces sharply the slack in the system for frivolous, irrational expenditures and, in so doing, raises sharply the inflammatory potential of such expenditures.

For some families, the kind that Angell would call well integrated, the pressures of rampant inflation might result not in familial strain but rather in closer cooperation and mutual support as the spouses make extra efforts to "make ends meet." In so doing, the tie between the spouses may grow stronger. It remains for empirical research to document the frequency of these outcomes and the conditions under which marital strains increase or lessen under inflationary pressure.

Apart from the relationship between spouses, rampant inflation is likely to have consequences for the relationship between parents and their children. The Depression studies documented that young adults were unable to find work and thus continued to live with their parents and those who had left home returned home. Rampant inflation may well have the similar effect of prolonging the period of dependency of children on their parents. Inflation is particularly likely to place a strain on the plans for higher education of children. College enrollments appear to be turning downward as many high school graduates find that their families cannot afford to send them to college. Rampant inflation may well be forcing youth who would have gone to college into the labor force and during the period that they are looking for work they contribute to unemployment, yet another way in which inflation is linked to the basic symptom of recession. The failure of grown children to leave home as they would in more normal times might well contribute to further strain in the family, this time between the parents and the children. Parents might well resent the frustrations stemming from the prolonged dependency of their children.

Modifications in Mental Health of Chief Wage Earner and Spouse

A major theme of the proposed research will be the impact of inflation on the mental health of the chief wage earner and his spouse. How do people feel when they find they must give up a wide range of aspirations (expensive consumption plans)? To what extent do people worry and suffer from anxiety because of the uncertainty of making ends meet? To what extent do housewives develop feelings of inadequacy because they are unable to cut down significantly on household expenses? To what extent do parents feel guilty because they must deny their children new clothes, summer camps, and expensive recreational activities, to say nothing of a college education?

Apart from the negative impact of rampant inflation on mental health, to what extent does it make a *positive* contribution to mental health? As noted, unemployment tends to undermine mental health by destroying the self-esteem of the breadwinner. But the psychological impact of inflation may be quite different for many people. Inasmuch as most breadwinners are still employed, they are likely to blame the system rather than themselves. In their efforts to make ends meet, both husband and wife may discover inner strengths and resources that they were unaware of, such as being able to make do with less expensive food, making one's own clothes, making household repairs, etc. Whether the negative consequences of rampant inflation for mental health outweigh the positive consequences and vice versa is again a matter for research. To some extent it will be possible to study these subtle psychological issues through standard form questionnaires in the household survey, but in this area, as in others, the proposed field work involving in-depth studies of 100 or so families will make a major contribution.

Modifications in Basic Value Orientations

Rampant inflation, for those who are vulnerable to its impact, represents a sudden, drastic reordering of life's priorities. In this process of rapid change it is quite possible that long-held, deep-seated value orientations may well change. The proposed research will seek to determine whether value orientations in four basic areas will have been modified by rampant inflation: (a) commitment to materialism, (b) the work ethic, (c) confidence in government, and (d) political orientation on a left—right continuum.

The dominant ethos of American society, one which served quite well until very recently, was a deep commitment to materialism, "getting and spending," acquiring in a never-ending way the symbols of the good life, from color TV sets to new cars and power boats and a home of one's own. Rampant inflation, like a deep recession, makes the pursuit of such consumer goals impossible. Many families not only must go without, but also a number of them may come to question the old values that told them that they should pursue these consumer goals. We may suggest that one consequence of rampant inflation is to seriously undermine the materialistic ethos that has been dominant in our society. In its place new dominant values may be emerging, such as a new sense of communality, kinship with others, or a commitment to simple pleasures, or a commitment to higher values, such as learning and the arts, as dominant goals of life. The impact of rampant inflation on materialistic value will thus be one theme of the research.

Another basic value that may be seriously threatened by rampant inflation is commitment to the work ethic. The sociologist, Richard Sennett, has suggested that the work ethic may well be undermined as people discover that their hard work not only fails to buy more goods, but also buys even less goods than formerly.[10] Americans are told from the time they are very small that if they work hard they will get the good things in life but rampant inflation tends to make a mockery of this precept. The man who was able to rationalize the aches and pains

---

[10] See *Time Magazine*, November 4, 1974, p. 104.

that he received from work on the grounds that his efforts would allow the family to buy a swimming pool may well wonder why he tolerates such aches and pains when the swimming pool is clearly only a pipe dream. He may decide not to work as hard and in the extreme to give up work altogether for some version of the "drop out" lifestyle. Again, attitudes toward work will be measured in the research to see if there is any merit to Sennett's idea.

Another basic value to be examined in the research will be confidence in government. In order for an administration to govern successfully there must be some minimal level of confidence in it. To what extent do those hurting from inflation turn cynical about government and political leaders because of government's inability to solve the problem that is hurting them? Economic issues have long been recognized as the most salient in the voting booth. To what extent is rampant inflation, coupled with recession, a force capable of making people cynical *about* the voting booth, that is, about their control over their lives and the democratic process itself. These questions border on the fourth basic value orientation to be considered in the light of rampant inflation, political orientation. Has rampant inflation coupled with recession, by pointing up fundamental weaknesses in our capitalistic economy, made people more ready to move to the left and consider socialistic solutions to their problem? Several questions will be asked of the respondents regarding their faith in capitalism and whether it has changed in recent years.

Interpretations of Inflation

Yet another major goal of the household survey and the field research will be to find out who and what people blame for rampant inflation. This was a major theme of Sieber's research of fifteen years ago and one of his major findings was that at that time even members of a militant union like the steelworkers union were as inclined to blame the excessive wage demands of their leaders as they were to blame

corporations for seeking excessive profits by raising prices. At the time of the Sieber study the culprits for inflation were limited to three groups — management, labor, and government. But today a fourth group and a new factor enter the picture, the Arabs and the energy crisis. The research will ask the respondents to rate the role of each of these groups in the current inflation. It will be extremely interesting to see whether there is now consensus within both the blue-collar and white-collar groups and whether these social classes hold similar or different views on the causes of inflation. The analysis of the data collected will deal with the relationships between the locus of blame and certain impacts of inflation crunch.

Methods of Procedure

The proposed research makes use of three well established research strategies: (1) a large-scale *sample survey;* (2) *case studies* in the form of repeated depth interviews with 100 "representative" families; and (3) *econometric analysis,* primarily of official statistics of cities and the economy as a whole but also of the survey data.

The Household Survey

At the heart of the proposed research is a large-scale sample survey of households. Instead of a national sample of households, we shall limit the survey to five cities of varying degrees of unemployment. In this way we shall be able to study the impact of inflation in the context of high and low unemployment. Two high unemployment cities will be selected (tentatively Detroit and Seattle) and two low unemployment cities (tentatively Chicago and Atlanta) with one city to represent the middle range of unemployment (tentatively New York). Within each city stratified random samples of 500 families will be selected, for a total of 2500 in all five cities. To insure adequate representation of the groups believed to be hardest hit by inflation, the poor and the retired, within each city, a random sample of 100 poor families and 100 retired persons will be interviewed. The remaining 300 interviews in each city will be split evenly between blue-collar and white-collar workers. Thus the final sample of 2500 households will consist of 500 poor families, defined as families living in the sampled cities who are earning below $8000 or so in the summer of 1976 when the survey will be conducted (by then such an income should be the equivalent of the $4000 poverty level set for urban families during the mid-sixties when war was declared on poverty), 500 retired persons, 750 blue-collar households, and 750 white-collar households. The survey of blue-collar and white-collar families will be limited to complete families, that is, those in which both the husband and wife are residing in the household. The reason for this is to permit examining the inflation strategies of having additional wage earners go to work and the stresses and strains that inflation may be imposing on marriages. The requirement of a complete family will be dropped in the samples of poor and retired persons. In at least half the cases the interview will be conducted with the chief wage earner and in the other cases with his or her spouse.

The research design specified above means that the city unemployment rate will be a key contextual variable in the analysis. We shall be able to assess whether the impact of inflation crunch is the same or different in high and low unemployment cities. It may well be, for example, that the specter of losing a job in a high unemployment community may make those who do have jobs more ready to accept the deprivations of rampant inflation. Given the sampling procedures described above it is quite likely that the final sample will contain several hundred or more households in which the chief wage earner has lost his job and thus we shall be able to compare the deprivations and feeling states of the unemployed with the employed who are experiencing severe inflation crunch.

The household survey will attempt to cover most if not all of the themes described above under "Specific Aims." It is anticipated that this will require about an hour-and-a-half interview employing a standard form questionnaire. This interviewing will be subcontracted to a national interviewing agency. Estimates of costs have been obtained from two such organizations. One gave a figure in the $50 to $60 per case range, the exact figure depending on when the interviewing is done, the length of the interview, and the number of cities in which the survey is done. The other national interviewing agency quoted a lower price, ranging from $42 to $52 per case, depending on similar contingencies. The estimated cost for the 2500 interviews in the budget section of this proposal is based on these estimates.

The Case Studies

Many of the themes enumerated in the discussion of the specific aims of the research, such as the shifting roles of family members as a result of inflation, the possible decline of authority of the chief wage earner within the family, and tensions between spouses, cannot be fully studied through a static interview employing a standard form questionnaire. Rather, depth interviews at different times with the same family are needed to study these more subtle effects of rampant inflation. For this reason we plan to interview in depth some 100 families at several different times over the course of the research. Approximately 20 of these will be poor families, 20 retired families, 30 blue-collar families, and 30 white-collar families. Each family will be interviewed at least three times at approximately four- or five-month intervals. These case studies will serve a number of functions for the proposed research. First, the information obtained from these depth interviews will be of great help in designing the questionnaire for the household survey. Second, these case studies will greatly enrich our analysis of the impact of inflation on families by providing qualitative information and even crude statistical data on the dynamics of familial responses to rampant inflation—recession.

Seventy of the 100 case studies will be conducted in the New York area, chiefly for reasons of economy. Thus the 20 poor families, the 20 retired families, and the 30 white-collar families will be recruited from the metropolitan area of New York. But the 30 blue-collar families that will participate in the case study will be recruited from among steelworkers in the Chicago, Gary, Joliet area, the district of the steelworkers union that was recently the scene of a triumph of union democracy as an insurgent, Edward Sadlowski, successfully challenged the old guard union leadership by winning an election by a two-to-one margin. It happens that the person who will be in charge of this field work, Professor William Kornblum, has a very close relationship with the new leadership in this district and many members of the union, stemming from his doctoral research.[11] By interviewing steelworkers in depth it will be possible to compare their responses to the current inflation with what Sieber found in his analysis of survey data collected from steelworkers in 1959 regarding their views of inflation. This comparison will be bolstered by the strong likelihood that a number of the 150 blue-collar workers to be interviewed in the Chicago sample of the household survey will also be steelworkers. In short, by taking advantage of Professor Kornblum's close ties with the steelworkers of Union District #31, we will be able to tie our research more closely to the earlier work of Sieber.

The repeated depth interviews with poor families and retired families should be particularly revealing. As our interviewers come to know these families they may well learn about practices that the families would at first want to hide, such as eating pet food or engaging in petty thievery in order to make ends meet.

The case studies are viewed as complementary to the household survey, adding depth to the statistical analysis with qualitative information on subtle processes. At the same time, the household survey can provide some idea of the frequency of certain themes or adaptations uncovered by the case studies.

Econometric Analyses of Inflation and Unemployment

Governmental agencies, particularly the Bureau of Labor Statistics, have kept a running record of inflation and unemployment, the two key economic conditions of concern in this research, over a number of decades. These data exist not only for the economy as a whole but also for most if not all of the large cities of the country. We propose to carry out a series of econometric analyses of these official statistics to learn more about the forces making for inflation and unemployment and the forces that may be establishing a positive, rather than the traditionally negative relationship between the two.

To some extent the econometric analysis will be based on time-series data dealing with the economy as a whole. For example, changes in the composition of the labor force, e.g., percent female, percent youth, etc., will be related to changes in unemployment. Similarly, variables such as productivity and wage settlements will be related to inflation over time for the economy as a whole. But most of the econometric analysis of inflation and unemployment will deal with data on cities in America. Under the direction of Professor Michael Aiken, a large data bank on over 1500 American cities is maintained at the University of Wisconsin. Each city in this collection is characterized by several hundred variables, ranging from demographic characteristics of its population to the kinds of industries it has, to the amount of federal funds it raises for various programs, etc. The Aiken city data bank is a vast resource for analysis of the causes and consequences of inflation and unemployment. By plugging in measurements of the rates of inflation and unemployment into the city data bank, it will be possible through econometric analysis to learn why some cities have high inflation and high unemployment; others, high unemployment and low inflation; others, high

[11] See William Kornblum, *Blue Collar Community,* Chicago: University of Chicago Press, 1974.

inflation and low unemployment; and still others, both low inflation and low unemployment. We have been assured by Professor Aiken that the information in his data bank will be available for this analysis. Most likely we shall deal only with the 100 largest cities or so for which time-series data on unemployment and inflation are readily available. The econometric analysis described above, like the case studies, will fill in the background picture of the household survey. The household survey will tell us what kinds of families are hurting from inflation—unemployment and how they are responding, but the analysis of the city data and the data for the economy as a whole will tell us about the forces that are causing the inflation—recession pressures which people are experiencing. A still more direct tie between the econometric analysis and the household survey is envisioned. The critical variables of the household survey, objective and subjective inflation crunch, will be subjected to the refined methods of econometric analysis to learn more about the forces that produce them and their consequences for families. In short, the economists on the research team will have a role to play in the household survey as well as in the analysis of city data.

The Research Team

Each of the three styles of research represented in this proposal — the household survey, the field work or case studies, and the econometric analysis — will be the responsibility of a leading expert in that research tradition. Dr. Caplovitz, the principal investigator, has had considerable experience conducting large-scale social surveys and has demonstrated his ability to translate large-scale research into significant monographs. He will be in charge of the household survey of 2500 families in five cities.

Dr. William Kornblum is a specialist in field work. His recently published book about blue-collar life is based on intensive case studies of the type envisioned in the proposed study.

Dr. Roger Alcaly is one of the better known members of the younger generation of econometricians. For a number of years he was closely associated with some of the leading econometricians at Columbia, Gary Becker and Jacob Mincner among them.

The principal investigator has had the good fortune of persuading Dr. Sam Sieber, the author of the only known investigation of inflation by a sociologist, to serve as a consultant to the proposed study. Dr. Sieber will serve several functions. He will contribute to the development of the questionnaire to be used in the household survey; he will consult with Dr. Kornblum with regard to the depth interviews of the steelworker families, and, on the basis of his extensive review of public opinion polls regarding inflation since World War II, he will prepare an appendix on this subject for the final report of this research. His dissertation summarizes many of these polls up through 1959. For the purpose of the planned appendix, he will update this review of poll data regarding inflation, taking the portrait of public opinion up to the seventies. The preparation of this appendix will be done by Dr. Sieber mainly during the second year of the proposed study.

Time Schedule for the Proposed Study

The first eight months of the proposed study will be spent on a variety of activities. These include analyzing in detail the empirical studies dealing with the effects of the Depression; devising the research instrument to be used in the household survey and pre-testing the various drafts of this questionnaire (experience indicates that the instrument for a study of this scope usually goes through five or six drafts); carrying out the first round of interviews with the 100 families selected for the case study, an activity that will contribute to the development of the household survey questionnaire; and collecting official statistics on inflation, unemployment, and characteristics of the labor force for the economy as a whole and for major cities, data that will be used in the econometric analysis. The last third of the first year will be devoted to the survey data and the official statistics on inflation and unemployment for computer analysis. By the end of the first year or so, the survey data and the data for the econometric analysis will be on computer tapes. During the second year of the study, the 100 families in the case study will be interviewed at least two more times and the various sets of data will be analyzed and research reports will be written. By the end of the project we envision a series of reports, at least one of which will be of book length and suitable for publication.

Significance

On at least two grounds, the proposed research promises to make a significant contribution to knowledge directly relevant to policymakers. First, the research program outlined above is intended to provide insights into changes in family lifestyles as a result of a crescive and chronic condition of modern society: inflation, currently coupled with an even greater economic evil, recession. How American families are adapting to and adjusting to these twin disasters and, equally important, how they are failing to adapt and adjust will be the primary foci of the research. This knowledge should prove of great value to policymakers who must devise programs that will help people cope with these problems. Second, our program of research may provide some answers to the most perplexing problem confronting economists today, namely, how it is possible to have both rampant inflation and a recession at the same time. Finally, apart from its value to policymakers, we envision our research as making an important contribution to knowledge. Just as the Social Science Research Council studies and many other studies documented the impact of the Great Depression on American life, so we believe that our research will achieve the same goal with respect to the rampant inflation of the seventies.

Facilities Available

The proposed research will be carried out at the Graduate School and University Center of the City University of New York. Not only will the Graduate School of CUNY provide space for the project, but also it will provide the graduate students who will serve as research assistants. In addition, the Graduate School of CUNY has at its disposal an advanced computer center. The system is so efficient that within minutes of our request for tables or any other form of computer output the relevant output will be forthcoming.

The undersigned agrees to accept responsibility for the scientific and technical conduct of the research project and for provision of required progress reports if a grant is awarded as a result of this application.

January 20, 1975
Date

David Caplovitz
Principal Investigator

*   *   *

Editor's Note. Attached to the application and not included here were curriculum vitae for Professors Caplovitz, Kornblum, Alcaly, and Sieber.

Blanket certification was on file with HEW attesting to the institution's compliance with Title VI of the Civil Rights Act of 1964 (Public Law 88-352), Form HEW 441, and Title IX of the Education Amendments of 1972 (Public Law 921318), Form HEW 639A (formerly Form HEW 639).

The institutional Indirect Cost Rate and Composite Fringe Benefit Rate had been previously negotiated with HEW.

Certification that the Human Subjects Committee approved the project was forwarded before the grant was formally awarded.

Engineering Ethics Study

Funded by: National Science Foundation, Office of Science and Society,
Ethics and Values in Science and Technology (EVIST)

Principal Investigator: Albert Flores, Assistant Professor of Philosophy, Rensselaer Polytechnic Institute,
Troy, New York
Proposal prepared by: Albert Flores and Robert Baum

HISTORY OF THE ENGINEERING ETHICS STUDY FUNDED BY NSF
by Albert Flores, Ph.D.

The idea for the research project described in the proposal that follows was an outgrowth of research that my colleague Robert Baum and I did for an anthology we edited entitled *Ethical Problems in Engineering* (Troy, 1978). In gathering materials for that volume, it became evident that a great deal of the literature in the field of engineering ethics focused almost exclusively on the duties engineers have to employers, the public, and their profession, or with examining case histories describing engineers' failures to fulfill these duties adequately. This was particularly evident in the area of how engineering activities impact on public safety, where understandably there is the greatest concern. What was missing were the details of how engineers succeeded in assuring that their work exhibited a paramount concern for public safety. Since the vast majority of practicing engineers in the United States are salaried employees of government or industry, it was clear that their behavior would be significantly influenced by their employers. With this in mind, the idea that became the research protocol for this project evolved into an examination of the ways in which a few organizations with outstanding product safety records influence their engineering staffs in designing products or processes that show maximum concern for safety. In this context, "safety" was understood to mean those special considerations employed during the design process to eliminate or reduce unreasonably dangerous conditions in products or processes affecting persons or the environment. By identifying those organizational mechanisms that have proved successful in promoting safety in engineering design, scholars concerned with the theoretical questions raised by the ethics of a profession could learn much about existing factors that positively affect the satisfactory fulfillment of professional ethical responsibilities. Moreover, such an objective seemed ideally suited in bringing to these discussions relevant empirical data that had until now been so sadly lacking in discussions of professional ethics.

Developing a Fundable Proposal

The National Science Foundation's program called Ethics and Values in Science and Tech-

Albert Flores, Ph.D., is Assistant Professor of Philosophy, Rensselaer Polytechnic Institute, Troy, New York. He is associated with the Human Dimensions Center at Rensselaer and co-edited (with Robert Baum) *Ethical Problems in Engineering.*

nology (EVIST), a division of the Office of Science and Society, was a program with which I was already quite familiar and that seemed a likely source for funding such a project. A central concern of this program is the examination of problems associated with the ethical principles and social standards that govern the conduct of scientists and engineers. In particular, one of EVIST's primary aims is to support research that examines, according to its Program Announcement, "the roles played by different types of scientific institutions and organizations in conditioning the ethical perceptions and responses of individual scientists and engineers."

With the encouragement and support of my colleague Robert Baum, I put together a draft proposal that could be used for discussion with other colleagues who might be persuaded to be a part of this project. Given the interdisciplinary nature of the research this project suggested, it seemed vitally important that the assistance of those experienced in important related disciplines participate in this research. After several discussions with a number of our colleagues, the idea for this project began to take definite form. A research team of four individuals from management, organizational psychology, and philosophy would undertake to develop descriptive models of how four typical engineering organizations influenced their engineers in matters of safety. (When the proposal was finally submitted, one of our colleagues withdrew because of other commitments.) These data were to be presented to a panel of recognized experts in engineering, management, psychology, sociology, and philosophy for their scholarly evaluation. A list of individuals with the necessary expertise and interest who might be members of this panel was compiled.

The Funding Process

A *preliminary proposal* of five pages was developed for submission to EVIST in early spring of 1978. EVIST will not accept a *formal* proposal unless a prior preliminary proposal is reviewed to determine its suitability in meeting the objectives of the EVIST program. This process successfully saves both the funding agency and those seeking funds a lot of wasted effort. It moreover gives the funding agency an opportunity to influence the final product before it is formally submitted for final determination. Since a preliminary proposal is regarded as an informal communication between an applicant and the EVIST program staff, it does not require the official endorsement of the applicant's institution. This facilitates an applicant's chances of getting a quick response regarding the fundability of a project without the need to go through the time-consuming process of obtaining all the various authorizations in order to submit a project for consideration.

The preliminary proposal contained four concisely worded sections: (1) a definition of the problem and a rationale for undertaking research in this area; (2) a general description of the project's design and its expected outputs; (3) the project staff and their qualifications were given; and (4) an initial budget, broken down into several general categories (wages, travel, supplies, honoraria, and indirect costs), across the three phases of the project. Included in the description of the project's activities were suggestions as to possible organizations that might be the subjects of our research. In addition, listed were the names of a few of the individuals we wanted to serve on our "panel of experts" who would be expected, as well, to act as an Advisory Committee for the project. It was felt that such a committee could serve a valuable function in keeping our research in proper focus and also that their involvement would help to assure the funding agency that its funds would be used effectively.

We submitted our preliminary proposal on 1 May 1978, the second closing date the EVIST program had set for initial submissions. Response was quick: by very early June we had received written positive encouragement from the EVIST program staff to proceed with submitting a fully developed formal proposal of the project sketched in our preliminary proposal. The quickness of the response normally affords applicants sufficient time before the next closing date to develop a formal proposal, which in this case was 1 August 1978. However, due to the special nature of the project we wanted to pursue, particularly in relation to what was needed to acquire the agreement of organizations that would be the subjects of our research, we let two closing dates pass before a formal proposal for funding was submitted on 1 April 1979.

I cannot go into all the details of what was involved in developing the formal proposal that follows, for it required a lot of advance work and the assistance of many individuals to secure the participation of four suitable organizations and to put together an Advisory Committee willing to take on the responsibilities involved in the project's second stage. Moreover, without the support received from my institution, from our university president who helped in making contacts with the appropriate representatives of several organizations, to the staff of the university's Office of Contracts and Grants who typed and reproduced the twenty copies of the formal proposal, asssisted in the preparation of the final budget, and facilitated the acquisition of the requisite authorizing institutional signatures, the task of putting together a formal proposal would seem an insurmountable task to anyone — especially someone inexperienced in the process of pursuing sponsored research. Finally, in writing the formal proposal, I was greatly assisted by the guidelines listed in the Program Announcement, which NSF has developed for all of its programs. By following this guide, I knew exactly what was required in order to develop a formally acceptable proposal.

After submitting the proposal, the first response we received from the EVIST program staff was a reply card indicating that they had received it satisfactorily. It is advisable that such a reply card be included when one submits a proposal to a funding institution (if they are not already required) in order to assure that the proposal reaches its destination.

By early July, we received our first substantial response in the form of a set of critical comments from outside reviewers, who NSF had requested to evaluate the merits of the project, and a summary of the review panel discussion. Of the ten reviewers, two recommended that the project be funded as proposed, five recommended it subject to revisions requested, and three reviewers recommended that it not be funded. In general, in addition to commenting on its merits favorably, the reviews contained a number of helpful suggestions, a few requests for clarification, and several critical comments for which a written response was requested. I carefully reviewed all of the comments and criticisms and drafted a five-page letter responding in detail to each of the points raised by the NSF reviewers.

Normally, a determination as to whether or not a project will be funded is made within six months of the date of formal submission. Our proposal was, however, caught in the middle of a restaffing change at EVIST in late summer 1979, thereby delaying formal notification of its acceptance until early November. In the interim, I had received by telephone informal confirmation that the EVIST staff had found the response to the reviews satisfactory and would likely fund the project, based on the recommendations of its staff, reviewers, and director. Ironically, I was surprised to learn later that the only required change made in the proposal that was originally submitted was in its title, a change that it was thought reflected more accurately the contents of the research project it described.

RPI Proposal No. 306(91R)3163(4A)

PROPOSAL TO THE NATIONAL SCIENCE FOUNDATION

FOR CONSIDERATION BY NSF ORGANIZATIONAL UNIT (Indicate the most specific unit known, i.e. program, division, etc.) Ethics and Values in Science and Technology Office of Science and Society	IS THIS PROPOSAL BEING SUBMITTED TO ANOTHER FEDERAL AGENCY? Yes ___ No _X_ : IF YES, LIST ACRONYM(S):

PROGRAM ANNOUNCEMENT/SOLICITATION NO.: SE 79-62	CLOSING DATE (IF ANY): 1 April 1979

NAME OF SUBMITTING ORGANIZATION TO WHICH AWARD SHOULD BE MADE (INCLUDE BRANCH/CAMPUS/OTHER COMPONENTS)

RENSSELAER POLYTECHNIC INSTITUTE

ADDRESS OF ORGANIZATION (INCLUDE ZIP CODE)

Troy, New York 12181

TITLE OF PROPOSED PROJECT

ENGINEERING ETHICS IN ORGANIZATIONAL CONTEXTS

REQUESTED AMOUNT $139,600	PROPOSED DURATION two years	DESIRED STARTING DATE 1/1/80

PI/PD DEPARTMENT Human Dimensions Center	PI/PD ORGANIZATION RENSSELAER POLYTECHNIC INSTITUTE	PI/PD PHONE NO (518)-270-6525

PI/PD NAME	SOCIAL SECURITY NO *	DATE OF HIGHEST DEGREE ACHIEVED	MALE*	FEMALE*
Albert W. Flores		Ph.D. 1974	X	
ADDITIONAL PI/PD				
ADDITIONAL PI/PD				
ADDITIONAL PI/PD				
ADDITIONAL PI/PD				

FOR RENEWAL OR CONTINUING AWARD REQUEST, LIST PREVIOUS AWARD NO.	IF SUBMITTING ORGANIZATION IS A SMALL BUSINESS CONCERN, CHECK HERE ☐ (See CFR Title 13, Part 121 for Definitions)

* Submission of SSN and other personal data is voluntary and will not affect the organization's eligibility for an award. However, they are an integral part of the NSF information system and assist in processing proposals. SSN solicited under NSF Act of 1950, as amended.

CHECK APPROPRIATE BOX(ES) IF THIS PROPOSAL INCLUDES ANY OF THE ITEMS LISTED BELOW:

☐ Animal Welfare   ☐ Human Subjects   ☐ National Environmental Policy Act

☐ Endangered Species   ☐ Marine Mammal Protection   ☐ Research Involving Recombinant DNA Molecules

☐ Historical Sites   ☐ Pollution Control   ☐ Proprietary and Privileged Information

PRINCIPAL INVESTIGATOR/ PROJECT DIRECTOR	AUTHORIZED ORGANIZATIONAL REP.	OTHER ENDORSEMENT (optional)
NAME Albert W. Flores	NAME Joseph M. LoGiudice	NAME Robert J. Baum
SIGNATURE *[signature]*	SIGNATURE *[signature]*	SIGNATURE *[signature]*
TITLE Assistant Professor of Philosophy	TITLE Director, Office of Contracts and Grants	TITLE Director, Human Dimensions Center
DATE 30 March 1979	DATE 30 March 1979	DATE 30 March 1979

Proposal to the National Science Foundation for project "Engineering Ethics in Organizational Contexts."

Project on

Engineering Ethics in Organizational Contexts*

<u>Project Summary</u>

An interdisciplinary team from Rensselaer Polytechnic Institute has designed a two-year project aimed at identifying and analyzing the various ways in which four typical organizations that employ engineers encourage and support their professional employees in designing products and services consistent with the need to protect the health and safety of the public.

The project is divided into three stages: In the first or descriptive stage, the research we will undertake involves isolating structural and policy aspects, and management practices, of several engineering organizations that have had proven records of developing safe and reliable products, to determine the mechanisms which these organizations use to influence engineering employees to fulfill their social, ethical, and professional responsibilities for safety. A questionnaire will be developed, pretested, and distributed to engineers and key administrators in the engineering hierarchy, in divisions of four study organizations that have consented to participate in this project. Based on our evaluation of responses, semi-structured interviews of twenty individuals in each organization will be conducted to identify more accurately the mechanisms that facilitate the engineer's acceptance of responsibilities for product safety. In the second or evaluative stage, we will present a formal report of our Committee, for its critical evaluation. Three workshops are planned to discuss and analyze the data and issues developed in this project. At the final conference-workshop, the Advisory Committee's position papers evaluating organizational mechanisms influencing engineers to design safe products will be presented and discussed. We intend to publish our research data and these positions papers in a volume for public distribution; this task describes the purpose of the third or summary stage.

Since the vast majority of engineers are employed in an organizational context, the systematic structuring of engineering activities raises important ethical questions never previously examined. The data we propose to develop here will aid us in better understanding how these organizations influence the conduct and perceptions of engineers. The outcomes of this project should thus be practically useful to practicing and aspiring engineers, to professional engineering societies, to organizations that employ engineers, to public regulatory agencies, and to the general public upon whose trust the engineering profession relies.

*Original title - Professional Responsibility in Organizations

Project summary.

ENGINEERING ETHICS IN ORGANIZATIONAL CONTEXTS

A Formal Proposal to the National Science Foundation's Program on Ethics and Values in Science and Technology

I. Introduction

The use of professional skills and knowledge entails certain social and ethical responsibilities. In situations where the relationship between the professional and the beneficiary of these skills is well defined, it is relatively easy to define one's duties and assign responsibility for their satisfaction. For example, in the medical context, it is generally accepted that the physician is ultimately responsible for the quality of the medical care the patient receives. There are, however, many professional contexts in which it is extremely difficult to determine the nature and extent of the responsibilities it is reasonable to expect of each individual. This is particularly true for engineers, who generally practice their professional skills within the context of large corporate or governmental organizations. These organizations require a micro-division of labor into distinct units within which each engineer contributes only a small portion of the work necessary to complete a project. The result is a diffusion of responsibility across various levels and units of the organizational structure, which complicates and affects the individual's general understanding of his or her responsibilities.

Since the vast majority of engineers are employed by governmental agencies or private corporations, the systematic structuring of the activities of professional engineers by these organizations raises some interestingly complex ethical issues which have never been rigorously examined. How does practicing within the context of an organization affect and influence the individual engineer's perceptions of and commitment to his or her social and ethical responsibilities? If each engineer is expected to practice engineering skills in accordance with a proper regard for the protection of the public's health and safety,

then how do the task responsibilities designated by the organization overlap and assist professional employees in the fulfillment of their social and ethical responsibilities to protect the public from products that may be harmful or injurious? Simply stated, what are the organizational mechanisms that can effect quality engineering? These questions briefly describe one of the fundamental problems of professional responsibility in organizations.

II. Project Objectives

To date, almost all research on this topic has focused exclusively on cases illustrating how engineers have failed in fulfilling their social and ethical responsibilities to design safe products. In an attempt to redress this imbalance, the goal of this project is to identify and analyze the ways in which typical public and private organizations that employ engineers encourage and support their professional employees in designing products and services consistent with the need to protect the health and safety of the public. The ability of these engineers to satisfy their social and ethical responsibilities, as defined by the profession's code of ethics, is directly affected by the operational and structural conditions that exist in these organizations. It is therefore important not only to understand the specific factors that affect engineering practice, but if we are to form a proper assessment of the profession's ability to satisfy its social and ethical responsibilities it is necessary that we know how these organizations condition their employees' perceptions of their responsibilities. This is particularly significant in the crucial area of product safety. In those organizations where there exists a proven commitment to engineering products that are safe and reliable, this can promote and enhance the engineer's acceptance of his or her responsibilities to safeguard the public's welfare. Understanding how in actual practice this is accomplished is the fundamental purpose of this project.

It is anticipated that this project will not only raise crucial questions not previously investigated, but it will clarify in greater detail some of the difficulties surrounding professional responsibility in organizations which are now only vaguely understood. By making explicit examples of commonly utilized organizational methods for insuring design and product safety, we may be able to begin to answer the following questions: How realistic are our idealizations of what we can and should expect from both engineers and engineering organizations in the area of design and product safety? If there is some optimum organizational method for assuring reliable and safe products, what other factors are there, external to organizational control, that can undermine its effectiveness? It is anticipated that the results of this study will be practically useful to a number of different groups. Undergraduate students of engineering are generally ignorant of the organizationally defined conditions that normally structure engineering activities. Since most of these students will be employed in organizational settings similar to those examined in this project, it is hoped that it can contribute to an improvement of their understanding. Perhaps, it may lead, as well, to some modification of the engineering curriculum. Engineering societies that must evaluate the efficacy of their codes and consider revisions in them cannot ignore the significance of the issues raised by this project. This study should also prove valuable to the engineers and managers of organizations where questions regarding appropriate standards of design and product safety and the mechanisms for insuring their satisfaction naturally arise, and to those regulatory agencies that oversee the quality of products and services which may potentially impact on the health and safety of the public. In general, the information and analyses developed by this project should prove to be the basis for much future research in this area.

III. Project Design

This two year project is divided into three stages: (1) a descriptive stage, to gather data on ways in which some typical organizations can and do encourage engineers to peform in an ethical way; (2) an evaluative stage, in which an interdisciplinary team of experts will analyze the collected data from the perspective of their separate disciplines; and (3) a summary stage, to edit and prepare the results of the previous stages for suitable publication and distribution. [*A Work Plan encompassing these three stages accompanied the proposal.*]

In the first year, *the descriptive stage,* the project staff will seek to identify those formal and informal mechanisms which four representative organizations use to encourage their engineering employees to design and develop products that display a proper regard for the health, welfare, and safety of the public. We have secured agreements to cooperate in our study from the following organizations: Monsanto; Boeing; United Technologies, Otis Elevator Division; and National Aeronautics and Space Administration, Manned Space Flight Program. (Monsanto and Boeing replaced two organizations that were originally part of the project but later withdrew.) [*Copies of their letters accompanied the proposal.*] The selection of these organizations was determined by the following considerations:

- these organizations employ large numbers of engineers and the activities of these employees play a crucial role in the quality of the products and services supplied by each organization;
- there is presently in the public record information regarding the activities and organizational structure of these organizations that if properly used will facilitate the process of developing our descriptive data, thereby minimizing the need for extensive new research;
- except for NASA where the effect is indirect, the kinds of products and services these organizations produce are extensively used by the public, which is dependent upon them to satisfy certain daily needs;
- these organizations are engaged in different types of engineering work, from both the private and public sectors;

- and finally, and most importantly, these organizations have long-standing records of engineering products and services that over the years have been consistently proven to be safe and reliable.

Our first task will be to review the relatively sparse literature and prepare an analytical summary of currently employed and suggested methods for encouraging engineers to attend to design and product safety. In order to assess the ways in which organizations actually influence their engineers, in this area, the project staff will survey and query a significant subset of engineers and certain key individuals at various administrative levels of the engineering hierarchy, within divisions of the four subject organizations. Among the questions we propose to ask, there are the following: How does the organization define design and product safety? How clear is its commitment to safety and what are the means by which this is communicated? How are responsibilities for safety incorporated into the normal task responsibilities of individual engineers? What quality control methods do organizations use to review and protect against substandard performance of these responsibilities? Are there procedures which allow an engineer to draw attention to and correct for possibly harmful products? How are conflicts, including technical disputes relating to safety standards, handled and resolved? What kinds of constraints exist which affect both the individual engineer's and the organization's ability to provide reliable and safe products? What are the organizational, professional, legal and ethical liabilities which engineers bear for unsafe products? What should be done to insure the development of safe products?

Two field research methodologies will be employed: (1) Based on our review of the literature on organizational methods for insuring design and product safety, a questionnaire will be developed aimed at identifying specific activities, procedures, and mechanisms employed by the subject organizations which facilitate ethically responsible behaviors on the part of engineers in the conduct of their organizationally defined responsibilities. The collection of

these data will rely on the descriptive techniques for data gathering developed by Van Dalen and Meyer (Van Dalen, D.B., and Meyer, W. J., *Understanding Educational Research*. New York: McGraw-Hill, rev. ed. 1966). (2) A stratified random sample of those completing the questionnaire will be selected for participation in semi-structured on-sight interviews, using techniques described by Borg (Borg, W. R., *Educational Research*. New York: David McKay, 1963). In addition to these formal procedures for data collection, the project staff will attempt to obtain from each participating organization any formal policy statements relating to organizationally defined responsibilities for safety which engineering employees are expected to satisfy and the enforcement procedures for assuring compliance with them.

In order to assure the reliability and validity of the questionnaire it will be pretested employing techniques suggested by Davis (Davis, R. L., *Survey Methodology*. New York: McGraw-Hill, 1971). Any revisions in the questionnaire suggested by the results of the pretest will be made and, after consultation with members of the Advisory Committee, a final questionnaire will be constructed. The project staff, in consultation with directors of the subject organizations, will identify the specific group or division of engineers and managers to whom the questionnaire will be distributed. Engineers at every level within that division of each of our subject organizations will be asked to complete the questionnaire. Arrangements will be made to have the questionnaire, along with a cover letter explaining the purpose of the questionnaire, signed by the project director and an appropriate representative of the subject organization, distributed through normal communications networks within the organization and to have it completed on company time. Questionnaires will be designed so that they will take no more than a half-hour to complete. Each respondent will be instructed to mail his or her completed questionnaire directly to the project director, in order to assure respondents that the confidentiality of their responses will be protected.

Project on Engineering Ethics in Organizational Contexts.*
Revised Work Plan

I. Descriptive Stage

1980

Jan.-Apr.
— Literature review and preparation of analytical summary.
— Development of questionnaire and pre-testing.
— Confirming arrangements for questionnaire distribution.

May
— Distribution of questionnaire.
— Assembling of organizational policy statements on product safety.
— Initial arrangements for on-sight interviews.

June-Aug.
— Completed questionnaire returned and evaluated.
— Analysis of formal mechanisms for assuring product safety.
— Development of interview format.
— Finalizing arrangements for on-sight interviews.

Sept.-Oct.
— On-sight interviews at four study organizations.
— Initial preparations for Stage-Two Workshops.

Nov.-Dec.
— Final evaluation of accumulated data and preparation of formal report for presentation to Advisory Committee.
— Finalizing arrangements for Stage-Two Workshops.

II. Evaluative Stage

1981

January
— First Two-day Workshop: Presentation of Stage-One report and identification of issues for analysis by Advisory Committee.

February
— Submission of abstracts on issues for analysis by members of Advisory Committee.
— Announcements for Conference/Workshop.

May
— Second One-Day Workshop: Discussion and review of drafts of Advisory Committee papers.

Sept.
— Three-Day Conference/Workshop on Engineering Ethics in Organizational Contexts: Presentation of Advisory Committee Papers.

III. Summary Stage

Oct.
— Advisory Committee revises papers for publication.

Nov.-Dec.
— Preparation of final report for publication.

*Formerly Titled: Professional Responsibility in Organizations.

Since the success of this initial phase of our project depends upon the cooperation and trust of those organizations and their employees who are participating in this project, every reasonable effort, consistent with a concern for the accumulation of accurate unbiased data, will be made to consult with and inform organization administrators of the kind of information being sought as well as the procedures we will use to obtain this data. The project staff expects to conduct its research in a manner that causes the least possible disruption to normal work routines.

We are, as well, sensitive to the legal concerns and the inherent rights of these organizations and their employees to protect the confidentiality of certain types of information, e.g., personal privacy, trade secrets, patent rights, and our assurances concerning these matters have been sincerely accepted. Our various contacts with high level executives of subject organizations indicates an unequivocal willingness to cooperate with the project staff in the development of useful accurate data. Indeed, these executives have expressed an enthusiastic interest in the goals of this project. We therefore anticipate the establishment of a good working relationship.

The complete questionnaires will be evaluated by the project staff and will form the basis for developing interview protocols to be conducted by the staff at each organization, in the spring of the first project year. Approximately 80 individuals (20 per organization) will be interviewed. In particular, a random sampling of engineers at each of the most important levels within the division studied will be selected to be interviewed. Some key management personnel will also be interviewed. Each interview will be conducted during regular working hours and should take approximately 30 to 60 minutes. These interviews will be semi-structured to allow for comparison of responses to certain questions and at the same time permit more extensive in-depth questioning where necessary. [Sample interview questions were included in the proposal.]

Upon completion of all on-sight interviews, the project staff will prepare a formal report summarizing the results of the data accumulated during the descriptive stage. This report will include a detailed analysis and comparison of questionnaire and interview responses and a description of the kinds of mechanisms, formal and informal, that are intended to insure that engineers design reliable and safe products. An evaluation of the efficacy of these mechanisms will also be included. Drafts of this report will be submitted to the subject organizations for their review, in order to assure that no inaccuracies are contained in it.

At the beginning of the second or *evaluative stage,* the project staff will present its formal report to an interdisciplinary group of nationally recognized experts and scholars who make up the Advisory Committee of the project. They will meet on the Rensselaer campus for a two-day workshop to discuss this report and identify significant issues it raises which each member of the Advisory Committee and the project staff will investigate in the coming academic year. Some of these issues are mentioned above. The primary purpose of these efforts will be to write papers which critically evaluate the descriptive models, previously developed, for assigning responsibility to engineers for design and product safety. The project staff will be responsible for coordinating and directing these investigations to make sure that they are completed and appropriate to the goals of the project.

Prior to the second workshop, members of the Advisory Committee will be asked to submit abstracts detailing the nature of the analysis they propose to undertake. These will be distributed to the Advisory Committee for review and comment. At the second one-day workshop, to be held in conjunction with a national meeting of an organization such as the American Association for the Advancement of Science (AAAS), the Advisory Committee will meet to discuss and review first drafts of its papers. Copies of these papers will be distributed prior to this workshop.

The Advisory Committee and the project staff will make its first formal presentation of the results of its investigations at a three-day Conference-Workshop, to be held at RPI in late 1981. Public announcements inviting interested persons to attend a Conference-Workshop on Engineering Ethics in Organizational Contexts will be placed in appropriate publications. In addition, ten nationally recognized experts will be invited to act as commentators.

The Advisory Committee is made up of the following individuals: Robert M. Anderson, Jr. (Ball Brothers Professor of Engineering, Purdue University); Michael D. Bayles (Professor of Philosophy, University of Kentucky); John Ladd

(Professor of Philosophy, Brown University); Seymour Melman (Professor of Industrial and Management Engineering, Columbia University); Ian Mitroff (Professor of Business and Administration, University of Pittsburgh); Robert Perrucci (Professor of Sociology, Purdue University); and Stephen Unger (Professor of Electrical Engineering, Columbia University). Three additional persons will be invited to become members of the Advisory Committee; selection will be based upon the recommendations of the EVIST staff.* [*Copies of letters from these persons indicating a willingness to participate were included in the proposal.*]

In the final and *summary stage* of the project, occupying the last third of the second project year, the project staff will edit and write a final report which will include: (a) a description of the research procedures and the results of the data collected; (b) the revised papers and summary of conclusions (and recommendations) of the Advisory Committee; (c) an analytical summary, describing the implications which this project might have for engineers and organizations where questions of design and product safety and the social and ethical responsibilities associated with these questions arise; and (d) a list the Conference-Workshop will provide an additional source of evaluation. It is also expected that some of the results of this project will be published in various professional journals or presented at suitable engineering conferences. We anticipate that some of the materials will be included in courses on engineering ethics and feedback on their utility will be solicited. At the final workshop, the Advisory Committee will also be asked to make recommendations on the significant issues raised by this project which should form the basis for directing future research in this area.

The project staff will write and edit its final report. This report, together with the final versions of the conference papers, will be published. We will consult with EVIST staff to review the method of publication, selection of publisher, and publishing agreement, prior to publication.

V. Project Staff

The project will be directed by Albert Flores, Assistant Professor of Philosophy, also associated with the Center for the Study of the Human Dimensions of Science and Technology, Rensselaer Polytechnic Institute. He has practical experience in dealing with problems of applied ethics, particularly in the fields of medical ethics, professional ethics, and engineering ethics. He is co-editor, with Robert Baum, of an anthology on engineering ethics entitled *Ethical Problems in Engineering*. Currently, he is associate director of the NEH National Project on Philosophy and Engineering Ethics, associate editor of the newsletter on *Business and Professional Ethics,* and officer and charter member of the Society for the Study of Professional Ethics.

The project staff is composed of:

Reginald L. Hendricks, Assistant Professor of Psychology, Rensselaer Polytechnic Institute, who specializes in the field of organizational psychology and statistics. His experience includes research and publication on the effects of organizations on motivation and productivity, as well as consultant to various private and public institutions concerned with assessing their management policies. His expertise in methods of data gathering and evaluation have been well tested in recent years.

Robert Baum, Professor of Philosophy and Director of the Center for the Study of the Human Dimensions of Science and Technology, Rensselaer Polytechnic Institute, is the third member of the project staff. He is recognized as one of the leading experts in the field of engineering ethics and has published and lectured extensively in this area. He is project director for the NEH National Project on Philosophy and Engineering Ethics, Editor of *Business and*

---

*Additional members are: Donald E. Wilson (Michael Baker Corp.) and George Sinclair (Chairman, Sinclair Radio Labs., Ltd.)

Professional Ethics, and on the advisory committee of a number of national engineering societies examining the ethical questions raised by engineering practice.

[*Curricula vitae of the above listed individuals were included in the proposal.*]

RPI Proposal No. 306(91R)3163(4A)
COST ESTIMATE — two years

Appendix D

SUMMARY
PROPOSAL BUDGET

March 1979

		FOR NSF USE ONLY
ORGANIZATION AND ADDRESS RENSSELAER POLYTECHNIC INSTITUTE Troy, New York 12181		PROPOSAL NO.

PRINCIPAL INVESTIGATOR/PROJECT DIRECTOR Dr. Albert W. Flores	DURATION (MONTHS)
	PROPOSED / REVISED

	A. SENIOR PERSONNEL (LIST BY NAME; SHOW NUMBERS OF PEOPLE IN BRACKETS; SALARY AMOUNTS MAY BE LISTED ON SEPARATE SCHEDULE) GPM 205.1b	NSF FUNDED MAN MONTHS			FUNDS REQUESTED BY PROPOSER	FUNDS GRANTED BY NSF (IF DIFFERENT)
		CAL.	ACAD	SUMR.		
	1. P.I./P.D. Dr. A. W. Flores		4.5	4.0	$	$
	2. CO P.I./P.D.				$	$
NSF USE	3. CO P.I./P.D.				$	$
	4. CO P.I./P.D.				$	$
	5. CO P.I./P.D.				$	$
11115	6. (1) ◄——— SUBTOTALS A1 - A5 ———►		4.5	4.0	$	$
	FACULTY AND OTHER SENIOR ASSOCIATES (ATTACH EXTRA SHEET IF NECESSARY)					
	7. Dr. R. Hendricks		4.5	4.0	$	$
	8. Dr. R. Baum		1.8	1.5	$	$
	9.				$	$
	10.				$	$
	11.				$	$
11117	12. (2) ◄——— SUBTOTALS A7 - A11 ———►		6.3	5.5	$ 27,770	$
	B. OTHER PERSONNEL (LIST NUMBERS IN BRACKETS)					
11141	1. ( ) POSTDOCTORAL ASSOCIATES				$	$
11149	2. ( ) OTHER PROFESSIONALS				$	$
11150	3. (1) GRADUATE STUDENTS				$ 10,200	$
11152	4. ( ) UNDERGRADUATE STUDENTS				$	$
11182	5. (1) SECRETARIAL - CLERICAL				$ 4,500	$
11183	6. (1) TECHNICAL, SHOP, OTHER				$ 3,000	$
	TOTAL SALARIES AND WAGES (A+B)				$ 61,845	$
11200	C. FRINGE BENEFITS (IF CHARGED AS DIRECT COSTS) (See ATTACHMENT)				$ 10,062	$
	TOTAL SALARIES, WAGES AND FRINGE BENEFITS (A+B+C)				$ 71,907	$
	D. EQUIPMENT (LIST ITEMS AND DOLLAR AMOUNTS FOR EACH ITEM) None					
23181	TOTAL EQUIPMENT				$ ---	$
	E. MATERIALS AND SUPPLIES Miscellaneous Items - $4,612					
32630					$ *	$
42111	F. DOMESTIC TRAVEL Staff $ 4,600 Advisory Committee Workshops 13,150				$ 15,014 *	$
	G. FOREIGN TRAVEL (LIST DESTINATION AND AMOUNT FOR EACH TRIP; GPM 731) None					
42112					$ ---	$

PAGE 1 OF 2 PAGES   21

*(See Individual year's budget for explanation)

Summary of proposal budget.

RPI Proposal No. 306(91R)3163(4A)
COST ESTIMATE – two years   March 1979

SUMMARY PROPOSAL BUDGET

	PROPOSAL NO.	

52500	H. PUBLICATION COSTS/PAGE CHARGES	None	$ ---	$
62315	I. COMPUTER (ADPE) SERVICES	None	$ ---	$

	J. CONSULTANT SERVICES (IDENTIFY CONSULTANTS BY NAME AND AMOUNT; GPM 516)		
	10 persons for 11 days each @ $150		
		$ 16,500	$

	K. PARTICIPANT SUPPORT COSTS, IF ALLOWED BY PROGRAM GUIDE (ITEMIZE) GPM 518		
	1. STIPENDS None	$	
	2. TRAVEL	$	
	3. SUBSISTENCE	$	
	4. OTHER - SPECIFY	$	
	5. TOTAL PARTICIPANT COSTS (K1 + K2 + K3 + K4)	$ ---	$

	L. ALL OTHER DIRECT COSTS (List items and dollar amounts. Details of subcontracts, including work statements and budget, should be explained in full in proposal.)		
		$	
	None	$	
		$	
		$	
65001	TOTAL OTHER DIRECT COSTS	$ ---	$

	M. TOTAL DIRECT COSTS (A THROUGH L)	$103,421	$

	N. INDIRECT COSTS (Specify rate(s) and base(s) for on/off campus activity Where both are involved, identify itemized costs included in on/off campus bases in remarks.)		
	58.5% of Total Personnel Payments (See ATTACHMENT)		
74100	TOTAL INDIRECT COSTS	$ 36,179	$

	O. TOTAL DIRECT AND INDIRECT COSTS (M + N)	$139,600	$
74500	P. LESS RESIDUAL FUNDS (If for further support of current project; GPM 252 and 253)	$ ---	$
75000	Q. AMOUNT OF THIS REQUEST (O MINUS P)	$139,600	$

REMARKS

*Total Materials and Supplies and Travel Costs are
$4,612 and $17,750, respectively. Of these amounts,
RPI will cost share $7,348 (5% of Total Project Costs).

NOTE: SIGNATURES REQUIRED ONLY FOR REVISED BUDGET (GPM 233). THIS IS REVISION NO.

SIGNATURE OF PRINCIPAL INVESTIGATOR/PROJECT DIRECTOR	DATE OF SIGNATURE	TYPED OR PRINTED NAME AND TITLE
SIGNATURE OF AUTHORIZED ORGANIZATIONAL REPRESENTATIVE	DATE OF SIGNATURE	TYPED OR PRINTED NAME AND TITLE

FOR NSF USE ONLY

INDIRECT COST RATE VERIFICATION			PROGRAM OFFICER APPROVAL
Date Checked	Date of Rate Sheet	Signature	

Grant Number	Amend No.	Institution	Organization	Fund Acct.	Program	Object	

	Proposal Number	Dur.	Chg.	Award Date	Proposed Amount	Prosd. Dur.	

PAGE 2 OF 2 PAGES

22

Summary of proposal budget. Continued.

TRAINING GRANTS

The three grant applications chosen for inclusion in this section offer as much variation as possible in type of program, funding organization, size and nature of grantee institution, and amounts of funds involved.

CETA Youth Employment Training Program

The Comprehensive Employment and Training Act (CETA) of 1973 has been under fire ever since it was created by the Congress and turned over to the Department of Labor to administer. The present administration seems determined to abolish it; some Titles have already been eliminated. However, the Henry Street Settlement proposal for support under Title IV contains elements that make it an excellent model for a training grant proposal to any agency in any sector.

Title IV of the CETA program aimed at providing employment for the long-term unemployed and those with job-market disadvantages. The proposal shown here, Henry Street Settlement's Youth Employment Training Program proposes a curriculum that provides for a combination of classroom and work experience to teach clerical and technical theater skills to young people with job-market disadvantages. In the selection of students, priority would be given to members of minority groups with poor work habits, educational handicaps, and with prior criminal justice system involvement, who nevertheless showed some potential for success. The objective was to prepare them to successfully enter employment in a skilled field.

The proposal was written by Donna Bonem Rich with the assistance of the Henry Street Settlement staff who would be involved in the training program. Ms. Rich's history of the proposal development, including details of the preapplication negotiations, an account of the writing, submission, and execution of the project is particularly informative.

Applied Social Research in Crime/Delinquency Program

The training grant application of Prof. Larry Adams and Barry Tuchfeld of Texas Christian

University, Fort Worth, provides a good model for training programs to be carried on in an university or college whatever the subject matter.

Paul Hennessey, former editor of the Grants Clinic wrote the history of this proposal and describes in detail the kind of negotiation and preliminary presentations that preceded the formal submission of the application. The pre-application discussion regarding the amount to be requested was particularly significant, and the advice given here is applicable to any grant request, especially if large sums of money are involved.

Health Advocacy Master's Program

Developing a Graduate Program in Health Advocacy at Sarah Lawrence College, Bronxville, New York was funded by the Florence V. Burden Foundation.

This Application, compared with those presented to the federal government, indicates one of the major differences between applications to foundations and to governmental agencies. Usually, no application form is used, and the applicant presents the proposal in a simple narrative description. In this particular case, no detailed budget was appended, but the fund request was stated in one short paragraph. For this application, this manner of presentation was appropriate, but for many proposals, a detailed budget would be essential.

An unusual feature of this example is the statement of Harriet L. Warm which precedes the application. Ms. Warm, Executive Director of the funding foundation, states exactly why they approved the request for the funds for this project. It is rare that foundation officials will be so open and frank about what they do and why they do it, and the Florence V. Burden Foundation is admirably unusual in this respect.

In the same issue of GRANTS MAGAZINE (September 1980) in which this proposal appeared, there is an article by Harriet L. Warm analyzing what all foundations are doing for the elderly. The information is tabulated by grouping foundation (large, medium, and small), and fifteen of the largest foundations making grants to the elderly are named. She also shows the amount given by each foundation during the most recent years for which data were available, 1976 and 1977.

Henry Street Settlement's Youth Employment Training Program

Funded by: Comprehensive Employment and Training Act (CETA), U.S. Department of Labor

Project Coordinator: Anne Dalton, Director, Youth Employment Service, Henry Street Settlement

Proposal Prepared by: Donna Bonem Rich with cooperation of Anne Dalton,

Mark Tilley, and Vito Perri

HENRY STREET SETTLEMENT'S YOUTH EMPLOYMENT TRAINING PROGRAM PROPOSAL

by Donna Bonem Rich

The Henry Street Settlement was founded in 1893 and today offers over twenty innovative programs including day care, mental health services, housing, and a variety of arts programs. The Settlement has been working in the field of youth employment for many years. Henry Street began by providing summer and year-round jobs that ranged from low skill activities — such as delivering interagency mail — to the more skilled positions of day camp counselor and clerical assistant. In the past five years, Henry Street has been enlarging its Youth Employment Service Program to pay attention to the development of work readiness skills in youngsters and to the provision of skill training and on-the-job work experience.

Henry Street has pioneered in the field of youth employment; it has also pioneered in many

Donna Bonem Rich is Associate Director of Development, Henry Street Settlement.

areas of social service (e.g., Mobilization for Youth began in 1959 at Henry Street). In 1975, long before most community-based agencies received government funding to operate youth employment programs, the Settlement ran a demonstration program called Supported Employment for Adolescents (SEA). Funded by the Law Enforcement Assistance Administration (LEAA), the SEA Program combined on-the-job training of court-involved youth (ages 14–16) with educational and counseling supports. The program served as an alternative to institutionalization for many young people.

The success of the SEA Program demonstrated the effectiveness of combining a mix of services with supervised supported employment in order to help young people make positive adjustments to school, work, their families and community. Using the SEA model, Henry Street then developed a program — focused on work readiness — for a general population of minority youth (ages 16–21) to help them make positive adjustments to the world of work.

In all, more than 100 young people between the ages of 16 and 21 are currently employed part-time or full-time (not including the summer employment programs) at the Settlement through a variety of governmental and privately-funded programs. All these youngsters have access to the educational, recreational, developmental, and health services offered at Henry Street. The Settlement provides an excellent base of support services for youth engaged in learning the skills and attitudes required by most work settings.

Since August 1979 Henry Street has been operating a Comprehensive Employment and Training Act (CETA) Youth Employment and Training Program (YETP) funded through the New York City Department of Employment (a CETA prime sponsor). The program involves the training of 60 young men and women — 40 in secretarial skills and 20 in technical theater skills. Targeted to serve out-of-school youth, the program provides vocational skills that will then open up unsubsidized job opportunities by the end of the training cycle. Several of the graduates of the clerical component have already accepted permanent employment and technical theater participants are working on actual productions of Henry Street's nationally acclaimed professional company, New Federal Theater.

YETP projects are funded locally throughout the country. These programs seek to enhance the job prospects and career opportunities of young persons — through employment and training services designed locally and adapted to local needs.

Background

In 1973 Congress passed legislation consolidating many of the existing employment and training programs. This legislation — the Comprehensive Employment and Training Act (CETA) — supports a variety of federal efforts through a network of local governments known as prime sponsors (for the most part cities or counties). New York City is such a prime sponsor and its CETA programs are administered by the Department of Employment. Localities are given control of a large portion of CETA funds, thereby enabling programs to be planned and administered according to the needs of local jurisdictions. Prime sponsors, in turn, look for organiza-

tions with the ability to deliver job services to those needing them.

One of the newest CETA programs is YETP (Youth Employment and Training Program), which was developed in 1977 as one of several parts of the President's Youth Employment Demonstrations Projects Act (YEDPA). Others are YCCIP (Youth Community Conservation and Improvement Projects); YIEP (Youth Incentive Entitlement Projects); and YACC (Youth Adult Conservations Corps). YEDPA was signed into law by the President in August of 1977 and was added to the original 1973 legislation as CETA Title III Part C. It is now CETA Title IV.

YETP projects concentrate on youngsters (ages 16–21) having the most difficulty in obtaining employment. The legislation mandates that special consideration be given to community-based organizations "with demonstrated effectiveness in the delivery of employment services." Congress emphasized the use of community-based organizations (CBOs) as it was felt they could reach individuals unlikely to be served by more traditional approaches. The end result of YETP projects must be job development and placement to secure unsubsidized employment, to the maximum extent possible, for participants. YETP programs require that comprehensive services be provided to youth.

New York City funds YETP projects once a year through an RFP (Request For Proposal) mechanism. In mid-October 1978 Henry Street learned that YETP applications would be due to the prime sponsor, the Department of Employment, by November 30. We called the department and ascertained that application kits and program guidelines could be picked up and that a technical assistance workshop on how to fill out the application forms was scheduled for November 1. We let them know Henry Street would be attending.

Development of the Proposal

At the November 1 training session on how to prepare the application we met YETP officials and had the opportunity to ask questions. This training session proved to be enormously helpful as the city was requiring, in addition to the narrative proposal reprinted here, a completed ten-page Program Operating Plan (POP), detailing budget expenditures and participant enrollment/ termination projections. The technical assistance workshop made it clear to us that the city was looking for well-designed programs. Agencies were requested to submit projects in one of four types of YETP programs: Classroom Training (involving intake, assessment of youngsters' academic capabilities, with training, to move them into entry level jobs); Work Experience, where youngsters learn a trade while working; On-The-Job Training (OJT), which involves work with private industry; and Career Employment Experience, designed to give in-school youngsters knowledge of the world of work. Applicants would be required: to develop a program that was primarily one type; to show employer involvement in the development of the proposal; to demonstrate their experience in running employment programs; to keep administrative costs to no more than 15 percent of the total budget; and to contribute in-kind services.

Between November 1 and November 30 Henry Street designed its classroom training program in clerical skills and theater technology for 80 young people aged 16 to 21. We proposed training youngsters for two occupations: secretary/ clerical (60 youngsters in two 22-week cycles of 30 each) and theater technician (20 young people in one 46-week cycle). The program would be targeted to out-of-school, economically disadvantaged youngsters to provide them with skills training, work training, remedial instruction, and support services. At the completion of the training cycles we would channel graduates to appropriate unsubsidized employment. For classroom training programs, the Department of Employment required youngsters to spend most (defined as at least 51 percent) of their time in the classroom. To have the youngsters with us and pay them stipends for 35 hours each week, we developed a program involving them in classroom skills training for about 20 hours a week. The rest of the time was to be spent in work ex-

perience training (mandated by the guidelines to be in the public sector) and in counseling.

The technical assistance workshop had also made us aware that the city wanted applicant agencies for YETP to show a 60 percent positive termination rate (defined as job placement, return to high school or college, entering another training program, or entering the military). Further, 50 percent of the youngsters enrolled had to be placed, at the program's termination, in unsubsidized jobs.

The city was looking for some type of agreement from employers as to what the jobs for which we were training required in terms of skills. While we realized that it was extremely important that work training programs be linked to real job opportunities, we realized that it is difficult with a classroom training program (as opposed to OJT) to get employer commitments to jobs after the training ends. What we felt we could reasonably obtain were letters from prospective employers indicating that they had reviewed our proposed curriculum for the training of youngsters and that if youngsters were trained in the manner being proposed, they would consider interviewing program graduates for suitable openings in their companies. We asked those who wrote such letters to give us suggestions for the proposed curricula materials. Too often, in youth employment training programs, voluntary agencies have either trained youngsters for jobs that did not really exist or for skills for which there was not really a need in that locality, or used a training curriculum which did not impart the skills or attitudes that would make youngsters employable and retainable by private industry at the end of the training program. The letters that Henry Street included in the proposal shown here indicate that project staff would maintain regular contact with the employers who helped in the development of the curriculum in order to ensure the appropriateness of the training as the program was proceeding. Drafts of both the clerical training curriculum and the theater technician curriculum were shared, as the proposal developed, with each of the prospective employers whose letters were included in our proposal.

We had also learned at the technical assistance

workshop that in a classroom training program, dropouts could only be replaced during the first two weeks of the program. Therefore, we had to be sure that we developed and spelled out in the proposal entry criteria which would target young people with some potential for success in the training course and those with post-training employability. At the same time we gave priority to youngsters with poor work habits, with educational handicaps, and with prior criminal justice system involvement. The positive termination rate (minimum 60 percent) and the job placement rate (minimum 50 percent) wanted by the prime sponsor was based on the number of students enrolled, not the number retained. Our selection criteria, as a result, had to target those who showed some promise of completing the program and attaining a certain level of skills. (In our Program Operating Plan, we had to specify exit criteria, such as a minimum typing level of 50 words per minute for the clerical graduates.)

The two fields we chose to train for were selected both because of Henry Street's prior experience and because of the strength we felt they would lend to our proposal. There is a large need for clerical workers in New York and theater technician is a skill for which Henry Street is uniquely qualified to conduct a training program. Further, we determined that technical theater was an area in which a need existed and for which economically disadvantaged minority youth were not generally being trained.

Why Did the Proposal Succeed?

The proposal that follows was tailored to the guidelines of the funding source. Having had the benefit of the technical assistance workshop, it was easier for Henry Street to develop the application and to understand better the intent behind some of the guidelines. (Information brought back from the workshop was also of enormous help to our fiscal officer in preparing the complicated budget forms.) We also tried to make the proposal as readable as possible. This meant preparing a typed, double-spaced, visually attractive document. We also made sure to emphasize in the proposal the benefits that would accrue to program participants. Measurable outcomes for all program participants were specified as well as outcomes specific to the clerical and to the theater components. We called attention to our unique capabilities by pointing to Henry Street's range of support services, our ability to serve those most-in-need, and the very unusual facilities offered by our architecturally-acclaimed Arts For Living Center (where the theater technician training would take place). It was extremely important, in our judgment, to describe Henry Street's particular capability as a training site for economically disadvantaged young people. This was done by emphasizing the following points:

- Henry Street has always worked with poor, minority young people.
- A settlement is an ideal setting within which to prepare young people for the world of work.
- Henry Street's experience in running government-funded programs and how that qualified us to provide skills training to urban youth.
- Our track record in the section of the proposal, "Administrative System," and our proposed project management plan.
- Our unique range of support services.

The proposal also contained endorsement letters from four companies for the clerical training component and several theaters for the technical component. For added emphasis we placed these letters immediately following the description of each curriculum, it being our belief that important support letters often get buried in the back of a proposal. We placed these letters near the front since the statement of prospective employers *before* the training actually got under way influenced significantly the identification of the skills to be embodied in our training program and the possibility that we could place at least 50 percent of the students in unsubsidized employment at the program's end.

We also took care to describe the specific work sites in which youngsters would be placed to practice the skills they would be learning in the classroom and what criteria would be used to choose these sites.

One of the most attractive components of our proposed program, as we subsequently learned from the Department of Employment, was the inclusion of the training component in the arts. Technical theater is an innovative area in which to train disadvantaged young people and one for which Henry Street is uniquely qualified to train. Henry Street has both the back-up services mandated for YETP projects (counseling, child care, High School Equivalency) and a wide-range of arts programs (including three high-quality professional theater programs and several well-equipped theaters). There are few community-based agencies that have Henry Street's range of social services and arts programs. Thus, our training of minorities in the theater arts — an area for which there has been some attention and concern on a national level — made our proposal unique and attractive. This, when coupled with four years of prior experience in operating youth employment programs (including a YCCIP program funded by the Department of Employment) helped strengthen the proposal.

Finally, we tried to make the project as cost efficient as possible. As a result, we kept administrative costs at around 9 percent of the budget, with 52 percent of the budget going for participant benefits, 28 percent of the budget allocated for training costs and 11 percent for services to participants. We also showed in-kind contributions to the project: we indicated that personal, family, and educational counseling would be given to program participants by Henry Street to augment the vocational counseling provided under the YETP contract. We also showed a contribution of 5 percent of the Executive Director's time for overall project management and supervision of the Project Director.

After the Proposal Submission

The proposal was submitted to the Department of Employment on November 29. We then wrote a three-page summary that could be sent to those whose support of the pending application we were seeking. The summary contained a description of the proposed program, the participants to be served, a description of both the clerical and theater technician training components, and an account of Henry Street's qualifications. In March we received word from the Department of Employment that our proposal had received favorable consideration and we were called into "contract negotiations." In the end, Henry Street was awarded a contract for $313,000, although we had initially requested $414,000. When the budget was reduced, we had to reduce the total number of youngsters we could train from 80 to 60.

At the end of the first clerical training cycle (January), 14 trainees, or 70 percent, had already been positively terminated, i.e., placed in unsubsidized employment, including one 18-year-old male who was hired as the secretary for Henry Street's Youth Employment Service. A young woman — the 17-year-old mother of a one-year-old child — was hired as a secretary at a large textile company in New York City and is already being considered for promotion. She is married to a former court-involved young man who found employment with the assistance of our prior LEAA-funded program. Others are working in private industry, and we are still working to place all trainees who complete the program.

The Theatre Technician Training Program provides a setting where students can learn skills in the classroom while working as interns on high quality, professionally produced plays, including those presented by Henry Street's Family Theatre and the New Federal Theatre. One trainee is an intern at the Equity Library Theatre. The program's job developer is constantly receiving calls for students to intern at theaters throughout the New York City area, and we have received many letters commending the students' work on theater productions.

* * *

YOUTH EMPLOYMENT TRAINING PROGRAM PROPOSAL

[In lieu of a cover page, the proposal was sent with a letter of transmittal, written on the stationery of Henry Street Settlement Urban Life Center, which contained the names of all officers, directors, and honorary directors of the Settlement. The letter was addressed to the New York City Department of Employment, the CETA prime sponsor. It was signed by the Executive Director of the Henry Street Settlement. The narrative portion of the proposal follows.]

OBJECTIVES

Statement of Purpose

Henry Street Settlement is proposing to operate a classroom training program in clerical skills and theatre technology for 80 young people ages 16 to 21. Training will be provided for two occupations: secretary/clerical (60 youngsters) and theatre technicians (20 youngsters). The proposed program will concentrate on those youngsters having the most difficulty in obtaining employment. The two classroom training programs at Henry Street will target economically disadvantaged youngsters and provide them with meaningful skill development and training experiences, thereby enhancing their long-term job prospects and career opportunities. The program will provide skills training, work-role training, counseling and remedial instruction combined with the provision of occupational and educational information. The overall goal of the program is to assist disadvantaged youth to overcome the barriers to entering the world of work and to achieving job stability and advancement.

Within the context of a classroom skills center at Henry Street, the young people would receive skills training, work training and a range of supportive services. Youth will be trained for the kinds of jobs they will hold after the classroom training program is completed. The program will foster specific job skills that trainees will use on subsequent jobs and the program will channel graduates to appropriate unsubsidized employment. Counseling and other supportive services will further enable youth to adapt to these jobs.

All eighty youngsters will be given productive skills training plus:

— Counseling
— High school equivalency preparation (where applicable)
— Child care and other supportive services
— Career information

The purpose of the classroom training will be to upgrade skills and to provide youngsters with remedial education. The supervised work training will assist youth to practice the skills of a particular occupation, while the counseling will further assist youngsters to adjust to the world of work. The overall goal of the program, the enhancement of the long-term employability of program participants, will be accomplished through:

— The provision of specific job skills
— Access to jobs for which participants will have received classroom and work training
— Counseling to assist youth to adjust to jobs
— Remedial education

The work role training will prepare youth to handle work situations as a complement to the classroom skills training. Program participants will develop vocational behaviors and appropriate work habits, while acquiring occupational skills.

While the primary emphasis of the program is on occupational training, the proposed program will include job and training-related remedial education, and high-school equivalency certification. All participants enrolled in the program will receive an allowance of $2.90 per hour for time spent in the classroom, in work training and in counseling. Part-time work training assignments will provide youth with a disciplined but supportive structure within which they can acquire work habits and skills and will be designed to enhance the employability of youngsters who have never worked or who have not been working for an extended period of time. The work training will provide youngsters with the opportunity to learn how to work. Work training assignments will enhance participants' employability, through supervision of work habits and the further development of skills of participants.

Participants to be Served

Program participants will be males and females between the ages of 16 and 21 who are out-of-school. Priority would be given in the program to young people who have experienced chronic unemployment as a result of:

(1) Poor or low level skills
(2) A history of poor work habits (high absenteeism, difficulties with supervisors, difficulty or inability to follow instructions)
(3) Racial and ethnic discrimination
(4) Juvenile and criminal justice system involvement
(5) School behavior problems
(6) Educational handicaps
(7) History of drug and alcohol abuse
(8) Dependent children

Preference would be given to youngsters whose families are economically indigent to insure that the project targets its services to youth suffering financial hardships.

EXPECTED RESULTS

Goals to be Accomplished

(1) To ready young people for the job market by teaching them the skills and attitudes necessary to get and hold a job.
(2) To improve youths' educational functioning with the outcomes of raising reading and math levels, acquisition of the equivalency diploma, returning to school.
(3) To assist youth to continue with education which may be required to strengthen basic skills or acquire new skills.

(4) To provide youth with career guidance and job-seeking training to insure their future stability in holding a job.
(5) To help youth to acquire information about and skills in interviewing, filling out job applications.

Implementation Outcomes

(1) Hire and train qualified project staff.
(2) Enroll 80 young people: 20 in a 46-week theater technology course and 30 in each of two 22-week cycles of clerical skills training.
(3) Develop and implement a complementary support services system.
(4) Select and monitor supportive work training assignments for all youth.

PROGRAM OUTCOMES

For all program participants:

(1) To positively terminate a minimum of 60% of the 80 enrollees.
(2) To place in unsubsidized employment a minimum of 50% of the 80 enrollees.
(3) To graduate clients who can achieve and maintain 90% attendance and punctuality.
(4) To graduate clients whose math and reading is minimally at the 8th grade level.
(5) To graduate youngsters who hold entry level positions for at least 90 days following placement in jobs.
(6) To graduate clients with appropriate work behavior and attitudes.

Program Outcomes for Clerical Component

(1) To graduate clients with 50 wpm typing and 80 wpm stenography skills.
(2) To graduate clients skilled in filing, use of telephone, use of business reference materials, basic operation of adding machine/calculator.

Program Outcomes for Theater Component

The project will graduate clients with the following skills:

(1) Tools and Equipment
  — Ability to use a variety of hand tools including hammers, various types of wrenches, pliers and screwdrivers, tape measure, framing and tri-squares, chisels, wood and metal hand saws, clamps, matt knife, etc.
  — Knowledge of and ability to use special tools such as trammel points, lighting instrument wrenches, cut-all.
  — Ability to use hand power tools: jig saw, circular (skill) saw, belt and orbital sander, hand drill.
  — Ability to use other power tools/equipment including table saw, radial arm saw, air compressor, band saw, drill press.
(2) Carpentry/Construction
  — Mastery of measuring, cutting, joints, glueing, fastening, finishing, wood grades; ability to apply techniques to theater situations.
(3) Electrics
  — Hanging and focusing various lighting instruments: fresnels, lecoes, scoops, beam projectors, slide projectors, follow spots, etc.
  — Basic a.c. wiring including lighting instruments, trouble shooting, simple special effects, e.g. flash pots, smoke pots, practical lamps.
  — Ability to operate all non-computerized lighting boards; familiarity with multi-cue board
(4) Sound
  — Ability to do basic recording and editing to make show tapes, miking and mixing of live shows, ability to operate basic theater sound systems, knowledge of sound wiring.
(5) Drafting
  — Ability to use T square, mechanical pencils, compass, drafting triangles (30-

60-90, 45-45-90, adjustable), French curves, drafting machine.
  — Ability to read detailed plans of sets and lighting plots, to draft three dimensional objects on paper, to create construction drawings from specifications.
(6) Production Techniques
  — Understanding of standard procedures in production work.
  — Knowledge of suppliers for production materials.

APPROACH

Selection of Work Training Sites

Clerical Component

Work training sites for the clerical skills trainees will be selected from among Lower Manhattan settlements and social service organizations, including Henry Street Settlement. Three major criteria will be used in selecting sites:

(1) The quality and range of work skill training available.
(2) The quality of on-site supervision.
(3) The availability of complementary support services for trainees during work training hours.

Prior to selection of work sites, visits will be made to a list of pre-screened (to determine interest and general suitability) organizations to enable project staff to meet with prospective supervisors, to visit specific work locations and to formulate prospective job descriptions and work training evaluation mechanisms. Final selection of work training sites will be made based on a rating of all sites with emphasis on developing a variety of work settings which complement the project's overall goals and objectives.

Theatre Component

To provide a broad background in technical theatre and to develop participants' skills to the fullest, students will be placed in various institutions (universities) and professional theaters, including:

— Marymount Manhattan Theatre
— Kingsborough Community College
— Lincoln Center
— The Public Theatre

Universities selected as work training sites must have an educational program in theatre, with particular strength in technical theatre and have the necessary facilities and supervision to insure the proper development of skills in program participants. All professional (non-profit) theatres selected as work training sites must have appropriate facilities to ensure the development of the students' skills and be able to provide adequate staff supervision.

Outreach and Recruitment

The program will be open to young people meeting the eligibility criteria,* with strong preference being given to young people from Lower Manhattan, because of the Settlement's commitment to its multi-ethnic neighborhood.

Notice of program openings will be given to public and private manpower services such as the State Employment Service, Vocational Foundation, Inc., Jobs For Youth, the Door, community and non-profit theatres.

Additionally, flyers will be distributed throughout settlements and community centers and with guidance staffs of local high schools, in order to identify recent high school graduates. Advertisements will also be placed in local newspapers.

Selection and Enrollment

All project trainees will be screened for enrollment according to: overall eligibility (age, income

*See previous section for "Participants To Be Served."

level, history of unemployment, etc.); skills and aptitudes (see program/course schedule); and basic attitudes and behaviors that would seem to indicate potential for success in the training course and for post-training employability. Information concerning course content, training methods, and support services will be made available to applicants at the outset, when overall eligibility is being determined. Subsequently, aptitude testing will be administered (it is expected that tests will be administered to approximately 40-50% more applicants than there are available spaces anticipating drop-outs) in each of the skill areas (e.g., clerical and theatre technology). During testing, project staff will be concerned not only with raw test scores but also with applicants' behavior and performance (e.g., punctuality, use of time, interaction with project staff and other applicants, etc.).

Following computation of test scores, eligible applicants will be asked back for individual interviews with a team of project staff including skill teachers and job development and counseling personnel. The interviews will attempt to explore an applicant's goals and motivation for program involvement.

While the components of the selection procedure as well as the structuring of the process are expected to yield necessary and appropriate information for final selection, care will be taken to avoid discouraging or frustrating applicants unnecessarily. Additionally, waiting lists will be maintained both in the event of drop-outs or terminations in the first two weeks of training, and for the second cycle of the clerical training course.

DESCRIPTION OF TRAINING AND SERVICES PROPOSED

Classroom Training

The Clerical Component

The following curriculum will be used for the clerical course:

I. Typing
- Basic knowledge and care of electric typewriter
- Typing training and drill with a goal of 50-60 wpm
- Instruction in setting up letters, spacing and centering, proofreading, use of carbons, etc.

II. Transcribing
- Basic stenography and transcription with a goal of 80 wpm
- Proper transcription of machine dictation

III. Record Keeping
- Alphabetical, numeric and subject filing systems
- Management of files: cross-referencing, retrieval and tracking systems, etc.

IV. Telephones
- Answering and placing calls
- Message taking
- Setting up appointments
- Maintaining telephone number and address files

FEDERAL RESERVE BANK OF NEW YORK

NEW YORK, N.Y. 10045

AREA CODE 212-791-5000

IN REPLY PLEASE REFER TO

November 28, 1978

Mr. Frank Seever
Executive Director
Henry Street Settlement
265 Henry Street
New York, New York 10002

Dear Mr. Seever:

We have reviewed your curriculum for the proposed clerical training program and are in accord with the objectives you set out. It appears to us that the curriculum is both comprehensive and appropriate.

If participants are trained in the manner you are proposing, our personnel department would be willing to interview program graduates as suitable openings occur. Further, should the proposal be funded, we would look forward to developing an ongoing relationship with your program staff in the months ahead.

With best wishes for success.

Sincerely yours,

Leo W. Van Beek
Training Director
Training Division

Fig. 1. Letter from Federal Reserve Bank of New York expressing an interest in the program and a willingness to consider graduates for employment.

V. Business English
   — Proper spelling, grammar, punctuation
   — Knowledge of reference materials
   — Proofreading
   — Preparing correspondence

VI. Use of Adding Machine and/or Calculator
   — Basic number accuracy
   — Ability to add, subtract, multiply and divide

VII. Basic Office Practices and Procedures
   — Punctuality and attendance
   — Co-worker relations
   — Appropriate dress
   — Handwriting
   — Organization and prioritization of work
   — Issues of confidentiality

Trainees will devote on the average, 15 hours weekly to skill training, 5 hours weekly to remedial and basic education, 5 hours weekly to supervised practice and drill sessions (counseling will also be scheduled during drill study time) and 10 hours weekly to work training. Two sections of 15 trainees each of the skill training class will be scheduled but trainees will be brought together for basic education and will overlap in drill periods. The two groups of 15 will have different work training schedules and some system of job-sharing may be attempted. A possible schedule is shown below:

	Group A	Group B
9-10 AM	Skill Training	Worktraining
10-11 AM	↓	↓
11-12 Noon		Drill/Counseling
12-1 PM	– – – – – – – Lunch – – – – – – –	
1-2 PM	– – – – – – Basic Education – – – – – –	
2-3 PM	Drill Couseling	Skill Training
3-4 PM	Work Training	↓
4-5 PM	↓	

There will be two 22-week course cycles. The first cycle will begin in the 5th week of the program following a four week start-up period for staff hiring and training, client intake and enrollment and project implementation. There will be a two-week break between the two cycles to allow for new intake with the second training cycle beginning in the 29th project week. The final two weeks of the project year will be devoted to closing out activities.

The clerical component which will train stenotypists, clerk-typists and secretaries was selected after a series of discussions with employer groups (see attached commitment/endorsement letters), and a review of employment listings in the local newspapers. Employers have consistently talked of the almost constant need for well-trained clerical workers and the proportion of clerical openings in the papers, generally significantly exceeding other types of openings, confirms this demand. However, it is also recognized that while clerical training involves a set of basic skills (typing, dictation, transcription, etc.) initially required for all positions, there is some specialization of vocabulary, work organization, etc. that varies. To insure the appropriateness of the training, the project staff will maintain regular contact both with employers who have already participated in the development of the training curriculum and with new employers identified by the project's job development unit.

[At this point in the application, four letters were inserted, three from business corporations and one from a bank, all agreeing to consider program graduates for suitable openings. Figure 1 shows the letter received from the Federal Reserve Bank of New York.]

Classroom Training

Theater Technician Training Program

Henry Street proposes to train technicians in the Technical Theater Department of the Henry Street Arts for Living Center. Twenty young persons ages 16-21 will be trained in a 52-week program (46 weeks of training).

These 20 youth will be trained as theater technicians with particular emphasis on two craft areas:

(1) Stage electrician/sound electrician
(2) Stage carpenter/property technician

In the course of the training, some exposure would also be given to trainees in the occupations of set designer, lighting designer, costume designer, property designer and technician. Training would consist of:

— Classroom time where new material would be introduced and questions by students could be answered in-depth.
— Hands-on classroom laboratory experience with equipment where trainees would be able to actively join in the use of tools and equipment at Henry Street.
— Work training where trainees would work in other theater organizations utilizing professionally equipped facilities.
— Field trips to professional shops and theaters where trainees would be able to see first-hand the opportunities available in the areas of their interest and different facility installations.

Skill building will include the following:
Carpenter/Props
— Use of hand and power tools used in the execution of theatrical scenery and props.
— Reading blueprints and translating blueprints into three-dimensional reality.
— Creating and building stage props.

Stage Electrician/Sound Technician
— Use and maintenance of stage lighting equipment.
— Reading lighting plots and "hanging" a show.
— Creating and wiring special effects equipment.
— Maintaining and using sound equipment.
— Making sound tapes.

The basic goal of the classroom training program will be to provide basic and advanced knowledge of technical theater and to develop basic skills in theater construction and electrics. Basic education in reading and math will be a regular part of the classroom experience. The theater curriculum was selected after consultation with several theatrical organizations including professional theaters, theater educational institutions, professional theater shops.*

Classroom instruction will consist of the following elements:
(1) Program Start-up/Intake of Participants — 4 weeks
(2) Introduction to Technical Theater — 12 weeks
Designed to provide participants with general understanding of technical aspects of theater and to begin basic skill building.
(3) Construction I and Electrics I — 6 weeks
Overall study of modern theater technology in electrics, construction, and drafting with development of basic skills in these areas.
(4) Construction II and Costumes, Electrics II and Production — 17 weeks
Intensive study of and skill development in construction/carpentry, electrics, overall production, costuming, with exploration of design and other specialized areas of technical theater.
(5) Independent Study/Job Placement — 7 weeks
Refinement and further development of knowledge and skills in areas of most interest to enrollees development of skills and techniques needed for obtaining and holding jobs, actual job interviews and placement.
(6) Program Closing — 2 weeks
Completion of program operation, report writing, termination of staff.

In addition, there will be a four week period of work training in an intensive work environment (summer stock), most likely occurring between (3) and (4) above.

Weekly schedule will consist of 3 days of classroom experience for all enrollees. On a rotating basis, 6 - 7 enrollees will receive intensive applied skills classroom training, and 13 - 14 enrollees will have a work training experience 2 days per week.

Counseling and basic educational curriculum will make up part of the classroom time. Class-

*Letters of commitment/endorsement follow curriculum.

'The Henry Street Settlement's carpenter (left) instructing a student in techniques of scenery building, for a production of the Settlement's Family Theatre.

room time will constitute 66% of the enrollees' activity.

The curriculum for each course follows:

Introduction to Technical Theatre

Weeks

1	Theatres and their physical plants, terminology, set plans, staffing and jobs.
2-5	Set construction, painting, rigging, theatre supplies, hardware, tools and reading plans.
6-8	Theatre electrics, lighting instruments, dimmer boards, special effects and reading plans.
9	Drafting and reading plans.
10	Sound (Drafting).
11	New materials, costumes.
12	Props and furniture, tours and discussion of theatres; scenic, sound and different lighting studios.

Theatre Electrics I

Weeks

2	Drafting and overview of stage lighting.
3	Current electrical theory.
4-5	Optics, stage lighting instruments, audio theory and sound equipment.
6	Lighting and audio control systems and installations.

Theatrical Construction I

Weeks

1	Drafting and overview of scenery.
2-3	Physical plant (building, rigging), Terminology, tools, hardware.
4	Structural physics (stress, tension, supports).
5-6	Methods of construction (material, cost, application).

Electrics II and Production

Weeks

1	Review of Electrics I.
2-3	Optics, color, color temperature.
4-5	Advance theory use of testing equipment.
6, 7, 8	Introduction to design, drafting.
9, 10, 11	Special problems (outdoor, limited facilities, road shows).
12, 13	Advanced design, project with plots.
14	Theater administration - publicity.
15	Fund raising, play selection, casting.
16	Stage management, unions.
17	Career opportunities and "tricks" of the trade.

14, 15, 16 } Production

Theatrical Construction II and Costumes

Weeks

1	Review of Contruction I
2, 3	Advanced structural physics.
4, 5	Special construction problems (weight bearing structures, special materials and their use i.e. steel and plastic).
6, 7, 8	Introduction to design for the stage, drafting.
9, 10	Props construction and materials (plastics, foam and card board).
11, 12	Advanced design.
13	Style of costumes through history and major periods of dress.
14, 15	Various materials, special problems, sewing machine. Color and design.
16, 17	Projects to be chosen by student.

Independent Study/Job Placement
(9 weeks)

During this period students will study specific areas of special interest to them in small groups and individually. Areas of interest can include model building, set designs, lighting designs, dimmer board analysis, prop construction and/or design, new construction materials and techniques, etc.

Participants will also devote about 30 to 40% of their time to job placement. Activities will include work habit counseling, interview role playing, resume writing etc. Students will then actively seek jobs in consultation and coordination with the staff.

A Typical Classroom Day (Introduction to Technical Theater)

9:00-10:00	Review the last meeting
	Class carpentry lesson
	Questions and answers
10:30-11:30	Skill building
11:30-12:00	Counseling or continuation of skill building
12:00-1:00	Review of standard problem
	Class electrics problem
	Questions and answers
2:00-3:00	Skill building
3:00-5:00	Basic education

The Applied Skills Workshops (classroom laboratory time) will be designed for intensive skill training in theatrical construction and electrics, including props and costumes. They will be conducted in small groups of 6-7 and will take place in the theatrical shop and Playhouse of the Henry Street Settlement. They will be held 2 days per week for a 14-week period for each group of participants. These will be organized and supervised by Henry Street's technical staff.

During most of the time, participants will be working alongside professional crews and involved on actual production work. There will also be skill training days, organized and conducted by the instructors and Henry Street technical staff.

Class and lab time will be conducted by an instructor/counselor, the Technical Director, Head Carpenter, Head Electrician, and by hourly teachers. Guest artist-professional persons known in the field for their work will conduct lectures and master classes.

Quality instruction will be achieved and maintained through the following:

— Selection of first rate experienced teaching staff.

— Regular observation of classes taught by technical director and subsequent consultation with teachers.

— Regular discussion and testing with participant of material covered to determine what has been learned. Following discussion and observation in curriculum areas where learning did not occur to determine if the teaching method employed was ineffective.

— Regular ongoing work training site visits by instructor/counselor and technical director to ensure that their work situation is conducive to maximum learning. There will be regular reports to staff from training site supervisory staff.

Field trips will include: professional theaters, the Metropolitan Opera (backstage), the American Place Theatre, shops (i.e Production Arts Lighting), a large scenic studio.

Students in the Henry Street Settlement's Technical Theatre Training Program preparing a flat for an upcoming performance.

Work training outside of Henry Street will be designed to provide enrollees with specific work skills, good work habits and an overall knowledge of theater production. Work training will take place 2 days per week and each enrollee will have two training placements lasting approximately 14 weeks each. One will be at a non-profit professional theatre and the other at an educational institution with a theatre department.*

The majority of the classes and the training will take place in the Henry Street Arts for

*See previous section "Approach" for criteria for selecting work training sites.

Living Center. Built in 1974, it is the nation's first arts center designed specifically for a predominantly disadvantaged multi-cultural population. There is no other cultural institution in New York, possibly in the entire country, with Henry Street's unique combination of many years of successful experience, a highly trained staff, and an all-encompassing arts program set in a remarkably culturally diverse neighborhood. Henry Street brings previous experience in theatre technician training. During the past six years, there have been formal and informal training workshops designed to train interested young adults in technical theatre. They have ranged in length from a 6-week introductory course to a year long skill training experience. A large number of these persons have become professionals in the field. We have also had almost continuous interns (1-3 at a time) from high schools and colleges in work experience training at Henry Street. They have come from as far away as Antioch College and as near as local high schools.

There is a need for well-trained technicians. At the moment the only training available is through a limited number of expensive professional schools, colleges and universities or by apprenticing in summer stock (which is generally non-paying) or by volunteering at small theatres. These opportunities are only available to those who have the where-with-all to survive while getting sufficient skills to secure meaningful long-term employment.

Henry Street is convinced that the young people we train as theatre technicians will find careers in live theatre (e.g. stage carpenter, property master, stage electrician). In addition, program graduates will be able to pursue careers in the service industry which supports the theatre industry including: building scenery, building properties, running shows (e.g. flying scenery), repairing lighting equipment, handling lighting equipment. Opportunities also exist for careers in film and in TV using similar skills. Further, trainees may find careers outside the Theatre Industry, in careers using the skills acquired during the training year at Henry Street.

PRODUCTION ARTS LIGHTING, INC.
636 11TH AVENUE
NEW YORK, NEW YORK 10036

(212) 489-0312

November 29, 1978

Mr. Frank Seever
Executive Director
Henry Street Settlement
265 Henry Street
New York, N.Y. 10002

Dear Mr. Seever:

After discussing your program to train youngsters as theatre technicians with Vito Perri of the Arts For Living staff, I did want to write to let you know that I found the proposed training curriculum to be both comprehensive and well developed.

As you know, there is a great need in this field for people who have been trained at places such as Henry Street where they can receive classroom and work training experience to develop appropriate skills. We will be very glad to consider with favor, graduates from your training program, as openings occur in our company. If your proposal is funded, we would like to talk with you further about the specifics of our cooperative relationship.

With best wishes.

Sincerely,

Peter M. Forward

Fig. 2. Letter from Production Arts Lighting, Inc., mentioning the need for trained theater technicians and expressing an interest in receiving applications from graduates of the program.

[Inserted at this point were four letters, two from college theaters and two from theater technology companies. Sample letters are shown in Figures 2 and 3. All the letters stated that the organizations would be willing to consider favorably program graduates for employment.]

Proposed Services

Henry Street will include the following services in its proposed training program:
(1) Outreach, assessment and orientation
(2) Counseling and guidance
(3) Occupational information

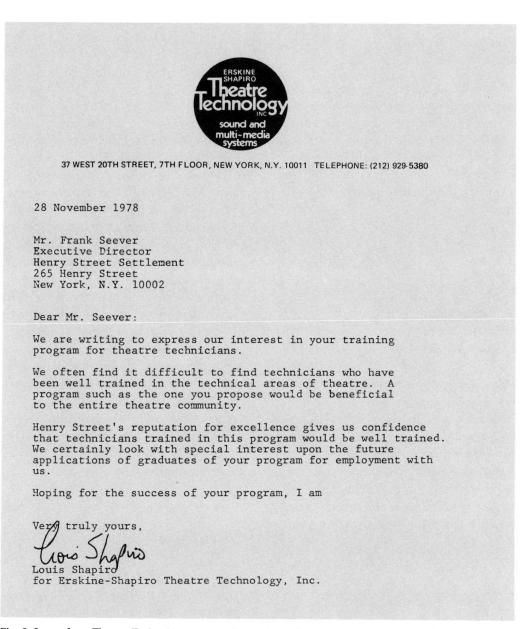

ERSKINE SHAPIRO
Theatre Technology INC
sound and multi-media systems

37 WEST 20TH STREET, 7TH FLOOR, NEW YORK, N.Y. 10011   TELEPHONE: (212) 929-5380

28 November 1978

Mr. Frank Seever
Executive Director
Henry Street Settlement
265 Henry Street
New York, N.Y. 10002

Dear Mr. Seever:

We are writing to express our interest in your training program for theatre technicians.

We often find it difficult to find technicians who have been well trained in the technical areas of theatre. A program such as the one you propose would be beneficial to the entire theatre community.

Henry Street's reputation for excellence gives us confidence that technicians trained in this program would be well trained. We certainly look with special interest upon the future applications of graduates of your program for employment with us.

Hoping for the success of your program, I am

Very truly yours,

Louis Shapiro
for Erskine-Shapiro Theatre Technology, Inc.

Fig. 3. Letter from Theatre Technology, Inc., stating that they have a special interest in receiving applications from graduates of the Henry Street theater technician training program.

(4) Job development and job placement services to secure unsubsidized employment opportunities

(5) Job referral information

(6) Services to help youth to retain employment

(7) Basic literacy training and equivalency preparation

(8) Child care and other necessary support services

Intake/Assessment

Youngsters would be assessed at program intake in terms of skill level, previous work history, school status, delinquency history. Both the vocational counselor and the job developer will be responsible for developing the program's intake structure, under the supervision of the project director. All the specialty instructors will participate, as well.

Orientation

There will be an orientation period at the beginning of the program which will be a time for case assessment and planning. The vocational counselor and the job developer will be the key staff responsible for referring participants for other services. Henry Street will be able to design a very effective experience for each of these 80 program participants because of the multi-faceted programs already in place. Provision would be made for services related to the social, educational, health, developmental and vocational needs of each youth. An exceptionally rich program tailored to variable individual needs is made possible by the variety of programs at Henry Street.

Day Care

For those trainees with dependent children, referrals would be made by program staff to the

Agency For Child Development for enrollment of children in day care. Additionally, staff would research available Head Start, nursery and kindergarten and baby-sitting services and assist program participants to link up with these services, as needed.

Job Development

A highly qualified full-time job developer will be involved from the inception of the program so that there is ongoing involvement between employers and program participants The job developer will be concerned with the development of labor market resources so that the best possible match is made between program graduates and employers. In developing appropriate private sector jobs, the Job Developer would draw upon Henry Street's existing contacts with those employers who helped in the development of the curriculum. In selecting prospective employers, emphasis would be placed on those employment settings which would offer youth a solid beginning work experience and options for future skill development and upgrading.

In addition to securing private sector jobs for program graduates, the job developer will run group and individual counseling sessions and work readiness workshops. The job developer will receive constant feedback on individual participant progress. In addition, the job developer will oversee the coordination of support services and skills training and will monitor, on an ongoing basis, each client's performance in the training program.

Job Placement

Youngsters who graduate from the program will be placed in jobs developed by the job developer and placement will be based on a youngster's skills and demonstrated ability to work.

Students in the Henry Street Settlement's Technical Theatre Training Program reviewing the plans for a stage set.

The program will work to set up a system of trial interviews with private sector employers to help youngsters learn how to interview. Additionally, workshops will focus on resume and application preparation, interviewing strategies and skills, appropriate dress, etc.

Counseling

Support services will include group and individual personal, educational and vocational counseling. Counseling workshops will be conducted on interviewing skills, resume and application preparation, resolution of conflicts with co-workers and supervisors, job finding, appropriate dress. Program staff will make education referrals, when needed, as well as referrals for psychiatric and psychological counseling, if required.*

The vocational counselor will convene periodic evaluation conferences with individual trainees

---

*The Community Consultation Center of Henry Street (a State-licensed mental health clinic) can provide treatment and diagnostic services for youth.

and the teaching staff and with the work training supervisors to insure that problems are accurately defined and that solutions can be agreed to by all concerned parties.

Post-Termination Follow-Up

Program graduates and employers will receive follow-up services during the 12 month contract period, particularly the first group of clerical graduates leaving in the 26th week of the program. However, because Henry Street feels that follow-up services should be available for approximately 90 days after course completion, efforts will be made to transfer follow-up responsibility to other Henry Street staff at the completion of the contract.

In either case, follow-up services will include:
— Regular telephone confirmation with employers and trainees to determine performance.
— Periodic conferences with employers and clients to evaluate work adjustment.
— Meetings with trainees during lunch periods and after work to resolve problems, provide ongoing support services, etc.
— Periodic evening meetings at Henry Street with groups of graduates to share experiences, solve commonly experienced work-site problems and to provide ongoing career guidance.

Medical

Special note should be made of two new Henry Street-related services which would serve as health resources for the proposed classroom training program. In cooperation with the Hunter College School of Social Work, Henry Street has developed a preventive service program for teenagers focusing on family planning, teenage pregnancy, health care and child care. Four MSW students are assigned to existing Henry Street youth-serving programs as counselors.

The second new program is the Betances Health Unit's HEW-funded Health Connection, focusing on health education and nutrition for adolescents. All youngsters in the proposed training program would be encouraged to receive a complete health assessment which would include family medical history, a nutritional assessment, a complete physical examination and a lab work-up. Referrals will be made by Betances staff for youngsters to specialty clinics in instances where diagnostic examinations are needed to determine if special health problems exist.*

It will be the responsibility of program staff to arrange for the preventive health examinations and to receive from the Betances staff suggestions of resources that might be appropriate for a particular young person. Thus, medical treatment would be coordinated with other support services.

ADMINISTRATIVE SYSTEM

Organizational Structure

The overall project administration will be the responsibility of the Executive Director of Henry Street, Frank Seever.† However, the Director of the Settlement's Youth Employment Service, Anne Dalton,† as Project Coordinator, will assume responsibility for project implementation, staff hiring and training, and overall project monitoring and evaluation. The Assistant Project Coordinator will be responsible for client intake, enrollment and orientation, will work with the training and services staff in the design and day-to-day operation of the project and will handle record-keeping and reporting. The clerical skills and basic education staff will report directly to the Assistant Project Coordinator. The theater technology staff will report to Vito Perri,† Tech-

---

*Betances also uses the services of its back-up hospital, Bellevue.
†Resumes included in Appendix A.

nical Director of the theater component who, in turn, will coordinate with the Project Coordinator.

The support services staff will report to the Project Coordinator through the Assistant Project Coordinator. Linkages with other agencies and Henry Street programs will be developed, as necessary, by the Assistant Project Coordinator.

Henry Street Settlement

Henry Street Settlement, founded in 1893, is a community-based organization of demonstrated effectiveness whose major purpose is to assist those least advantaged in the solution of crucial personal, social and economic problems. Today, Henry Street offers over 20 innovative programs ranging from day care, to mental health services, to housing, to job training programs for adolescents, to a variety of arts programs.* Henry Street has piloted many social innovations over the past 85 years; and because of this experience is an excellent base from which to operate this innovative demonstration program.

Program participants will have the opportunity to participate in Henry Street's wide range of recreational, cultural and athletic services and programs. These activities will provide youngsters with important opportunities to acquire new skills and interests and to benefit from group activity with peers.

The Youth Employment Service

In January, 1978 Henry Street established a Youth Employment Service based on its Supported Employment for Adolescents (SEA) program, and LEAA-funded demonstration supported work program for delinquent adoles-

*See attached Guide to Programs for a complete description of Henry Street.

cents. SEA, the nation's first supported work project for juveniles, provided paid, part-time community service work, with each adolescent being assigned to a work crew under staff supervision. The goal of the program was to reduce delinquent behavior by improving the youngsters' social functioning, helping them to develop good work habits and prevocational skills and encouraging them to return to school or to improve their school functioning.

At the end of the three-year demonstration period, the project was institutionalized through a contract with the New York State Division for Youth. Seeking to expand, based on SEA experiences, the Youth Employment Service was established. Presently, the Service employs 20 youth in supported work projects funded by the Division for Youth and the Department of Social Services. An additional 17 youth are employed in Henry Street's CETA-YCCIP project. These youth are undertaking major renovation and rehabilitation of the East River Park as well as maintaining neighborhood street trees.

In September of 1978, the Youth Employment Service undertook a second grant from the Division For Youth which provides employment for 24 youths designed to enhance their work readiness functioning in combination with support services in education, counseling, vocational preparation and related referral services. Twenty of the youth have been placed in part-time public sector jobs and four are placed in full-time public sector jobs. Youth function in individual job assignments in areas such as tutoring children, teaching and supervising recreational, athletic and play activities, day care and clerical and maintenance support.

An additional project of the Youth Employment Service is a job counseling and placement demonstration operated jointly with Jobs for Youth, Inc. under a grant from the Lavanburg-Corner House Foundation. Neighborhood youth who are job ready and available for full-time employment receive vocational counseling and support services while being referred out for job placement.

Other Programs

Apart from the Youth Employment Service programs, the Settlement has operated several other employment programs including CETA Title I and VI, SPEDY, Summer Work Training Program and Urban Corps. The Henry Street School offers an experience-based career education program to its senior high school division students, the Youth Development Exchange employs approximately 20 adolescents in the operation of cultural, recreational, athletic and youth leadership activities for youth and about 80 young people are employed yearly in the Settlement's arts programs.

Through the variety of employment programs, Henry Street has gained a great deal of knowledge about the methods and strategies for the employment of youth and the relationship between work and other developmental tasks. Critical areas where we have gained expertise include:

— Types of job tasks available to and suitable for youth.

— Types of supervisory strategies and staffing patterns appropriate for different types of youth (youth with no prior work experience, the younger adolescent, the adolescent with court problems, the adolescent with educational handicaps).
— The relationship between work skills and academic skills.
— Mechanisms for identifying and assessing youth's needs and wants and then integrating with work the services required.

APPENDED MATERIALS

[In addition to the material reproduced here, the following documents were sent with the application:

- *Appendix A, which contained resumes of all principal project personnel.*
- *A 10-page Program Operating Plan.*
- *A Department of Employment (New York City) questionnaire regarding the organization and management of Henry Street Settlement.]*

Applied Social Research in Crime/ Delinquency Programs

Funded by: Center for Studies in Crime and Delinquency, National Institute of Mental Health (NIMH),

Alcohol, Drug Abuse, and Mental Health Administration (ADAMHA)

Program Director: Barry S. Tuchfeld, Assistant Professor, Department of Sociology, Texas Christian University,

Forth Worth, Texas

Proposal Prepared by: Larry Adams and Barry Tuchfeld

HISTORY OF THE PROPOSAL
by Paul Hennessey

This project trains graduate students and local professionals in effective evaluation research. The genesis of the idea came about as a result of a visit by Dr. George Weber of the National Institute of Mental Health (NIMH) to the Texas Christian University (TCU) campus in fall, 1975. According to Dr. Larry Adams, one of the project designers, Dr. Weber talked of the current "time of accountability" in research programs, and expressed NIMH's interest in a project to train researchers to improve their research and evaluation skills.

Soon after this visit, Adams sat down with Dr. Barry Tuchfeld to discuss ways TCU could help NIMH meet this need. Out of these discussions came the idea of a training project in research evaluation.

Before writing the application, Adams and Tuchfeld accomplished three important things:

1. They examined their own interests, backgrounds, and credentials to make sure they were prepared to administer a program of this kind.
2. They carefully examined where their discipline was moving, and made sure their project idea reflected the most current sociological knowledge.
3. They investigated all other potential funders, and made sure NIMH was the most appropriate. This investigation was done primarily by phone and in-person contact. After careful research they chose the NIMH Center for Studies in Crime and Delinquency (CSCD) as the most logical funding source.

Adams and Tuchfeld then drafted a concept paper. Before writing their application, however,

---

Paul Hennessey is a Program Coordinator at the University of California, Berkeley. He was formerly Vice President of the Institute for Fund Raising, San Francisco.

they had further in-depth discussions with CSCD. Based on feedback from CSCD's Eckford Voit, they submitted their first application in February, 1977. In June they received word: Their proposal had been approved, but not funded. In spite of this setback, they were encouraged to rewrite and resubmit the application.

According to Tuchfeld, reviewers saw five problem areas in the application:

1. The *need* for the program hadn't been demonstrated in enough detail.
2. The issue of *student recruitment* hadn't been discussed in enough detail.
3. The extent of *interdepartmental collaboration,* an important element in the project's design, was not clear.
4. The project's *evaluation design* was too sophisticated considering the relatively small number of trainees and short project time frame.
5. There were no *letters of support* from the community agencies expected to participate in the project. (Interestingly, Tuchfeld notes that "This information had been forwarded in an appendix, but by the time it was routed through DHEW, the decision had been made.")

As you can see, the rewritten application presented here incorporates changes based on the reviewers' comments. It was resubmitted in July, 1978, and a grant of $224,000 was made.

The Importance of Being Unique

Like proposals reviewed in past GRANTS CLINIC, "Applied Social Research in Crime/Delinquency Programs" stood above its competition because it offered reviewers something new and different. According to Tuchfeld, the main problem he faced in writing this proposal was answering the question "What are we providing NIMH that has some unique value?" Adams echoes this: "Most training grants are 'plain

vanilla.' I've found it's crucial to get a slant or angle to make your proposal different."

Tuchfeld and Adams developed a number of unique features in their program application:

- Local community agencies were asked to participate, adding a "real world" orientation to the project.
- A detailed evaluation of the program model was included; this evaluation pays special attention to the "demonstration" aspects of the project — the involvement of local agencies, and the student field placements.
- The curriculum was designed to include a unique combination of theoretical and practical courses. This includes "supervised field internships" at local agencies.

According to both proposal writers, these unique aspects of the program made their idea much more attractive to NIMH. Emphasis on these key points in the proposal, and attention to the recommendations of NIMH officials, helped insure the application's success.

Other Lessons from the TCU Experience

Based on the experience of designing, funding, and running this project, Adams and Tuchfeld have a number of suggestions for those applying for training grants.

First, both sociologists feel their program benefited by involving community agencies in its design and implementation. According to Tuchfeld, it provides good public relations for the university, helps local agencies improve their services, and "adds realism to a program that could easily become heavily technical."

Adams and Tuchfeld also feel writers of training grant applications should prepare for potential budgeting problems. The insert below outlines the three main problems they faced. In all cases budget problems were avoided through careful and detailed discussions with NIMH before the final proposal was written.

The Application

The success of the Texas Christian University training grant presented here depended on three key factors:

- Community involvement in the project.
- Designing a unique project and stressing the unique features in the application.
- Discussing the project's design and budget with the funder before submitting the application, and incorporating the funder's suggestions into the proposal.

Larry Adams and Barry Tuchfeld's experience reflects that of many successful grant seekers. Therefore, the lessons of this proposal can be applied not only to training grants in sociology, but to proposals for different types of projects in other fields.

Budgeting a Training Grant

Adams and Tuchfeld found three major difficulties in preparing budgets for training grants. Here is how they suggest dealing with them:

1. *The funder's desire to negotiate.* This problem was avoided by detailed, relatively informal discussions with NIMH on project design *before* the final application was written. The eventual $224,000 award was made without formal budget negotiations; all differences had been worked out in advance.

2. *Fiscal year differences.* The federal fiscal year runs 1 October to 30 September, while most academic projects run from 1 September to 31 August. If you don't plan either to start early or to negotiate deferred payment, you may end up with unspent funding during your training period's early months. In this case, the probem was dealt with in pre-proposal negotiations.

3. *Tuition increases and inflation.* When budgeting a training grant involving student stipends, it is important to include second and third year inflation increases, including increases in tuition. Adams and Tuchfeld recommend two strategies for dealing with this: (a) agree in advance with your funder on a predetermined percentage increase in the tuition lines in your budget, or (b) be prepared to shift money from a direct expense account (like "supplies") to a stipend account. Adams points out that "DHEW policy now lets you shift money into, but not out of, student lines in your budget."

Remember, funders have different views of budget strategies like these. Your best defense against budget problems? Discuss your budgeting ideas with your funder well in advance of submitting a formal proposal.

SUPPLEMENT TO TRAINING GRANT APPLICATION

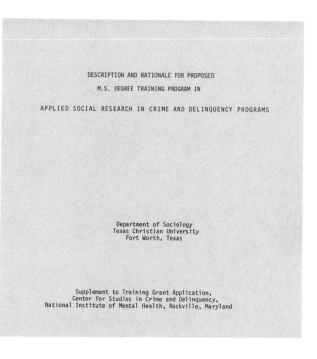

DESCRIPTION AND RATIONALE FOR PROPOSED

M.S. DEGREE TRAINING PROGRAM IN

APPLIED SOCIAL RESEARCH IN CRIME AND DELINQUENCY PROGRAMS

Department of Sociology
Texas Christian University
Fort Worth, Texas

Supplement to Training Grant Application,
Center for Studies in Crime and Delinquency,
National Institute of Mental Health, Rockville, Maryland

SUMMARY OF TRAINING PROPOSAL

14. TYPE AND LEVEL OF TRAINING PROGRAM

14A. Primary Purpose	14B. Degree Training	14C. Non-Degree Training	14D. Discipline, Specialty or Field of Training
TRAINING FOR:		Postdoctoral: ☐ Pre M.D. ☐ Post Ph.D.	Sociology
☐ Service	☐ Associate (AA, AS, etc.)	☐ Residency	
☐ Teaching	☐ Baccalaureate	☐ Continuing Education (Short Term)	14E. Sub-discipline, Sub-specialty or Sub-field of Training
☐ Administration	☒ Master's ☐ Pre M.D.	☐ Inservice/Staff Development	
☒ Other (Specify)	Doctoral: ☐ Pre Ph.D.	☐ Technical	Evaluation Research
Research		☐ Conference, Workshop	
	Specify Degree(s) Sought	☐ Diploma	
	Master of Science	☐ Other (Specify)	

15. BRIEF DESCRIPTION OF TRAINING PROGRAM (Limit to space provided)

15A. Purpose and Program Characteristics

This multidisciplinary program in Applied Social Research in Crime and Delinquency Programs is a 42 hour training sequence (21 mos., 4 semesters, and a summer session) at the M.S. degree level. The program has been designed as a demonstration model of training in evaluative research on social programs in crime and delinquency. The training sequence is directed through the Dept. of Sociology and integrates substantive and methodological coursework with supervised on-site field research experiences. The methodologies studies include qualitative and quantitative techniques. The curriculum entails a minimum of 5 courses (15 hrs.) in the substantive area, 3 courses (9 hrs.) in advanced methodology, including participant observation and nonparametric and parametric statistics, 3 courses (9 hrs.) in applied and evaluation research, and 3 semesters of credited fieldwork. The last 2 semesters of fieldwork involve 15 contact hours per week (minimum) internship and the production of a research report acceptable to agency representatives and the University training committee. A collateral dimension of the training program is to assess a strategy aimed at facilitating student awareness and appreciation of issues that affect research in an applied setting, e.g., communication problems and socio-political realities. Moreover, program administrators and policy makers of criminal justice agencies will participate as fellow students in a proseminar designed to address critical issues. The evaluation of this strategy will also involve an initial assessment of the impact that combined trainee-practitioner involvement may have on facilitating the utilization of research findings in crime and delinquency programs.

15B. Trainees Two cohorts of 5 trainees each will be recruited in 2 consecutive years. Trainees must meet University and Departmental graduate admission requirements and have an expressed interest in applied, programmatic research. Trainee cohorts will be heterogeneous with regard to race and sex. Special efforts will be made to recruit interested applicants with prior experience in agencies dealing with crime and delinquency, social deviance, etc. All students will take 9 hrs. of instruction per semester during their traineeships and will be involved in a progressive amount of field activities and research. Fieldwork is integrated with the training curriculum, beginning with 6-9 contact hrs. of community and agency acclimation and culminating with 15-20 contact hrs. of resident internship. Program functioning will be routinely monitored, assessed and evaluated.

15C. Training Facilities and Procedures The primary facility is the Dept. of Sociology at TCU, including Departmental library and remote data processing equipment. Collaborating units include the Depts. of Psychology, Economics, and Political Science and the School of Business. Representatives from these units will also serve as an Advisory Committee for the Program. Auxiliary University facilities include the Computer Center, the Institute of Behavioral Research, and the Library. Participating crime and delinquency and related agencies providing sites for resident internships are defined as secondary facilities. A resident internship requires trainees to conduct and satisfactorily complete an approved project in programmatic research. Special arrangements will be made to accommodate those trainees whose prior working experience has included responsibilities for the conduct of such research projects. The training committee consists of the Program Director, a Co-Director in crime and delinquency, a Co-Director for evaluation, and a Co-Director in participant observation. A community advisory committee also will be organized to provide constructive input into the program.

PHS-2499-1
Rev. 7-75
PAGE 2

DEPARTMENT OF HEALTH, EDUCATION, AND WELFARE
PUBLIC HEALTH SERVICE

TRAINING GRANT APPLICATION

TYPE	PROGRAM	NUMBER
REVIEW GROUP		FORMERLY
COUNCIL (Month and Year)		DATE RECEIVED

TO BE COMPLETED BY PROGRAM DIRECTOR (Items 1 through 7)

1A. Title of Training Program (Not to exceed 53 typewriter spaces)
Applied Social Research in Crime/Delinquency Programs

1B. Federal Agency Program (If same as 1A, so state) (See Instructions)
Center for Studies in Crime and Delinquency, NIMH

3. Dates of Proposed Project Period (This application)
From: 9-1-78   Through: 8-31-81

2. PROGRAM DIRECTOR

2A. Name (Last, first, initial)
Tuchfeld, Barry S.

2B. Degree(s)
B.S., M.A., Ph.D.

2C. Social Security No. (See Instructions)

2D. Title of Position
Assistant Professor: Sociology

2E. Mailing Address (Organization, street, city, state, zip code)
Dept. of Sociology
Texas Christian University
Fort Worth, TX 76129

2F. Telephone: Area Code 817 Number and Extension 926-2461, ext.540,549

2G. Department, Service, Laboratory or Equivalent (See Instructions)
Dept. of Sociology

2H. Major Subdivision (See Instructions)
AddRan College of Arts and Sciences

4. Performance Site(s) (See Instructions)
Department of Sociology
Texas Christian University
Fort Worth, Texas 76129

5. Head of Sponsoring Department, Service, Laboratory, or Equivalent (Name, Degree, Title and Telephone No.)
Larry D. Adams, Ph.D., Chairman
Dept. of Sociology
Texas Christian University (817)926-2461

6. Human Subjects Involved (See Instructions)
A. ☐ No   B. ☒ Yes

7. Inventions (Renewal Applicants Only – See Instructions)
A. ☐ No
B. ☐ Yes, not previously reported
C. ☐ Yes, previously reported

TO BE COMPLETED BY RESPONSIBLE ADMINISTRATIVE AUTHORITY (Items 8 through 13)

8. Applicant Organization (Street, city, state, zip code) (See Instructions)
Texas Christian University
Fort Worth, Texas 76129

9A. Name and Title of Official Signing for Applicant Organization
William Koehler, Acting Dean of the
Graduate School and Director of
Research Coordination

9B. Telephone: Area Code 817 Number and Extension 926-2461, ext. 303

10. Type of Organization (Check applicable item)
☐ PUBLIC INSTITUTION (Specify)
☒ PRIVATE NONPROFIT INSTITUTION

11A. Name, Title and Address (Street, city, state, zip code) of Official in Business Office Who Should Also Be Notified If An Award Is Made
Joe L. Enochs, Business Manager
Business Office
Texas Christian University
Fort Worth, TX 76129

11B. Telephone Area Code 817 Number and Extension 926-2461, ext.217

12. Entity Number 1-75-0827465-5

13. CERTIFICATION AND ACCEPTANCE. I certify that the statements herein are true and complete to the best of my knowledge and accept, as to any grant awarded, the obligation to comply with the enabling legislation, applicable regulations, Public Health Service policies, and conditions, if any, placed on the award.

SIGNATURE   Signature of Person Named in Item 9A
Date 9/13/77

PHS-2499-1
Rev 7-75

DETAILED BUDGET FOR INITIAL BUDGET PERIOD
(USUALLY 12 MONTHS)

DIRECT COST ONLY — SEE INSTRUCTIONS

APPLICATION NUMBER (Leave Blank)

BUDGET PERIOD DATES From 9-1-78 Through 8-31-79

ITEMIZE PERSONNEL (Do not list trainees)

NAME	TITLE OF POSITION	TIME OR EFFORT %/Hrs.	AMOUNT REQUESTED (Omit Cents) SALARY	FRINGE BENEFITS	TOTAL
Academic Year / Summer	Program Director	20% / 1.5 mo.			
Academic Year / Summer	Co-Director	15% / 2 mo.			
Academic Year / Summer	Co-Director	25%			
Academic Year / Summer	Faculty	10% / 1.5 mo.			
Secretary (to be named)	Secretary	50%			
(Subtotals)					

Enter Total Salary Amounts Plus Fringe Benefits → $ 28,768

CONSULTANT COSTS (Include Fees and Travel)
(fees for two days = $200; travel = $250) → $ 450

EQUIPMENT (Itemize)
Electric typewriter for secretary and trainee use ($750); two portable taperecorders for field research ($250); tape transcription unit ($415) → $ 1,415

SUPPLIES
Paper and materials for data collection and trainee reports → $ 200

STAFF TRAVEL
Domestic: Local agency travel ($250) and travel for program director to national meeting ($250) → $ 500
Foreign: $ 500
TOTAL TRAVEL EXPENSES → $ 500

ALTERATIONS AND RENOVATIONS

OTHER EXPENSES (Itemize) Trainee recruitment brochure ($200); duplication of materials and research reports ($300); computer costs for 1 hour at $180/trainee ($900); planning, pre-test, implementation and initial evaluation of program and proseminar ($1,000) → $ 2,400

(A) Subtotal – Non Trainee Expenses → $ 33,733

TRAINEE EXPENSES – (See Instructions)

		No. Proposed		
STIPENDS	Predoctoral M.S. degree	5	$ 19,500	
	Postdoctoral	No Proposed	$	
	Other (Specify)	No Proposed	$	
	TOTAL STIPENDS		$	

TUITION AND FEES 24 semester hours at $80/hr. Tuition per trainee & $190 Univ. fees/yr. ($2,110/trainee) → $ 10,550

TOTAL TRAINEE COSTS → $ 30,050

TRAINEE TRAVEL (Describe) Local travel to agencies ($200) and travel to regional professional meeting ($300) → $ 500

(B) Subtotal – Trainee Expenses → $ 30,550

TOTAL DIRECT COST (Add Subtotals (A) and (B)) → $ 64,283

PAGE 3

BUDGET ESTIMATES FOR ALL YEARS OF SUPPORT
REQUESTED FROM PUBLIC HEALTH SERVICE
(Direct Cost Only – Omit Cents)

APPLICATION NUMBER

DESCRIPTION	FIRST PERIOD (Name on Page 1)	2nd YEAR	3rd YEAR	4th YEAR	5th YEAR
PERSONNEL (Salaries and fringe benefits)	28,768a	31,645a	34,810a		
CONSULTANT COSTS (Include fees and travel)	450	450	450		
EQUIPMENT	1,415	--	--		
SUPPLIES	200	400	200		
STAFF TRAVEL Domestic	500b	500b	500b		
STAFF TRAVEL Foreign	--	--	--		
ALTERATIONS AND RENOVATIONS					
OTHER EXPENSES	2,400c	2,400c	2,200c		
SUBTOTALS OF NON-TRAINEE EXPENSES	33,733	35,395	38,160		

TRAINEE EXPENSES (Enter number proposed and dollars)

		No.		No.		No.		No.		No.	
TRAINEE COSTS	STIPENDS Predoctoral	5	$19,500	10	$39,000	5	$19,500				
	STIPENDS Postdoctoral										
	Other (Specify)	No.		No.		No.		No.		No.	
	TUITION AND FEES	10,550		18,700d		8,150e					
TOTAL TRAINEE COSTS		30,050		57,700		27,650					
TRAINEE TRAVEL		500		1,000		500					
SUBTOTALS OF TRAINEE EXPENSES		$ 30,550		$ 58,700		$ 28,150					
TOTAL EACH YEAR (Add the two subtotals)		$ 64,283		$ 94,095		$ 66,310					

TOTAL FOR ENTIRE PROPOSED PROJECT PERIOD $ 224,688

BUDGET JUSTIFICATION Justify all costs especially for the first year for which the need may not be obvious. For future years, justify any item of equipment as specified in the instructions, as well as any significant increase in any other category. If a recurring annual increase in personnel costs is requested, give percentage. (If additional space is needed, use a separate sheet numbered 4A.)

a. Increases in personnel costs reflect ten percent projected salary increases each year.

b. Additional costs for staff travel to consult with Dr. William Erickson and Dr. George McCall prior to the initiation of the first year of the training program will be absorbed by TCU.

c. Reflects costs of recruiting trainees during the first two years and costs of evaluating the training program during the three years.

d. Trainees in first cohort will be taking 18 hours of academic credit during second and final year. Trainees in the second cohort will be taking 24 hours as this is their first year in the training program.

e. Trainees in the second cohort will be taking 18 hours of academic credit during their second and final year.

IS INDIRECT COST REQUESTED ☒ Yes ☐ No IF "YES" AT 8 RATE OF TDC

PHS 2499-1
Rev. 7-75

PAGE 4

Training Grant Application (Department of Health, Education, and Welfare/Public Health Service)

DESCRIPTION AND RATIONALE FOR PROPOSED M. S. DEGREE TRAINING PROGRAM IN APPLIED SOCIAL RESEARCH IN CRIME AND DELINQUENCY PROGRAMS

by Larry Adams and Barry Tuchfeld

Introduction

Overview

During the past decade an increasing societal commitment has been made to various social action programs designed to ameliorate problems involving deviant and/or maladaptive behaviors. In particular, much public attention, monetary commitment, and professional effort have been directed toward agencies and programs dealing with individuals who have violated criminal and

Dr. Larry Adams and Dr. Barry Tuchfeld are faculty members in the Department of Sociology, Texas Christian University, Fort Worth, Texas.

juvenile laws (cf., Miller, 1973). Efforts to evaluate the effectiveness of these social action programs have enhanced our knowledge of factors that contribute to problems of crime and delinquency. For certain, these activities have revealed many of the complexities of program operations. Nevertheless, Glaser (1973:182) has observed that

> Evaluations too often are formulated in noncomparable terms, are reported in widely scattered publications, and consequently, provide only disconnected bits of knowledge that are noncumulative.

Inconsistencies in research methodologies and disparate reporting are not the only factors that have restricted the utility of our evaluative endeavors. Tuchfeld (1976), among others, has criticized the social sciences for their resistance in providing specialized training in evaluative research. Moreover, the absence of specially trained personnel who can take an active research role in ongoing crime and delinquency programs is still a limiting factor to the accumulation of knowledge in this area.

The context in which social action programs exist requires that even the technically competent researcher be cognizant of the socio-political realities that affect the research process and subsequent utility thereof. Tripodi *et al.* (1975:21-22) maintain that the failure to appreciate the environment of evaluative efforts is likely to result in wasted efforts:

> Just as political realities are necessary considerations in the planning of social programs, they are also important in evaluation. . . . Naive evaluators without political sophistication may draw up evaluation plans that are irrelevant and unrealistic for decision makers.

While specialized training and experience with socio-political realities are necessary, a third dimension of evaluative efforts is all too often neglected. Research findings must be communicated effectively if the efforts are to have any utility to program personnel. However, Weiss (1972:122) has noted that effective communication of findings from evaluative efforts is "far from common practice." Moursund (1973: 131) is even more vehement about this issue:

"Research, no matter how painstakingly carried out, is worthless unless the results are communicated."

In summary, the successful completion of evaluation research and the utilization of knowledge gained through such efforts require that the following criteria be fulfilled:

1. Personnel specially trained in a variety of methodologies and techniques suitable to evaluative efforts;

2. Personnel experienced and sensitive to the realities of the socio-political contexts that operate in crime and deliquency programs; and

3. Personnel oriented to the effective communication of research findings.

These criteria are not merely theoretical platitudes; they have emerged from the experiences of a variety of individual researchers and also, from the experience of prior attempts to produce evaluation personnel. In particular, the review of a previous training project by NIMH at the University of Missouri at St. Louis clearly demonstrated the efficacy of specialized training (cf., Erickson *et al.*, 1976). Similarly, a training program sponsored by NIMH at the University of Texas at El Paso identified the need for a variety of field placement opportunities and experiences in crime and delinquency agencies.

This proposal is for a two-year program in Applied Social Research at the Master of Science level. The program has been designed as a demonstration model of instruction for training personnel to participate in evaluative efforts of social action agencies in crime and delinquency. The comprehensive program will integrate substantive coursework and methodological training. Two strategies will be used to train students to fuse academic skills and knowledge with agency realities. For one, students will have an extensive involvement, in the form of direct field experience, with agencies coping with problems of crime and delinquency. Second, an integral part of the instructional model is the involvement of relevant agency personnel, in one of two capacities, as active components in

the formal learning process. These personnel will either participate with students in a specially designed Proseminar in Applied Research, or they will serve in a more traditional role as occasional outside resource personnel invited to address the Proseminar. In an attempt to discover the optimal form of agency personnel involvement, the contribution of the two modes of agency participation to learning will be evaluated. Further, the effectiveness of the general model of instruction will be evaluated in light of the criteria specified in this proposal.

The proposed training program is at the Master of Science level. As a result of interactions with a variety of social service agency managers, it was determined that there is a need in the Fort Worth/Dallas Metroplex for personnel trained at the Master's level. The concerns were that the relatively few existing personnel at that level had been exposed both to substantive coursework in crime and delinquency *and* to the variety of methodological strategies necessary to conduct programmatic research. The perceived tendency for doctoral level personnel to "overstudy" programmatic and policy issues and budgetary limits of agency operations added further support to the need for the proposed training program. After extended consideration of the sentiments and expressed needs of Metroplex representatives, it was decided that thoroughly trained Master's level persons, sensitized to the needs and limitations of crime and delinquency agencies, would satisfy local agency needs and maximize the likelihood of successful placement in crime and delinquency positions. Moreover, these conclusions are clearly supported by the letters (in Appendix C) which represent the general sentiments of agency directors and administrators with whom we have interacted.

The program is to be administered by the Department of Sociology of Texas Christian University, Fort Worth, Texas. Representatives of collaborating University units will constitute an Advisory Committee for the program and each representative will serve as a liaison with the training program. The location of the University in the Dallas-Fort Worth Metroplex is considered a strong asset as numerous opportunities for the placement of interns in relevant agencies are available. Further, the lack of any similar training program in a 600 mile radius suggests that the program will attract some trainees with prior working experience in crime and delinquency related agencies.

NIMH funding of the proposed program will provide the Department with the resources necessary to

1. Attract highly qualified students,
2. Conduct and supervise resident internship for students,
3. Involve relevant agency personnel in the training process, and
4. Evaluate the utility and efficacy of the program as a model for training students in evaluation research.

Moreover, this special program would significantly expand the opportunities for specialized training in crime and delinquency as our current Master of Arts degree program in the University does not allow for the intensive training and breadth of experience that would be provided in the proposed program. A description of the Sociology Department at Texas Christian University and its present degree programs are contained in Appendix A.

Program Objectives and Strategies

The goal of the proposed model of instruction is to provide comprehensive and integrated training which will equip students with the knowledge and skills required to conduct effective research in crime and delinquency and related agencies. A critical assumption underlying the model is that programmatic research should be conceived as an active and integral component of contemporary social service delivery. Such a view requires that trainees be provided with more than technical research skills. Thus, the proposed model is designed to give students extensive exposure to socio-political realities of agency operations and to emphasize the necessity of effective communication with the most appropriate audience(s). Moreover, trainees must learn to appreciate the complexities of agency operations and the need for having a comprehensive view of agency functioning that incorporates all aspects of service delivery.

To attain these objectives, supervised field internships will require the conceptualization and completion of programmatic research by each trainee. Additionally, appropriate representatives of crime and delinquency agencies will participate in the Proseminar in Applied Research, thereby integrating practical experience with academic instruction. In brief, the fusing of field and classroom will provide opportunities for students to benefit directly from their field experiences and coursework while benefiting indirectly from the experiences of the agency representatives. The rationale, description, and evaluation procedures of these strategies will be detailed in subsequent sections of this proposal.

An equally important dimension that contributes to a comprehensive view of programming is the training model's distinction between evaluation and assessment research. This contrast is akin to Suchman (1971) and others' dichotomy of "outcome and process evaluation." Our distinction, however, focuses on the more formal, and generally more quantitative approach required for acceptable evaluation of program "outcomes." The concept "evaluation" is thus restricted to a more specific content area. "Assessment" is meant to connote mainly administrative monitoring which is best facilitated by qualitative methodologies. While not mutually exclusive, our distinction between assessment and evaluation *per se* more clearly communicates the different (though interrelated) domains of programmatic research. Moreover, trainees are to be prepared to conduct evaluations of program impact emphasizing the description and explanation of program outcomes. This is to be accomplished via the requirement that they actually conduct an evaluation project with some crime and delinquency agency. Furthermore, trainees must be capable of conducting assessments of agency functioning by analyzing processes internal to routine agency operations. This is to be accomplished via their participation in projects conducted during their summer-long classroom training in strategies of qualitative methodology. The training model, therefore, incorporates preparation in quantitative and qualitative research skills that are necessary to address the variety of research questions one might expect to encounter as a researcher in a crime and delinquency agency. And to maximize trainees' preparation, the curriculum entails supervised field experience in conjunction with technical classroom preparation.

The use of qualitative skills is viewed as central to the analysis of process variables that contribute to program outcomes. For example, analyses of patterns of organizational communication, of labeling and delabeling processes operative within an agency, and of inter-program or inter-agency relations are most amenable to qualitative field research. Also, the qualitative approach may contribute intensive, in-depth information that can help clarify the quantitative data required for an extensive, generalized evaluation of service program outcomes.

To demonstrate abilities in qualitative and quantitative analysis, trainees will be required to participate in two field experiences. The major field experience requires two semesters of internship in the second year of the program culminated by the completion of an evaluation research report on some aspect of the sponsoring crime or delinquency agency. The summer prior to that internship, students will study that agency using qualitative field research methods. While the qualitative analysis of a selected aspect of functioning will be required prior to the fall inception of the internship, it is expected that the summer experiences will contribute substantially to the design and completion of the major field project in evaluation research. As will be discussed in the next section, those with prior responsibilities for the conduct of evaluations in crime and delinquency agencies may be granted a waiver of the internship requirement.

Program Design and Implementation

Student Recruitment and Agency Participation

The training program will recruit five new trainees in each of two academic years. All recruits must have an expressed interest in preparing for careers in applied, i.e., programmatic, social research. A prerequisite for admission to the program is possession of a Bachelor's degree from an accredited college or university with an academic record meeting the standards established by the Graduate School of the University. A condition for admission is that all trainees must have successfully completed either a course in elementary statistics or in basic social research methodology. Scores on the Graduate Record Examination and recommendation letters from former professors of the applicant will be used as an aid in the overall evaluation of the applicant's potential for successful completion of the Applied Social Research Program.

Recruiting procedures will include public contact via brochure announcements and direct contact with Metroplex crime and delinquency agencies and related social service agencies. The brochure describing the program will be mailed to universities and colleges in the United States which offer sociology or criminal justice majors. Special presentations by the training staff will be made to the relevant Metroplex agencies and programs.

Prospective trainees will be informed about the nature and philosophy of the program and funding opportunities for selected trainees. The cooperation of employers will be encouraged with particular emphasis on their arranging for leaves of absences for successful applicants whose position and experience warrant special consideration.[1] To facilitate such persons' progress through the training program, relevant experience will be considered as substitutable for the six

---

[1] Some agency administrators have expressed to us a willingness to consider such leaves of absence.

credit hours and research project required by the internship. To obtain such credit, experienced persons must have been primarily responsible for the conduct of an evaluation project in some aspect of crime and delinquency programming. The report on that project will be subject to review by the training program faculty and an oral defense of that project will be required in order for the trainee to obtain credit for the internship and project requirement. Furthermore, this opportunity would enable experienced personnel to complete the program with a one year leave of absence and then part-time course participation during Year Two when he/she returns to employment.

While prior work experience in crime and delinquency agencies is considered desirable, the experiences must have been clearly related to the thrust of the training program in order for a trainee to undertake an altered curriculum. This stringency is necessary in order to maintain the integrity of the training program as a model of instruction for future training and to maximize the cohesiveness of training cohorts. For trainees who have related work experience but have not been primarily responsible for an evaluation research project, employers will again be encouraged to grant a one year leave with the understanding that these persons' internships may be satisfied by their return to employment and the successful completion of a relevant research project.

Appropriate Federal, State, and local crime and delinquency agencies within the Dallas-Fort Worth Metroplex will be asked to participate in the training program.[2] It is expected that the agencies that will participate will represent each component of the criminal justice process. Thus, at least one agency would be included from the police, probation, prison, interim parole treatment, and parole aftercare components. In particular, such programs or agencies may include the Fort Worth Police Department, Tar-

rant County Juvenile Probation Department, U.S. Probation Office, and U.S. Federal Correctional Institution, and the Tarrant County Mental Health/Mental Retardation Centers. Programs eligible for inclusion may also include administrative agencies such as relevant components of the Regional Office of NIMH in Dallas and the North Central Texas Council of Governments. Comprehensive social service agencies which are contractually involved as a formal extension of a criminal justice component would also be eligible for inclusion. Such agencies as the Volunteers of America and Family and Individual Service would fall into this category.

Program Curriculum

The student training program described in this proposal involves 42 semester hours, including 9 semester hours of internship and field research in community based agencies. The program will require two academic years, including a mid-program session, for completion. The curriculum schedule for a trainee cohort is outlined below and descriptions of course content are included in Appendix B.

Curriculum Schedule for Trainee Cohort

Fall, 1978 (September-December)
Soc.   6053 Proseminar in Applied Social Research
Soc.   5433 Social Research Methodology
Psy.   5423 Advanced Statistics

Spring, 1979 (January-May)
Soc.   5443 Evaluation Research Methodology
            xxxx Elective in Deviant Behavior Analysis and Criminal Law Policy
Econ.   5293 Economics of Urban Problems and Policy Evaluation
or
Pol. Sci.   6093 Advanced Methodology in Political Science

Summer, 1979 (June-August)
Soc.   6670 Directed Readings in Anthropology: Techniques of Participant Observation and Field Research
Soc.   6970 Directed Research in Sociology: Crime and/or Delinquency Program Participant Observations

---

[2] The supervision of trainee internships in any of these agencies is discussed in a subsequent section of this proposal. Also, participation in a proseminar is discussed in a special section.

Fall, 1979 (September-December)
Soc.   7213 Internship in Applied Social Research
            xxxx Elective in Deviant Behavior Analysis and
                   Criminal Law Policy
            xxxx Elective in Deviant Behavior Analysis and
                   Criminal Law Policy

Spring, 1980 (January-May)
Soc.   7313 Internship in Applied Social Research
            xxxx Elective in Deviant Behavior Analysis and
                   Criminal Law Policy
            xxxx Elective in Deviant Behavior Analysis and
                   Criminal Law Policy

Note: The electives in Deviant Behavior Analysis and
            Criminal Law Policy may be selected (with ad-
            visement) from the following courses:

Crim. Jus. 5403 Issues and Problems of Criminal Law
                     Policy
Crim. Jus. 5603 Administration of the Courts (Pol. Sci.)
Soc.   5483 Social Structure and Personality
Soc.   5773 Seminar in Urban Affairs: Social Policy
                     Planning for Metropolitan America
Soc.   6623 Seminar in Deviant Behavior
Soc.   6970 Directed Readings in Sociology: Crimi-
                     nology

The conceptual framework of the program is presented in Figure 1. As previously mentioned, the program is designed to integrate substantive coursework with extensive field experiences. The first semester involves (in addition to the coursework) opportunities for community and agency acclimation. This acclimation entails bi-weekly meetings of the trainee cohort, the training staff, and invited representatives from the Dallas-Fort Worth Metroplex community and crime and delinquency programs. The objective of these sessions is to provide students with an overall concept of crime and delinquency operations in the Metroplex as well as a more in-depth introduction to specific crime and delinquency operations. To implement the latter objective, acclimation will take place at the site of the particular crime and delinquency program scheduled for the date of the meeting.

The second semester requires that the student trainee make a tentative selection of two crime and delinquency agencies in which the trainee will conduct his/her internship and field research. Trainees will be required to make biweekly visits to each crime and delinquency agency. (Agency visitations are to be staggered so that a trainee will visit one agency every week.) These

	First Year		Second Year	
Fall Semester	Spring Semester	Summer Session	Fall Semester	Spring Semester
CURRICULUM				
Proseminar in Applied Social Research Social Research Methodology Advanced Statistics	Evaluation Research Methodology Substantive Elective Economics of Urban Problems and Policy Evaluation OR Advanced Methodology in Political Science	Directed Readings in Anthropology: Techniques of Participant Observation and Field Research Directed Research in Sociology: Agency Participant Observations	Substantive Elective Substantive Elective Internship in Crime and Delinquency Agency	Substantive Elective Substantive Elective Internship in Crime and Delinquency Agency
FIELDWORK				
Community and Agency Acclimation	Tentative Agency Selection	Participant Observation in Agency	Agency: Data Collection	Agency: Data Analysis and Feedback to Crime and Deliquency Agency Closure

Fig. 1. Conceptual framework of program.

visits are to involve casual conversation with agency employees and clients. Summaries of each week's experiences are to be noted by the Director of the training program, revised if necessary, and then accumulated in a notebook summarizing the trainee's contacts, experiences, and impressions. At the end of the semester, the staff of the training program will meet with each student to discuss his/her agency preference. The training program Director will be responsible for verifying the acceptability of a trainee with the crime and delinquency agency the student has selected as his/her preference. If the student trainee's first preference cannot be arranged, then the second preference will be pursued. The final selection of an agency in which a trainee will intern and conduct field research thus incorporates the student's preference, the training staff's concurrence, and the acceptability of the student to the crime and delinquency agency.

The summer session involves training in techniques of participant observation and the completion of a qualitative, ethnographic study by each student trainee in the agency in which they will be interning. In addition to sensitizing the student trainee to process variables that may be central to the routine functioning of the agency, this field research will also provide students with a more in-depth comprehension of the different types of research that might be beneficial to crime and delinquency program managers. Too, these experiences will provide an interpretative framework for the research to be conducted during the second year internships. Trainees will be required to write the results of their experiences in a descriptive, ethnographic account of the particular aspect of agency operations selected for study. The project Co-Director in charge of this training dimension will provide supervision throughout the research.

Course descriptions are included in Appendix B. While all courses are directly relevant to the goals and objectives of the instructional model, one course is of particular note: the Proseminar in Applied Social Research. This course addresses substantive issues as integral to the development and implementation of evaluation and assessment endeavors. Throughout the seminar, the pervasive theme is directed toward increasing trainees' awareness and sensitivity to the socio-political contexts of evaluation. Subsequent trainee experience, especially in the field, will expand upon this theme; participating program personnel will continually alert the trainees to the necessity of articulating technical knowledge and skills with pressures and limitations that are operative in agencies in the field.

The Proseminar is a central part of the training model and is the testing ground for the optimal utilization of agency resource personnel. Because of its importance, the tentative outline for the Proseminar is presented below:

   I. Introduction
      A. Contribution to Rational Decision Making
      B. The Elements of Assessment and Evaluation
      C. Divergent Points of View on Evaluation Research
  II. The Context of Evaluative Research Efforts
      A. The Participants in Evaluation Research
      B. The Socio-Political Context
      C. The Organizational Context and Communication
 III. Comparison Between Evaluation and Other Research
      A. Experimental and Survey Designs
      B. Quantitative and Qualitative Approaches
      C. Examination of Illustrative Cases
  IV. Issues in the Implementation of Evaluation Research
      A. Substantive Issues in Research Design
      B. Determining Program Parameters
      C. Measurement Issues
   V. The Utilization of Research Findings
      A. The Consumers of Research Findings
      B. Research, Social Innovation and Change
      C. Ethical Issues of Evaluation Research

The course will use a seminar-discussion format, directed by the Project Director with routine participation by the training staff. The tentative texts for the course are Lazarsfeld and Reitz (1975), Franklin and Thrasher (1976), Weiss (1972), Rivlin and Timpane (1975), and O'Toole (1971). The course, to meet one evening per week, will be offered during the fall semesters of 1978 and 1979.

In addition to substantive coursework in crime and delinquency, the second year of the program includes the resident internship for trainees in a crime and delinquency agency and the completion of an evaluation research project in that agency. Details of this field placement and its supervision are discussed in the following section.

Field Placements and Supervision

Two semesters of resident internship are required by each student in the program.[3] These internships will occur during the second year of the program by which time students will have completed all required methodology courses, some of their substantive coursework, and will have had extensive and some intensive exposure to crime and delinquency agencies.

There is an historical relationship between the TCU Department of Sociology and many of the crime and delinquency and related agencies in the Dallas-Fort Worth Metroplex. These relationships have resulted from our reliance on agency personnel as part-time instructors of special courses offered through the Department's Criminal Justice Program, field placements of students in the Department's Undergraduate Social Work Program, and personal and professional contact with agency/program staff and administrators. Letters reflecting support for the current endeavor and willingness to participate in internship supervision are included in Appendix C.

Field Placements for internships will be based on the following considerations:

1. The student's interest in a particular agency and that agency's acceptance of the particular student,
2. The presence of a person within the agency who will commit himself/herself to supervise the trainee and to evaluate that student's performance, and
3. The commitment of a program manager, director, or other relevant administrator of that agency to participate in some capacity in the workshop/proseminar which is designed as part of this proposed model of instruction.

Given the exposure to the crime and delinquency agencies discussed previously, it is reasonable to expect trainees to be adequately informed about available alternatives that exist in the Metroplex community. Of course, requests from students with previous working experiences would be based on an even more informed foundation. In any case, the training staff will serve an active supervisory role.

The training staff will be directly responsible for supervising trainee placements, and the Program Director will be charged with coordinating communication among the training staff, the trainees, and the participating agencies. Supervisory responsibilities of training staff members are outlined in particular job descriptions. It is notable that trainees are required to conduct a research project for the satisfactory completion of the internship courses and of the training program Trainee research proposals must be prepared and formally approved by the staff prior to the initiation of the research. To facilitate substantive research, the relevant agency representative will participate as an equal member of a student's training committee, both in the initial stages of the proposal and in the final assessment of the acceptability of the research report. Each participating agency is, therefore, required to contribute at least one qualified person who will assume on-site super-

---

[3] Credit hour substitution for students with directly related work and project experience was discussed in the section on Student Recruitment and Agency Participation.

visory responsibility and is further willing to participate as a student's committee member.

In keeping with the thrust of the program in producing personnel who can take an active role in crime and delinquency agencies, it was decided that trainees and participating agencies would benefit most by learning to communicate research findings in a manner that would be meaningful to agency program managers. Consequently, rather than requiring a research report prepared in accord with academic standards of style and format for theses, the research conducted during the internship must be reported in a style conducive to communication with program managers and agency personnel. This will involve the preparation of a formal final report, executive summaries and policy implications that can be directly consumed by program managers and other relevant agency personnel. An oral presentation of the report will also be required.

Each semester of internship will require an assessment of a trainee's performance by the supervising agency representative. The assessment will include three dimensions:

1. An assessment of awareness of research needs in the agency;
2. An assessment of the trainee's comprehension of research limitations given the constraints operating within an agency and his/her ability to develop alternative research strategies; and
3. An assessment of the student's active participation in the agency and ability to work effectively with other agency personnel not directly engaged in research.

Assessments will be communicated in writing and orally. The training staff and direct supervisor will also be responsible for seeing that students understand their shortcomings and are aware of areas needing improvement. The training program Director will regularly communicate with each student and his/her internship supervisor so that particular problem areas can receive immediate attention.

An integral part of the internship experience will be a University based seminar. The biweekly seminar will serve as a forum to share common experiences and difficulties and to discuss aspects of research being conducted in the different agencies. The seminar will be directed by the Program Director and all members of the training staff will participate. This strategy is to facilitate comprehensive supervision of the internships as it will help integrate the on-site experiences (and supervision) with the classroom preparation. Again, the strategy is in keeping with the intent of the instructional model by providing an opportunity to integrate curriculum instruction with field experiences.

Personnel Participation and Responsibilities[4]

Program Director (Tuchfeld): 20 percent training grant administration during academic year. Includes coordination of trainee recruitment and selection; coordination of regular training faculty and faculty-student meetings; active liaison with current and potentially participating community agencies; coordination of training program evaluation; oversees conduct and analysis of students' evaluation research projects; coordination of course scheduling, teaching assignments, etc.; and responsible for semester progress reports to funding agency representative.

1.5 months training grant administration and field research during summer months. Includes regular administrative duties; involvement in training students in qualitative research methods; and providing technical support to Co-Director of Assessment and Evaluation.

Teaching responsibilities include Soc. 5543, Soc. 6053, Soc. 7213, and Soc. 7313. (See course descriptions for contents.)

---

[4] The University will assume responsibility for instruction of relevant courses for trainees in the program. Consequently, the teaching responsibilities identified for each of the training staff are not included as budgeted items.

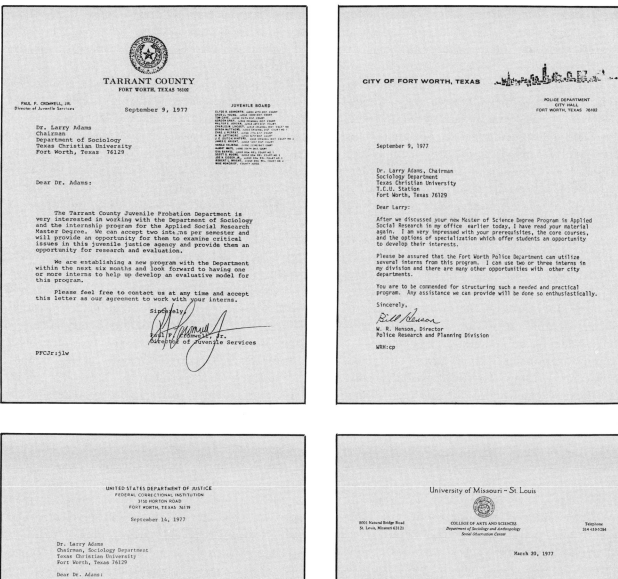

Some letters of support that accompanied the application

Co-Director of Crime and Delinquency (Regoli): 25 percent program development in crime and delinquency during academic year. Includes participation in trainee recruitment and selection processes; consultation with individual trainees in regard to specialty area; development of sensitivity to substantive and research issues in crime and delinquency; active participation in regular faculty and faculty-student meetings; development of community advisory committee and continual liaison to them; participation in regular conferences of training staff; participates in evaluation of design, implementation, and data analysis of research component on use of resource personnel in training program; participates in training staff supervision of trainees' evaluation research projects; and responsible for obtaining preliminary information on impact of training program on crime and delinquency agencies' utilization of evaluation research.

Teaching responsibilities: all advanced courses in crime and delinquency. (See curriculum outline for course electives and section on course descriptions.)

Co-Director of Evaluation and Assessment (Henley): 15 percent training program monitoring and evaluation during academic year. Includes direction of research component on evaluating alternative strategies of using agency resource personnel in training model; development and administration of trainee and participating crime and delinquency agencies evaluation instruments; coordination with outside consultants; and participation in regular conferences of training staff and in faculty-student meetings. Responsible for annual progress reports and final evaluation report on the instructional model.

Two months research and reporting during summer months. Includes analysis of routinely collected monitoring information and of periodically collected evaluation data; and production of reports of those analyses and findings.

Co-Director of Qualitative Field Research (Miracle): 10 percent program participation during academic year. Includes responsibility for community acclimation of trainees; participa-

tion in regular training staff and faculty-student meetings; and responsibility for development of field sensitivity skills with respect to qualitative research methods.

Responsible for teaching and directing ethnographic field research during interim summer semester. Goal is to expand appreciation of agency process variables that are relevant to evaluation and assessment of crime and delinquency programs. Project to provide interpretative framework for conduct of second year research project by interning trainees.

Community Advisory Committee: Voluntary group of 6-10 members formally affiliated with crime and delinquency and related agencies. Would serve as primary community contact and function as liaison between academic and social service communities. Would have input to evaluation of training program; ready access to Program Director, and be expected to provide input in regard to program needs and refinement.

Secretary (to be appointed): 50 percent program participation providing secretarial support to trainees and faculty associated with training program.

University Advisory Committee: In addition to the Program Director and one Program Co-Director (each faculty members within the Department of Sociology), one member from each other participating unit will serve on an Advisory Committee. This arrangement will foster interdepartmental cooperation in the administrative coordination of the training program, and provide multidisciplinary input pertinent to the operation and content, including review and planning efforts, of the program. A list of the Committee composition is contained in Appendix D.

Participation in Professional Meetings

Recognizing the need for professionalization as well as technical preparation, trainees will be expected to attend at least one professional meeting during each of their training years. Regional meetings in the Southwest will be emphasized in order to minimize expense. Further, students will be encouraged to present papers, particularly during their second year in the training program. To facilitate such presentations, a special section will be requested for trainees. Because of the special nature of the training program and its model of instruction, it is anticipated that such a session would be well-received.

In addition to outside speakers on evaluation research who will be sponsored by the University, the Program Director will annually attend at least one national meeting which has relevant program sessions. Tentatively, that meeting would be the annual meeting of the newly formed Evaluation Research Society of America. The Program Director would be required to relay the content of the meetings to the trainees and the training staff. In these ways, it is anticipated that trainees will have input beyond the confines of the more localized aspects of the training program.

Evaluation of Training Program Model

Overview

The responsibility for evaluating the training program model will belong to the Co-Director in charge of that program component. That Co-Director will provide NIMH with a final report which will include:

1. An overall evaluation of the apparent effectiveness of the model of instruction. When possible, a comparison will be made with available information about other instructional models, e.g., at St. Louis and the University of Texas at El Paso;
2. An evaluation of the unique component of the training model, i.e., the relative utility of two alternative forms of involving agency personnel in the academic side of training; and
3. An assessment of routine program functioning encompassing such variables as inter- and intra-program communication and

maintenance of the proposed integration of coursework and field experiences.

The evaluation Co-Director will also be responsible for monitoring the participating agencies and the community advisory staff and obtaining direct feedback from trainees. Much of the assessment and evaluation will be descriptive in nature, and will be oriented to the accurate depiction of process variables central to the training program. (As will be discussed subsequently, instruments and scales to measure program objectives will also be used whenever possible.) Student input will be obtained in an effort to maximize the relevance and significance of coursework to student fieldwork. It is expected that the internal, descriptive assessment will optimize feedback to the training staff.

Prior to the initiation of the first year of the training program, the Co-Director responsible for evaluation and the Director of the project will consult with Drs. George McCall and William Erickson. These persons were responsible for the NIMH training program at the University of Missouri in St. Louis. Their experiences will help sensitize us to potential problem areas and desirable program modifications.

Furthermore, after the initial consultation, one of these individuals will serve as an independent consultant and will conduct and annual site visit. The visit will entail examining the functioning and progress of the training model toward its stated objectives. The written results and analysis of the site visit will be provided by the consultant.

Evaluation of the Overall Training Model

The evaluation of the training model will include the following types of information:

1. A description and assessment of the selection and recruitment of five students in each of two academic years;
2. A record of the employment careers of graduated trainees, especially in crime and

Fall 1978	Spring 1979	Summer 1979	Fall 1979	Spring 1980	Summer 1980	Fall 1980	Spring 1981
First Cohort Entry	B_1 B_2 D_1		C_1	B_1 A D_2 C_2			
			Second Cohort Entry	B_1' B_2' D_2'		C_1'	B_3' A' D_2' C_2'

A = Evaluation of Projects
B = Simulated Research Problems
C = Agency Evaluation of Trainees
D = Trainee Evaluation of Program

Prime letters identify data for the second cohort.
Numerical subscripts denote data from a time series.

TOTAL PROGRAM EVALUATION

EVALUATING PROSEMINAR VARIATIONS

Final Performance Levels

Short-Run Impacts (Direct Effects)

A & A'; B_3 & B_3'

B_1 vs. B_1'

C_2 & C_2'; D_2 & D_2'

D_1 vs. D_1' (Proseminar evaluation only)

Performance Improvement

Long-Run Impacts (Additive and/or Interactive Effects)

$B_3 + B_3'$ vs. $B_1 + B_1'$

A vs. A'; $\dfrac{C_1 + C_2}{2}$ vs. $\dfrac{C_1' + C_2'}{2}$

$C_2 + C_2'$ vs. $C_1 + C_1'$

D_2 vs. D_2'; $B_2 - B_1$ vs. $B_2' - B_1'$

Fig. 2. Schedule for collection of data used in training program evaluation.

delinquency agencies. (It is recognized that such records will be incomplete and potentially misleading at the time when the initial evaluation report is due. However, the maintenance of such records will be a regular part of the long-range efforts at monitoring program success, and their judicious use at an early stage may be informative); and

3. A variety of measures including skills acquired by trainees, evaluations of trainee performance during internships, and trainee evaluations of the program. These measures, when disaggregated by training cohort, will constitute the basis for evaluating the relative utility of the two modes of involving agency personnel in academic instruction. Details of these measurement procedures are presented below. A graphic representation of the collection and use of these data are contained in Figure 2.

(a) Evaluation of Project Conducted During Internship. During the internship each trainee will be required to conduct evaluations of agency impact, emphasizing the description and explanation of agency outcomes. The adequacy of each research project will be judged independently by program personnel, by an outside consultant, and by the participating agency.[5] In addition to an overall assessment, each project will be judged on the following criteria: (i) the technical quality of the research design and its individual components; (ii) the degree to which the report is organized and written so as to communicate effectively with the target

[5] In the event that the internship is waived for a student, his/her evaluation project that justified the waiver will be submitted for judgment along with those completed by the remainder of the trainees during their internships.

audience, i.e., the relevant person(s) in the participating agency; (iii) the degree to which the research design and report are addressed to the evaluation, alteration, and/or formulation of agency policy; and (iv) the extent to which the trainee report is actually used by the participating agency in its ongoing activities.

(b) Trainee Performance on Simulated Applied Research Problems. At the beginning and the end of the second semester, and near the completion of the internship, trainees will be presented with simulated problems and given a limited amount of time to prepare a research proposal. Students will work independently, but they may rely upon whatever non-human resources they find suitable. All members of the cohort will receive the same problem at a particular stage in their training; of course, problems at points one, two, and three will be different. Use will be made of program personnel and an outside consultant, all working independently, to evaluate the trainee proposals. (Whenever possible, judgments will be made without the knowledge of cohort or individual identity.) In addition to an overall assessment, each proposal will be judged on the following criteria: (i) feasibility, given time and resource limitations, (ii) technical adequacy of the research design; (iii) plans to access helpful individuals inside or outside the agency described in the simulation; (iv) reliance on existing literature and data; (v) flexibility of design, e.g., back-up data sources and alternative analytical tools; and (vi) suitability of design for evaluating and (re)formulating policy of the agency in the simulated problem.

(c) Agency Evaluations of Trainees. At the end of each semester of internship, those agency personnel working most closely with the student in a guidance capacity will be asked to assess the student's performance along three dimensions: (i)

awareness of research needs in the agency; (ii) comprehension of research limitations given the constraints operating within the agency and the student's ability to develop alternative research strategies; and (iii) level of active participation in the agency and ability to work effectively with other agency personnel who are not directly engaged in research.

(d) Trainee Evaluations of the Program. As each cohort nears completion of the second and final semesters, trainees will be given questionnaires to measure their perceptions of benefits derived from the program as a whole as well as from its constituent parts. The individual dimensions to be measured include the following: (i) awareness of socio-political constraints in applied research, (ii) ethical/legal considerations and limitations, (iii) resource limitations and alternative avenues of access, (iv) problems and techniques of accessing information, (v) awareness of key individuals who can expedite research efforts, and (vi) problems in translating data based analyses into reports having clear implications for policy evaluation and/or (re)formulation.

Efforts to assess the impact of the training program and its variations, like all applied research endeavors, is problematic. The small size of the cohorts, the inability to randomize trainees into cohorts as well as into internships in agencies, the likelihood of variations over time in factors that are external to the program, and the difficulty of quantifying the degree of learning all introduce uncertainty into assessments of the program. Additional difficulty in conducting a definitive assessment stems from the recognition that the Proposed Program is in a pilot stage where flexibility and innovation are most appropriate. Under these conditions, evaluation should have a "primary emphasis upon the 'feedback' of results for program changes. This does not mean that success or failure are not to be judged but that the basis of such judgments need not depend upon rigorous experimental designs" (Suchman, 1971:106).

Any single approach to assessment is likely to contain an unknown amount of measurement error due to less than ideal level of validity and reliability. However, if multiple, independent measures[6] are employed and different techniques (e.g., rating and ranking scales) are utilized, greater confidence can be placed in the conclusions about the impact of the training process.[7]

Evaluation of the Proseminar Component of the Training Model

Proseminar variations. The involvement of agency personnel in the Proseminar in Applied Social Research is an essential component of the training model. It is expected that such participation will significantly enhance the trainees' abilities to articulate technical skills and knowledge with the limitations and practical considerations that ultimately confront the evaluation researcher in service delivery settings. In an attempt to identify the optimal manner of such involvement, two modes will be employed:

1. The more traditional form in which agency persons are occasionally brought into the class as outside resource individuals, and
2. A more prolonged and intensive form in which select agency personnel regularly attend the Proseminar along with trainees.

Only those agencies working in the areas of crime and delinquency (as described in an earlier portion of this proposal) will have

personnel eligible to attend jointly with trainees in the Proseminar. Insofar as is possible, efforts will be made to involve a variety of agencies. Selection of an individual from each agency will be made by program personnel in consultation with the director(s) of the agency under consideration; regardless of titular status, the participant selected will be one significantly involved in a capacity for which evaluation and implementation are most pertinent.

It is hypothesized that the latter mode, hereafter referred to as the combined Proseminar format, will be a more efficacious training method.

Measuring the impact of the Proseminar. In order to assess whether the combined Proseminar format contributes more to the learning process than sporadic appearances of agency personnel in the role as outside resource persons, a conservative quasi-experimental design has been incorporated within the program. Of the initial two entering cohorts, only the first will have the presumed benefit of meeting jointly with agency personnel in the Proseminar continously through the semester. In other aspects, the training experiences of the two cohorts will be identical except for the one year lag time. Thus, to the extent that trainees in the first cohort demonstrate superior ability to apply their technical knowledge when constrained by a host of practical or political factors, the positive contribution of the combined Proseminar format will have been documented.

The conservative nature of assessing the contribution of the combined format stems from the temporal sequence to be employed. Although this proposal calls for two cohorts being processed sequentially through the same program (except for the Proseminar format variation), there will, no doubt, be other differences as well. The net effect of these changes from the first cohort to the next should be in the direction of improving the training experience. Such a net gain should be produced by modifications in course content and teaching based on experience with the first cohort, improvement and stream-

---

[6] The use of multiple measures, or "triangulation" as it has been called (Webb *et al.,* 1966), is experiencing increased acceptance in the type of research with which this training program is concerned.

[7] The use of multiple measures and techniques is not without risks. There exists the rather disconcerting potential that each will yield unique results, thereby making interpretation equivocal. Nonetheless, the risk is warranted; greater confidence is attained when multiple approaches yield consistent findings in contrast to the level of uncertainty which always accompanies the use of a single measurement procedure.

lining of relationships between program personnel and participating agencies, increasing proficiency in the manner in which agency personnel work with trainees during the internship period, etc. In short, except for the combined nature of the Proseminar for cohort one, the second cohort should be exposed to an improved training program.[8] Therefore, a superior performance of the first cohort would indicate the superiority of the combined Proseminar format as a training aid.

Four different types of data will be employed to evaluate the impact of the combined Proseminar format upon trainees. (As indicated previously, these data for both cohorts combined will be used in the evaluation of the overall program.) The data gathering sequence is portrayed graphically in Figure 2; schematic designs at the bottom of Figure 2 symbolize the approaches that will be taken in the analysis of the efficacy of the two forms of agency personnel involvement in the Proseminar.

In the analysis of short run or direct effects, assessing the unique impact of Proseminar variations will be somewhat limited, given the fact that the two cohorts may have entered the program with unequal prior training and experience. However, tentative conclusions can be based on cohort comparisons of:

1. Differences in trainee evaluations of the Proseminar, and
2. Performance on simulated research problems.

Assessment of long-range impacts of the Proseminar is even more problematic than the short-run view. Initial training advantages might fade away in the succeeding year or they might be enhanced through interaction with subsequent training experiences. More complex intra-cohort interactions might also occur. However, some indication of the long-range worth of the Proseminar variations can be gained from further examination of abilities to handle simulated research problems, inter-cohort comparisons of the internship projects, and agency personnel evaluations of the members of the two cohorts.

In summary, multiple measures and analytical approaches will be used in evaluating the efficacy of the overall training model as well as its specific components. While it is recognized that the follow-up is restricted by the limited duration of the program, it is expected that the knowledge gained will be useful in laying foundations for other training programs in crime and delinquency.

References

Erickson, William L., Richard Ferrigno, and Joe Harding (1976) "Evaluation Training: A Symposium on Conducting A Training Program in Sociological Evaluation Research." Symposium presented at the meetings of the Midwestern Sociological Association, St. Louis.

Franklin, Jack and Jean Thrasher (1976) *An Introduction to Program Evaluation.* New York: Wiley and Sons.

Glaser, Daniel (1973) *Routinizing Evaluation: Getting Feedback of Effectiveness of Crime and Delinquency Programs.* Rockville: National Institute of Mental Health.

Lazarsfeld, Paul and Jeffrey Reitz (1975) *An Introduction to Applied Sociology.* New York: Elsevier.

Miller, Walter B. (1973). "Ideology and Criminal Justice Policy: Some Current Issues," *Journal of Criminal Law and Criminology,* Vol. 64, No. 2:141-162.

Moursund, Janet P. (1973) *Evaluation.* Monterey: Brooks/Cole Publishing Company.

O'Toole, Richard (ed.) (1971) *The Organization, Management, and Tactics of Social Research.* Cambridge: Schenkman.

Rivlin, Alice and Michael P. Timpane (eds.) *Ethical and Legal Issues of Social Experimentation.* Washington: The Brookings Institution.

Suchman, Edward A. (1971) "Action For What? A Critique of Evaluation Research" in O'Toole, R. (ed.), *The Organization, Management, and Tactics of Social Research,* Cambridge: Schenkman.

Tripodi, Tony, Phillip Fellin, and Irwin Epstein (1971) *Social Program Evaluation.* Itasca: F. E. Peacock Publishers.

Tuchfeld, Barry S. (1976) "Putting Sociology to Work: An Insider's View," *The American Sociologist,* II (November):188-192.

Webb, Eugene, Donald Campbell, Richard Schwartz, and Lee Sechrest (1966) *Unobtrusive Measures: Nonreactive Research in the Social Sciences.* Chicago: Rand McNally and Company.

Weiss, Carol H. (1972) *Evaluating Action Programs.* Boston: Allyn and Bacon, Inc.

---

[8] One could also identify factors which might reduce the quality of training for the second cohort: waning of initial enthusiasm among the administrators of the program and the participating agencies, experimenter effects (wherein the experimenters themselves unintentionally alter the program or the means of program assessment in the direction that will support the hypothesis), and the like. Nevertheless, the expectation, is that the net effect, if different from zero, will be in the direction of program improvement as time passes.

Appendix A. Description of Texas Christian University and the Department of Sociology

The Sociology Department

The Department contains nine full time faculty members, and offers five undergraduate degrees:
B.A. in Sociology
B.S. in Sociology
B.S. in Social Work
B. S. in Criminal Justice (Interdisciplinary program)
B.S. in Urban Studies (Interdisciplinary program)
An M.A. program has existed within the Department since 1937. Recent recipients of the Master of Arts degree have subsequently pursued the Ph.D. in sociology in such schools as Arizona, Florida State, Michigan State, Texas, Washington State, and Yale.

Texas Christian University

The University is composed of five undergraduate schools and colleges (Arts and Sciences, Business, Education, Fine Arts, and Nursing), and two schools at the graduate level (the Graduate School and Brite Divinity School). Support facilities include a library with approximately 900,000 items (with additional materials readily accessible via cooperative systems with neighboring academic and public libraries), and an expanding Computer Center which houses a Xerox Sigma Nine machine and attendant software. (Some data processing equipment is housed in the Department of Sociology.) Over 300 full time faculty are employed at TCU, with 80 percent holding the doctorate or some other highest degree available in their field.

Appendix D. University Advisory Committee for the M.S. Degree Program in Applied Social Research

Eugene J. Alpert (Ph.D., Michigan State U.), Assistant Professor, Department of Political Science.

Floyd W. Durham (Ph.D., U. of Oklahoma), Professor, Department of Economics.

James R. Henley (Ph.D., Florida State U.), Associate Professor, Department of Sociology.

Lawrence R. James (Ph.D., U. of Utah), Associate Professor, Department of Psychology and Research Associate, Institute of Behavioral Research.

E. Leigh Secrest (Ph.D., M.I.T.), Professor of Management Science, School of Business.

Health Advocacy Master's Program

Funded by: Florence V. Burden Foundation (Planning funds had been previously provided by J. M. and Helena Rubenstein Foundation)

Project Director: Joan Marks, Co-Director, Health Advocacy Program, Sarah Lawrence College, Bronxville, New York

Proposal Prepared by: Joan Marks

DEVELOPING A GRADUATE PROGRAM IN HEALTH ADVOCACY
by Joan Marks

In the past decade, over 1400 hospitals in the United States have instituted health advocacy programs in response to the growing awareness that our complex health care systems frequently fail to meet the needs of patients. With doctors, nurses, and administrators already overburdened with a multitude of medical responsibilities, patients increasingly find themselves treated with a brisk impersonality that can be both confusing and frightening. The demand for a new kind of health worker, the health advocate (a generic term for a variety of positions, for example, patient representative) represents a nation-wide effort to resolve this problem and to improve the quality and delivery of health care services.

The idea of developing a training program for health advocates at Sarah Lawrence College has been germinating since 1976 when I became aware of the role of the hospital patient representative. As Director of the Human Genetics Program, I realized that the genetic counselors we were training were advocates for patients with genetic disease and were a vital resource for families overwhelmed by the birth of a child with "a family disease." These families were

usually unable to organize the medical or family resources the family needed to deal with the genetic crisis, and the skilled genetic counselor assumed an advocacy role for such families as they dealt with the confusing, often inadvertently inhumane, medical facility.

Joan Marks is Director of the Human Genetics Program and Co-Director of the Health Advocacy Program at Sarah Lawrence College.

Further explorations into the ways in which uninformed, foreign-speaking, and elderly patients manage to obtain health care for themselves convinced me that all people in need of health care need someone to serve as their ombudsman or advocate. Visits with patient representatives around the country indicated that this advocacy role takes many forms but the most effective role is that which allows advocates to effect changes in the delivery system within their institutions once problem areas have been recognized. These "change agents" usually report directly to senior hospital administrators and thus require skills that can only be learned at the advanced level.

Sarah Lawrence College chose to develop an eighteen-month interdisciplinary program with a 1000-hour fieldwork component in New York City health delivery settings. Since the elderly occupy 37 percent of New York City hospital beds, we naturally developed a curriculum and field component with strong emphasis in this area. The need for patient advocates in the nursing home industry was, of course, painfully evident.

The Health Advocacy Program is designed for people who are committed to improving the delivery of health care, for those who are interested in beginning careers in health advocacy, and for those already in this or related fields, such as patient representation, who are seeking advancement. Students can earn either the Master of Arts or Master of Professional Studies degree. Graduates will be prepared to organize and direct programs of health advocacy in such institutions as hospitals, ambulatory health facilities, health maintenance organizations, nursing homes, prisons, schools, as well as in government and voluntary health agencies.

Health advocates assist patients in negotiating the health system and act on their behalf in securing appropriate medical care. They educate health care consumers to a better understanding of their rights and responsibilities in the use of health resources. They serve as an interface between the needs of consumers and the capabilities of health care institutions. They are trained to evaluate and effect changes from within the health care delivery system in an effort to make the system more responsive to patient needs.

In seeking funds to develop the Health Advocacy Program we turned first to our "friends," that is, foundations that had previously recognized the Human Genetics Program as an innovative concept designed to serve an unmet need. One of these, the J. M. Foundation, agreed with our assessment of the need and recognized our track record in establishing the field of genetic counseling at the allied health level. With planning funds for six months and for the first year of the program, we were subsequently able to interest two other New York City foundations (the Helena Rubinstein and the Florence V. Burden foundations) to provide modest support that will allow us to recruit applicants from a broad segment of society, particularly those populations that are so disadvantaged in getting health care.

The main problem I see in obtaining foundation support is the initial request. Generally, this takes the form of a short letter of inquiry. My experience is that this approach has never been successful for Sarah Lawrence; what has been productive is a telephone call to someone associated with a foundation who is willing to listen to you and perhaps put you in touch with a specific foundation where you can use the name of the referral source. Even this can be useless since so few foundations are really willing — or able — to be responsive to ideas that do not fit neatly into their defined areas of interest.

The response to the announcement of the Health Advocacy Program has been impressive. We have recruited a highly qualified faculty, challenged by the opportunity to teach in an innovative, interdisciplinary curriculum. Applicants are diverse, highly motivated, and talented. One of our applicants is a young Puerto Rican woman working in a hospital who felt personally deprived of a relationship with grandparents who were left in Puerto Rico. She has since "adopted" a grandfather in New York with whom she visits regularly. This led to her interest in the fate of elderly Puerto Ricans and to her plans to work with the elderly, probably in a nursing home. Nearly one hundred hospitals have written to express their interest, to request our help in advising them, or to request that we let them know when our first graduates will be available for employment. Our first class will begin in September 1980 with fifteen to twenty women and men and we look forward to the impact they may have as they serve in hospitals, nursing homes, community health centers, and mental health programs.

* * *

COMMENTS ON THE HEALTH ADVOCATES PROPOSAL

by Harriet L. Warm

This project has an interesting history. It was first brought to us in 1978 when Sarah Lawrence was seeking planning funds to develop a master's degree training program for health advocates. Since the Burden Foundation is relatively small and concentrates its funds almost entirely in the fields of aging and crime and justice, we were not in a position to consider this initial request for support because it addressed the problem of health care in a general way.

During the following year, the Foundation became increasingly aware of the extent to which older persons constitute a high proportion of the hospital population. We also saw a growing need to provide nursing home residents with assistance in solving some of the problems of daily living. Finally, we recognized that there was a strong desire on the part of many active elderly persons for a second career that emphasized assistance to others.

We saw a way to respond to all three of these concerns together and suggested to Sarah Lawrence that if the proposal could be revised accordingly, we might be able to provide some of

Harriet L. Warm is Executive Director of the Florence V. Burden Foundation. Her article, "Foundation Grantmaking for the Elderly," appears in this issue of *Grants Magazine*.

the support needed to start the program. As a result, the proposal was modified to include a clear emphasis on preparing patient representatives, as they are also called, for work with elderly patients. There was also a decision to actively recruit a group of older students and to supplement their tuition as necessary. Our grant of $15,000 is helping to pay for some of these costs, supplemented by funds from other sources.

Since the Burden Foundation is generally able to fund only about 2 percent of all requests, it may be useful to summarize the specific reasons why we ultimately selected this project as opposed to others within our fields.

- First, Joan Marks, the project's director, had an excellent track record. She had previously developed an outstanding training program for genetics counselors that has been copied by a number of other colleges and universities. Sarah Lawrence itself has had substantial success in training and then finding jobs for mature students, as well as for younger ones.

- Second, the proposal and budget were carefully thought out and clearly written. They anticipated many of the problems that could occur during the development of the program. A strong Advisory Committee had been selected and was helping to guide decisions about course content and faculty.

- Finally, the problem of humanizing health care for older people seemed to us an important one and the use of well-trained patient advocates appeared to be one way of solving it. As conceived by Sarah Lawrence, the health advocate was not intended to be an adversary of the management of the hospital or nursing home, but a practical problem-solver who could both assist individual patients and lay the groundwork for systematic change and for greater cost efficiency as well.

The growing interest around the country in the use of both volunteer and paid health advocates and the passage of legislation in some states requiring their use persuaded us that there was a growing market for trained professionals in this field. While it is too early yet to judge the program's success, we hope that it will establish a pattern for the recruitment and training of patient representatives that can eventually be copied in other parts of the country.

* * *

HEALTH ADVOCACY MASTER'S PROGRAM
Sarah Lawrence College, Bronxville, New York
January 1980

Sarah Lawrence College plans to offer innovative training in the field of Health Advocacy. Planning funds from the J. M. and Helena Rubinstein Foundations have enabled the college to organize a Masters Program in Health Advocacy with an entering class scheduled for September 1980. The program will be of 18 months duration and will consist of an interdisciplinary curriculum, coupled with fieldwork, leading to a Master of Professional Studies or Master of Arts Degree.

The Health Advocacy Program developed in consultation with a Board of Advisors prominent in the health care field, is designed to train advocates for responsible health care in a broad range of settings. These might include hospitals, HMO's, nursing homes, health planning agencies, prisons, and the work place. Because 25 million Americans are 65 years old or older, a major service area of health advocacy will concern the elderly. Learning to serve this population in an innovative way will be greatly facilitated if some of the trainees in the program are themselves mature individuals.

For this reason, we would propose that the Burden Foundation consider funding up to five individuals who are qualified and interested in professional advocacy work with the elderly in health care settings. These students could be named as Burden Trainees in Health Advocacy. The curriculum as presently conceived (see attached outline) will prepare such individuals

specifically for work with the elderly and their fieldwork would be concentrated (though not confined) in areas serving this age group.

The recruitment of students for this program will be a key factor in developing the field of health advocacy. It is hoped that some students will be drawn to the program from their previous experience in the health field. Others will be sought who desire a new career in their later years. Such individuals will be approached through contacts with major corporations in the New York area and could be an important source of students appropriate for Burden Traineeships. Such individuals, when appropriately positioned in the health care system upon completion of the program, could make major contributions toward improving the delivery of services to the elderly and could, in turn, train others to assume these roles. Such individuals may be unable to invest the necessary financial resources to seek this training. Your support will greatly facilitate recruiting such individuals into the field.

Field work, or on-the-job training, will be a prominent component of this program. Students will spend about 1000 hours of supervised work in a variety of settings. A primary affiliation is presently under negotiation with Mt. Sinai Hospital so that many students in the program would spend at least 250 hours at that institution where one of the leading programs in patient representation is offered. Other affiliations are being developed at other major New York hospitals and nursing homes.

Partial support for 4-5 Florence Burden Traineeships in Health Advocacy coupled with modest program support to launch this new program and to recruit trainees could be achieved with a grant of $15,000. Other program support to date is $40,000. Five year program support from the Fund for the Improvement of Post-secondary Education is under consideration at this time.

Student Body

Applicants will be sought who have the following qualifications:

Academic Bachelor's degree reflecting a high level of achievement

Evidence of success in at least one substantive course in each of the following areas:

Biology
Psychology
Sociology/Anthropology
Economics
Language—preferably Spanish

Evidence of a commitment to working with people, preferably on-the-job in a health setting or as a peer advisor

Applications will require thoughtful essays. Interviews will be an essential tool of selection along with transcripts and letters of recommendation. The program would encourage applications from people of all ages, all social and cultural backgrounds and a broad geographic area. Scholarship funds are budgeted to assure the diversity of professionals needed to enter this challenging field.

Curriculum and Course Outlines

First semester

4 credits	The History of Health Care in America
2 credits	Human Anatomy and Physiological Systems
2 credits	The Language of Patient Care
3 credits	Health Care Organization and Concepts for Change
3 credits	Introduction to Health Advocacy

14 credits

Second semester

4 credits	The Psychology of Interpersonal Communications
4 credits	Health Law
3 credits	Problems in Health Advocacy
4 credits (fieldwork)	Practicum - 2 days a week

11 credits + 4 fieldwork credits*

Summer Internship—4 fieldwork credits—minimum of 5 weeks full time

Third semester

4 credits	Priority Problems in Health Care
4 credits	The Economics of Health
3 credits	Advanced Seminar in Health Advocacy
4 credits (fieldwork)	Practicum - 2 days a week

11 credits + 4 fieldwork credits

36 credits + 12 fieldwork credits - Total

*Each fieldwork credit equals 50 hours on the job.

Human Anatomy and Physiological Systems

After thoroughly covering human anatomy, this course will teach the physiology of normally functioning systems and introduce the effects of pathological conditions.

The Language of Patient Care

Approaches to diagnosis and treatment will be covered in this course along with the medical, pharmacological, and technological terminology central to communicating in a health care setting.

Introduction to Health Advocacy

Concept and Philosophy of Patient Representation
Background
Development
Growth

Access to Health Care
Information and Referral
Outreach
Community
Ambulatory Patients
Hospital Patients
Others

Cultural Factors in Health Delivery
Life Styles and Nutritional Patterns
Ethnicity Related to Acceptance and Use of Health Care
Herbalists
Acupuncturists
Spiritualists

Psycho-Social Needs of Hospitalized Patients
Impact of Acute and Chronic Illness on Patients and Families
Humanizing the Hospital Environment
Working with Patients and Families
Death and Dying
Family Interaction

Eliciting Patient's Perceptions of Care
   Analyzing Complaints. Comments

Organizational Staffing and Administrative Priorities
   The Roles of the Professional, the Para-professional and the Non-professional

Coping Patterns of Health Care Staff

Health Care in
   Ambulatory Care Settings
   Emergency Rooms
   Clinics and HMO's
   Long Term Care Facilities
   Prisons
   Schools
   Work Place

Interdepartmental Collaboration
   Influencing Staff Attitudes
   Negotiating the System
   Documentation
      Purposes and Methods

Patients Rights and Responsibilities
   Legal and Moral
   Informed Consent

Working with the Aged, Handicapped, Chronically Ill, Children, the Emergency Patient and their Families

The Psychology of Interpersonal Relations

The study of human relations invariably involves an analysis of interpersonal communications. Consequently the subject matter of the course will be an examination of the factors which affect the ways in which human beings perceive and judge one another. The particular topics under consideration will be: impression-formation, verbal and nonverbal communication, self perception, attribution and equity theory, and liking and attraction.

Health Law

This course seeks to enhance the capabilities of students in two ways: (1) making students understand basic health law issues and instructing them on how to find legal information when necessary (by using lectures on substantive health law and by surveying written, organizational and library health law resources); (2) teaching how to think and speak effectively in the hospital setting as an advocate (by using the case method/argumentation approach to review current health law, particularly in the area of patient rights).

I. The first part of the course will focus on (a) paralegal skills such as how to use health law resources; how to read statutes and basic legal language; how to dig up legal information quickly; how to document cases properly; knowledge of legal and administrative procedures which can be taken by patients against an institution; and (b) such substantive health law issues as the legal structure and organization of an institution; standard hospital rules and regulations; medical malpractice doctrines; licensing and regulation of professional staff; patient liability for hospital bills; state regulations affecting hospital services and reimbursement; legal differences in hospital auspices (voluntary, proprietary, municipal).

II. The second half of the semester will focus on evolving doctrines in the area of patients' rights. As this law is unsettled and changing, it is critical that students develop a sense of advocacy rather than a mastery of particular rules. "Advocacy" includes the ability to represent a point of view in writing or orally and to understand and diplomatically and effectively deal with opposing views. The following patients' rights questions will be debated: right to information prior to treatment; right to refuse treatment; rights affecting women, children, minorities and special patients, such as long term care and terminally ill patients; rights of the mentally ill; human experimentation; confidentiality and privacy; access to medical records.

Problems in Health Advocacy

Organizational Rules, Official and Unofficial
Medical Education and Medical Ethics
Representation of Psychiatric Patients
Legal Implications of Advocacy
Malpractice
Patient Grievance Mechanisms
Risk Management and Quality of Care
Advocacy for the Aged
  Disadvantaged Economically
  Handicapped
  Children and Youths
  Prisoners
The "Difficult" Patient

The Economics of Health

I. Medicine is a Market
  Measure of "product" or "output"
  Measures of inputs
  Non-price competition
  Supply and demand—how relevant?

II. Financing and Reimbursement Structure
  Health insurance programs
  Use of cost controls through reimbursement
    system
  Various approaches NYS & AHA
  Voluntary efforts methodologies

III. Allocation of Resources in the Medical
     Market
A. Fee-for-service vs. service unrelated to fee
B. Non-profit vs. profit-making
C. Fixed costs vs. variable costs
D. Regulation of resource allocation
E. Can one put more competition into the
    medical market?

The courses listed above are being developed as a core curriculum for the Health Advocacy Program. Each will be approached as an academic study of the subject, set in a historical and theoretical context. Assigned readings will be from multiple sources, including current literature, and each course will require the writing of substantive library research papers.

Although specific approaches to functioning in a health advocacy role will be dealt with in advanced practicums and fieldwork placements (in lieu of thesis), the core curriculum is designed to provide historical background and a conceptual framework that will enable graduates to think creatively about problems of delivering care to patients in various health settings.

The following descriptions are the result of consultations with people qualified to and interested in teaching. Further refinements are expected as the process of recruitment of faculty continues.

The History of Health Care in America

Currently health care is in crisis in this country. Questions are being asked and solutions sought to the newly-perceived problems of costs, access to and availability of health care services. This course will focus on the past, when the roots of the contemporary system took shape, in order to understand some of the characteristics which define current expectations of our health care system, as well as some of the factors upon which it is built. Examining attitudes toward sickness, death and health from the eighteenth century to the present, we will discuss historic changes in the medical profession; the organization of health care services; the growth of mental health as a distinct specialty; the impact of illness, illustrated through literature, demographic changes and large social and political movements (public health and sanitation); the role of the patient. In addition to reading historic narrative and theory, we will draw from original sources as much as possible, especially for research papers.

The Organization of Health Care and Concepts for Change

Both public and private aspects of the current U.S. health care system will be covered in this course. Beginning with a study of the federal responsibility for public health programs and for health planning, the course progresses to the organization and management of institutions which deliver health care, such as acute and long term care facilities, community health centers, tertiary and specialty care centers and private practitioners. Various kinds of health professionals, the services they perform, and how they interrelate will be included, as well as the administrative supports required.

Proposals for major change in our current system will be analyzed where possible, by studying societies which now employ such programs as national health insurance and socialized medicine.

Advanced Seminar in Health Advocacy

    Organizing a department
    Objective setting
    Staff training and supervision
      Paid staff
      Volunteers
    Developing a departmental manual
    Accountability
      Data collection
      Statistics
    Budgeting
    Power theory and institutional change

    Assessment
      Effecting systems change
      Cost benefits
      Staffing needs
    Conflict resolution
    The role of the change agent
    Patient education

Priority Problems in Health Care

In this senior seminar the class will deal with widely recognized health care problems such as spiraling costs and inequality of access to and allocation of resources.

Each student will be required to present a major paper on a specific problem encountered on the job, to thoroughly research the issue, its background and possible solutions and to develop a plan of action for resolving the problem.

Practicums

All field training (a total of 600 hours) will be supervised by professionals in advocacy programs. Several settings will be selected as training centers but primary affiliation with Mt. Sinai Hospital is under discussion at this time. The planning period will be used to establish linkages with non-hospital settings which students might elect for their second and/or third placement.

THE ARTS

The fiscal year 1982 budget proposal of the President called for a fifty percent reduction for the National Endowments for the Arts and the Humanities. Seldom has an administrative move electrified a constituency to the extent that this budget cut excited the artists and arts administrators in this country. Seldom has a group been so united in a common cause as was this group in its effort to save the NEA. Led by Theodore Bikel, an aggressive lobby was mounted and the voice of the artist and arts organizations was heard throughout the land, in the halls of the Senate and the House of Representatives, as well as in the White House. The result was that the Arts and Humanities Endowments ended up with budgets approximately the same size that President Carter had recommended. The proposed budget cuts for 1983 were similarly opposed, and both Endowments have remained at about the same budget levels. However, when inflation is taken into account, they are funding fewer projects.

Without a crystal ball, or even with one, it is impossible to know what will happen in the future, but those seeking support for the arts have already begun to explore other sources of support to replace anticipated losses of federal funding which appear to be inevitable. Some states have passed record appropriations for the arts, and corporations and foundations are being urged to increase their arts programs. Corporations have responded well, but they have gone to great lengths to insist that it will be impossible for them to replace federal support because arts activities not only need federal funds but the imprimatur of governmental approval is important to decision makers in corporations. They prefer to sponsor artistic events jointly with the federal government instead to taking on the entire responsibility.

Fortunately, a great deal can be done in arts fields with relatively small sums of money. Many communities in this country now have their own opera, ballet, theater, and music organizations — thanks, at least in part, directly or indirectly to the existence of the NEA — and the American public is no longer dependent upon visits to the large cities in order to look at paintings and sculpture, hear music, and see plays.

Community and private foundations as well as local business organizations have a stake in supporting the arts in their own geographic locales and many of them restrict their support to those places in which they have an interest or a headquarters.

The four documents presented here include: *The Opera Participation Project—Involving Bay Area Youth in the Vocal Arts,* which was funded by three northern California foundations, is a fine example of a proposal that gives small foundations an opportunity to jointly support a program in which they all have an interest. The planning and presentation of this proposal which was designed to attract multiple funding is described by Paul Hennessey in the article, *Adding Excitement to Your Proposals,* which here precedes the application itself.

Small Arts Projects is the heading given to three applications funded by the National Endowment for the Arts to Friends of the Graduate Center Mall, City University of New York Graduate Center Mall.

The background of these three separate proposals is given by Ray Ring, Director of Exhibitions of The Mall, who prepared the applications. One of these proposals was to support an exhibition by an artist who works with sound, Liz Phillips, to "create an interactive sound environment specifically for the Graduate Center Mall." Ms. Phillips was not unknown at that time, but has become even better known since that exhibition. Her latest piece called "Windspun" is housed in a windmill in the midst of a composting plant in the South Bronx and was unveiled on May 13, 1981. *The New York Times* headed its review of the event "Avant Garde: Liz Phillips Sound" and the reviewer stated that Ms. Phillips "is becoming one of the best known practitioners" in her field and that the off-beat location "doesn't detract from its charm."

Although all three applications in this group are from the same organization and all were funded by the NEA, they are quite different in what they propose, particularly as to scope and design. The budgets are particularly useful guides for arts groups who approach the National Endowment for support.

The third *Grants Clinic* feature in this group begins with an article, *The Film Fund: What It Is and What It Does,* by Terry Lawler, Director of The Film Fund, Inc. It is the organization's story of how they are set up to receive, review, and participate in the execution of grants, and the criteria they use in determining which to approve. The article is followed by an example of a proposal The Film Fund found to meet its criteria in every respect and which they therefore funded.

One of the common failings of grant seekers is an inadequate understanding of the objectives of the grantmaking institutions which they approach—a failing that usually results in the presentation of proposals that do not meet the criteria of the grantmaker, and failure to obtain support. Ms. Lawler's article tells how the Fund is organized, what their objectives are, and how they select the proposals they fund. Such precise information is not always available from funding organizations, but it is well worth asking for, and if it is available well worth following. It will make the job of the application process immeasurably easier.

The Living Stage Theatre Company's proposal to expand one existing improvisational theatre workshop and launch another at two penal institutions in the Washington, D. C. area exemplifies several significant elements in successful grant getting.

The applicant, that is, Living Stage, is affiliated with a nationally known and highly regarded theatre, the Arena Stage. At the time this project was designed, Living Stage had 12 years of successful experience behind it. The director, Robert Alexander, had come to the attention of people interested in the theatre and officials in funding organizations knew of the accomplishments of his company. When he approached The Ford Foundation, he knew Richard Sheldon, then a program officer in arts at the foundation. At that time, Ford was interested in supporting projects for incarcerated men and women. In other words, all the elements were in place for a successful negotiation. Following the pre-application negotiations, Mr. Alexander and Elizabeth Brunazzi wrote an explicit, imaginative proposal containing background information, a precise outline of the proposed activity and the arguments in favor of its approval. The section headed "Goals and Philosophy" should be studied for its effective arguments in favor of the project, its reasons why the foundation should support it.

This is one point where many applications are weak according to funding officials—they fail to make a case for their proposed activity strong enough that it stands out among the multitudes of applications that flood the offices of foundations, corporations, and government agencies.

The Opera Participation Project—Involving Bay Area Youth in the Vocal Arts

Funded by: Three Northern California Foundations

Project Director: Rudolph Picardi, Artistic Director, The Talent Bank, San Francisco.

Proposal prepared by: Staff of the Talent Bank Foundation

ADDING EXCITEMENT TO YOUR PROPOSALS
by Paul Hennessey

With the passage of California's Proposition 13, and the movement for tax relief in many other states, arts organizations are finding it increasingly difficult to find grant support. When funding cutbacks occur in local school budgets, arts programs are often labeled "luxuries" and eliminated.

The arts group whose proposal is discussed in this Grants Clinic, The Talent Bank, is the kind of group most affected by such funding cuts. The mission of this San Francisco-based organization is to bring opera, one of the least salable arts, into parochial schools that receive little or no funding for arts programs. This proposal helped them fund a $20,000 project from three northern California foundations. The Talent Bank submitted a well-written, ex-citing grant application tailored to the potential funders, and succeeded while others were failing.

Before the Proposal Was Written

The Talent Bank set out to find private support for a program to expose elementary school students to a participatory opera experience. Before writing and submitting proposals, however, they did four important things:

1. They "creatively cross-indexed" their project.
2. They budgeted their program in several ways.
3. They did research to locate the best potential funding sources.
4. They made personal contact with potential funders.

The Talent Bank drafted their proposal after these four steps were thoroughly worked out.

The first step, "creative cross-indexing," began with the question, "How, other than as an opera group, can The Talent Bank present itself?" The answers were:

- "a Catholic/parochial schools project" — because of their emphasis on bringing opera in-

---

Paul Hennessey is a Program Coordinator at the University of California, Berkeley. He was formerly Vice President of the Institute for Fund Raising, San Francisco.

to schools that have no public funding for arts programs

- "a project for disadvantaged youth" — because of their emphasis on low-income areas
- "a music program" — because of the program's training aspect for musical performers

These redefinitions allowed them to increase the number of likely funders for their Opera Participation Project. Rather than present themselves as a simple "opera" project, they could locate and approach funders interested in disadvantaged youth, training for young musicians and singers, as well as those who believe in music education in schools.

The second step was to draw up a number of budget strategies for the project, designed to appeal to funders with different granting patterns. The budget was drawn up in three ways:

- *a three-part budget broken down by* **phase**. This was used to "market" different kinds of educational activities at different costs. The proposal shown here asks for $4,250 for the project's intimate second-phase "demonstration projects." Another similar proposal asked a different funder for almost $8,000 for the third phase, a full-scale production of an opera.
- *a budget broken down by* **school**. This covered the cost of the full three-phase project at one school; at a modest price, a small foundation could support the program at a single school.
- *a budget broken down by* **line item**. This was presented to foundations interested in funding "musicians" or "singer training."

After completing these first two steps, The Talent Bank had an increased number of possible funders. Now, instead of asking for $20,000 for their "opera" project, they could ask several funders with different interests for varying amounts of money.

The Talent Bank's research, the third step, involved a thorough search of *The Foundation*

Directory, The Foundation Grants Index, state foundation directories, and IRS-990 forms. According to their researcher, the most important part of this search was a phone call to confirm data: "The most recent foundation data I could find was often one or two years old. By calling before submitting a proposal, I found out all kinds of information about interests, priorities, and application procedures."

The final step before writing the proposal was to make personal contact with the best prospects. A Board of Directors' meeting was called, and a list of trustees from likely foundation funders was circulated. It turned out that a Talent Bank board member knew at least one trustee in about 75 percent of the targeted foundations. Board members set up formal or informal meetings with the foundation people they knew, either to discuss the project in detail or to pave the way for proposal submission.

Based on the results of these combined actions — research, phone contacts with funders, and board members' personal contacts with foundation personnel — individually tailored proposals were prepared for each of the most likely funders for the Opera Participation Project. The proposal that follows is one of them.

* * *

THE OPERA PARTICIPATION PROJECT — INVOLVING BAY AREA YOUTH IN THE VOCAL ARTS

by The Talent Bank

Summary

Students in San Francisco's lower income parochial schools have traditionally been under-exposed to the arts, especially opera. When they *are* given a chance to experience the arts, it is usually as spectators — and almost never as participants.

The Opera Participation Project breaks this pattern. As its name implies, it is designed to help students understand and appreciate opera through *participation in actual opera performances* at the school sites. During the past four years, we have reached 10,000 disadvantaged 4th, 5th, and 6th graders in over fifty San Francisco parochial schools with a unique three-phase program that teaches through involvement, and excites through participation.

At the same time, we give a number of talented Bay Area singers expert, individualized training. They learn to improve their art by performing. They learn to teach children about opera by helping run music demonstrations in schools. They get expert coaching every step of the way. And they are paid for all performances they give through the Opera Participation Project.

What are the benefits of the Opera Participation Project? For students, heightened excitement and interest in music, as well as increased self-confidence and oral expression skills. For our singers, an opportunity to gain performance experience at the same time they support their artistic training. For our community, the promise of arts support tomorrow from students we reach in today's Mission District classroom.

We will be taking our unique project into thirteen schools in the Mission District in 1978. In order to help us reach these children with our program, we are requesting a grant of $4,250 from [   ] to support the second
phase of our three-phase Project — a series of instructional demonstrations that take place on-site at the thirteen schools we work with. We give three demonstrations in each school. They are designed to teach students to appreciate music by introducing them to the basics, and then having them actually sing with our teachers.

These demonstrations are the central learning experience of our project. They offer students the opportunity to observe and perform with trained opera singers. Our demonstrations are the logical prelude to the climactic final production of Britten's "Noye's Fludde," which involves students from all participating schools.

At [   ]'s suggestion, we submit this proposal for funding under the category "Performance and Instruction of Arts and Music at the School Site." We think you will agree the Opera Participation Project is an exciting way to bring musical instruction to parochial school students in San Francisco.

The Need

Most elementary school students, despite efforts made on their behalf, are never "turned on" to good music. In some cases — especially in parochial schools — they are never exposed to it at all.

This is a problem for a number of reasons:

- These *students are missing out on an important part of their education:* personal artistic expression. This artistic experience, important in itself, also affects students' motivation to learn in other areas. According to a recent $300,000 study funded by 15 American foundations and corporations, students exposed to the arts perform better in *all* scholastic areas. (See *San Francisco Chronicle,* 4 October 1977, page 21.)

- *Parochial school students should not be deprived of training* in the performing arts. They deserve as full an educational experience as students in tax-supported public schools. They are equally entitled to the opportunity to experience the arts in their schools.

- If the arts in general, and opera in particular, are to survive in the future, *audiences must be developed now.* If we expect the arts to prosper through the 1990s, we must involve and excite young audiences in 1978.
- Along the same lines, *we cannot expect to produce future opera singers from minorities if we do not excite them* about opera at an early age.

Finally, there are a number of young *opera artists in the Bay Area needing performance exposure and training.* There are too few opportunities for gifted artists to perform, especially for compensation. The Opera Participation Project meets these needs by matching talented young singers with needy audiences. We expose children in San Francisco's Mission District parochial schools to the joy of music. Everyone wins -- students, teachers, and singers.

The Opera Participation Project

The Opera Participation Project is a unique three-phase program that gets disadvantaged elementary school children excited about — and involved in -- opera. We bring talented young Bay Area singers into schools in San Francisco's Mission District; these singers encourage students to learn by having them actually participate in operatic performances. As our name implies, the emphasis is on opera *participation . . .* and that is where we are unique.

This is how the Opera Participation Project works:

Phase 1: Talented opera artists from around the Bay Area perform Donizetti's *Rita* in twelve parochial schools and one public school in the mission district, at the school sites. This opera, written in English for easy comprehension, has proven a favorite of students everywhere it has been staged.

Phase 2: Four singers return to the schools a second time; they conduct instructional demonstrations in which students learn about music and opera *through participation.* Students learn simple harmony patterns, invent operatic dialogue, improvise with our singers, create movements to match their music, and make up their own recitatives.

Phase 3: As the climax of the Project, our singers, *along with students,* perform Benjamin Britten's *Noye's Fludde.* Mission District students get a chance to actually sing in the chorus and play in the orchestra of this full-scale production.

The Opera Participation Project has involved over 10,000 students during the past four years. The best gauge of our success comes in the numerous letters we receive from enthralled students and gratified teachers. We have enclosed samples for your examination.

We work in the Bay Area, a national center for such opera companies as the San Francisco Opera and Western Opera Theatre. The Opera Participation Project has a number of features making it a unique, important, and complementary part of San Francisco's opera community:

- *Students actually participate in our opera performances.* They don't just sit and listen; they learn to know and appreciate opera by becoming a part of one!
- *Bay Area singers are trained and paid for their efforts.* This gives the young talented singers a chance to perform and grow, and helps them support their own training.
- *The Program brings an involving opera experience in English to disadvantaged parochial school students.* The racial breakdown of students we work with is: Black — 25 percent; Chicano/Spanish — 35 percent; Oriental — 10 percent; other — 30 percent. Twelve of the thirteen schools we work with get no public support for arts programs. The Project opens new avenues of musical awareness and appreciation; it also improves students' self-confidence and oral expression skills.

In short, the Opera Participation Project helps artists grow today . . . at the same time it instructs, involves, and excites the audiences of tomorrow.

Full 1978 Budget for Opera Participation Project for Thirteen Schools

First Opera Production — Three Performances

Cast: 6 Singers @ $100/Performance	$1,800.00	
Music Director	600.00	
Stage Director	400.00	
Coaching	250.00	
Narration	150.00	
Performance Fee	390.00	
Rehearsal Pianist	150.00	
Technical Crew	250.00	
Truck Rental	150.00	
Set and Costumes	1,000.00	
Rights and Rental	400.00	
Contingency	300.00	
		$5,840.00

Demonstration Workshops

13 Schools
  3 Demonstration Workshops per School

13 Workshops @ $130/Workshop	$1,690.00	
26 Workshops @ $85/Workshop	2,210.00	
Music Director Preparation	250.00	
Stage Director Preparation	100.00	
		$4,250.00

Final Opera Production. *Noye's Fludde* — Two Performances

Cast: 8 Singers @ $75/Performance	$1,200.00	
1 Speaking Part @ $50/Performance	100.00	
Music Director	600.00	
Stage Director	600.00	
Coaching	300.00	
Narration	100.00	
Performance Fee	260.00	
Rehearsal Pianist	300.00	
Orchestra	2,000.00	
Technical Crew	400.00	
Truck Rental	150.00	
Set and Costumes	500.00	
Rights and Rental	300.00	
Piano Rental, Insurance, Tuning	175.00	
Production Coordinator	150.00	
Choreographer	50.00	
Music Teachers, 4 @ $50	200.00	
Contingency	400.00	
		$7,785.00
Project Coordinator	$1,000.00	
Music Preparation Materials for Schools	200.00	
Posters, Flyers, and Prizes	300.00	
Talent Bank Administrative Expenses	1,200.00	
		$2,700.00
TOTAL		$20,575.00

Dear Talent Bank,

I was very much impressed by your performance because I just thought that opera was just loud singing, but once I seen your play I have realized what real opera is.

The opera seemed very realistic, at one moment at the play I thought that it was a true story.

I hope you come next year.

Your Friend,
George Suarez
Corpus Christi School
Grade 6

---

655 Elizabeth Street
San Francisco Calif. 94114
March 16, 1977

Dear Mr. R Picardi,

The opera "Pepito" was good. When Manuelita slapped Miguel in the face it looked like it was real. Then after the opera when everybody asked questions and Manuelita and Miguel showed us how they did it it was really neato! I would like to see another opera composed by Jacque Offenbach. Adrian Metings played by Allen Parker looked like he was really fat with that pillow under him. Manuelita played by Julie Yeager and Miguel played by Dan Jensen looked neat in the story. I hope that next year I can see another opera preformed by these same players.

Sincerely
Florence Refuerzo

"Papetto"

What I liked about the opera is the costumes they were very creative. They fit the parts just right. And the voices were loud and clear. And the words could be understood. I wish I had an opera voice. And if I do I hope I find it and fast. Thank you for letting the 5-B class see the show

Holy Name 5 B

Dear Opera,

I like the girl she was pretty and the star she gave the fat guy and the scenerey and the girls shop and the cafe second thing I like was the piano player and the high voice like la capito it was very very very very very nice you all do a good job of doing plays I hope you come and see us soon but I still remeber Julie and alan it was sort of a good education for kids like us 4th graders It was a story like that one the book was called legend of opera stories. the end

Paul

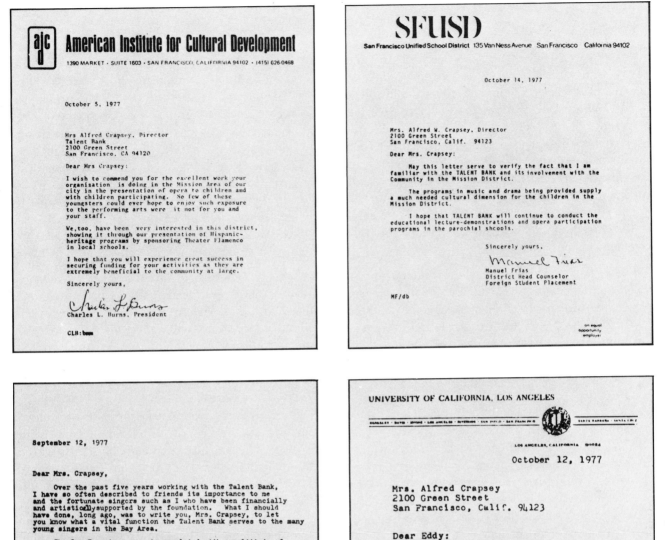

American Institute for Cultural Development

1390 MARKET · SUITE 1603 · SAN FRANCISCO, CALIFORNIA 94102 · (415) 626-0468

October 5, 1977

Mrs Alfred Crapsey, Director
Talent Bank
2100 Green Street
San Francisco, CA 94120

Dear Mrs Crapsey:

I wish to commend you for the excellent work your organization is doing in the Mission Area of our city in the presentation of opera to children and with children participating. So few of these youngsters could ever hope to enjoy such exposure to the performing arts were it not for you and your staff.

We, too, have been very interested in this district, showing it through our presentation of Hispanic-heritage programs by sponsoring Theater Flamenco in local schools.

I hope that you will experience great success in securing funding for your activities as they are extremely beneficial to the community at large.

Sincerely yours,

Charles L. Burns, President

CLB:bm

SFUSD

San Francisco Unified School District 135 Van Ness Avenue San Francisco California 94102

October 14, 1977

Mrs. Alfred W. Crapsey, Director
2100 Green Street
San Francisco, Calif. 94123

Dear Mrs. Crapsey:

May this letter serve to verify the fact that I am familiar with the TALENT BANK and its involvement with the Community in the Mission District.

The programs in music and drama being provided supply a much needed cultural dimension for the children in the Mission District.

I hope that TALENT BANK will continue to conduct the educational lecture-demonstrations and opera participation programs in the parochial shcools.

Sincerely yours,

Manuel Frias
District Head Counselor
Foreign Student Placement

MF/db

on equal
opportunity
employer

September 12, 1977

Dear Mrs. Crapsey,

Over the past five years working with the Talent Bank, I have so often described to friends its importance to me and the fortunate singers such as I who have been financially and artistically supported by the foundation. What I should have done, long ago, was to write you, Mrs. Crapsey, to let you know what a vital function the Talent Bank serves to the many young singers in the Bay Area.

The San Francisco area is populated with a multitude of talented performers attempting to acquire the experience, repertoire and exposure so fundamental to a thriving career. Talent Bank has admirably fulfilled these needs in an area where the support funds and opportunities are often difficult to find. There are so many fine and highly respected singers in the Bay Area — Marianne Marsh, Donna Pederson, Steve Covington to name a few — who have worked for the Talent Bank throughout their careers and have looked to the Talent Bank to maintain their artistry and financially sustain their careers.

For me, the foundation has satisfied some very personal and unique needs. As a mother of two small children, an instructor of microbiology and a wife, my normal choice would be quite simple -- stop singing. Without the presence of the Talent Bank there would be no opportunities for me to continue to sing and singing is a very important part of me.

For all the the consuming hours at the expense of your own personal needs a simple thank you sounds quite empty. For myself, for all the countless singers before me and for all who will follow with the Talent Banks support, thank you.

Sincerely,

Mrs. Carol Drew
1075 Annerley Road
Piedmont, California
94610

UNIVERSITY OF CALIFORNIA, LOS ANGELES

BERKELEY · DAVIS · IRVINE · LOS ANGELES · RIVERSIDE · SAN DIEGO · SAN FRANCISCO   SANTA BARBARA · SANTA CRUZ

LOS ANGELES, CALIFORNIA 90024

October 12, 1977

Mrs. Alfred Crapsey
2100 Green Street
San Francisco, Calif. 94123

Dear Eddy:

Having been absent from San Francisco for quite some time Beta and I were happy to see you at the War Memorial Opera House and to hear that TALENT BANK is still flourishing.

I have expressed myself many times in the past in favor of TALENT BANK. This organization has made a most important contribution to professional opera on the West Coast. With so much young vocal talent hereabouts, and only a few opportunities to get performance experience and to be heard in public, TALENT BANK has filled an important niche and should receive full support from all who love opera and who would want to see our young American singers get to "first base". I, for one, am an enthusiastic supporter of the organization.

Yours cordially

Jan Popper

The Demonstration Workshops — Central Phase of the Opera Participation Project

After seeing Donizetti's *Rita,* we find students ready and eager to involve themselves in the second phase of the Opera Participation Project — the Demonstration Workshops. We stage three different demonstrations at each school site. Our goal is to instruct and excite students about music through interesting vocal demonstrations by our singers, lecturettes [*sic*] by our musical director, and student participation.

The three Demonstration Workshops in each school are designed as an involving and progressive learning experience:

- *The first workshop* teaches students about operatic singing: the different voice ranges; the nature of singing; how singers use their lungs, vocal chords, and diaphragms. Singers demonstrate various singing techniques, then show students how music is used to create mood and atmosphere. Students get a chance to guess the mood and content of arias in foreign languages, and then hear these arias sung in English.
- *The second workshop* in each school emphasizes the operatic recitative. Students learn what a recitative is, hear examples, and then create their own. Each student is assigned a role in a dramatic plot situation, and is asked to improvise both dialog and melody to fit that role.

Schools Participating in the 1978 Opera Participation Project

Anza School
Brandeis-Hillel
Corpus Christi School
Lycée Français
Mission Dolores School
St. Anthony's School
St. Charles' School
St. James School
St. John's Lutheran
St. Paul's Intermediate School
St. Philip's School
Zion Lutheran School

- *The third Demonstration Workshop* teaches students the basics of music — then introduces them to *Noye's Fludde.* They first learn about harmony, counterpoint, and canon by participating in "rounds" like "Row, row, row your boat." We break students into small groups for this exercise, each group under the direction of one of our singers. Students then learn the eight-part canon from *Noye's Fludde.* After performing the canon, they are taught how it fits into the opera. Students also get a chance to see a scale model of the stage set we use for the full-scale production of *Noye's Fludde.*

Our students, sensing the informal atmosphere of these Demonstration Workshops, respond warmly and enthusiastically with questions, ideas, and rapt attention. Their excitement is evidenced in their willingness to participate in improvisations. A great number enthusiastically volunteer to join the production of Britten's *Noye's Fludde,* third and final stage of the Opera Participation Project.

The Demonstration Workshops are the central learning experience of the Opera Participation Project. The musical exposure students get in these intimate workshops helps them appreciate music, and inspires them to join our full-scale performance of *Noye's Fludde.* In short, the Demonstration Workshops are the epitome of our instructional method: teaching through student participation is music.

The Talent Bank: Sponsors of the Project

The San Francisco Talent Bank, sponsor of the Opera Participation Project, is a nonprofit organization founded in 1959 under the auspices of the San Francisco Opera Guild. It is now administered by The Talent Bank Foundation. Our mission is twofold:

- *To assist young Bay Area singers in securing performance experience,* professional training, and income. We act as a referral agency

Vita
Rudolph Picardi

Rudolph Picardi, Music Director, received his early musical training in San Francisco studying the violin and piano as a child and later continuing his training in teaching and piano at the San Francisco Conservatory of Music, a pupil of Alexandre Raab and Charles Cooper. His early training as a conductor was under the tutelage of the late Gastone Usigli. Picardi is a graduate of the Vienna State Academy of Music, a conducting student of Hans Swarowsky. He has also attended the Music Academy in Munich, Germany, and the Cherubini Conservatory in Florence, Italy, where he was a composition student of Vito Frazzi and studied piano with Eriberto Scarlino.

While attending the Accademia Chigiana in Siena, Italy, he was a student of the conductors Paul van Kempen and Alceo Galliera. The Italian conductor, Franco Ferrara, with whom Picardi studied in Italy and in Hilversum, Holland, has had a strong influence in his musical training. Picardi was Assistant Conductor and Coach for the Vienna Chamber Opera and has also been on the musical staff of the San Francisco Opera's Merola Program for nine years. He has also served as Director of the Opera Workshops of the University of Texas and the University of Redlands. As Musical Director and Conductor, he has headed the San Bernardino Symphony and the Redlands University/Community Symphony.

for local artists, give free coaching for operatic roles, and sponsor performances of our singers. We pay our singers for every performance they give, including those connected with the Opera Participation Project.

- *To build an audience for all types of music in the San Francisco Bay Area.* We accomplish this through a number of sponsored performances for San Francisco youth. The Opera Participation Project is one such program.

Our artists are selected through public auditions held a number of times each year.

Professional guidance for our present and future activities comes from Mr. Rudolph Picardi. Mr. Picardi, our artistic director for the past four years, brings an enormous amount of experience to The Talent Bank program. His *vita* is enclosed.

Future Plans and Future Funding

Based on the continuing success of the Opera Participation Project, The Talent Bank has now undertaken an expansion program. Our plan includes:

- *Creating an apprentice program* to train managers, directors, and designers in opera production.
- *Expanding the Opera Participation Project* into other areas in Northern California.
- *Videotaping the Opera Participation Project.* Tapes would then be rented to schools we cannot reach with our normal three-phase program. This would supply us with income at the same time it helped us reach more disadvantaged students in both parochial and public schools.

We also plan to undertake a follow-up program in the thirteen schools we work with in 1978. It will be a logical extension of the *participatory* program emphasis. This program will involve a production of Aesop's Fables in which students create the sets, staging, costuming, props, and even the libretto! This program, unique in the United States, offers students an opportunity to work with several art forms in the creation of their own opera.

We are approaching a number of local foundations for support of our current program, and already have a commitment from the [   ] for $5,000. We plan to fund our expansion through a combination of foundation support and other proven fundraising techniques. These include: increasing the size of our membership through large mailings, enlarging our speaker's/singer's bureau, and staging more fundraising events.

Your support now will allow us to bring our expanded program to more parochial school students in years to come. It will also help many talented Bay Area singers receive invaluable training and performance experience.

Why Did This Proposal Succeed?

First of all, The Talent Bank tailored the proposal to the interests of and average grant amount given by each foundation they approached. This tailoring is apparent in a number of places:

The summary. This is where the specific request to *this* funder is made and explained. Note the fact that this request is for funding for the second phase of a three-phase project. Also note that the name of foundation "contact" is mentioned, along with the exact funding category under which the proposal is being submitted. (This information was gleaned by phone and in personal contacts with foundation staff).

The specific description of the Project Phase being funded. This important part of the proposal, the Demonstration Workshops — Central

Phase of the Opera Participation Project, highlights the benefits of the particular phase The Talent Bank is asking the funder to support (the second phase "demonstrations"). Because it is a self-contained, independent section of the proposal, it would be easy to replace it with another, describing a different phase of the project. This is a simple, striking method of quickly creating tailored proposals for different funders.

The budget. Note that the budget is broken down by phase, to correspond to the nature of the grant request. This could be converted into a request for $2,100 to bring the project into one school and the budget would then be broken down by costs per location.

Tailoring of this kind is important, especially when asking smaller funders for support. The "personal touch," your obvious concern with *their* needs, increases your fundability significantly.

Perhaps the most striking thing about The Talent Bank proposal is its exciting, involving text. Many of the techniques used here are suitable for any grant proposal. There are five of special note:

1. *Readability.* Note the short words, sentences, and paragraphs. The layout of the proposal is also excellent. It is double-spaced, has wide margins, and makes liberal use of headings, underlinings, and indentations. All these features make it enjoyable reading — which can be quite important when your proposal is competing with many applications that may have very appealing programs to offer.

2. *Emphasis on benefits.* There is little discussion of what The Talent Bank *does.* Much more space is devoted to the client benefits of the program: disadvantaged students exposed to the arts, and apprentice singers given a chance to perform and receive an income. The actual mechanics of the program are explained only after these benefits have been described and redescribed in the Summary and Need sections.

3. *Emphasis on unique features.* After a strong description of the project need, the three-phase Talent Bank project is described, "the Opera Participation Project." Note the emphasis on the

uniqueness of the planned opera-in-schools idea. The actual description of the three-phase project is "sandwiched" between two paragraphs emphasizing how it is different and better than others like it. This tells the funder, "This project is a good investment. By funding it, you'll be doing something really special, something you can do no other way."

4. *Discussion of future potential.* In addition to its excellent discussion of client benefits and unique features, this proposal also includes a powerful description of its future potential, outlined here under the heading "Future Plans and Future Funding." There are three notable features of this section of the application: (a) its description of what the project will evolve into after the grant ends, (b) its mention of funding already received, and (c) its brief discussion of plans for future support. This indicates that the project will survive and continue its good works long after the grant money is spent. To put it another way, The Talent Bank promises the funder that their investment will pay "dividends" long into the future. Most proposals include too much discussion about what their organization has done in the past, and the mechanics of what it plans to do with the funders' money. Few emphasize the two things that encourage giving: client benefits of the proposed project and potential for increased effectiveness after the grant ends.

5. *Endorsements.* Most good proposals, especially those from local projects, include endorsements from civic leaders and people in the field. What sets this proposal apart is its *endorsement letters from clients.* The letters from fifth-grade students who have experienced The Talent Bank Opera Participation Project attest to the project's benefit better than pages of dry prose. Whenever possible and appropriate, letters from people who have benefited from your work will strengthen your appeal, and increase your fundability.

These five features make this an outstanding proposal. They do much more than show the funder how the Opera Participation Project works. They illustrate the direct client benefits of the program, show its uniqueness, and point out its potential for future growth.

Applications

What can we conclude from the Opera Participation Project proposal? Whenever possible, include discussion of the following key points in your application:

- *Include the benefits to clients from the project, preferably stated in their own words.* You might consider including case histories or quotations in boxes within the text of your proposal.
- Make your proposal *visually attractive* and *readable.*
- Show the funder why you are *unique,* and better suited to do the job than anyone else.
- Show the funder *how you will survive after the grant ends,* and the good works that will continue into the future because of today's grant.

Finally, remember that the success of this proposal (like others discussed in THE GRANTS CLINIC) is due in great part to planning, research, and personal contact.

Small Arts Projects: Marjorie Strider Exhibition, "City Flow: A Work in Sound" - Liz Phillips, and Six Exhibitions by Contemporary Artists

Funded by: National Endowment for the Arts

Project Director: Ray Ring, Director of Exhibitions, Graduate Center Mall, Graduate School and University Center, City University of New York

Proposal prepared by: Ray Ring

NEA SUPPORT FOR THE SMALL ARTS PROJECT
by Ray Ring

The skepticism that accompanied the establishment of the National Endowment for the Arts has gradually dissipated, and most knowledgeable people now recognize the valuable contributions it has made to the arts, particularly in the mounting of impressive exhibits at well-established art museums across the country, and through support of major musical, theater, and opera companies.

What is less well-known, however, is the extent to which small museums and other institutions are supported by the Endowment.

The Graduate School and University Center houses many of the doctoral and research programs of the City University of New York, a publicly supported institution offering undergraduate and graduate education. The Center is located opposite the New York Public Library, on 42nd Street near Fifth Avenue in the historic old Aeolian Hall Building, which was renovated in 1969. The designers created a ground floor, walk-through mall that was to become the interface between the school's population and the New York City community. The Mall is a unique architectural space, and has been the recipient of many distinguished awards for design. It is open on either end, to 42nd or 43rd Streets, allowing an uninterrupted passage of pedestrian traffic in both directions. The Mall is a protected space equipped with a variable lighting system, a hanging system for paintings, and adjustable gates to provide security. In 1970 the first art exhibition was held; and by 1972 a continuous program of exhibitions had been established.

Not only is the Mall's architectural environment unique, but its audience is as well. Since pedestrians use the space to walk to and from 42nd Street, the exhibitions are seen by many who would not ordinarily be exposed to art in the course of their normal daily activities. It is estimated that approximately 3,000 people a day view the exhibitions in this space in the heart of New York's midtown business center.

Many different types of exhibitions were mounted in the space at first, but it soon became apparent that large works created by artists who dealt with architectural environment were the most suitable. Once the word went out that less established artists who worked in this way were being sought, we were approached by many artists who wanted to create works especially for the Mall. It became obvious that there was a need in New York City for an institution other than the commercially-oriented gallery or museum where artists who were not established personalities could show their works. We, therefore, joined the ranks of what are now called alternative spaces, where artists can realize their ideas and visions. The major problem with creating alternative spaces, however, is finding the money to support such projects.

By 1974 New York City was in financial crisis. The Mall program, which had originally been funded by the city, found its funds drying up. In 1973 an application to the New York State Council on the Arts was disqualified because of Mall was seen as part of a school, although it was in reality a community activity. At the suggestion of the Council, a nonprofit community funding group was formed, which was eligible for Council funds. The Council also advised turning to the National Endowment for the Arts as an additional funding source.

When we received the NEA guidelines it was apparent, much to our dismay, that although the Mall fit into many of the NEA categories generally, it did not qualify for any one specific program. In June of 1974 we made a trip to Washington to seek advice. The Endowment staff turned out to be most willing to help. They were aware of both the growing alternative space movement in New York and of artists' need for such a movement. Two such projects had already been funded in 1973 — The Clocktower and 112 Greene Street — but the guidelines were not clear-cut. The Mall was not a museum because it did not have a permanent collection of art objects. It was not financially secure enough to handle the Projects for Public Space; the Artist Services category was a possibility, but this program had very limited funds. We were not very encouraged.

In 1976 a major exhibition of artist Marjorie Strider's work was being planned in the Mall. This was to be in part a mini-retrospective of the artist's earlier works, and in part a work to be created especially for the space. We had some funds available to us from the New York State Council on the Arts, but not enough to cover the new piece. It seemed, unhappily, that the new work would have to be cancelled, when one of the artist's friends suggested applying to the NEA. We contacted the Workshop Program; the staff was well aware of Strider's excellent reputation and was indeed interested in funding the work. The application was sent in immediately and the Mall received its first NEA grant, $1,000.

The Strider exhibition was a great success. It received excellent coverage in the press and art journals. The NEA suggested that future applications be sent to the Museums Program under the category Aid to Special Exhibitions. Since the Endowment had now funded one successful project for us, it was more willing to show some flexibility about fitting the Mall into the guidelines of an established category.

We submitted the application shown here (Fig. 1) accompanied by illustrations of Marjorie Strider's work, reviews of previous exhibitions, and examples of posters, invitations, and flyers we had produced for other Mall exhibitions, and received a $1,000 grant.

With this encouragement we applied for two new projects. One was a commission for a new work by environmental-sound sculptor, Liz Phillips; the other was a program involving a series of six exhibitions, works created specifically for the Mall.

The Phillips commission was an expensive proposition. It required engineers, custom-made electronic mixers, and the rental of other complex sound equipment. We had already received some funds to begin the project, but $8,000 was needed to finish it. We discussed the proposal with an NEA staff member by telephone, and explained that we also wanted to present a large proposal but we were concerned about the two interfering with each other. The NEA was inter-

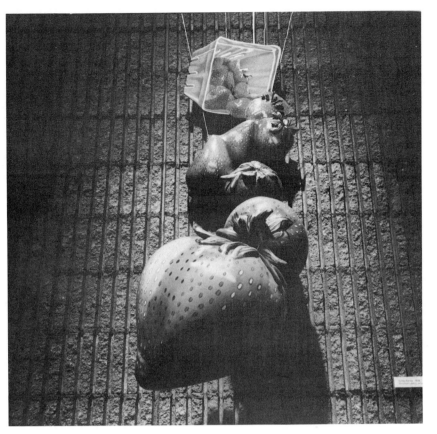

Spilled Berries (Strider, 1975), styrofoam, epoxy, oil paint, and steel rods, was included in the 1976 Strider exhibition in the Mall. Photo: Peter J. Harris.

ested in Ms. Phillips' work, which they knew well, and encouraged us to submit both applications.

The Phillips' proposal (Fig. 2) was also accompanied by biographical information about the artist, reviews of her past exhibitions, and photographs and documentation of our own past work. We were awarded the $8,000 we requested.

When we first visited NEA in 1974, our main objective was to obtain funding for the program of exhibitions involving works commissioned specifically for the Mall by up-and-coming artists. Two years later the proposal for this project was submitted. We requested $20,000 in funds over a two-year period, during which six different artists would be presented. In this way the grant would be for a program, not for

the exhibition of the work of one artist. We told NEA which artists we were considering for the series, but made it clear that they represented examples of the type of work we were interested in and not final selections.

This proposal (Fig. 3) was accompanied by photographs of past exhibitions including the Strider show, reviews of other exhibitions, posters, and invitations produced for past Mall shows, and photographs of the kind of works we wanted to present in the future.

The grant, which was funded in full, was right for our needs and philosophy, enabling us to help artists create new, exciting works which would be presented to a large and mixed audience.

At the time we first approached NEA in 1974, they were not familiar with our program, and the most important first step was to establish our

An untitled work by Peter Berg, constructed for the first Mall show in 1976, presented with support from the Aid to Special Exhibitions NEA grant. The top photograph shows the construction in progress — the wooden frame. The bottom photograph shows the completed work, after the frame was covered with plaster board.
Photos: Peter J. Harris.

The custom-made electronic control board built for Liz Phillips' 1977 Mall show, "City Flow: A Work in Sound."
Photo: Peter J. Harris.

credibility with the agency. Our first break-through was the request for funds to exhibit the work of Marjorie Strider, an artist in whom the Endowment was already interested. Once that exhibition was presented successfully, it opened the door to future NEA support.

In 1974 the Endowment had been sincerely interested in our concept, but when it came to the actual application, they (and we) had the problem of fitting our concept into the established NEA categories. An important and gratifying revelation during all our negotiations was that the Endowment does keep track of new developments in the art world, and is willing to show flexibility in interpreting its guidelines in order to support a worthwhile project. Until such a

circumstance occurs, i.e., until NEA is convinced of the merit of a proposal and the credibility of an organization as happened as a result of our Strider exhibition, they will be cautious. In the arts fields, funding needs are constantly changing; it is the nature of a creative endeavor that this be so. There is an inevitable lag between the types of funding requests coming into the NEA, and the guidelines for such funding. It is to the credit of the NEA that it does keep up with such changes, and constantly updates its guidelines. It is also to their credit that the informed and interested staff is willing to make the effort to assist applicants whose projects they approve, even though a particular proposal might not *exactly* fit a current category.

NEA-3 (Rev.)

I. APPLICANT ORGANIZATION (name and address with zip)
Friends of the Graduate Center
Mall
33 West 42 Street
New York, New York 10036

PROJECT GRANT APPLICATION
NATIONAL ENDOWMENT FOR THE ARTS
WASHINGTON, D. C. 20506

II. PROGRAM UNDER WHICH SUPPORT IS REQUESTED
Workshop Program - Visual Arts

III. PERIOD OF SUPPORT REQUESTED

| START | March | 1 | 1976 | END | April | 15 | 1976 |
| | MONTH | DAY | YEAR | | MONTH | DAY | YEAR |

IV. SUMMARY OF PROJECT DESCRIPTION (COMPLETE IN SPACE PROVIDED. DO NOT CONTINUE ON ADDITIONAL PAGES.)

Continuing our efforts to bring new art to the public, created specifically for our exhibition space at the Graduate Center, we are presenting the work of Marjorie Strider. Ms. Strider will exhibit many small and large-scale works, some of which have not been shown for several years. She will also create a major new foam piece for the space. The work she will create deals with the architectural environment of the Mall. The Mall is a pedestrian arcade connecting 42nd and 43rd Streets in midtown Manhattan. The City University Graduate Center with the aid of the New York State Council on the Arts and our corporate neighbors, have been sponsoring artists to do works in our public space for the last five years. We are requesting aid from the National Endowment for the Arts to help meet the expenses for this exhibition.

V. ESTIMATED NUMBER OF PERSONS EXPECTED TO BENEFIT FROM THIS PROJECT approximately 2000 per day

VI. SUMMARY OF ESTIMATED COSTS (RECAPITULATION OF BUDGET ITEMS ON PAGES 2 AND 3)

TOTAL COSTS OF PROJECT (rounded to nearest ten dollars)

A. DIRECT COSTS

SALARIES & WAGES	$ 1666.66
FRINGE BENEFITS	
SUPPLIES & MATERIALS	1000.00
TRAVEL	
SPECIAL	
OTHER	1240.00
TOTAL DIRECT COSTS	4056.66
B. INDIRECT COSTS	$ 894.42
TOTAL PROJECT COSTS	$ 4951.08

VII. TOTAL AMOUNT REQUESTED FROM NEA $ 1000.00

VIII. ORGANIZATION TOTAL FISCAL ACTIVITY

	ACT. MOST RECENT FISCAL PD	EST. FOR NEXT FISCAL PD.
A. EXPENSES	1. $ 195,850	2. $ 250,525
B. REVENUES GRANTS & CONTRIBUTIONS	1. $ 195,850	2. $ 250,525

DO NOT WRITE IN THIS SPACE

Est. of prior yearly project(s) [1] [2] [3] [4]   PYS $ _____   CPS $ _____   Audit Report [1] [2]

(OVER)

X. BUDGET BREAKDOWN OF TOTAL ESTIMATED COSTS OF PROJECT AS SUMMARIZED ON PAGE 1 (continued)

4. Special (list each item separately)
DETAIL NOT REQUIRED WHEN REQUESTING $10,000 OR LESS ON A PROJECT OF $20,000 AND LESS.

	Amount
	$
Total Special	$

5. Other (list each major type separately)
THIS SECTION MUST BE COMPLETED ON EVERY APPLICATION

	Amount
Printing	$ 300.00
Mailing	200.00
Advertising	200.00
Transportation of Art	300.00
Phone	15.00
Misc. Display Expenses	75.00
Artist's Honorarium	150.00
Total Other	$ 1240.00

B. Indirect Costs
1. Rate established by attached indirect cost allocation plan

	Amount
Rate ____ % Base $ _____	$
2. Rate established by attached rate negotiation agreement with Federal agency	
Rate 53 % of S and W Base $ 1666.66	$ 894.42

X. CONTRIBUTIONS, GRANTS, AND REVENUES (FOR THIS PROJECT)

A. Contributions
1. Cash (do not include direct donations to NEA)

	Amount
Graduate School and University Center - City University of New York	$ 2951.08

2. In-kind Contributions (list each major item)

Graduate School and University Center - City University of New York (pro-rated rent and guard service) - this figure does not appear in total	[$10,625.00]
Total Contributions	$

B. Grants (do not list anticipated grant from NEA)

	Amount
New York State Council on the Arts	$ 1000.00
Total Grants	$

C. Revenues

	Amount
	$
Total Revenues	$
Total Contributions, Grants, and Revenues	$3951.08

Fig. 1. Application submitted to NEA for support of the Strider exhibition in 1976.

PROJECT GRANT APPLICATION
NATIONAL ENDOWMENT FOR THE ARTS
WASHINGTON, D. C. 20506

OMB 128-R0005

NEA-3 (Rev.)

I. APPLICANT ORGANIZATION (name and address with zip)

Friends of The Graduate Center Mall
33 West 42 Street
New York, New York 10036

II. PROGRAM UNDER WHICH SUPPORT IS REQUESTED

Aid to Special Exhibitions

III. PERIOD OF SUPPORT REQUESTED

START July 1 76   END June 30 77
MONTH DAY YEAR   MONTH DAY YEAR

IV. SUMMARY OF PROJECT DESCRIPTION COMPLETE IN SPACE PROVIDED. DO NOT CONTINUE ON ADDITIONAL PAGES.

An interactive sound environment created specifically for the Graduate Center Mall, is being designed by artist Liz Phillips. Ms. Phillips has been experimenting in sound and space since the late 1960's. Her work has been exhibited at many galleries and universities including Artists Space, The Kitchen, the State University of New York at Albany, the Everson Museum in Syracuse and the Wadsworth Atheneum in Connecticut.

The sound installations she creates involve the presence and movement and/or the absence and stillness of the audience in areas of space. Motion within defined areas is radiated and detected by radio frequency fields to voltage regulators. Voltages will first reflect movement, and then to change pitch, duration, timbre or loudness of sounds that are electronically generated or processed. The interaction of people within the environment determines the combinations of forms within the sound-space. In this way, through both sound and physical activity, an installation is composed and realized for both the audience and the artist.

One of the most exciting aspects of this installation at the Mall is that the space is designed specifically for continuous movement of people. Unlike a closed gallery, with limited audience participation, the Mall was created as a throughfare for thousands of workers and visitors in transit each day in midtown. It is this continuous feedback situation tuned to the street traffic sounds which make an exhibition of this magnitude very exciting for the public and the artist.

V. ESTIMATED NUMBER OF PERSONS EXPECTED TO BENEFIT FROM THIS PROJECT

VI. SUMMARY OF ESTIMATED COSTS (RECAPITULATION OF BUDGET ITEMS ON PAGES 2 AND 3)

A. DIRECT COSTS	TOTAL COSTS OF PROJECT (rounded to nearest ten dollars)
SALARIES & WAGES	$ 4737
FRINGE BENEFITS	947
SUPPLIES & MATERIALS	5000
TRAVEL	
SPECIAL	
OTHER	14835
TOTAL DIRECT COSTS	$ 25519
B. INDIRECT COSTS	2510
TOTAL PROJECT COSTS	$ 28029

VII. TOTAL AMOUNT REQUESTED FROM NEA $ 8000

VIII. ORGANIZATION TOTAL FISCAL ACTIVITY

	ACT. MOST RECENT FISCAL PD	EST. FOR NEXT FISCAL PD
A. EXPENSES	1. $ 195,850	2. $ 250,525
B. REVENUES GRANTS & CONTRIBUTIONS	1. $ 195,850	2. $ 250,525

DO NOT WRITE IN THIS SPACE

End of prior year(s) project(s)   1 2 3 4   PYS $ _____   CPS $ _____   Audit Report 1 2

(OVER)

IX. BUDGET BREAKDOWN OF TOTAL ESTIMATED COSTS OF PROJECT AS SUMMARIZED ON PAGE 1

A. Direct Costs

1. Salaries and Wages

DETAIL NOT REQUIRED WHEN REQUESTING $10,000 OR LESS ON A PROJECT OF $20,000 AND LESS

Title and/or Type of Personnel	No. of Personnel	Annual or Average Salary Range	% of Time Devoted to this Project	Amount
Exhibition Coordinator	1	$ 15,000.	10	$ 1,500
Asst. Exhibition Co.	1	10,000.	10	1,000
Graphic Designer	1	15,000.	2.5	375
Public Relations	1	14,000.	2.5	350
Graphic Facilities	3	14,000. per person	1	420
Administration	1	15,000.	1	150
Engineer Services	1	30,000.	1	300
Photographer	1	13,000.	1	130
Music Coordinator	1	12,000.	2.5	300
Secretary	1	8,500.	2.5	212
		Total Salaries and Wages		$ 4,737
		add fringe benefits		947
		Total Salaries and Wages including fringe benefits		$ 5,684

2. Supplies and Materials (list each major type separately)

DETAIL NOT REQUIRED WHEN REQUESTING $10,000 OR LESS ON A PROJECT OF $20,000 AND LESS.

	Amount
Electronic Components (custom made) and rental of electronic equipment	$ 5,000
Total Supplies and Materials	$ 5,000

3. Travel

DETAIL NOT REQUIRED WHEN REQUESTING $10,000 OR LESS ON A PROJECT OF $20,000 AND LESS.

Transportation of Personnel

No. of Travelers	from	to		Amount
				$
		Total transportation of personnel		$

Subsistence

No. of Travelers	no. of days	daily rate	Amount
			$
		Total Subsistence	$
		Total Travel	$

4. BUDGET BREAKDOWN OF TOTAL ESTIMATED COSTS OF PROJECT AS SUMMARIZED ON PAGE 1 (continued)	
4. Special (list each item separately) *DETAIL NOT REQUIRED WHEN REQUESTING $10,000 OR LESS ON A PROJECT OF $20,000 OR LESS*	Amount
N.A.	$
Total Special	$

5. Other (list each major type separately) *THIS SECTION MUST BE COMPLETED ON EVERY APPLICATION*	Amount
Artists fee $100 per day 20 days.	$ 2000
Engineer (electronic consultant) fee	1500
Mailing	250
Advertising	200
Transport of equipment	100
Phone	15
Insurance	145
Rent, Guards & Maintenance	10625
Total Other	$ 14835

8. Indirect Costs	Amount
1. Rate established by attached indirect cost allocation plan	$
Rate _____ % Base $ _____	
2. Rate established by attached rate negotiation agreement with Federal agency	
Rate 53 % S & W Base $ 4737	$ 2510

X. CONTRIBUTIONS, GRANTS, AND REVENUES *(FOR THIS PROJECT)*	
A. Contributions	Amount
1. Cash (do not include direct donations to NEA)	
Individual and Corporate Contribution	$ 833
2. In-kind Contributions (list each major item)	
City University Graduate Center	18530
Total Contributions	$

B. Grants (do not list anticipated grant from NEA)	Amount
NYSCA	$ 666
Total Grants	$

C. Revenues	Amount
	$
Total Revenues	$
Total Contributions, Grants, and Revenues	$ 20029

Fig. 2. Application for support of artist Liz Phillips' exhibition, "City Flow: A Work in Sound."

IX. BUDGET BREAKDOWN OF TOTAL ESTIMATED COSTS OF PROJECT AS SUMMARIZED ON PAGE 1

A. Direct Costs
1. Salaries and Wages

DETAIL NOT REQUIRED WHEN REQUESTING $10,000 OR LESS ON A PROJECT OF $20,000 AND LESS.

Title and/or Type of Personnel	No. of Personnel	Annual or Average Salary Range	% of Time Devoted to this Project	Amount
Exhibition Coordinator	1	$ 15,000	36% over 2 years	$ 10,800
Asst. Exhibition Co.	1	10,000	36% over 2 years	7,200
Graphic Designer	1	15,000	7.5% over 2 yrs	2,250
Public Relations	1	14,000	7.5% over 2 yrs	2,100
Graphic Facilities	3	14,000 per person	3.75% over 2 yrs	3,150
Administration	1	15,000	3.75% over 2 yrs	1,125
Engineer Service	1	30,000	3.75% over 2 yrs	2,250
Photographer	1	13,000	3.75% over 2 yrs	975
Music Coordinator	1	12,000	7.5% over 2 yrs	1,800
Secretary	1	8,500	7.5% over 2 yrs	1,275
Total Salaries and Wages				$ 32,925
add fringe benefits				$ 6,585
Total Salaries and Wages including fringe benefits				$ 39,510

2. Supplies and Materials (list each major type separately)
DETAIL NOT REQUIRED WHEN REQUESTING $10,000 OR LESS ON A PROJECT OF $20,000 AND LESS.

	Amount
$1166 per artist per exhibition	$ 7,000
Total Supplies and Materials	$ 7,000

3. Travel
DETAIL NOT REQUIRED WHEN REQUESTING $10,000 OR LESS ON A PROJECT OF $20,000 AND LESS.

Transportation of Personnel

No. of Travelers	from	to	Amount
6 artists		New York	$ 1,500
Total transportation of personnel			$ 1,500

Subsistence

No. of Travelers	no. of days	daily rate	
6 artists	5 per artist	$50.00	$ 1,500
Total Subsistence			$ 1,500
Total Travel			$ 3,000

NEA-3 (Rev.)

I. APPLICANT ORGANIZATION (name and address with zip)
Friends of the Graduate Center Mall
33 West 42 Street
New York, New York 10036

PROJECT GRANT APPLICATION
NATIONAL ENDOWMENT FOR THE ARTS
WASHINGTON, D. C. 20506

II. PROGRAM UNDER WHICH SUPPORT IS REQUESTED
Aid to Special Exhibitions
Museum Program

III. PERIOD OF SUPPORT REQUESTED
START July 1 1976 END June 30 1978

IV. SUMMARY OF PROJECT DESCRIPTION (COMPLETE IN SPACE PROVIDED. DO NOT CONTINUE ON ADDITIONAL PAGES.)

The Graduate Center of the City University of New York is expanding the scope of our exhibition program in the Mall, beyond giving the public a sampling of the kind of art being created today, by displaying artists existing works, from a variety of fields. We have in the past been fortunate enough to commission artists to create works specifically for their exhibit at the Mall. George Trakas designed a new work for his show last year, and Marjorie Strider has agreed to do a new foam piece in the Mall for her show in February, 1976. In recent years, as more artists exhibit in the Mall and become aware of the potential of the arcade as a challenging architectural space, more and more artists have expressed interest in creating works in their medium, designed with the Mall in mind.

At this time, we would like to formalize a program of six exhibitions over the next two years, involving artists working in a variety of media, creating works specifically for this unusual environmental space. Our funding needs involve: announcing the project to the art community through published announcements in art journals and mailings; reviewing the proposals to evaluate them on the basis of financial feasibility, physical applicability to the space, and variety of media; and execution of the exhibits (each would run for a two-month period), including transportation for the artist's materials and tools, honorariums for the artists, misc. installation expenses, announcements, publicity as well as two catalogs of the installations for each season. Selection of the exhibitions would be made by the Mall Committee, consisting of faculty and students from the Art History Doctoral Program, Exhib. Coordinators & artists in visual & performing arts.

V. ESTIMATED NUMBER OF PERSONS EXPECTED TO BENEFIT FROM THIS PROJECT 2,000 per day

VI. SUMMARY OF ESTIMATED COSTS (RECAPITULATION OF BUDGET ITEMS ON PAGES 2 AND 3)

A. DIRECT COSTS — TOTAL COSTS OF PROJECT (rounded to nearest ten dollars)

SALARIES & WAGES	$ 32,925.
FRINGE BENEFITS	6,585.
SUPPLIES & MATERIALS	7,000.
TRAVEL	3,000.
SPECIAL	
OTHER	74,800.
TOTAL DIRECT COSTS	$ 124,310.
B. INDIRECT COSTS	17,450.
TOTAL PROJECT COSTS	$ 141,760.

VII. TOTAL AMOUNT REQUESTED FROM NEA $ 20,000.

VIII. ORGANIZATION TOTAL FISCAL ACTIVITY

	ACT. MOST RECENT FISCAL PD.	EST. FOR NEXT FISCAL PD.
A. EXPENSES	1. $ 195,850.	2. $ 250,525.
B. REVENUES GRANTS & CONTRIBUTIONS	1. $ 195,850.	2. $ 250,525.

DO NOT WRITE IN THIS SPACE

Eval. of prior year(s) project(s) 1 2 3 4   PYS $ ___   CPS $ ___   Audit Report 1 2

(OVER)

IX. BUDGET BREAKDOWN OF TOTAL ESTIMATED COSTS OF PROJECT AS SUMMARIZED ON PAGE 1 (continued)

4. Special (list each item separately)
DETAIL NOT REQUIRED WHEN REQUESTING $10,000 OR LESS ON A PROJECT OF $20,000 AND LESS.

	Amount
	$
Total Special	$

5. Other (list each major type separately)
THIS SECTION MUST BE COMPLETED ON EVERY APPLICATION.

	Amount
Artists Fee $1000 per exhibition	$ 6,000
Mailing	700
Advertising	1,500
Transportation of Materials	1,000
Telephone	100
Insurance	1,750
Rent, Guards and Maintenance	63,750
Total Other	$74,800

B. Indirect Costs

1. Rate established by attached indirect cost allocation plan

	Amount
Rate _____ % Base $	$
2. Rate established by attached rate negotiation agreement with Federal agency	
Rate _53_ % of S & W Base $32,925	$17,450

X. CONTRIBUTIONS, GRANTS, AND REVENUES *(FOR THIS PROJECT)*

A. Contributions

1. Cash (do not include direct donations to NEA)

	Amount
Corporate and Individual Contribution	$ 5,000

2. In-kind Contributions (list each major item)

Graduate School and University Center of the City University of	107,760
New York	
Total Contributions	$ 112,760

B. Grants (do not list anticipated grant from NEA)

	Amount
New York State Council on the Arts	$ 5,000
Total Grants	$ 5,000

C. Revenues

	Amount
Sale of Catalogs	$ 2,000
Rental of Exhibition	2,000
Total Revenues	$ 4,000
Total Contributions, Grants, and Revenues	$ 121,760

Fig. 3. Application for $20,000 for Aid to Special Exhibitions submitted to the NEA Museum Program. These exhibitions involved the works of several up-and-coming artists.

On The March

Funded by: The Film Fund

Project Director: Lucy Winer, Independent Filmmaker

Proposal prepared by: Lucy Winer

THE FILM FUND: WHAT IT IS AND WHAT IT DOES
by Terry Lawler

The Film Fund, which was established in 1977, is committed to assisting independent filmmakers, distributors, and community organizers in the production and use of films, slide shows, and videotapes as creative and educational instruments for social change. Through tax-deductible contributions from individuals and through support from foundations and the film industry, the Fund helps individual film artists and the growing number of community-based institutions that use film to give wider visibility to social issues.

Visual media, particularly mass-distributed theatrical films and television, exert an exceptional influence on public opinion in our society. Increasingly, these media are dominated by large multinational interests that are generally inaccessible and unaccountable to the public. The Film Fund is the only privately established funding aid for visual media projects on contemporary — and often controversial — issues like nuclear policy, racial and sexual justice, labor struggles, southern African liberation, environmental abuse, and economic democracy.

The directors, staff, and supporters of The Film Fund believe that independently produced visual media should be more widely supported because, in a powerful and unique way, they can support social change by providing the public with viewpoints and visions often ignored by the commercial media.

Specifically, The Film Fund gives priority to documentary and fiction films that take hard looks at pressing social issues, that try to expand peoples' perceptions of what is real or possible, that encourage activity rather than passivity. We are interested in films that respect the intelligence of viewers, combine intellectual clarity with skillful and imaginative filmmaking, and that will reach a broad audience. Following are some of the themes with which the The Film Fund is concerned. (The list is meant to be suggestive, not exclusive.)

Racial and national discrimination
Women's rights
Urban and rural health care, unemployment, poverty
Consumer rights
Work and the labor movement
Civil liberties and constitutional rights

Terry Lawler is Acting Director of The Film Fund, Inc., and was coordinator of the 1980 grants program.

The Film Fund: 1980 Grants Awarded

The Board of Directors of The Film Fund approved the following grants at its Spring 1980 meeting, held May 22–23 in New York City:

1. *An Interest in Life*, by Mirra Bank. A dramatization of the daily efforts of economically and socially disenfranchized women to achieve dignified survival in a society that seems to validate dominance and material wealth over all else. $4550.
2. *The Atomic Cafe*, by Jayne Loader, Kevin Rafferty and Pierce Rafferty. A feature documentary which examines the history of the "atomic age" as it has been reflected in American media and culture. $4550.
3. *Clarence and Angel*, by Robert Gardner. A dramatic film about the failure of the public school system in teaching black and hispanic children, and one student's attempt to teach another to read. $7280.
4. *A Day in the Life of the Dollar*, by Paula Longendyke. An educational film that interviews qualified economists critical of the U.S. economy and uses their analysis to construct a model to explain cash flow and the need to democratize the economy. $4550.
5. *Farmworker Women Slide Show*, by Adela Serrano. A program depicting the special problems and struggles of farmworker women in Maricopa County, Arizona and San Luis, Mexico. $1221.
6. *First Run Features*, by Stewart Bird and Deborah Shaffer. Assistance towards the establishment of a distribution company specializing in independently produced feature films. $4550 (loan).
7. *Housekeepers*, by Cara DeVito, Lillian Jimenez and Jeffrey Kleinman. A documentary depicting the process of organizing the first Household Workers Union through the lives of five key characters, black and latin women residing in the South Bronx. $4550.
8. *Independent Feature Project*, by Joy Pereths. The Independent Feature Project is a service and advocacy organization dedicated to stimulating new funding and distribution for socially important American independent feature films. $2861.
9. *KKK Film*, by Thomas Sigel and Pamela Yates. A documentary on the resurgence of the Ku Klux Klan and the implications of this development. $4550.
10. *La Operacion*, by Ana Maria Garcia. A documentary about the problem of massive, forced sterilization of Puerto Rican women. $6825.
11. *Latinas*, by Sylvia Morales. A one-hour documentary about the ways in which Chicana women are perceived and shaped by institutions both inside and outside their culture. $5460.
12. *Media, Messages and Networking*, by Katherine Kinsella. A three-day series of intensive workshops designed to introduce basic communications methods to progressive public interest, labor and community organizations. $1365.
13. *National Conference of Black Film and Video Artists*, by Terry Williams and Warrington Hudlin. A national conference to be held in New York City in the summer of 1980 consisting of five days of working sessions on problems and issues of concern to Black media artists. $4550.
14. *Nuclear Weapons and Power Slide Show*, by David Goodman, NARMIC. A slide show describing the nuclear fuel cycle, the nature of nuclear weapons and nuclear power, the connections between them and their impact on people around the world with an examination of alternatives to present policies. $2275.
15. *Out of Order*, by Robert Epstein. A film documenting the emergence of the gay and lesbian community as a political force as seen through a specific series of events in California. $4550.

(*continued*)

The Film Fund: 1980 Grants Awarded, Continued

16. *The Roxbury Response,* by Alonzo Rico Speight. A 60-minute documentary about racial violence and rights violations by the police in the Roxbury section of Boston. $5460.
17. *The Teamster Film Project,* by Gail Sullivan. A film document on the Teamsters for a Democratic Union. $4550.
18. *To Claim the Future,* by Dave Davis. A documentary on U.S. foreign policy towards Africa, particularly southern Africa. $6825.
19. *Vieques,* by Marcos Zurinaga. A film about the struggle between the people of the island of Vieques and the U.S. Navy, a dramatic conflict underlying the colonial domination of Puerto Rico by the United States. $6825.
20. *When I Get Out,* by Carlos Penichet. This docudrama follows a young Chicano as he looks at the world around him, with its discrimination, unemployment, conflict in values and the day to day contradictions which he shares with his peers who are part of a Chicano gang. $4550.
21. *Women Coal Miners,* by Elizabeth Barret. A film on women coal miners, their reasons for entering this workforce and the problems they encounter. $4550.
22. *Women and Pornography,* by Lucy Winer. A 30-minute documentary on the relationship between sexism and pornography and the anti-pornography organizing of the feminist movement. $5915.
23. *Workers and Technology,* by Lawrence Daressa, California Newsreel. A film designed for use by trade unionists and teachers to reevaluate traditional assumptions about technological development and its relation to democratic participation in the process of technological change. $4550.

Total Grants Awarded: $106,912

Environmental issues
Structuring and restructuring the economy
Changing international systems
Community and workplace organizing

The following interview, conducted between Cheryll Greene, a New York-based writer and editor, and this writer, appeared in the Summer 1980 *News from The Film Fund.* It is reprinted here as a further effort to describe the criteria used by The Film Fund in making its grants decisions. Following the interview is an Application for a Media Project Grant that we feel ably illustrates our requirements.

Would you describe the decision-making process for awarding grants?

We received 440 proposals this year and divided them among three staff people for preliminary evaluation — Jennifer Lawson, myself, and Barbara Zheutlin in our California office. We reviewed them and eliminated all but 144 of them, based on whether they were inside the guidelines — some were not, and they were easy to eliminate — and whether they were within the priorities of The Film Fund. Even though a project could be defined as a social issue film, it would not be a priority for us if there was no organizing around the issue, if it wasn't going to reach a wide audience, and if it didn't seem likely the filmmaker would be able to get additional money to complete the project.

Let me just interrupt here. How do you determine that, because there's not a lot of organizing around an issue at this time, it's not an important issue?

We don't say it's not an important issue, just that it's not a priority for The Film Fund.

The Fund was established to help get media to community groups that are organizing around issues. It doesn't have to be national organizing, it could be local. But the project has to fit within the priorities we have at this time.

Another thing: We might get a proposal for, say, an hour-long film budgeted at $150,000; the filmmaker hasn't raised any money except for his/her own volunteer contribution, and he's/she's looking for the first $10,000. And, the subject is one we can't see will attract a lot of additional money unless the filmmaker really hustles. That proposal would have a very low priority, because that film may never get made.

Is that because the filmmaker is looking for the first batch of money or because you believe the project as a whole is not fundable?

It's the combination of both. If it's, for instance, an anti-nuke film, we know money is available from many sources, and the film has a chance of going somewhere, so we might be the ones to put in the first $10,000. But if it's a more obscure topic, and we don't know of any way the person can raise money, and he or she is not putting out a lot of effort to do so, then it's not likely we'd give him the first $10,000. If that person reapplied in a year or two, having raised $70,000, and was looking for completion money, his or her chances would be much greater.

The other thing the staff considers when evaluating proposals is the filmmaker's ability. If it's a brand-new filmmaker, we'll want to know who he or she's working with to help iron out problems.

If a project meets most of the criteria I've outlined, the staff passes on the proposal to the screening panel. The panel has a harder job than the staff, because the proposals they see meet all or most of the criteria, and they have to evaluate higher and lower priorities.

At the same time, we send to the board of directors and to the screening panel a list of all the proposals received, with the project title, project director's name, and the one-sentence project description we ask for on each application. The board and the panel have the option, then, of recalling any proposal the staff has eliminated. And so does the rest of the staff. In other words, the board and the panel get a list of every proposal, broken down into recommended ones and eliminated ones. They can then recall any eliminated proposals. Usually, about ten projects a year are recalled. This procedure is the check against mistakes by the three staff members who first read all the proposals.

Then, the nine-member screening panel is divided into four subcommittees of two or three people each. And the proposals are divided into four groups, based on the issues they address. Each subcommittee gets about a quarter of the proposals, or about 38 each, and they rate them, and each member chooses seven to 12 best out of the 38. They may all end up choosing different ones, and in fact this almost happened this year — there were very few overlaps.

This is prior to looking at any footage?

Yes, each panelist rates his or her top seven to 12 based on the proposal. They also give me a list of proposals they feel they can't evaluate without seeing footage, even if they're not in their top seven to 12. Then we write for footage to all the applicants whose work has been recommended by the panel for screening. This makes about 80 semifinalists, plus an additional 15 who can't be evaluated without footage.

After the semifinalists are chosen, each one is interviewed by one of the panelists. They're asked for any necessary clarification of their proposal, about fund raising strategies, budget changes, affiliations with community groups, and other matters.

Then we inform the board and each subcommittee of the panel who the semifinalists are. We ask them for any additional information they may have about the projects and if they want to recall any that weren't chosen. At this point, we add those for which footage

With Babies and Banners: Story of the Women's Emergency Brigade, was a project of the Women's Labor History Film Project, Lorraine Gray, director. This 45-minute documentary on the important role women played in the Great General Motors Sit-Down Strike of 1937 received a $3000 distribution grant from The Film Fund in 1978. Photo: *With Babies and Banners,* distributed by New Day Films.

has been requested. Then the whole screening panel meets to view the footage and make final recommendations to the board. About 100 out of the 154 proposals originally recommended by staff to screening panel were actually screened this year (1980).

After the panel makes its final recommendations to the board, the board is asked again for questions or recalls. This year, a few more projects were recalled at this stage. Those, along with the panel's final recommendations, were voted on by the board at its May meeting. Also, they considered 16 projects the screening panel didn't consider — special projects

such as festivals, conferences, publications. Three of these were funded.

Many applicants, who don't make the semi-finals, are upset that you don't look at their footage. Is The Film Fund trying to remedy this in any way?

We're recommending to the board, for next year, that we request footage from all of the projects recommended by the staff to the screening panel, and that at least two staff people look at all of the footage. We have a volunteer screening panel, and it doesn't seem possible to ask them to look at so much footage, and it doesn't seem they'd ever have the time to screen over 150 projects — they meet here in New York for only two days. As it was, it was extremely taxing for them to have to look at 90 or 100. Another possibility might be to ask an outside group of people, who were not considering the proposals, to do a qualitative evaluation of the footage or something like that. But that doesn't seem to be a very effective method if the proposals haven't been read.

We're also considering, for next year, having each of the four screening panel subcommittees select, by consensus, ten semifinalists, instead of each individual member selecting seven to 12. That would cut the total number to 40, and with the recalls, it would probably end up being about 50. That's a reasonable 25 projects a day to screen — it would give the panel significant time to look at all of the footage and take a second look if necessary. If we do this, we'll probably ask each semifinalist for more footage than we do now.

Have you considered enlarging the screening panel so that it can in some way look at more footage?

What we've asked ourselves is, is it better to look at more footage or have the whole panel look at the footage that's really under consideration. We used to have two screening panels — one in the   east and one out west — but that didn't work well. They never met all together, and the combined panels never saw all the footage under consideration. Each recommended for its region, and then the board of directors considered their recommendations and made its decision, but without actually looking at the footage. So it seems fairer to me to have the panel look at everything together and make recommendations to the board. As it is, there's never going to be enough money to fund all of the good films. At least, with the nine-person panel, we feel the process is fair and representative and that we can stand behind it, because they came to their decisions together in a democratic way.

Another thing: We could have the panel meet more days to look at more footage, but we can't ask people to meet more days for free. We could pay panelists $75 a day, like NEA does, but that's still not much in terms of the actual work — voluminous reading and intensive screenings. If we were paying for more than two days, the amount would start to come to as much money as we could give to another film. So I don't know if it's really cost-effective.

Many people have complained about the application form. Are you planning to change it, too?

The application has proven to be much too much work, considering the return even for grantees and considering the small number of people who get money as a result of it. Some of the applications are so long, it may cost $20, $30, even $50 for applicants to just reproduce them. Following the screening panel meeting this year, staff and panel evaluated the form, and the panel all felt they could have gotten as much real important information from, say, one or two pages of summary.

They also thought it important to have a fill-in-the blank budget. The applicants do a lot of work, and some are more specific than we need them to be. Enough of the panel and staff are filmmakers so that we can tell if a budget is realistic.

So, we want a more fill-in-the-blank kind of application form and just two or so typed pages of project summary. We'll see how that works next year. Meanwhile, we hope people will send us their criticisms of the old form and suggestions for a new form.

Another part of the form that's been criticized is the guidelines.

Yes, some applicants have said they aren't clear about how a film must be used in an organizing context. Others didn't understand what we meant by "sponsored" projects. Some thought that if they were working with a community group, we wouldn't fund their film. That's not true at all.

Would you define "sponsored" project?

It's a project an organization is sponsoring in order to promote itself or its work or to get new members exclusive of other groups doing the same work. A project can be about an organization, and that organization can be working with the filmmaker, but if it's going to be used to exclusively promote that group and not to deal with the issue and raise people's consciousness about it, then we wouldn't support it.

Another area that needs clarifying is about submitting footage. Some filmmakers who became semifinalists this year sent us previous works when footage was requested, although their proposals were for works-in-progress. In next year's guidelines, it'll be stipulated that the actual work under consideration must be submitted.

How do you determine whether a filmmaker's affiliation with a particular community group or movement is what he or she says it is?

The only way we have of determining it, unless someone on the panel knows the group from experience, is through the interview with the filmmaker – and this would come up only with the semifinalists. Usually the panelist gets a sense of the applicant's involvement from his or her responses.

If someone has not been working directly with a community group, but it's clear that certain issues are very important in the area the filmmaker comes from, and that a film would be used by activists, is that sufficient?

Sure, you don't have to be working directly with a group. We try to encourage contact

Hito Hata, chronicles the contributions and hardships of Japanese people living in the United States. The first docudrama in the *Nation Builders* series, it received a grant from The Film Fund in 1979. Photo: Visual Communications.

between filmmakers and activist groups, but it's not a prerequisite.

Could you talk a little more about using the fundraising ability of an applicant as one of the main criteria for funding? It seems like a kind of vicious cycle: We won't hire you without experience, but we won't give you the opportunity to get any, either.

Some people may think that The Film Fund was established to help filmmakers, but that's not actually its purpose. It is to get media to community groups that are organizing. If you look at it from that side, to invest, say $10,000 in a project that may never happen would go counter to the organization's goal, which is to get the media out there. If a filmmaker doesn't seem to be committed to the kind of long-term work that is necessary to raise money for a project, and if it doesn't seem likely that it will be easily funded, then The Film Fund probably won't fund that project. We've gotten proposals in different years for the same $10,000 start-up money. Obviously, that applicant hasn't explored all the alternatives. The screening panel's not going to react favorably to the project because they know if the filmmaker isn't behind it all the way, then chances of finishing it are not great.

Of course, sometimes we take risks. If the panel feels the issue is really crucial, if the filmmaker has demonstrated real commitment, even if other fundraising steps haven't panned out, we would consider the project favorably. Last year, for example, we funded Ana Maria Garcia's project about sterilization abuse of Puerto Rican women. She was a brand-new filmmaker, brand-new to the funding world, but the issue was viewed as very important, and she had demonstrated her commitment to fundraising to complete the film, although up to now she hasn't been able to raise as much as she'd planned. So, it's not an inflexible rule.

I want to add a general comment: We welcome criticisms and suggestions about how this whole evaluative process can be modified. We'd like to hear from people with alternatives to the solutions we've come up with so far — ideas that won't increase the amount of money we have to spend in order to give out the amount we do in grants.

ON THE MARCH

Application Form

Project Description

Project Personnel

Explanation of Budget

Budget Summary

Itemized Budget

Supporting Materials

THE FILM FUND
APPLICATION FOR MEDIA PROJECT GRANT

This application is for:

Pre-production ☐   Production ☒
Completion ☒   Distribution ☐
Special ☐   Other ☐
(Check more than one where appropriate)

Name (first)   (last)
Project Director: **Lucy   Winer**

Address: 157 Garfield Place   11215
           Brooklyn, N.Y.   (zip code)

Film ☒   Video ☐   Proposed length:
Slides ☐   Other ☐
                                    min

Phones:
Office 212 780-5665   Organization (if any)
                          On The March Productions
Home 212 768-2228   Address
                          255 6th Ave. NY NY
                          10014

Total project budget
    $ 29,820

Proposed starting date:
    10/6/79

Amount raised to date: $ 12,768
Amount needed to complete: $ 5,539
Amount requested from The
Film Fund: $ 11,513
*included deferrals & equipt. donations

Projected completion date:
    10/80

One sentence description of project:

A thirty minute, 16mm, color documentary, demonstrating how and why pornography
is a feminist issue.

Summary of proposed project. (Confine description to this space.)

We are in mid-production on a thirty minute film which will serve as a conciousness
raising vehicle and an organizing tool, identifying the social values and attitudes
which equate the sexual objectification and victimization of women with entertainment
and even sexual liberation. The target of our film is not merely the porn industry
(though that industry outgrosses the record and film industries combined), nor the local
porn districts (though they are visually its most blatant manifestation). The film will:

1. Explore the nature of pornography, establishing the critical connection between
   pornographic and popular images of sexual objectification.

2. Examine the ways in which pornography profits from and perpetuates racial and
   class stereotypes. (While no women are exempt, the actual exploitation within
   industry falls heaviest on those women with the least social status-- Third
   World and working class white women.)

3. Examine the numerous and complex ways in which pornography has affected women's
   lives.

4. Illustrate organizing tactics used by feminists in recent years to raise public
   consciousness on this issue.

APPLICATION FORM (continued) 2

How does this project differ from previous works on the topic?

There have been films dealing with violence against women and the sexist representation of women by the media. But there exists no film which focuses on the multi-billion dollar industry of pornography and the historically recent efforts of women to identify and challenge the anti-female messages of pornography.

Why is the medium you selected appropriate for dealing with this subject or theme?

For the film to raise public consciousness on the issue of pornography, we feel it crucial for our audience to explore visually a district which finds its economic base in the exploitation and degradation of women. As an organizing tool we feel the film derives its greatest dynamism from the coverage of the march. Our footage of October 20th succeecs in conveying the size and intensity of the event, the varied responses of the bystanders, and the misogynist backdrop against which the action took place.

Is the completed project likely to be used in an organizing context?
Why/why not? This work will be used by women organizing against pornography all around the country.

DISTRIBUTION

Who is the audience and/or constituency for this project?

We are already in contact with a national network of women's centers and feminist organizations, women's studies programs, gay activist groups, community centers and cultural associations, all of which have already expressed a strong interest in the film.

Do you plan to self-distribute? _____

Distribute through a cooperative? Yes _____

Distribute through a company? _____

Don't know yet? _____

List possibilities:

Do you have a working relationship with any of the audiences or constituencies that might use this project?

Describe: Since the march, we have developed a close working relationships with the Women Against Violence Against Women and Women Against Pornography. Lynn Campbell, our script consultant, was the principal organizer of the march on Times Square.

Do you have other works in distribution?
                              No.
For example:

APPLICATION FORM (continued) 3

AVAILABLE SUPPORTING MATERIALS:

Give title, short description, length and format. Also note whether the work relates to this project by demonstrating personnel's technical ability or your perspective and familiarity with subject of this application. DO NOT SUBMIT SAMPLES UNLESS REQUESTED TO DO SO.

> ON THE STREETS: a 16mm, color documentary about the lifestyles of street performers in New York City. This project indicates Ms. Winer's ability as a documentary director and editor. 30 minutes.

CHECKLIST:

To complete the application, please attach the following:

1. Table of contents
2. Project Description
3. Project Personnel
4. Budget
5. Verification of Tax-Exemption (if any)

CERTIFICATION

It is understood and agreed to by the applicant that:
1. The primary purpose of the proposed project is educational, artistic or charitable.
2. Any funds granted will be used for the purposes stated in this proposal.
3. Substantial alterations in this project, as stated in this proposal, must be mutually agreed to by the applicant and The Film Fund.

date   1/28/80   _____

/s/ Lucy Winer _____
Project Director Signature

Project Description

Film Treatment

The film opens with a highly stylized montage of the Times Square area. Beginning at dawn and continuing well into the night, we examine the streets, porn shops, commercial billboards and businesses which comprise the heart of New York's pornography industry. As the day progresses, the growing visual and aural tensions of the area are traced through the flashing lights, the neon glare, the blare of disco, the building traffic and the emergent activity of the street hustlers and evangelists. The pre-dawn quiescence gives way to the day's hustle and business activity which, by evening, takes on an air of danger, power and excitement.

To the sound of pinball machines, transistor radios, sirens, and the interminable coaxing of the street barkers ("Sextacular acts! Check 'em out, beautiful girls inside waiting for you!"), images of hard-core pornography (taken from movie marquees, peep show store fronts and bookstores) will be juxtaposed with more acceptable sexist images found in advertising and media (taken from display ads, billboards, amusement arcades and legitimate storefronts). In one sequence, we observe a marquee announcing "House of Psychotic Nurses" and the grainy but graphic stills of bare-breasted young nurses streaked with blood which are displayed to lure customers. As the camera pulls back we see that this marquee's display is but one of many. We see an enormous billboard overhanging the center of Times Square advertising designer jeans. The billboard features a beautiful woman posed down on her hands and knees with her buttocks upended and prominently angled toward the camera. Directly alongside this billboard is a second billboard of a young man advertising the same designer jeans. The young man, however, stands upright.

The images captured and examined in the opening montage are taken only from those displayed on the streets and sidewalks of Times Square available and unavoidable to all inhabitants and passersby. In the process of examining these images, the camera also records, but does not pursue, the physical attitudes and actions of the many people in the area: the women on their way to work or home who walk with their eyes directed toward the ground or staring blankly ahead, the assured stance of the men (both businessmen and hustlers) as they walk down the street, the neatly dressed businessman with briefcase who matter-of-factly enters Peep Land ("Live Sex Shows — Twenty-Five Cents!") after checking his wristwatch, the two tired-looking women who leave one porn establishment and walk into a nearby coffee-shop.

The film cuts from the deliberate and highly stylized montage to a faster-paced, brisk and ironic historical overview of pornography. A voice-over narration accompanies the depiction of Grecian urns with pornographic images, gold-bound editions of de Sade, Egyptian cave walls, etc., acquainting us with the longevity and cross-culturalism of pornography as well as its elitist and aristocratic roots. This section includes the filming of a college-level class on Renaissance literature. The professor's grandiloquent lecture on Boccaccio ("his glorious treatment of the pursuit, seduction and occasional rape of virgins provides us with a sense of the exuberant challenge he posed to the mores of his society") is contrasted with the quiet comments of a young female student of art history. Using the standard college text (which, she notes, contains no works of women artists), she points out and discusses the treatment of women in works by Rubens, Ingres, and Picasso. In this section we also take a look at the "porn of the future", the new home technologies such as video cassettes and discs which are expanding the home porn-viewing market at an exponential rate.

In a dramatic shift to a realistic, spontaneous style, the film then cuts to the interior of the Women Against Pornography storefront in Times Square, where the tour leader is preparing a small group of women for their tour of the district. The group will be followed as they are led through the bookstores, peep shows and sex carousels. The response of the women is at first usually very constrained, hesitant, nervous. With the guidance of the tour leader and the support of their small group, they are able — the majority for the first time in their lives — to examine the images of their sexuality being bought and sold, and they are overwhelmed. Often the store managers try to bar the women from entering these traditional male sanctums, or attempt to intimidate them into leaving; when the tour leader asks the police for assistance, citing the appropriate section of civil law guaranteeing equal access to public establishments, the police frequently refuse to help. The isolation and vulnerability felt by these women is captured by the camera. With great care, the tour leader points out the diversity of the clientele as well as the diversity of the products being sold. The models pictured on the walls on bondage magazines and the actresses featured in the twenty-five cent film loops represent every conceivable ethnic, racial, age and class group. The bookstores reflect the care of an industrious librarian: magazines, books and video-cassettes are arranged by theme and subject matter, so that the genres of bondage, child porn, Nazi porn, and racial stereotypes have their own sections on the walls. Within each genre there are specialties and variations which are announced by their titles. For example, the bondage section includes "Black Bondage," "Women in Chains," "Rope Games," etc., while the racial stereotypes section includes "Black Bitch," "Blonde Pussy," "Oriental Jewels," etc. The film loops, shown in "private viewing booths," advertise their content with a title card (complete with picture and blurb) on the outside of each booth. Like the magazines and books, the films offer specialties; in addition to those already cited, popular themes include the abduction and rape of young virgins, gang rapes, bestiality, sado-masochism, etc. As the women read the titles and — at the urging of the tour leader — select a film loop to view, the normal business of the establishment continues. We

Paula de Koenigsberg, cinematographer of *On the March* (on ladder) with members of the film crew. Photo: Sarina Scialabba.

see the men entering and exiting the booths, and the janitors moving into each vacated booth with a mop and a bucket of Lysol.

As the women prepare to leave each establishment, the tour leader calls their attention to the sexual paraphernalia and accessories (inflatable life-size dolls, rubber vaginas, and night sticks) displayed in glass cases near the proprietor's desk. As the women leave, the men (employees and customers) frequently make remarks ("You need one of those fifteen-inchers, baby?," "Hey, how about a real man?," etc.)

The sequence of the tour will be intercut with interviews. Tour organizers and former participants will describe the origin and rationale for the tours and recall past experiences; one porn proprietor who has agreed to be interviewed will describe his impression when the first W.A.P. tour entered his store; an anthropologist whose specialty is male bonding and pornography will give his analysis of what function the porn places serve for their clientele.

Following the tour the women return to the storefront for a consciousness-raising session. The talk is wide-ranging, and the tone ranges from the analytical to the profoundly emotional. Some of the women connect the images and sights just viewed to encounters with pornography in their own lives, past and present. As the women pick up on the theme of the pervasiveness of pornography in their lives (touching on certain ads which bother them, their husbands' use of *Hustler* and *Playboy*, the centerfold pin-ups in their places of work), their words introduce and overlap with the next segment of the film, a montage which recalls and echoes the first but which is more generalized in its subject.

Moving away from the Times Square area into mainstream society, in this montage the camera records the multitude of ways in which women are objectified, including menus which describe dishes in terms of the parts of women's bodies, laundromats and boatyards in which the machines and boats are labelled with women's names, art galleries which feature graphically realistic paintings of fragmented parts of women's bodies in their windows, gas stations which have centerfold pin-ups in the offices, ads covering the full lengths of New York City buses displaying a row of women's backsides encased in jeans, grafitti which express sexual hatred of women, etc.

Part-way through the montage we hear the voice-over of an organizer explaining that the most difficult thing for women to see and accept is "how and to what extent the ideas and themes underlying pornography permeate our culture." This opens up a major section of the film which explores the effects, internal and external, pornography has had on women. This section employs interviews with women

in their homes and workplaces and footage from conferences and consciousness-raising sessions. The feeling of being visually assaulted by these images is expressed repeatedly and finally connected with the idea of access. As one woman says, "Pornography may not make men do anything, but it's proof that men think they're entitled to have access to our bodies, anywhere, in pictures, pin-ups, real life. What woman doesn't have to deal with sexual harassment on the job or on the street, and the constant fear of rape?"

Her question leads into a sequence in which the camera adopts a highly subjective persona. In this sequence, we explore what it means to be female in this society and to have internalized the very real condition of constant vulnerability. As the camera moves through what may be a typical route home for a woman (leaving a subway, walking alone through a neighborhood full of shadows), the man-made world is revealed as being filled with the constant threat of violence, all of which is familiar and everpresent for women. This type of scene — a woman walking alone on a darkened street — has been frequently employed in "thrillers" which exploit violence against women. The familiarity of the scene is intended in part to shock the audience into a recognition of the scenario, but whereas such scenes usually equate danger with excitement, the subjective use of the camera will identify with the woman's experience rather than exploit the situation.

The final segment of the film examines what women have been doing to fight pornography. The actions range from educational discussions to networks of guerrilla activity in Europe and the United States. Beginning in a low-key tone and building with excitement, this section utilizes stills, interviews and footage from our extensive coverage of the October 20th March on Times Square Against Pornography (1979). Interviews with the organizers of the march will be intercut with the footage of the assemblage and reactions of bystanders. The footage of the march itself — the stunning visual impact of thousands of women marching on an area which has long existed at their physical and psychological expense — is a dramatic demonstration of not only the profound emotions stirred by this issue but also of the level of activity and achievement possible when women mobilize to act and organize.

Project Personnel

Director: Lucy Winer

Lucy Winer is a freelance cinematographer and teaches film at Brooklyn College and Pratt Institute. For the past six years, she has been actively involved in the feminist and gay movements. She was the founder and playwright for the New York Feminist Theatre Troupe (1974-76), a group which produced two of her works, *But Something Was Wrong With The Princess,* and *In Transit* in New York, Connecticut, and New Jersey. In the summer of 1974 she organized a cooperative theatre troupe of American and Canadian Women who toured western Canada. This summer, with Claudette Charbonneau she completed an article on the troupe which will appear in *Women In American Theatre* (Crown, fall 1980). She is a member of the National Association of Lesbian and Gay Filmmakers and the National Coordinating Committee of the Alternative Cinema Conference. Through the former group she has been involved in the formation and actions of the Coalition To Make Public Television Public and has assisted Shiela Roher in organizing the anti-*Windows* demonstrations. Her recent film credits include *Forty Strokes a Minute,* a film about women's rowing, and *Sunset Park: The Story of a Neighborhood.*

Cinematographer: Paula de Koenigsberg

Paula De Koenigsberg, cinematographer, studied in Argentina and at Pratt Institute. Her current projects include *Sound of the Bugle,* an anti-nuclear film concerning the exploitation of Indians in the Southwest. Recent film credits include *Marathon Woman,* a biographical film of marathon runner Micki Gorman, and *Sunset Park,* a documentary film about a neighborhood in transition. Ms. de Koenigsberg also does promotional photography for a New York art gallery.

Writer: Shiela Roher

Shiela Roher's political work began with the anti-war movement; in 1968 she worked as coordinator of the Youth for McCarthy and in the ensuing years also worked on the presidential campaigns of Udall and Harris. The organizing skills developed during these experiences have for the last ten years been applied to her organizing work in the feminist and gay rights movements. She sees her work in developing and running an abortion information center (Sarasota, Fla.) and a rape crisis center (Austin, Texas) as not only important and satisfying, but as a crucial prelude to her current involvement in the anti-pornography campaign.

Her political interests have also found expression in the theatre. She was the founder of Up Against The Fourth Wall Theatre (70-72), and directed *Smiles,* an original work, and *Waiting For Gidaut,* for the British Drama League (72). In 1973 she co-directed Deborah Fortson's *Baggage,* at Theatre For The New City, where she also worked as a lighting designer. Her play, *Past Tense, Present Imperfect,* has been produced on several college campuses, most recently in Santa Cruz, Ca.

During the past year, Ms. Roher has become and active member of W.A.P. She organized the anti-Sloane's action and persuaded Mr. Rose, president of the Sloane's chain to remove *Playboy, Penthouse* and *Oui* from his stores. She was crucially involved in the initiation of the anti-*Windows* demonstrations, and organized a coalition of feminist and gay organizations, the Coalition Against Violence Against

Women, to protest the film. She leads tours and delivers slide show presentations and talks for the group on a regular basis. Her months of work on the issue of pornography with W.A.P. will insure a firm ideological basis for film.

Script Consultants

Lynn Campbell. Co-ordinator of the first national feminist conference on pornography and Take Back The Night march in San Francisco in Nov., 1978; Co-founder and staff organizer of Women Against Pornography in New York City, and helped organize the march on Times Square, Oct. 20, 1979.

Claudette Charbonneau. Women's Studies Department, Brooklyn College; Co-founder of the New York Feminist Theater Troupe.

Project Consultants

Charlotte Bunch. Feminist theoretician, founder of feminist quarterly *Quest.*

Susan Brownmiller. Author, *Against Our Will: Men, Women and Rape;* Co-founder of New York Women Against Pornography.

Film Budget Summary. *On the March,* 16mm color, 30 min, 1/25/80

Item	Total cost	Raised	To be raised
Director/producer	$5,000	Deferred	
Research and script	$ 750	Deferred	
Consultant	250		
Writer/researcher	500		
	750		
Pre-production/location scouting	200	$200*	
Crew	150		
Expenses	50		
	200		
Production	$10,071	$3,819	$6,252
Crew	3,675	2,495**	
Equipment	2,495	1,323*	
Raw stock/tape	1,431		
Location	200	3,818	
Laboratory	2,270		
	10,071		
Post-production	$8,088		$8,088
Personnel	3,000		
Editing	1,200		
Laboratory	2,121		
Mix and completion	1,767		
	8,088		
Administrative	$3,000	$3,000**	
Direct costs	$27,109	$7,019	$14,340
10% overhead/contingency	$ 2,711		
TOTAL	$29,820		

*Individual donations.
**In kind contributions.

Itemized Budget. *On the March*

Director/producer		$ 5,000
Research and script		$ 750
Consultant	$ 250	
Writer/researcher	$ 500	
	$ 750	
Pre-production/location scouting		$ 200
Crew	$ 150	
Expenses (gas, garage, food)	$ 50	
	$ 200	
Production		$10,071

10 days (7 days + 3 days with additional MOS camera and crew)

Crew		$ 3,675
4 people @ $75 per day, 10 days	$3000	
3 people @ $75 per day, 3 days	$ 675	
	$3675.	
Equipment rental		$ 2,495
1 Frezzolini with accessories @		
$125/day, 10 days	$1250	
1 Bolex with accessories @ $30	$ 90	
1 Tripod & head @ $40/day, 10 days	$ 400	
1 Nagra with accessories @ $25/day,		
10 days	$ 250	
1 Sennheiser mike @ $13/day, 10 days	$ 130	
1 EV omni mike @ $10/day, 5 days	$ 50	
Lighting equipment @ $25/day, 5 days	$ 125	
Miscellaneous supplies	$ 200	
	$2495	
Location		$ 200
Gas, parking, food	$ 175	
Con Ed	$ 25	
	$ 200	
Production supplies		$ 1,431
(Shooting ratio 9:1)		
Raw stock 9200 ft.	$1270	
1/4 in. tape	$ 161	
	$1431	
Laboratory		$2270
Picture – develop and work print	$1757	
Sound – transfer	$ 420	
Ink code	$ 93	
	$2270	
		$10,071
Post-production		$ 8,088

9 weeks (6 weeks editing and 3 weeks completion to answer print and release prints)

Personnel	$3000	
Editing expenses	$1200	
Room, Steenbeck	$ 750	
Projection	$ 250	
Supplies	$ 200	
	$1200	

Itemized Budget. Continued

Laboratory		$2121	
1st Answer print	$ 497		
Corrected print	$ 281		
CRI	$ 767		
Check print	$ 194		
2 Release prints	$ 382		
	$2121		
Mix and completion		$1767	
Mix	$ 350		
Optical track	$ 117		
Opticals	$ 300		
Titles	$ 500		
Negative cutter	$ 500		
	$1767		
Administrative			$ 3,000
Legal		$ 650	
Insurance		$2000	
Public relations		$ 350	
		$3000	

Julia London. National Coordinator, Women Against Violence Against Women.

Explanation of Budget

We are requesting $11,513 in finishing funds: $2378 to cover the remaining production expenses in stock, tape and processing; $8088 to cover post production; $1,047, 10% overhead/contingency.

1. *In kind contributions:* The majority of the equipment (camera gear, tape recorder, lights), are owned by the filmmakers. The remainder will be donated by friends, and all of it is already insured. Both a lawyer/accountant and a printer have donated their services.
2. *Individual donations:* These funds were offered in response to a letter of appeal and screening of the rushes of the march.
3. *Raw stock:* We were able to purchase raw stock for the march at $40 a roll.

Since then, the price of 7247 has gone up by 35%.

We will be submitting proposals to other progressive foundations with interest in women's issues and/or an interest in the organizing efforts of grassroots organizations (i.e., The Joint Foundation For Support and The Lucius and Eva Eastman Fund, Inc.). We will also be approaching groups with a New York regional orientation (i.e., The Fund for the City of New York). Finally, we will request funds from groups in the area (i.e., The Broadway Theatre Producers Alliance). We are currently cutting a trailer from the march footage to be used for a series of fundraising screenings, and we feel confident that these events will bring in approximately $2000 to $3000. Having seen the rushes of the march and rally, Lynn Campbell (the principal organizer of the march) has agreed to write a second letter of appeal for the project which will be sent to previous W.A.P. donors, and a long mailing list of possible contributors.

The Living Stage Theatre Company—A Proposal to Work with Incarcerated Men and Women

Funded by: The Ford Foundation

Project Director: Robert Alexander, Director, The Living Stage Theatre Company

Proposal prepared by: Robert Alexander and Elizabeth Brunazzi

THE HISTORY OF THE LIVING STAGE THEATRE COMPANY PROPOSAL
by Susan A. Hellweg

Long before any proposal was written, the Living Stage Theatre Company was formed. Established in 1966 by its director Robert Alexander, The Living Stage is an interracial improvisational theatre company based in Washington, D.C., as part of the Arena Stage. Originally developed to provide small, intensive workshops to minority children, it has expanded this work to a broader range of groups. Through these workshops and performances, the company has brought its participatory program to physically handicapped, blind, deaf, emotionally disturbed, mentally ill, and drug-addicted individuals; the theatre program has also been able to involve runaway teenagers, senior citizens, and incarcerated men and women.

The participation of incarcerated individuals in the program was initiated in 1969. Alexander, in collaboration with Ken Kitch, Executive Director of the Barbed Wire Theatre Cage at San Quentin, put together the first theatre project for inmates in Lorton Reformatory in Lorton, Virginia. As a result, Inner Voices, a theatre company initiated and maintained by the prisoners, was developed. This company was the only one of its kind to be funded by *Project Culture* for 1977–78, a federal program supported by the Law Enforcement Assistance Administration as a means to provide incarcerated individuals with creative leisure time activities. Since the early beginnings of this unique relationship, the Living Stage has been able to expand its work at Lorton Reformatory from three 3-hour performance-workshops per year to 16 all-day workshops per year.

The company of the Living Stage has also initiated a series of performance-workshops for female prisoners at the Women's Detention Center in Washington, D.C. This activity has grown from performances two or three times per season initially to nine times per season at present.

Early in 1978 a proposal to sustain the activities of the Living Stage Company at the Lorton Reformatory in Lorton, Virginia, and the Women's Detention Center in Washington, D.C., was pre-

Dr. Susan A. Hellweg is Assistant Dean for Academic Affairs for the College of Professional Studies and Fine Arts and Assistant Professor of Speech Communication at San Diego State University. She has performed numerous consulting activities in grant proposal development for various educational and community agencies. She has been involved in the direction of grant activity at the university level for the past six years and has several publications in this area.

pared by Robert Alexander and Elizabeth Brunazzi. The original proposal was submitted to approximately 50 private foundations for review. Subsequently, the Ford Foundation funded $18,000 of the approximately $37,000 requested for the period from July 1, 1978 through June 30, 1979. After a second application was submitted, the Foundation awarded another $18,000 for the period from July 1, 1979 through June 30, 1980. The project was supported jointly for the two years by the Office of the Arts and the Division of National Affairs within the Foundation.

What led to Elizabeth Brunazzi's contribution to this proposal? Simply put, she says: ". . . my knowledge of prison life (I have conducted writing workshops in women's prisons and reviewed prison literature for several magazines); thorough experience of Living Stage's work and a high level of conviction as to its worth; and long training, experience, and skill as a writer all combined to produce such a proposal."

What took place in the negotiations and pre-award discussion between Robert Alexander (Living Stage Company) and Richard Sheldon (at the Ford Foundation)?

When Mr. Alexander was asked to make a statement concerning these contacts, he declared that he had known Mr. Sheldon for many years and that they had attended the same theatre conferences. When the proposal was written, he sent it off to quite a few foundations in hopes that the work would be supported.

When Mr. Sheldon was asked about the negotiations, he recalled that he knew Mr. Alexander from professional meetings, that the Ford Foundation was very interested in supporting projects for incarcerated men and women, and that the Foundation sent an evaluator to observe the Living Stage Company at work. Based upon the evaluator's recommendations, and the proposal presented in the following pages, the project was funded.

A PROPOSAL TO WORK WITH INCAR—CERATED MEN AND WOMEN FROM THE LIVING STAGE THEATRE COMPANY

by Robert Alexander and Elizabeth Brunazzi

Purpose

Living Stage is seeking funding for the purpose of (1) expanding an existing program of regular workshops in improvisational theatre at Lorton Reformatory in Lorton, Virginia, and (2) implementing a program of regular workshops in improvisational theatre at the Women's Detention Center, Washington, D.C. The overall objective of this project is to provide a level and quality of creative activity within these institutions which will give participating men and women personal and professional skills required for their survival and growth as fully functioning human beings.

History and Nature of Living Stage Improvisational Theatre Company

(1) Living Stage is a professional, multi-racial improvisational theatre company founded in 1966 as the educational and outreaching arm of Arena Stage in Washington, D.C. Over the past 10 years the company has brought its unique, parti-

Robert Alexander is Director of the Living Stage Theatre Company and also the Director of the Arena Stage's continuing Improvisational Workshop program, which has served over 75,000 children, teenagers, and adults in its 14 years of operation. Bringing 35 years of theatre experience to his work, Mr. Alexander has served on the National Endowment for the Arts Task Force for the White House Conference on Handicapped Individuals; the Theatre Panel, D. C. Commission on the Arts and Humanities; and the Advisory Panel, Special Projects, National Endowment for the Arts.

Elizabeth Brunazzi has had a variety of grant-writing, teaching, and creative experiences. Most recently a Writer-in-Residence and Instructor of Creative Writing for the D.C. Commission on the Arts and Humanities, she has numerous academic honors (Doctoral Fellow at Stanford University, Honors Diploma at McGill University among them) and publications to her credit. She has served in various development capacities—as director for educational programs in Fairfax County Public Schools and development consultant for the D.C. Public Schools.

LIVING STAGE
THEATRE COMPANY
Robert Alexander, Director

a venture of
ARENA STAGE
Zelda Fichandler
Producing Director

6th & Maine Ave., S.W., Washington, D.C. 20024   Telephone: (202) 554-9066

A Grant Proposal
to work with incarcerated men and women

from

THE LIVING STAGE THEATRE COMPANY

C/o Arena Stage
6th and Maine Avenue, SW
Washington, D.C.   20024
(202) 554-9066

Theater for Children and Youth   •   Teacher Training Programs   •   Improvisational
Theater Workshops   •   Educational Consultants for Theaters, Schools and Museums

Fig. 1. Cover sheet for proposal.

cipatory form of theatre to thousands of children, men, and women ranging in age from 2 to 85. Living Stage has performed widely and conducted workshops, lecture/demonstrations, and seminars both in the United States and in Europe. Director Robert Alexander has initiated and conducted numerous community projects in the Washington Metropolitan Area, including programs for individuals in a variety of institutional settings: the handicapped, the mentally ill, the addicted, the aging, and the imprisoned.

Living Stage has been involved in providing creative, habilitative environments within prisons since near the inception of theatre programs for incarcerated men and women in the nation. In 1969 Robert Alexander collaborated with Ken Kitch, a pioneer in the "Barbed Wire" theatre movement at San Quentin, to create the first theatre project for inmates at Lorton Reformatory in Lorton, Virginia. A signal result of their collaboration, effort, and vision was the formation of "Inner Voices," a theatre company initiated and maintained by and for inmates at Lorton and which drew on Living Stage methods and techniques as a model for its program.

The close personal and working relationships established between the members of Living Stage and the men at Lorton, whose company is currently entitled "Lorton Voices," and continuous cooperation between the company and prison administration have enabled Living Stage to gradually expand its work there from 1971 to 1977: from giving three 3-hour performance/ workshops per year (1971–75) to three all-day workshops (1975–76), and nine all-day workshops during the past season (1976–77). Although there has long been a desire on the part of the men and that of Living Stage to further expand and deepen this work, to bring it to an authentically professional level, and although Living Stage involvement in the Lorton work/release program has been discussed at the administrative level, any such innovation is, at the present time, blocked by a lack of funds.

Living Stage has also provided a series of performances for women at the Women's Detention Center in Washington, D.C., going to the facility two or three times per season during the past four years. Although a willingness to implement an expanded program has existed on the part of all parties involved, the company's work there has been severely limited due to logistical problems arising from a lack of funds. With adequate funding, Living Stage could develop the artistic and administrative resources necessary to implement a demonstration program for women on the model of the one already begun at Lorton. There is a great lack of all resources and programming, educational, recreational and creative, at the women's facility and thus a great need, both individual and institutional.

(2) The nature of Living Stage's work is an artistic dialogue between the actor-artist-human being and the participant-artist-human being. The number of participants in any given workshop is limited to 25, so that an atmosphere of sharing and trust can be created. When the number of participants is larger, the experiential thrust of the work is lost. During the period of the workshop, the men and women who comprise Living Stage are there for the participants; are there to create an environment where it is impossible to be wrong; and are there to create an environment where men and women can take a chance and express how they feel about the world and the people in it, using their bodies, voices, minds, and hearts. The members of Living Stage take the men and women they work with very seriously as creators, and they ask these men and women to take themselves very seriously as artists.

Living Stage workshops are designed to actively encourage all participants to discover their own creativity through the art of theatre— the artistic expression and communication of one's point of view using the sensory, physical, vocal, emotional, and intuitive apparatus of the human being. The members of the company are trained to create and demonstrate to participants a ritualistic theatre that attempts to reveal human behavior on its deepest level. The particular "language" of this theatre is a vocal expression of feelings and thoughts encompassed in a highly structured form combining consonantal and vocalic sounds. This "language" is used to

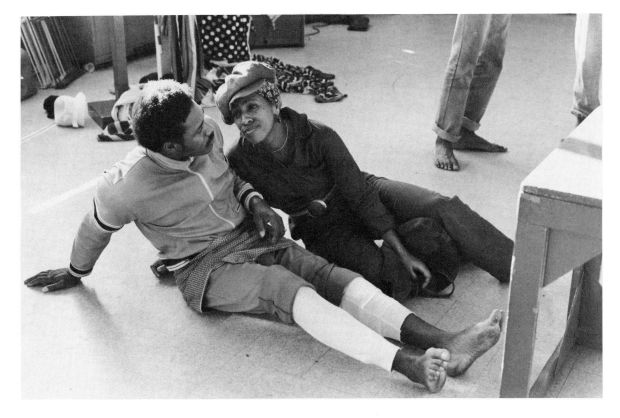

Living Stage Theatre Company's Associate Director/Actress, Rebecca Rice, in an improvised scene with a member of Lorton Voices, an inmate theatre company. The scene is from a larger improvisation about people in a primitive society being transformed into men, women, and children who live in a big city in modern America. In this scene, Ms. Rice and Lorton Voice actor are boy and girl friend in the middle of a disagreement about his continuing to be a cab driver and feeling thwarted from his own ambition to be a writer. The theme of this improvisation was suggested by a member of the Lorton Voices. Photo by Tess Steinkolk.

communicate essences of feelings between the characters that emerge in the course of the workshops. Although the men and women who work with Living Stage are encouraged to express their feelings in verbal form, poems, and original lyrics, for example, it is through the use of a ritualistic "language" that they begin to become aware that the voice is an instrument of expression and that the tone of the word is as important as the word itself.

All Living Stage workshops include improvised scenes between members of the company and the participants. No scripts are used for these scenes; participants volunteer their own ideas and concerns as subjects and subsequently become the characters who make them come alive. In this way participants vividly experience the effects and results of personal choices.

When asked to identify the most difficult aspect of prison life, incarcerated men and women frequently respond that the lack of emotional release is the most difficult.[1] Living Stage believes that together with the physical confinement, the emotional confinement of prison life is not only difficult and painful but also over the long-term destructive of even the potential health of the organism. The work of Living Stage exists in large measure to aid those with whom it works to directly contact their feelings: the life of the emotions is the source of all creativity, it is the substance out of which all art is made.

[1]"The Female Ex-Offender," *Fortune News,* February, 1977.

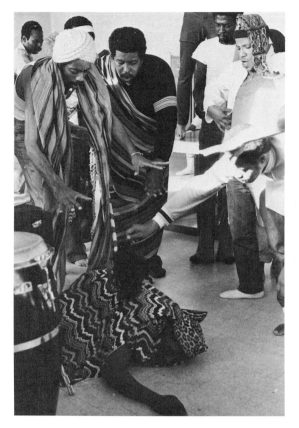

Members of the Lorton Voices in a Living Stage workshop. They are improvising a scene in which they are the first people of the planet earth. One of their community has been killed by evil forces and the wise men, the men of spirit, are creating a ritual in order to bring him wholeness and life. Photo by Tess Steinkolk.

Goals and Philosophy

Living Stage believes that the needs of incarcerated men and women are not different from those of people on the outside. The majority of prisoners are neither evil nor psychotic. But the human, emotional, social, and aesthetic needs of incarcerated men and women, if not different in kind, are different in degree: they are indeed greater. Most prisoners are quite poor. Many have little education. They lack basic communication skills and have, in any case, little sense that what they feel and express is of value. Most feel that they are "losers" and have accomplished little, if any thing, that they can be proud of. Women suffer particularly from the guilty sense that they have failed their children. Most men and women in prison have learned what survival skills they possess from the street: their surest response is a quick defense, a cuff. In prison they too often find the conditions of the street replicated in distilled form. Cut off from close relationships, constantly called upon to defend themselves, lacking rights to basic privacy and respect for individuality, constantly required to control their emotions, they find few channels for expressing and channeling how they feel. Most are starved for human exchange in which they are relieved of the defenses they must usually exhibit; and most are starved to accomplish something.

When members of Living Stage first encounter imprisoned men and women, they find people who literally are not in possession of their lives. It is the view of Living Stage that they can be "given back to themselves," that they can be given a sense that it is possible for them to take control of their lives through, in the workshop, a radical re-creation of available environment. The principal, most immediate goal of Living Stage within this project, and whenever it enters a prison, is to create and demonstrate an environment which encourages mutual trust and freedom of individual expression. It is an alternative environment completely unlike that of "normal" prison life, one in which prison "games" have no valid currency, one in which no one can be "put down" for what they say, how they look, move or sound, or for whatever they attempt in improvisational exercises and scenes. It is an environment vibrating with music, sound, and movement, a rhythmically colored environment which invites participation and involvement by those present. Thus, it is an attitudinal as well as a specific physical environment.

The establishment of this "Living Stage" makes the accomplishment of other goals possible:

— To aid each man and woman to gain a sense of identity and self-worth through the exercise of an expressive skill, the art of theatre.
— To impart to each man and woman the confidence that they can learn to work and concentrate very hard in the interest of their own

ideas, feelings, perceptions, and concerns.
— To impart to each man and woman the idea that to imagine a solution to a problem is one of the most important survival skills that they can acquire.
— To impart to each man and woman the skill of collaborating with others in the interest of expressing a group feeling or ideas.
— To impart to each man and woman the experience of overcoming obstacles, of going beyond themselves, both physically and imaginatively, so that they may understand that they are not bound by past failure.
— To aid each man and woman to integrate physical and emotional responses.
— To convince each man and woman within the workshop environment that once they have begun to solve difficult artistic problems, they also have a ready tool for solving life problems.
— To demonstrate to the men and women working with Living Stage that they can affect others and gain understanding through the mastery of a difficult art.
— To aid each man and woman to understand that the different, sometimes unfamiliar characters which they create out of and beyond their own conscious personalities represent different potentials within them.
— To impart to each man and woman the knowledge that they can establish a new environment for themselves out of their own creative potential.

These are the most important, immediate operant goals in the Living Stage theatre demonstration program. Longer range goals are:
— To impart to each man and woman the emotional flexibility, strength, artistry, determination, and interest necessary to take the skills gained in the workshop out into their daily lives within the institution and, on release, into their lives in the world.
— That the skills gained in the workshops will be instrumental in decisions of the participants to never allow themselves to be imprisoned again.

— To contribute to a heightened awareness on the part of prison administrators of the need for programs recognizing and encouraging the potential creativity of imprisoned men and women, and thus to broadly contribute to a humanizing of relationships within correctional institutions.
— And to, through creation of an artistic and administrative model, open up administrative channels and create further public and private support for creative efforts within correctional institutions.

Need for Assistance

(1) $37,541.00 will be needed to fund the entire Living Stage Demonstration Project, including both the Lorton and Women's Detention Center segments, with $6,291.00 to be drawn from operating funds of Living Stage. It should be kept in mind that this funding is not being sought for the purpose of maintaining a professional theatre company for a period of 12 months. Living Stage is able to deliver an intensive, professional theatre program to the institutions concerned only because it receives yearly funding from other sources, preeminently the National Endowment for the Arts and the D.C. Commission on the Arts and Humanities, which has allowed it to maintain itself as a cohesive, professional ensemble for the past 10 years. The amount of the grant is being sought so that existing artistic and administrative resources can be allocated to the operation of the demonstration project.

(2) Living Stage must be able to work with participants on a frequent, regular, and on-going basis in order to accomplish the professional, artistic, habilitative, and administrative goals outlined above. The quality of artistic effort and the personal growth of participants are functions of time spent in the endeavor. Men and women in prison who work with the company on a more frequent basis will not simply be getting more of the same. They will be getting a higher quality and greater depth of artistic experience. They will

have a strengthened opportunity to carry new skills and vision out into the institution. They will have the opportunity to begin to think and perceive as artists, rather than as prisoners who occasionally attend a theatre workshop.

(3) There is a manifest need for the demonstration of ways in which creative energies may be released, channeled, and concentrated at both Lorton and the Women's Detention Center. Professional arts programs, except for the involvement of Living Stage, are nonexistent at both institutions. At the Women's Detention Center, minimal recreation programs are not fully operational. The situation at the Women's Detention Center lends vivid support to recent contentions that the female prisoner is nationally "the forgotten offender."[2] There is a particular national urgency to publicize the needs of female offenders and to provide services to women's institutions.

Plan of Action

(1) Location and Population to Be Served

A. *Area to be served:* Metropolitan Washington Area

B. *Population to be served:* (1) Twenty-five men at Lorton Reformatory, Lorton, Virginia. (2) Twenty-five women at the Women's Detention Center, Washington, D.C.

(2) Statement on Program Approach

A. *The Workshop.* Every Living Stage workshop begins with a musical, verbal, and vocal "jam" session in which staff and participants improvise lyrics and movement on a theme chosen for that particular workshop (for example, the theme of "drugs"). To an outside observer, this segment of the workshop would look like just any group of people having a very good time together. It is in

[2]"The Female Ex-Offender," *Fortune News,* February, 1977.

Rebecca Rice, Associate Director/Actress of the Living Stage Theatre Company, and a member of the Lorton Voices, an inmate theatre company, as part of an improvised jam that was created collectively by the Living Stage Theatre Company and the Lorton Voices. Photo by Tess Steinkolk.

fact designed to have precisely that atmosphere but at the same time has a serious purpose: to put participants at their ease; to create a sense of trust; and to loosen up their bodies and imaginations. The jam is a "warming up" period, physically, mentally, emotionally, and socially. It is designed to get participants involved and to help them lose fear and inhibitions.

The "jam" is followed by a series of additional "warm-up" exercises. These include "sculptures," in which participants are asked to select single-word themes such as "love," "hate," or "freedom" and then to "throw" their bodies into a physical posture expressing their feeling about that theme. In these sculptures participants make physical contact with one another and are asked to deeply feel the group impulse at work. In order to pursue

Two members of the Lorton Voices, an inmate theatre company, participating in a Living Stage workshop and a human sculpture on the theme of pain which was suggested by the man to the right. Photo by Tess Steinkolk.

collective feeling, the members of the sculpture are asked to make sounds or words expressing how the sculpture feels and, again on a group impulse, to bring the "sounding sculpture" to a close at the same moment. They are further asked to imagine, from the posture in which they find themselves in a given sculpture, the identity of a character they would like to become, the character's age, where the character is, and what the character is doing.

The most important part of each session is work in improvised scenes, in which participants select and develop their own characters. In this segment of the workshop, the members are asked to both participate in scenes with the staff and other members of the workshop and also to comment on and make suggestions about the characters and situations created by others. They are always asked to supply endings to scenes created by the staff. In this way, they become

aware of what they would like to see happen and are able to act on, act out, and participate in what they would like to see happen.

The value of learning "what one would like to see happen" is illustrated by a recent incident in a Living Stage workshop at Lorton. An exercise had been selected in which four members of the workshop were to stand up and simultaneously begin to tell a story about something they were very proud of. One of the purposes of the exercise is to aid participants to develop different points of simultaneous concentration: each participant in the exercise tells his story while "listening" to each of the other three stories being told, all four bringing their stories to a close at exactly the same moment. It is a difficult exercise. But it was particularly difficult for one participant, an inmate, because, as he said, he could not think of anything he had ever done that he was proud of. He was instructed to "imagine it, then," and he proceeded to tell a story of beautiful accomplishment. In imagining accomplishment, he in fact accomplished something that he *could* be proud of.

The Living Stage program is hard work, mentally, and physically. It is neither a diversion nor a time-filler. It presents a unique combination of emotional and physical release of energy, but unlike recreational programs involving, for example, calisthenics, it is not designed to get inmates to simply "blow off steam." It demands a serious commitment; and it involves the whole organism in the pursuit of an accomplishment, the practice of an art form. The rewards are correspondingly greater. This approach offers participants the opportunity to take an activity and themselves seriously.

(3) Projected Sequence of Activities

A. Duration of the Project: A 12-month period beginning June 1, 1977 and ending May 31, 1978.

B. Phases of the program: 1. Phase I: June 1977–July 1977. Components of this phase include planning; meetings with Mike Pearlman, Corrections Program Associate for Lorton and coordinator for the Living Stage project at Lorton, and Betty Richardson, staff psychologist at the

Women's Detention Center and coordinator for the Living Stage project at the Women's Detention Center, and with other appropriate administrators; coordination with independent evaluators who will act as consultants to the project and establishment of an observation schedule for these evaluators; development of a communications system and schedule for dissemination of information regarding the project within the institutions; and dissemination of information regarding the project to the general public by the Living Stage Director of Development.

August, 1977. Preparation of artistic staff and equipment; rehearsals; development of new material; maintenance work on bus, musical instruments, and set pieces.

2. Phase II: September, 1977–April, 1978; Operation of Workshops.

(a) Lorton: Two workshops per month lasting seven hours each; to be given two Saturdays out of each month from 9:00 AM to 4:00 PM.

(b) Women's Detention Center: Monthly workshops of three hours each; to be given on one Thursday out of each month from 1:00 PM to 4:00 PM. There is a possibility that these workshops can be expanded to seven hours but at this writing Living Stage has no confirmation that they will be. The monthly workshops at Women's Detention Center will be divided into two segments of approximately four months each, in order to accommodate incoming inmates, assure continuity of membership and insure full membership. Living Stage will initially accept only participants who want to volunteer to be in the workshops for a four-month period and will not accept new participants after the start of the first series of workshops. At the end of the first series, those remaining in the workshop may continue in the second half, if they wish. Any vacancies will be filled with arrivals or others wishing to take the workshop for a four-month period. This has seemed the best way to structure demonstration workshops in a short-term facility.

(c) Each workshop will be followed by an evaluation or "note" session among the artistic staff lasting up to five hours (See *Evaluation*).

(d) Independent evaluators acting as consultants to the project will observe the project at intervals during this phase (See *Evaluation*).

3. Phase III: April 31–May 31; *Evaluation.* Final evaluation of the project (See *Evaluation*); Preparation of final report; Dissemination of results of the project.

(4) Unique Feature of the Project

A. Living Stage demonstrates a form of theatre that is unique in its physical flexibility and mobility. The company, together with musical instruments and set pieces, can be transported into the institution with minimal logistical arrangements. The company requires only a spacious room cleared of all obstacles to movement and with no exposures such as picture windows or sliding glass doors in order to work with participants.

B. Living Stage provides both highly individualized, personal contact as well as intensive group interaction to participants.

C. Living Stage presents a unique combination of physical, mental, and emotional outlet.

(5) Contingencies

A. *Factors which might accelerate the work:* 1. The presence of participants in the workshops who take a high degree of initiative in supporting and publicizing the program. 2. Extraordinary continuing rapport with prison administrators; energetic support on the part of program coordinators.

B. *A factor which might decelerate the work:* 1. Closing of institutions to outside visitors, groups and educational consultants due to violence within the institution.

Expected Benefits of the Project

It is expected that participants in the program will gain:
— Increased ability to express and communicate verbally and physically.

— Increased ability to concentrate mentally and physically.

— Increased determination and ability to solve problems, both as individuals and in a group context.

— Increased ability to trust, enter into, and utilize a group process.

— Greater ability to project a future, because they will have imagined it.

— Greater ability to connect the past with the future.

— An understanding that toughness is not necessarily strength.

— Experience of a variety of enjoyment, the aesthetic, which is neither self-punitive nor self-destructive, i.e., that it is not necessary to use drugs to escape to obtain pleasure.

and that:

— Prison administrators will be able to perceive these changes and will thus value the demonstration.

— The net result of the demonstration will be increased interest in and support for authentically creative programs in correctional institutions.

Evaluation

(1) Types of Data to Be Collected

A. After workshops have been in operation for two months, each member of the Living Stage artistic staff will contribute an initial, written profile of each participant rating participants on approximately ten dimensions of their personal, social and creative functioning. They will then add interim reports on the participants' activity at intervals of two months during the course of the workshops and at the termination of the project will prepare a final, written evaluation of each participant, comparing the initial profile with subsequent data.

B. The basis of the profiles will be the following aspects of the participants' personal, social and creative functioning:

— Quality of the individual's self-image.

— Ability to express self-concept in symbolic form.

— Extent of withdrawn or outgoing behavior.

— Degree and quality of physical response to verbal stimuli.

— Degree and quality of interaction with staff artists and other participants.

— Ability to establish working relationships with others in the interest of expressing an individual or a collective idea.

— Ability to establish functional, creative relationships with the objective environment, whether actually present or imaginatively suggested.

— Quality of wishes expressed; who/what they would like to be; what they would like to see happen; what they feel they need.

— Quality of characters portrayed; who they are; where they come from; what their past and future are.

C. The artistic staff will contribute comparative data in the same 10 areas on younger vs. older participants in the project to the final report.

D. The artistic staff will contribute comparative data in the same 10 areas on men vs. women in the project to the final report.

E. A record of all exchanges between prison administration and Living Stage staff will be kept and made a part of the file.

F. All reports will be typed by the Living Stage secretary and filed in the Living Stage office.

(2) Methodology for Evaluating Effects of the Project

A. All observations and evaluation will be discussed orally among Living Stage artistic staff and taped in evaluation sessions following each workshop and lasting for from three to five hours, after which each individual staff member will arrive at his or her independent, written evaluation. Participants' progress in the project will be measured against their expressed capacity at the beginning of the workshops as reflected in the profiles established by the artistic staff. Living Stage considers as important indicators of the degree of success in meeting its objectives:

—Degree of participation by workshop members, both as reflected in attendance and in energy exerted during the workshop period.

—Degree of self-initiated activity in the workshop.

—Degree of self-initiated activity outside the workshop related to the workshop process, for example poems and characters generated and brought into the workshop.

—Degree of self-generated, as opposed to received, imagery expressed.

—Degree to which participants form mutually supportive artistic relationships during the workshop period.

—Degree of effort and interest exhibited over time by prison administrators as reflected in recorded statements and concrete actions.

B. Initial profiles and measurements will be made available to three independent evaluators acting as consultants to the project who will observe the workshops at intervals as described in *Projected Sequence of Activities* (see *Staffing* for names and titles of evaluators). These evaluators will be asked to submit written reports comparing their findings with the data established by Living Stage staff to the Director of Living Stage. Evaluators will also be asked to compare their findings with other programs with which they are familiar. Reports of independent evaluators will be made part of the final report on the project.

Staffing

(1) Positions

A. *Artistic and Administrative Director.* To oversee all areas of the program and to make final decisions affecting all areas of the program. Will work with artistic staff, oversee all logistical arrangements and make all decisions of an artistic and evaluative nature.

B. *Assistant Artistic Director.* A member of the acting and teaching staff who will also be responsible for conducting rehearsals,

preworkshop warm-up exercises for the company and self-evaluation or "note" sessions for the company.

C. *Actor-Educators.* Four professional actors who have worked together for from two to seven years and are trained to create environments that aid participants in discovering their creative energies. Actor-educators will work as a group and will also split up to work on a one-to-one basis with participants. Actor-educators function flexibly within the workshop setting and will work with participants in ratios of one-to-one, one-to-two and one-to-three, whenever it is necessary to stimulate creative interaction. Participants who initially cannot function well within the group setting are enabled to explore and discover their own creative potential by working one-to-one with the members of the Living Stage staff.

D. *Musical Director.* A professional musical director and pianist who is equipped to improvise on themes and songs throughout the period of the workshop. This position is essential to the functioning of a Living Stage workshop as music accompanies all the exercises designed for participants in any given session. Participants will join the Living Stage staff in creating original lyrics which express the participants feelings and concerns.

E. *Production Manager.* To be responsible for logistics, for maintaining and setting up equipment, and for maintaining and driving the Living Stage Volkswagen bus. This staff member will also be responsible for giving actor-educators their daily calls for reporting to work; will be in charge of all logistics during the workshops; and will be in contact with prison staff coordinators concerning any change in scheduling or procurement of space that might affect the logistics of the workshop.

F. *Developmental Director.* Will be responsible for disseminating information and creating interest about the project in the area served and also nationally.

G. *Administrative Liaison.* Will be responsible for all communications between Living Stage, prison administration, and independent evaluators; for all meetings between Living Stage, prison administrators and independent evaluators; and for all evaluative materials. This staff member will coordinate with the production manager and the developmental director, and will be directly responsible to the artistic and administrative director.

H. Secretary. Will be responsible for typing all evaluative reports and all correspondence between Living Stage, prison administration, and independent evaluators. This staff member will also be responsible for keeping an accurate, up-to-date file on the entire program. He/she will work for the artistic and administrative director, the production manager, the developmental director and the administrative liaison.

I. Consultants. Three professionals in the field of theatre arts programming in correctional institutions who will act as independent evaluators of the project. Will observe the project at intervals during its operation and submit written reports of their findings.

(2) Personnel

A. Project Director. Robert Alexander, 6th & Maine Avenue, S.W., Washington, D.C. 20024; Telephone: 554-9066 (all project staff should be contacted at the same address and telephone number *except consultants,* for whom individual addresses are supplied below). Mr. Alexander brings over 30 years of artistic and administrative experience in the theatre to this project. Since coming to Arena Stage to direct Living Stage in 1966, he has directed and administered numerous theater programs for a wide variety of community groups. Along with Ken Kitch, he was a prime mover in initiating a theatre program for inmates at Lorton Reformatory. He has also been a member of the White House Conference on Children and the National Endowment for the Arts Task Force on the White House Conference for Handicapped Individuals.

B. Assistant Artistic Director. Rebecca Rice. A professional actor-educator who has been a member of Living Stage for the past seven years.

C. Actor-Educators. Rebecca Rice, Jennifer Nelson, Larry Samuel, and Greg Jones. Professional actor-educators who have been members of the Living Stage staff for seven, five, four and three years respectively.

D. Production manager. Roberta Gasbarre. A member of Living Stage for the past three years.

E. Musical Director. Joan Berline. A professional pianist/flutist who has been a member of the Living Stage staff for the past three years.

F. Administrative Liaison. Elizabeth Brunazzi. Development Officer responsible for national touring and grants management for the company for the past two years.

G. Development Director. Applicants will be interviewed for this position.

H. Secretary. Portia Iverson. A member of the staff for the past two years.

I. Consultants. Larry Dye, Deputy Director, New York State Executive Department, Division for Youth, 84 Holland Avenue, New York, N.Y.

Nancy Gabor, Director, Street Theatre, 13 East 16th Street, New York, N.Y. Ms. Gabor has administered theatre programs in the New York State prison system.

Ken Whelen, Director, Creative Alternatives, 13 East 16th Street, New York, N.Y. 10003. Mr. Whelen was executive director for the Barbed Wire Theatre "Cage" at San Quentin. Creative Alternatives deals with arts in prisons on a national level.

(3) Salaries

All Living Stage staff are paid in accordance with an Equity Contract Association League of Resident Theatres contract under the subcategory Theatre. See *Budget* (in Table I) for breakdown of salaries.

Appendices to the proposal included staff resumes, an organization chart (see Fig. 2.), and letters of support (for an example, see Fig. 3.).

Critique of the Proposal

The proposal convincingly demonstrates the need for support. While there are no *measurable*

Table I. Living Stage Projected Budget for 1977–78.

Title and/or type of personnel	Number of personnel	Annual or average salary	% of time devoted to project	Amount
Artistic director/administrator	1	$24,700	25	$ 6,175
Assistant director/actor-educator	1	14,300	25	3,575
Actors-educators	4	11,502 (each)	12.5	5,751
Musical director	1	11,502	12.5	1,437
Production manager	1	11,502	25	2,875
Director of development	1	11,502	25	2,875
Administrative liaison	1	13,000	25	3,250
Secretary	1	7,280	25	1,820
Total salaries and wages				$27,758
Fringe benefits				2,775
Total salaries and wages including fringe benefits				$30,533
Supplies and materials:				
Cassette tapes for evaluation				150
Total supplies and materials				$ 150

Number of trips	Number of travelers	From	To	Purpose	Amount
4	3	N.Y.C.	Wash. D.C. and return	Evaluation	$1,200
30	11	Lorton and Women's Detention Center and return		Workshops	127
Total transportation of personnel					$1,327

Number of Travelers	Number of Days	Daily Rate	Amount
3	8	$30.00	$720
Total travel			$2,047
Direct costs			$32,730
Indirect costs (14.7%)			4,811
Total Budget			$37,541

objectives given, the intent of the cited goals is relatively clear. The 14 goals, however, could have been more articulately phrased. The methodology is carefully delineated, so that the reader has a sense of the sequence of activities that will take place over the proposed 12-month period. The evaluation is relatively well detailed in the proposal, although some of the measurement techniques are not fully described. Additionally, there is no one-to-one discussion between each objective and the evaluation procedures. The method of project dissemination is also not totally clear. A number of potential benefits of the projects are outlined in the proposal; these are generally clear, though one in particular seems somewhat remote from the project (connecting the past with the future). The budget appears reasonable and is very adequately detailed. The project staff, as reflected in the resumés appended to the proposal, are an asset to the program.

The basic strengths of the proposal lie in the project itself, what it was designed to accomplish, and its long-range potential. Especially critical,

GOVERNMENT OF THE DISTRICT OF COLUMBIA

THE DEPARTMENT OF CORRECTIONS

Correctional Complex
Lorton, Virginia 22079

March 8, 1977

Mr. Robert Alexander
Director
Living Stage
6th and M Streets, S.W.
Washington, D.C. 20024

Dear Mr. Alexander:

Pursuant to your letter of February 21, 1977, I welcome
the opportunity to express my appreciation to the Living
Stage for their work with selected residents of the
Lorton Central Facility, Lorton, Virginia. Your company's
efforts over the past two years have been characterized by
a continuing interest in members of our resident pupula-
tion and a dedication to providing them a viable experience
in the creative arts. Our prison drama group, the Lorton
Voices, has expressed a feeling that your monthly workshops have assisted them in improving their own performance.
From a managerial standpoint, your dependability in terms
of keeping your committments and the seriousness with
which you undertake your task are recognized and very much
appreciated. Your understanding and adherence to institutional security procedures is another area in which you
have been most cooperative.

We welcome your further participation with our Institution.
We will continue to provide you with all possible support,
(workshop space, preparing of work area, etc.). We are
satisfied with the voluntary participation of our residents
with the Living Stage Company and trust that this will
grow. At some future date, perhaps we can also consider
a similar involvement to interested members of our staff.

Wishing you every success in your future efforts.

Sincerely,

Salanda V. Whitfield
Administrator

Fig. 2. Sample letter of support.

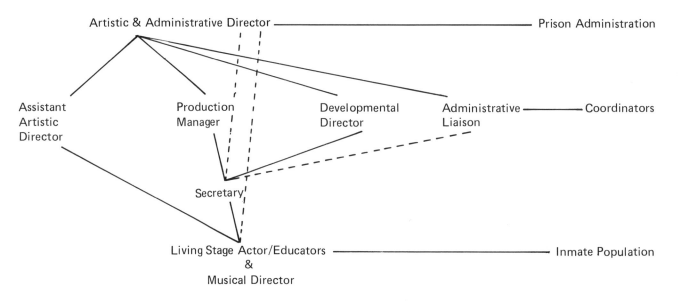

Fig. 3. Living Stage Theatre demonstration project organizational chart.

the project *already had a history of success!* When the Ford Foundation evaluator came to visit the Company, he found a well-established program—in operation. Infusion of Ford funds, at that point, would serve to continue and expand a worthwhile activity to which the Living Stage Theatre Company had already committed substantial talents and resources.

It is important to keep in mind in reviewing the proposal that it was intended as a submission to a foundation, rather than a governmental source. The less public the granting agency, the less critical an evaluation component becomes. The orientation becomes more flexible and less bureaucratic. Therefore, the fact that the proposal does not contain measurable objectives becomes less of an issue. The structure and form of the proposal is more at the option of the applicant in this case.

Although the project was not fully funded, it received two years of consecutive support (an exception to the Ford Foundation's usual policy of providing funds for one year).

This project has been the fortunate beneficiary of support from the National Endowment for the Arts, the Bureau of Education for the Handicapped, and the Washington, D.C. Commission on the Arts and Humanities. Hopefully, continued visibility of the project will lead to its continued support.

THE HUMANITIES

The one application presented here in the Humanities area is, *Proposal for a Three-Quarter Sequence of Interdisciplinary Humanities Courses for General Students*. This Pilot Grant was supported by the National Endowment for the Humanities and was designed to meet the needs of an institution by improving its humanities offerings. It appeared in the June 1979 issue of GRANTS MAGAZINE (Vol. 2, No. 2).

A critique of the proposal by Myra Ficklen comments on the care with which the proposal was prepared and on the other elements that probably had a great deal to do with its acceptance. She particularly mentions the institutional commitment to the program which many funding institutions consider crucial to the success of a project.

The project director, Prof. John F. Fleischauer, has prepared a short history of the proposal, beginning with the moment the idea was born in an airport cocktail lounge in Columbus, Ohio. His step-by-step description of the negotiations indicate the trial and error, the changes in plans, the rethinking and rewriting, and above all the consultation with others that go into the preparation of a plan that turns out to be acceptable to a funding agency.

The humanities is an area that many find confusing, and since the National Endowment for the Humanities (NEH) has done so much to bring the fields included in that term to public attention, we have added to this presentation an article written by John Lippincott of the NEH, "Grantmaking at the National Endowment for the Humanities", which appeared in the June 1981 issue. Mr. Lippincott's article makes a clear statement about the subjects of interest to the NEH, and tells precisely the way it goes about making decisions about grants.

A Three-Quarter Sequence
of Interdisciplinary Humanities Courses
for General Students

Funded by: National Endowment for the Humanities

Project Director: John F. Fleischauer, Chairman, Humanities Division, Columbus College, Columbus, Georgia

Proposal prepared by: John F. Fleischauer

THE HISTORY OF THE INTERDISCIPLINARY HUMANITIES PROPOSAL
by John F. Fleischauer

In smaller schools these days, most academic grants begin to take shape when the grants officer notices that a deadline is approaching and starts looking for a faculty member who might supply expertise and details to flesh out a more or less pre-established format — say in bilingual instruction, or the implementation of the current Administration's solar energy program by a high-school class. This particular proposal was born during a moment of quiet reflection in an airport cocktail lounge in Columbus, Ohio. I had just completed a week of intense and exciting involvement in the Ohio Conference on the Humanities — itself a program funded by the National Endowment for the Humanities (NEH). That conference contributed several elements to

Dr. John F. Fleischauer, the Project Director of the proposal featured in this issue, is Chairman of the Humanities Division of Columbus College, Columbus, Georgia, and has provided a history of the conception of this Pilot Project and the application process.

my own concept; it seemed such a perfect use of support funds for the humanities that I want to describe it briefly.

The Ohio Conference, directed for four years by two far-sighted Ohio Univeristy English professors, brought together an invited cross-section of ordinary but interested citizens for a summer week to consider from a humanistic viewpoint some general but nagging social issues. An audience of about fifty teachers, plumbers, mayors, journalists, and mothers gathered in 1976 to hear lectures upon social aspects of the origin and history of the Constitution presented by noted scholars and public officials. Humanities teachers like me were brought in to hear the lectures and then lead intensive discussions on the topics, supported by outside reading in history and literature to help focus group reactions. Then we consolidated our sense of the progress of the discussions and reported back to the conference at large. The week was capped by a public program on the Constitution featuring readings by James Earl Jones.

It was all very heady. Real learning took place. Ordinary people asked questions and expanded their awareness instead of griping about "the way things are." Sitting there afterward over my martini in the airport, I realized how important such eclectic — and interdisciplinary — experiences are to learning and yet how hard they are to create in the college environment, with its separated departments and career-oriented students. My own college, of which I am Humanities Division Chairman, did not even have a humanities course — only competing courses in literature, art, music, history, and political science, all struggling to gain student enrollment. And pity the student who wanted (and would benefit from) a sense of the relationship between art and social values, or between ethical theories and modern material technology.

By the time I reached the olive, I had jotted notes for the grant proposal printed here. My own sense of inadequacy while preparing for the Ohio Conference suggested that although I could collect a faculty, we would need to train each other to talk more confidently to students about the interplay of diverse intellectual and social forces. Such a faculty should be broadly representative, but I knew that we would flounder without direction or agreement unless we had some guidance. So I concocted Phases I and II, an initial period of planning and defining followed by a more intense summer of seminar meetings visited by experienced humanists who could give us tips and evaluate our progress. This was the best idea of the whole grant. The visiting humanists not only helped us understand how to be interdisciplinary in our approach, they also showed us by their own example that success would come from diffidence — that our goal should be to learn with our students new questions and perspectives rather than to dictate to them sets of values or truths of which we ourselves were unsure.

The writing of the grant proposal posed several problems which I did not immediately solve. The program itself was sound, if not well enough defined, and the faculty I recruited were excited and eager to begin. A benevolent college administration gave its blessing once I explained matching funds in terms of "in kind" contributions and fractional salary allocations. Still, in my inexperience, I failed at first to anticipate

the reactions of the NEH review panel in the areas of total budget, faculty qualifications, and definition of objectives.

The proposal, in spite of helpful suggestions from the NEH central office, was rejected in the fall of 1976. The reviewers' comments were helpful, but disappointingly conservative in their demand for identification of specific methods, materials, and objectives *before* the planning phase of what was designed as an experimental program. They also demonstrated peculiar concern about local politics, born, I am sure, out of cynicism developed from experience in larger university communities. They noted that some of the faculty lacked Ph.Ds. Many of our college faculty do. We are a new school, a community college, and we employ many ABD (all but dissertation) instructors who fit right in while they complete their advanced academic work. But the reviewers, applying an AAUP point of view, worried that these supposedly untenured instructors, pulled out of their disciplines for such a program, might fail of selection. Actually, all but one of us were tenured, only two of the seven lacked doctorates, and inclusion in the program was seen by department heads (three of whom volunteered for the program) as a distinctive example of professional commitment and development. The problem was not in our program but in communication of our environment — our ecology, so to speak — to a misapprehending panel. So in the revision of 1977, I added several paragraphs showing our progress in planning and emphasizing the value of the program to the participants as well as to the students.

The suggestion for more specific description of methods, scope, and materials led to a prototype course I taught after the first proposal had been rejected. It also turned out to be a valuable corrective to the scope of the proposal as a whole. Under a "Special Topics in Literature" heading, I tried my own wings at a course that would encourage students to come to grips with cultural diversity by focusing on several points of cultural conflict in history. The course plan was too ambitious, and the students, although excited by the exposure to so many new ideas and so much information, felt bewildered and overwhelmed by the end of it. We studied the collapse of Hellenism in Palestine under Roman occupation during the Maccabean period; the adaptation of Italian aesthetics in England during the Renaissance; the effects of European colonial exploitation in Nigeria and the Congo; the American rehabilitation of Japan after WWII; and the student revolution of the American 1960s.

By the end of the course it was obvious that one could not teach the world's wisdom and ignorance in one quarter. Scope must be narrowed and materials selected in advance to provide representative rather than complete exposure to a very few interdisciplinary topics. So while I was revising the grant proposal, I also began meeting with the potential faculty to settle on a more concrete series of course topics. We finally agreed that the first course would focus on America in the sixties and seventies, since students had some interest but little direct knowledge of the counter-culture, and attractive materials were readily available. The second would focus on urbanization, primarily because we are an urban college but also because Urban History is the specialty of one of the program faculty. The third, in an effort to recapture some of the spirit of the Ohio Conference, would focus on apparent conflicts between technological expansion and the humanities, with some polemical effort to stress the need for humanistic perspectives, but without any preconceived "lesson" to be learned. It would be a "problems" course with more questions than answers. These new focuses gave a more solid sense of direction to our program but still left enough flexibility for adapting it to the chemistry of discovery in progress.

The budget problem was simple. We were at first not asking for enough money. Although the project was ambitious for Columbus College, it was modest by NEH Program grant standards, and in the revision I learned how to play the budget game. We did not cheat or pad, really, but we did not scrimp. Secretarial services were included, as were replacement funds for the instructors in the program — in the form of re-

leased time — although we might have absorbed such expenses. It occurred to me much later that I had neglected to write in compensation for myself as director. Had I been more experienced in such things, I would have — not so much for the additional income, about which I have ethical questions, but rather to defray the expenses of entertainment when consultants came and went or when the faculty met to evaluate and plan. I believe now that the satisfactions of the program compensated me adequately for such expenses and for the time spent; but as a guide for future projects, I feel the need to suggest that the purpose of federal support for academic programs such as this is precisely to avoid the necessity for compensation in metaphysical satisfaction as a return for physical, intellectual, or financial effort. Humanists must eat, too, and in our tolerance of relativity we tend to let others eat first and best.

I would change only one aspect of the proposal in hindsight. The public element, in which our visiting experts returned to speak in the courses and also to give public lectures, was not very satisfactory. My idea was to include some of the public education experience I had admired in the Ohio Conference and to obtain a little PR mileage for the program and the college. Unfortunately, not many Columbus citizens were interested in conflicts between traditional and popular art, so the first lecture was not well attended. But it had not been heavily advertised either. So the second quarter, I obtained additional funds from the Georgia Committee on the Humanities and held a forum on local civic values, featuring local civic leaders, whose comments were then focused by our visiting urban values expert. The more dramatic and topical nature of this program helped, as did the extra promotional funding, but the program threatened to become too grandiose and trendy for the sake of publicity at the expense of educational benefit, so the final public program was gratefully cancelled when our expert had difficulty scheduling his return. Another case of too much missionary ambition on my part to reach the world while I had the floor!

Over all, the program was a major success, both for me personally and for the college. The humanities series has become a part of the elective curriculum, and a small but active core of students continues to demand it. We are having some trouble determining a plan for long-term direction of the sequence, as we seek a way to control faculty selection and preparation without inhibiting interest and turnover. But these are good problems to work on. I'm not certain what the secrets of our success were — perhaps excitement, for one thing, and willingness to compromise with alien perspectives, for another. Certainly persistence, and an honest appraisal of our own weaknesses as they turned up. At any rate we did succeed and created, with the help of NEH, something of value.

* * *

NEH PILOT GRANT – COLUMBUS COLLEGE PROPOSAL FOR A THREE-QUARTER SEQUENCE OF INTERDISCIPLINARY HUMANITIES COURSES FOR GENERAL STUDENTS

Background

Columbus College, begun in 1958, achieved senior status in the University System of Georgia in 1965. It has grown to a size of 5500 students, primarily out of an urban community interest in an institution which can provide a comprehensive education beyond the limits of the traditional two-year community college. Its philosophy is essentially practical if not technical, and the student body tends to seek out majors in professional and pre-professional disciplines such as Education, Business Administration, and Criminal Justice, more than in the liberal arts. The Humanities Division, while sponsoring about eighty majors, acts primarily as a service unit for other academic divisions.

We have departments of Art and Music, Nursing, Dental Hygiene, and so on, with separate faculties whose members are appointed as experts in particular specialties within given fields. Excerpts from a recent Review of Academic Programs for the English major demonstrate the usual departmental view of faculty responsibility:

> The program has faculty members who have specialized in every traditional area in British and American literature. In addition, we have specialists in linguistics, creative writing, literary criticism, drama, and film.

> With the hiring of a creative writing specialist for 1975-76, the program's last weak area has been covered. It would be nice to have specialists in folklore, minority literature, and bibliographical methods as well, but there is not enough student demand in these areas to justify the cost.

The point of view exhibited is totally segmented, ignoring overlaps of influence in disciplines, seeking even further specialization in the event of faculty increases.

The course structure, though comprehensive, is diverse and fragmented. It contains duplications (courses on the psychology of reading are offered in three different departments) and serious gaps — especially gaps of perspective. The fragmentation most seriously affects the humanities. Nowhere can the original concept of the eclectic and organic study of man's achievements be found. In order to obtain even the most superficially integrated sense of the development of civilization, a student at Columbus College must take more than eight different courses in the arts, humanities, and social sciences. And then he must do the integrating himself. Such diversification has injured the attractiveness of humanistic study by overwhelming potential students in complexity, time, and expense.

Such a curriculum is self-defeating, because it dissipates the available pool of beginning potential humanities students into a variety of more limited courses which often must be cut at registration time for insufficient enrollment, whereas the combined total may be more than sufficient to warrant continuation. In the Fall Quarter, 1975, for example, six lower level sections in world literature, art, drama, music, and history

```
WASHINGTON, D. C. 20506              DATE RECEIVED:      LOG NUMBER:
                                       12/6/76          H-27322
TELEPHONE: 202-382-5891            ─────────────────────────────────
                                   1. PROJECT DIRECTOR (NAME, ADDRESS & ZIP)
GRANT APPLICATION FACE SHEET
  PROGRAM GRANT                       Dr. John F. Fleischauer, Chairman
(X) PILOT            ( ) PROJECT NEW   Languages-Humanities Division
( ) DEVELOPMENT      ( ) PROJECT RENEW Columbus College
( ) PROJECT RESUBMISSION              Columbus, Georgia 31907

                                   TELEPHONE:  (404) 568-2054
───────────────────────────────────────────────────────────────────
2. INSTITUTION (NAME, ADDRESS & ZIP) 3. AUTHORIZING OFFICIAL (NAME, ADDRESS & ZIP)

    Columbus College                  Dr. Thomas Y. Whitley, President
    Columbus, Georgia  31907          Columbus College
                                      Columbus, Georgia  31907


───────────────────────────────────────────────────────────────────
4. FUNDS REQUESTED (FIRST YEAR & TOTAL) 5. PAYEE (CHECK TO BE MADE PAYABLE TO:)
                                        Columbus College
FIRST YEAR:   $36,063               CHECK TO BE MAILED TO:

TOTAL:        $36,063               NAME AND TITLE: James O. Sanders, Comptroller
                                    ADDRESS:        Columbus College
                                                    Columbus, Georgia 31907
───────────────────────────────────────────────────────────────────
6. INCLUSIVE DATES OF GRANT:
FROM:   June      1,     19 77    THROUGH:  June       1,    19 78
       MONTH     DATE                       MONTH     DATE
```

TITLE:
    A Three-Quarter Sequence of Interdisciplinary Humanities Courses for General Students

BRIEF DESCRIPTION:

    Columbus College will complete development of a three-course sequence of inter-
disciplinary, inter-cultural humanities courses designed to provide a balance for the
current curriculum, which reflects traditional specialization and students interest in
career preparation courses. Released time will be provided for selected faculty from
English, Philosophy, Art, Music, Histroy, and Sociology to meet during one quarter in
a seminar which will devise course syllabi, select teaching materials, and train participants in the broader areas and syntheses necessary for interdisciplinary instruction.
Notable guest humanists will be invited to advise and stimulate the seminar. The
course sequence will address culture conflicts, urbanization, and technocracy. Each
course will be taught by a team of two of the Program faculty with occasional assistance
from the others and guest lectures from the visiting humanists. The program will be
evaluated by students, consultants, and a workshop involving Program faculty.

STATEMENT: IT IS UNDERSTOOD AND AGREED THAT ANY FUNDS GRANTED AS A RESULT OF THIS REQUEST
ARE TO BE USED FOR THE PURPOSES SET FORTH HEREIN. FURTHERMORE, THE UNDERSIGNED AGREE, AS
TO ANY GRANT AWARDE, TO ABIDE BY THE RELEVANT NATIONAL ENDOWMENT FOR THE HUMANITIES POLICIES
AS PRESCRIBED.

SIGNATURE: PERSON NAMED IN ITEM 1   SIGNATURE: PERSON NAMED IN ITEM 3

John F. Fleischauer   *Thomas Y. Whitley*

Application Cover Sheet

were cut. Their combined enrollment at the time of cancellation was thirty-five. The conclusion is that the College could support a beginning humanities program, but is not serving interested students sufficiently with its variety of unrelated and uncoordinated specialized course offerings.

Within the last several years, an increasing number of educational theorists (including such men as Morse Peckham, O. B. Hardison, and A. D. Van Nostrand) have suggested developing interdisciplinary programs in the humanities, even to the extent of Ph.Ds in humanities which might fight the shrunken college job market by providing scholarly factotums able to teach wherever there are vacancies. Disregarding possible cynicism about the motives of the new

Columbus College has developed plans for an interdisciplinary, intercultural
sequence of three courses designed to provide general students with a broad introductory understanding of the relationship between the humanities and their practical
interests. The College developed out of community interest in comprehensive education beyond the limits of the two-year school. Its philopsophy is practical, and
majors predominate in professional and pre-professional areas rather than in the
liberal arts. The Humanities Division consequently acts primarily as a service unit.
Further, the faculty and curriculum reflect the concern of the 1960s for specialized
separation of disciplines; this fragmentation has discouraged potential humanities
students by denying them any integrated view of civilized culture. Even the de-
partmentalized humanities courses in Art, History, Literature, etc. must often be
cancelled for lack of enrollment, because the available pool of interested students
is necessarily dispersed. In order to provide an honestly interdisciplinary
humanities sequence and to minimize the biases and limitations of particpating
faculty specialists, we have set out a three-phase program of planning, faculty
retraining, and cooperative team teaching. Additional guidance and stimulation for
both faculty and students will come from well-known, visiting humanists who can
demonstrate the effectiveness of humanistic education in social action. In Phase I,
begun Fall, 1975, the Program faculty--one professor each from the Art, Music,
English, Philosophy, History and Sociology departments--were selected and met as a
committee with the Program Director to design three complementary but non-traditional
course themes suitable for both interdesciplinary investigation and a variety of
possible instructional approaches. The courses include: HUM 101: The conflicts
and syntheses of cultural imposition (counter-cultures); HUM 102: Urbanization and
a variety of city cultures; HUM 103: The problems of the humanities in a technocracy. Examination of possible texts and other useful materials will continue
focusing the tentative themes and objectives of the sequence. Phase II will begin
Summer Quarter, 1977, if funded by the NEH. It will provide this group with partial
released time to establish detailed syllabi and complete selection of teaching
materials, but primarily this phase will allow them to meet regularly in seminar to
learn from each others' specializations, developing a keener sense of relationships
among the various disciplines represented, at least in the areas of the sequence.
This effort will be augmented by outside consultants--men of some national stature
in non-academic areas--who can advise and stimulate the Program faculty as they
refine the course and their roles. The consultants will visit during the refinement phase and return as guest lecturers during the teaching phase, providing the
community with a public address as well. In the teaching--Phase III, scheduled for
academic year 1977-1978--the six faculty will devide into teams of two for each
course to ensure balanced perspectives. They will develop their own presentation
arrangements for best instruction, and each team will draw on other members as
necessary for additional viewpoints and variety. The Program faculty includes
J. Fleischauer, Chairman, Humanities, Project Director; T. Jordan, English;
J. Thomas, Philosophy; J. Howard, Art; J. Anderson, Chairman, Fine Arts, Music;
J. Murzyn, History; and T. Hefner, Sociology. The evaluation of the program will
be derived from students responses, critiques of the guest consultants, and a workshop of Program faculty after each course is completed. NEH funds will help
provide released time during the refinement-retraining phase, consultant fees, and
some initial instructional materials.

Application Summary Sheet

tendency to return the stress of the humanities curriculum toward the direction of its origins, we must note that the thrust of the new trend demands interdisciplinary programs. These programs attempt to counter functionalism by forcing students into a broad-spectrum experience which includes not only practical technique but also the contexts and significance of learning.

Plan

Facing our technocratic complexity from a humanist perspective presents an unnerving, but exciting, challenge. In order to address this challenge and provide the humanities disciplines in the Columbus College curriculum value beyond service for technically oriented programs, we plan to establish an interdisciplinary, intercultural series of courses emphasizing the relationship of the humanities to the practical concerns of higher education and social activities in America today. The exact nature of the course sequence has been designed in an effort to reflect and respond to locally felt needs and priorities by the methods described below. In its general conception, however, the sequence will introduce lower level or "general" students to the interrelationships of their own interests in philosophy, the arts, letters, and social sciences. Further, it will make a coherent effort at demonstrating that the universalities of the humanities not only have spawned present science and technology, but contain within them the balance needed for the maintenance of progressive but responsible civilization.

The course sequence will provide exemplary evidence that the humanistic disciplines are practical pursuits rather than the will-o-the-wisps of bygone cultures — evidence offered partly by means of guest lecturers who are themselves successful and effective humanists from a variety of respected modern fields. The goal of the sequence is not blatantly to sell the humanities, but to develop an appreciation for their significance and relevance. The specific approaches will be determined by the faculty involved; the general forms have been tentatively identified. Given the infinite possibilities for organization of such a sequence, a committee of faculty have agreed to focus upon a group of conceptual themes in world culture and to avoid a purely chronological survey. The committee, composed of potential teachers of the sequence, has established the following descriptive guidelines:

1. *Counter-Culture.* An examination of the effects upon society when the values and forms of one social order are imposed upon those of another. Focus will be on (a) the Hellenistic era in the eastern Mediterranean, with attention to the Roman occupation of Greece and Palestine; (b) The English Renaissance, in which the flourishing culture of Italy was consciously borrowed and adapted by an influential oligarchy of courtiers, scholars, and the Tudor monarchy; (c) The encroachment of white European powers in Africa in the twentieth century, including colonialism, rapid technolgical revolution, Christianization, and the resultant disintegration of native African tribal mores; (d) The American counter-culture of the 1960s, investigating the attempt of a sub-culture to rise to independence, its failure, and the reverberations of the conflict in contemporary art, ethics, and other cultural conventions.

2. *Urbanization.* A look at the various cultural identities of some of the great cities of the world and at the evolutionary trend from a pastoral or agricultural to an urbanized civilization. In its historical perspective, this course will survey Semitic, South Pacific, and some African nomadic societies, then examine Greek city-states, imperial Rome, Tenochtitlan, London, and the modern cities of Paris, Rio de Janeiro, Sydney, Leningrad, Rome, and ultimately the Boston-New York-Washington megalopolis.

3. *Culture and the Technocracy.* A "problems" course aimed at stimulating student response to a number of social and artistic dilemmas borne of the technological advances of the twentieth century and the natural shifting of consciousness toward the quantitative, functional, and practical. Students will observe hybrid art — geodetics, cybernetic design, random musical composition — as well as protests in art and ethics and what is called the "crisis of the humanities." Emphasis in faculty guidance will be on the need for balance and interrelationship of varying cultural values rather than domination of either humanities or sciences over other aspects of culture; but in this course students will not be provided with easy solutions.

The course sequence is being developed in three phases by an interdisciplinary group of faculty, who will also provide the core of instruction. A Pilot course in area 1 above has already been taught to test feasibility of some of the goals of this program and to sample student reaction. A second, in area 3, is scheduled for Spring Quarter 1977. Inferences based upon these experiments are discussed later.

Phases of the Program

Phase I — Planning

In the first phase a series of meetings is being conducted during the 1976-77 academic year. These meetings include two representatives from each of the three academic divisions most involved in the humanities: Thornton F. Jordan, Assistant Professor of English; John J. Thomas, Assistant Professor of Philosophy; James B. Howard, Head, Department of Art; John H. Anderson, Chairman, Fine Arts Division and

Professor of Music; John S. Murzyn, Associate Professor of History; and Ted C. Hefner, Assistant Professor of Sociology.

The group members have investigated the possibilities, areas of demand, forms, and feasible concentrations for interdisciplinary study at Columbus College. They have already decided upon subject areas for the sequence of three courses as described above and in the same process have developed a tentative list of applicable works for selection of texts, audio-visual aids, and resource materials. In order for the faculty to apply their efforts fruitfully and conscientiously in the development of teaching materials, however, they will be granted released time in Phase II equivalent to two courses in their normal teaching load. The meetings are moderated by the Program Director, John F. Fleischauer, Chairman of the Humanities division and Associate Professor of English, who will receive the same released time.

Phase II — Coordination and Training of the Faculty Team

The second phase, which requires the assistance of the National Edowment, is scheduled for Summer Quarter, 1977. In it, as in Phase I, work will be undertaken in the seminar format. Participants will include the faculty participating in Phase I or replacements if necessary, with the addition of outside leadership provided by three distinguished guest consultants to the program. Other faculty from the College will be invited to contribute as well, where appropriate. The goal of this phase is to develop, in what are now disparate specialists, a keen and feasible sense of the relationships among their specialties so that they can teach with conviction and confidence a blend of interests and areas of knowledge. Further aims of this phase will be to assign faculty teams to individual courses, to finalize selection of texts and materials, and to refine the syllabi for the courses.

Faculty members of Columbus College, like those of many small colleges, have traditionally been selected for their potential teaching ability more than scholarly promise. The intimacy of the small college environment coupled with the professional rather than academic goals of the students tend to encourage development of classroom expertise at the expense of (but not to the exclusion of) scholarly professional growth. As a result, many excellent faculty demonstrate rather meager credentials on paper; many never complete their doctorates. Recent trends in the job market and rapid growth of the college are changing this tendency, but in the meanwhile the Interdisciplinary Program, like the rest of the college curriculum, will depend on the energy, broad-ranging curiosity, and experience of the selected faculty for success. They are among our best. It should be pointed out that five of the seven persons involved are tenured and four are senior faculty. Participation in this program will enhance rather than detract from the faculty's opportunities for promotions because of its reflection of teaching ability, creative effort, and interest in the development of curriculum.

The function of the outside consultants will be two-fold: first, they will bring to the faculty team fresh perspective and expertise in the practical uses of the humanities. They will suggest definitions and adjustments peculiar to the translation of humanistic inquiries into social realities; and they will develop a bond with the College which will help to make the sequence succeed; for having assisted us in the birth of the program, they will be invited later (see Phase III) to participate in the nurturing of their child, and their involvement will lend both a credence to the skeptical and an example of what we value to the rest of the campus and community. Their specific duties in the second phase, however, will be to give advice about emphases and approaches, recommend other resources, and assist in the process of expanding the articulateness of the faculty team beyond their accustomed boundaries. The consultants named may change depending upon their schedules, but we have received interested responses from Yates

Hafner, former Dean of Monteith College, Wayne State University; Harrison Sheppard, Assistant Executive Director, San Francisco Regional Office of the Federal Trade Commission; James Earl Jones, actor; Samuel Crowl, Professor of English, Ohio University; Betty Adcock, poet and editor.

Phase III – Implementation of the Course Sequence

With the completion of the planning and coordination of Phases I and II, a sequence of three interdisciplinary humanities courses — HUM 101, 102, 103, — will be scheduled and advertised at Columbus College. Each course will be self-contained but will lead to the next one in the sequence; each will emphasize one of the areas determined previously. The courses will be open to all students regardless of major. The sequence will be accessible in a more practical sense because it will fulfill Humanities distribution requirements in the lower-level general studies core curriculum. It is estimated that with priority scheduling during its infancy, the program will draw forty students in the fall quarter and twenty-five to thirty in the winter and spring.

In order to maximize the combined interdisciplinary expertise of the Program faculty, we have agreed to teach the course in flexible teams. A group of two will be assigned to each course to finalize lesson plans and reading assignments as well as supplemental class materials. The two will agree on a suitable classroom format — generally a combination of lecture and group discussion, but perhaps also dialogue, debate, or field work. Other members of the Program faculty will be asked to provide guest presentations from time to time in the course in order to provide highlights, new perspectives, or simply variety. The underlying purpose of the teams is to avoid the narrowness and superficiality likely in the intruction of a specialist; the flexibility of arrangements is designed to overcome some of the problems of format, grading,

etc., which are often encountered in prescribed team teaching situations.

In fact, flexibility within a controlled continuum is a guiding principle of the Program itself. The humanities teach us that through both self-discipline and risky exposure to new ideas, man will reach his highest moments. The course sequence ought to reflect that commitment of ours not only in the exhortation of lectures but in the adaptability of curriculum and faculty to the students in their efforts to absorb ideas. Course objectives will include not only specific knowledge on, say, the development of the urban community, but also demonstration of the tolerance those who call themselves humanists possess for alternate points of view.

In addition to the Program faculty, each course will include at least one guest lecture by a noted humanist presently engaged in practical administration of an educational, political, or scientific institution. These guest lecturers, of course, should be the same outside consultants who provided guidance to the development of the program in Phase II; their involvement in the program should also permit us to induce each of them to present a public address during his visit for the course. Such addresses, one per quarter during the academic year, will contribute significantly to the cultural environment of Columbus, to the relationship between the College and the community, and to a general interest in the humanities among students, faculty, and citizens.

This plan is solid and feasible. Its success on campus and as a model for other colleges and universities will depend on the care and seriousness of participation of all involved in Phases I and II, but also on the support of the College in publicizing the course and the presentations of the guest experts. A trial course was taught Winter Quarter, 1976, by the Project Director. The syllabus followed the plan of the first course in the sequence (described earlier), in an effort to determine: (1) whether Columbus College students were willing to broaden their learning experience in a general humanities course; (2) what kinds of evaluation techniques are suit-

Budget for Columbus College Interdisciplinary Humanities Program

Item	NEH	College	Total
A. Salaries			
1. Two-thirds of contracted salaries for six faculty members and Program Director during Summer Quarter 1977:			
Dr. A		3,508	
Dr. B		3,462	
Dr. C	3,662		
Mr. D	2,500		
Dr. E	2,460		
Mr. F	2,600		
Dr. G	2,780		
Subtotal	$14,002	$6,970	$20,972
2. One-third released time for six faculty members and Program Director for one quarter during 1977-78 academic year	4,300	8,458	12,758
3. One-half time secretarial assistance for development (Phase II) and operation (Phase III)		2,900	2,900
4. Fringe benefits:			
(a) 18% of $18,302	3,294		3,294
(b) 18% of $18,328		3,299	3,299
B. Travel:			
1. Program Director: One trip to Southern Humanities Conference to discuss this program and study related interdisciplinary curricula		200	200
C. Supplies:			
1. Planning resources, reports, syllabi	500		500
2. Instructional materials (A/V)	1,600	400	2,000
D. Other:			
1. Consultant fees:			
Phase II — 6 days @$100	600		600
Per diem — 6 days @$25	150		150
Travel — 4,900 miles @$12 per mile	588		588
2. Phase III — Honoraria, per diem, and travel	1,338		1,338
3. Stipends for incumbent guest participants	300		300
4. Communications (telephone, mail, etc.)	500	500	1,000
Subtotal	$27,172	$22,727	$49,899
E. Indirect cost: Up to 50.5% of salaries in accordance with negotiated agreement with HEW dated 1/20/77	8,891	9,256	18,147
	$36,063	$31,983	$68,046

able to judge both students and the course; (3) the availability of and feasible uses of teaching materials; (4) the limitations actually experienced by an interested specialist attempting to develop an unbiased, eclectic articulateness for our students.

Although the course was not widely advertised, word of it spread and the actual enrollment was twenty-three. The students came from a wide variety of majors in the liberal arts spectrum but also from business. Evaluations were unanimously enthusiastic by students and the instructor, and over half the class have continued since the course to ask for a sequel. The pilot project fell short of the planned presentation in that faculty could not be released for team experimentation. However, a member of the art faculty did visit to discuss composition and expressive themes in contemporary art and sculpture, and two students teamed up voluntarily to perform a very successful vocal-guitar medley of protest songs of the sixties and their 1970s offspring. The course outline is attached, along with examinations and some student comments, as an indication of one very possible format for the course.

The knowledge gleaned from this course experience will greatly assist the Program faculty in the refinement of the humanities sequence for its first independent scheduling. A second effort, at the third course (the "Problems" course), is scheduled for Spring 1977, if faculty can be spared. But a full-scale, coordinated plan is needed. If students are attracted by their awareness of the planning and by the promises of the sequence, and if they feel that their exposure to the humanities has been educational in the subjective sense of stimulation, growth, and profit, they will continue to register. The College Curriculum Committee has already approved the concept of the sequence. If the sequence proves its value, it will be incorporated into the curriculum of the College, and operational expense will be borne by the College after the first year, except that state legal limitations on consultant fees may force us to seek outside support — from the National Edowment, the Georgia Com-

mittee for the Humanities, or private patrons — for the quarterly guest speakers, and we will need some program assistance once our direction is sure in order to develop a library of teaching resource materials for subsequent instructional staff.

Evaluation

The evaluation of the program will consist of four assessments: (1) Student registration figures over the first year of operation will indicate attractiveness of the sequence; (2) Student evaluations at the end of each course will assist instructors and the Program Director in adjusting methods and objectives; (3) Responses from the outside experts will focus on the worth of their participation in Phases II and III and the overall merit of the program from their perspective; and (4) Program faculty will conduct self-assessment through individual reports during all three Phases and in an evaluative workshop session at the end of each course.

Conclusion

We have at this point gone as far as the approved College budget and the duties of our faculty will allow if we are to avoid sacrificing the possible excellence of this program to expediency. We need to be able to release the Program faculty to apply their time and attention to the effort responsibly; we need to go out to discuss our plans with others for perspective; and we need to begin training our faculty in the broader awareness and articulateness required of a true humanities curriculum. Some of the College's share of the enclosed budget has been not only allocated but spent in the development of the plan to date, an indication of the seriousness of our commitment. We hope to find the National Endowment interested in our effort and willing to share in it.

CRITIQUE OF THE INTERDISCIPLINARY HUMANITIES PROPOSAL

by Myra Ficklen

The Columbus College proposal is an excellent example of an NEH Pilot Grant, a program designed to meet the local needs of an institution by improving its humanities offerings. Columbus College developed an interdisciplinary program in keeping with its professional and pre-professional orientation. The proposal demonstrates that a careful needs assessment has been made and that sufficient planning has taken place to ensure successful implementation. Further, there is strong evidence of institutional commitment to the program.

The proposal is presented in a clear, jargon-free style. It is concise, yet provides enough detail for the reader to visualize what the director wants to do. The writer followed carefully the NEH guidelines, providing all the relevant information, with each section leading logically to the next.

Proposal Summary

The summary in the Columbus College proposal is especially effective in that it provides a capsule of the entire proposal. From this brief description, the reader knows precisely what the proposal is about.

Background

In this section of the proposal the writer has introduced Columbus College by indicating the unique qualities of the institution and its mission. "Its philosophy is essentially practical, if not technical, and the student body tends to seek out majors in professional and pre-professional disciplines such as Education, Business Administration and Criminal Justice, more than in the liberal arts." Thus in planning the humanities program, the project director developed courses appropriate to this type of institution, where humanities would be primarily service units for other academic divisions. The appropriateness of the project to Columbus College is one of the strengths of the proposal. The proposal writer is realistic about what can be achieved.

The idea for the project is based on a need determined by the faculty review committee after a careful examination of course offerings:

> The course structure, though comprehensive, is diverse and fragmented. It contains duplications (courses on the psychology of reading are offered in three different departments) and serious gaps — especially gaps of perspective. The fragmentation most seriously affects the humanities.

The problem is further documented by the enrollment figures. While several of the more limited humanities courses had to be dropped, the combined enrollment indicated sufficient interest in a beginning humanities course to justify restructuring the offerings to provide a more integrated approach to the humanities. Thus, Columbus College has adequately established the need for improvement in its humanities offering.

Plan

Columbus College is very clear about the goal of its humanities program. "The goal of the sequence is not blatantly to sell the humanities, but to develop an appreciation for their significance and relevance." While the specific approaches are to be determined by the faculty involved, there is ample evidence that the program has been carefully planned and thought through. A series of interdisciplinary, inter-

Myra Ficklen, Director of the Federal Resources Advisory Service of the Association of American Colleges in Washington, D.C., is the analyst of this proposal. Ms. Ficklen is the author of a series of federal funding guides in selected disciplines: arts and humanities, social sciences, biological sciences, physical and mathematical sciences, and education. She is the editor of the Federal Resources Advisory Service monthly newsletter *News Notes*.

cultural courses "emphasizing the relationship of the humanities to the practical concerns of higher education and social activities in America today" have been planned around the following themes: counter-culture, urbanization, and culture and technology. Since Columbus College has already initiated a pilot program in counter-culture, with favorable results, there is an excellent indication that the other portions of the program will also be successful. The proposal writer has given adequate evidence that this plan is likely to improve the humanities program, by providing a more integrated approach to courses with practical aspects of the humanities included.

The proposal provides a step-by-step description of how the program will be implemented. Phase I is a planning stage, with the specific faculty members already indicated. However, much of the initial brainstorming has already taken place. This planning will be for further development of teaching materials and details of the courses. Phase II is for faculty training in team teaching, with the assistance of outside consultants. The faculty will further refine the syllabi and courses. Phase III is the implementation of the courses. Columbus College will begin with three interdisciplinary courses, designed for forty students in the fall quarter and twenty-five to thirty in the winter and spring.

By presenting its plan in this manner, Columbus College is able to show the reader exactly how the program will develop. Attention to detail and careful planning are evident. The proposal answers questions which the reviewer will have about who will be involved in the project, the time frame, and types of courses to be developed, etc. Since faculty will be engaged in teaching interdisciplinary courses, the faculty workshops and extensive planning are necessary to give the agency evidence of the feasibility of this project.

The proposal also emphasizes the appropriateness of the faculty to carry out this project, because of their experience in teaching. The use of outside consultants is justified on two grounds:

to bring to the program an added perspective and expertise beyond that of the faculty in the planning stages and to serve as guest lecturers for the courses.

Evaluation

The evaluation section, while not elaborate, is indicative of the type of evaluation expected by NEH. Since the need was documented by low student registration figures in limited humanities courses, one indication of the success of the program will be the registration for the new course sequence. Student evaluations will provide a further indication of the attractiveness and effectiveness of the offerings. The instructor will be able to determine if the goal of developing an appreciation for the significance and relevance of the humanities is being met. This feedback will also help determine any needed course alterations. The outside consultants' evaluation will provide a more objective assessment of the program. And finally, through the faculty evaluation workshop, faculty will provide another indication of how successful the program has been in alleviating the fragmentation and ineffective course offerings.

Conclusion

The institutional commitment to the program is evident throughout the proposal, from the pilot program already implemented to the substantial planning effort involved. Columbus is specific as to why it needs outside support: released time; training for faculty; outside consultants. Yet once the program is implemented, Columbus College will incorporate it into the regular curriculum of the college, thereby supporting the program from institutional sources.

There is a strong sense of merit throughout the proposal. Careful planning, commitment to an idea, and evidence of likelihood of successful implementation contribute to the effectiveness of this proposal.

GRANTMAKING AT THE NATIONAL ENDOWMENT FOR THE HUMANITIES

by John Lippincott

When Pat Bates first considered applying to the National Endowment for the Humanities for a Public Libraries grant, she was intimidated by the prospect. "I thought it was out of my league. I was overwhelmed and scared."

But she had two things going for her. She had the encouragement of the Vermont Council on the Humanities, which was familiar with her highly successful reading/discussion program at the Rutland Free Library. And she was naive; "I didn't know it would be such hard work."

The encouragement and naiveté prompted her to call NEH. She spoke with a Libraries Program staff member and outlined her proposal to conduct public discussions with humanities scholars on literature related to contemporary social issues. She proposed implementing the program in 20–25 Vermont public libraries and preparing program packets for distribution throughout the state.

The program officer sent her the application guidelines and requested that she submit a short written prospectus for the project. Countless phone conversations and four drafts of the proposal later, she was ready to submit the formal application.

"There were many times when I was ready to give up, but the NEH staff was very supportive, and I had the encouragement of two successful applicants I'd contacted at the Endowment's suggestion."

The hard work paid off. Pat Bates says she is still "on a high" from receiving the grant last August, that the dissemination of her program to other Vermont libraries is going well, and that she is now working on a follow-up grant request to NEH.

Pat Bates' experience demonstrates many things, among them that the Endowment staff is approachable and ready to help potential applicants work through the sometimes complex grant-making process. This article will attempt to provide other prospective grantees with insight into the Endowment's grant-making process. It will not offer the assurance that applying will be easy, but it will clarify and demystify the steps involved in receiving an NEH grant.

Pre-Application Contact

The success of Pat Bates' application was in part due to the step-by-step guidance she received from an NEH program officer. That guidance is available to all eligible applicants, but first they must determine the appropriate program within the Endowment to contact.

There are more than 30 programs in the six NEH Divisions — Education, Research, Fellowships and Seminars, Public Programs, Special Programs, and State Programs. The programs provide support for a wide range of projects including:

- curriculum development and faculty training to strengthen the teaching of the humanities at all levels;
- long-term, collaborative research in all humanities disciplines as well as development of research resources and materials;
- fellowships and seminars for college teachers, independent scholars, and professionals to pursue study in the humanities;
- programs at museums, historical organizations, and libraries and on public radio and television interpreting the humanities for large, public audiences;
- innovative programs linking scholarly research with public activities; and
- programs exploring the relationship among science, technology, and human values.

Descriptions of all the programs along with general eligibility requirements are included in the NEH Program Announcement, available free upon request from the Endowment's Public Affairs Office.

John Lippincott is a Public Affairs Specialist in the Public Affairs Office of the National Endowment for the Humanities.

NATIONAL ENDOWMENT FOR THE HUMANITIES

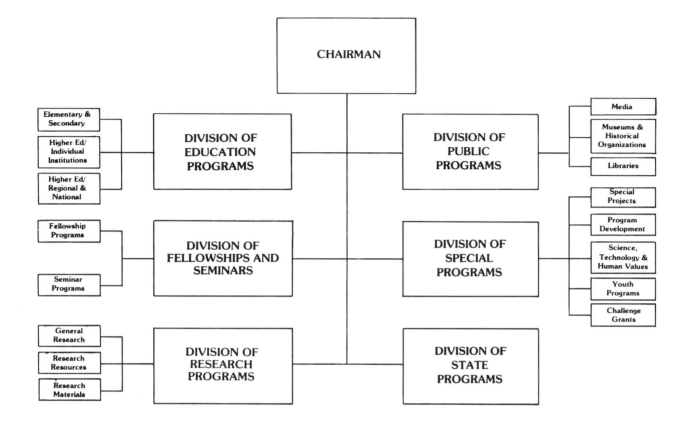

After reviewing the program material, applicants are encouraged to contact a program officer by phone or letter giving an outline of the proposed project to be sure that it is eligible for funding and properly formulated.

Contacting and working with NEH staff members during the application process will not prejudice the applicant's chances for a grant. The staff's role is to facilitate, not to evaluate.

Application

The formal application must be submitted by the specified deadline for the appropriate NEH program. Program deadlines are published in the agency's annual Program Announcement and in the NEH bimonthly periodical *Humanities,* available by subscription.

Endowment staff have found that successful applications:

1. clearly and fully state the role of the humanities in the project;
2. relate the budget closely to the activities described in the narrative;
3. use objective arguments in support of the project that do not assume reviewers are predisposed to the subject matter;
4. give a clear plan of work with a logical sequence of specific tasks;
5. explain the dissemination/distribution of the end-products of the project;
6. are neat, accurate, and complete.

Inflated rhetoric is often seen by reviewers as camouflage for a lack of substance. A straightforward description of the proposed project is always preferable.

Table of Contents

Pat Bates heard a recurrent theme in her discussions with a program officer: be explicit about the project activities, especially in defining the role of the humanities. As she clearly learned, "The hard work it takes to develop a proposal will be wasted if the information is in your head but not in the application."

The specific contents and length of the formal application for an NEH grant will depend greatly on the nature of the proposal and the program to which it is being submitted.

An annotated table of contents for an application submitted to the Higher Education/Regional and National Program is reproduced below. The project, awarded a major grant in November 1980, is to develop curricular materials in Chinese and Japanese languages with a focus on business practices in the respective cultures.

The application, submitted by Adele Rickett at the University of Maryland, is exemplary for several reasons:

1. it gives a clear and compelling argument concerning the need for the project on a national level;
2. it provides concrete examples of the material to be produced under the grant;
3. the budget is detailed, complete, and reasonable;
4. plans are given for national dissemination of the curricular materials;
5. all information is complete, including vitae for all project principals.

Application Review

Because formal proposals for NEH grants far exceed the funds available — on average three out of ten applicants receive grants — applications undergo a stringent review process.

Proposals are evaluated for the contribution the project will make to an understanding of the humanities and the ability of the project director or team to carry out the proposed activities. All applications are measured against standards of scholarly and professional excellence, as defined by the Endowment's peer review process.

Grants are made impartially on the basis of individual merit.

Most applications go through a four stage review process: (1) processing of the application by NEH staff; (2) review by panelists and, in many cases, by outside specialists; (3) review by the National Council on the Humanities; and (4) review by the NEH Chairman.

While some elements of the review process differ among the NEH programs, an example of a typical NEH application followed through the calendar of its review stages will provide a general understanding of the process.

In 1976, Earl Labor, author and editor of several books on Jack London and a professor at Centenary College in Louisiana, and Milo Shepard, executor of the Jack London estate, began discussing the need for a definitive new edition of London's letters. Growing scholarly interest in the American novelist, short story writer, adventurer, and social crusader suggested that an annotated edition of selected letters would be a valuable resource.

Labor and Shepard invited Robert Leitz of Louisiana State University, who had edited the correspondence of William Dean Howells, to help them with the project. Shortly thereafter, the team signed a contract with Stanford University Press to publish their proposed three-volume work.

The team undertook a nationwide search, collecting and examining London's letters and related materials. Having examined over 3,000 letters and selected 1,200 for publication, Leitz and Labor began the second phase of the project — transcribing and annotating the selected letters and preparing the appendix. They found they needed help, in release time and financial assistance, to complete the work, so in 1979 they approached NEH.

1979

May. Leitz and Labor contact NEH requesting information on Research Division grants. Project clearly fits guidelines for Editions Program, so Leitz calls the program officer. At staff mem-

NEH — APPLICATION COVER SHEET
Form OMB-128-R-0071

1. Individual Applicant/Principal Project Director
a. Name and Mailing Address

Rickett,   Adele   A.
(last)   (first)   (initial)

Oriental and Hebrew Program, University of Maryland

College Park   Maryland   20742
(city)   (state)   (zip)

Director and Associate Professor
title/position

f. Telephone
(   )   -   ext.

g. Citizenship
1. ☒ USA 2. ☐ Other Specify:

b. Date of Birth
/   /
mo day year

c. Major Field of Study
Chinese

Literature

d. Highest Degree Attained
Ph.D.   5 /67
mo year

e. Education
University of Pennsylvania

(For NEH use ONLY)

Date Received   /   /
Application #
Initials

2. Type of Application

1. ☒ New   2. ☐ Revision
*3. ☐ Renewal *4. ☐ Supplement
*If 3 or 4 (above) enter previous grant #

3. Program To Which Application Is Being Made

Higher Education

4. Type of Applicant

1. ☐ Individual

*2. ☐ Institution/Organization

5. Requested Period

6 / 1 /81   7 /31 / 83   Total Months 26
From: mo day yr   To: mo day yr

6. Audiences (Direct Beneficiaries)

a. Teachers of Chinese and Japanese
b. Undergraduate students

c. Graduate students

7. Requested Amount

Outright $ 132,241.00

Gift & Match $

NEH Total $

Cost Sharing & Other Contributions $ 26,034.00

Total Project $ 158,275.00

Congressional District   Fifth

* If (2) above (inst./org.) enter -
Type: University
Status: Public

8. Field of Project

Chinese and Japanese Language

9. Location Where Project Will Be Completed

College Park, Maryland

10. Public Issues Of Project

11. Topic (Title) of Project

Course materials for Chinese and Japanese Business Language and Communication

12. Description of Proposed Project (Do not exceed space provided)

To meet the rising need for American business personnel trained in the language and culture of China and Japan, the project staff will prepare materials for two two-semester courses, one Chinese, one Japanese. They will combine third-year level language training with cultural/economic information, including 3-5 page introductory essays in English, oral and written language texts, cross-cultural communication lessons (farewell banquets, etc.) to educate students in the customs of China/Japan, and a teacher's manual. Materials will be prepared in 1981-82, tested in classrooms at the Universities of Maryland/Pennsylvania in 1982-83, including outside evaluation, and presented in a workshop in July 1983.

The goals are to train students in language and communication and teach them how to continue to learn while on the job.

13a. Have you submitted, or do you plan to submit a similar application to another NEH Program? If yes, provide name(s):[year(s) when applicable]

No

13b. Have you submitted, or do you plan to submit a similar application to another government or private entity? If yes, provide name(s): [year(s) when applicable]

No

IMPORTANT — READ INSTRUCTIONS CAREFULLY BEFORE COMPLETING BLOCKS 14 & 15

14. Authorizing Official (name & mailing address)

Victor Medina
Office of Sponsored Programs
University of Maryland
College Park, Maryland 20472

Certification: I certify the statements herein are true and correct to the best of my knowledge and belief:

Sig. _____ Date   /   /
authorizing official/applicant   mo day yr

15. Institution/Organization (name & mailing address)

University of Maryland
College Park, Maryland 20742

Type Ins./Org.: Public Higher Education

ber's suggestion, Leitz and Labor submit written prospectus for project.

June. Project team corresponds with NEH to clarify details of the application form and process. NEH staff requests a draft of the application.

July. Project directors send draft proposal to Editions Program. NEH staff suggests some minor revisions in the narrative and budget portions of the draft.

September. Formal *London Letters* application is submitted in time for Editions Program's October deadline and logged in by NEH staff.

October. Editions Program officer begins process of identifying reviewers for proposal. (As in most NEH programs, applications must be reviewed by a panel of peers in the field and by individual specialists in the subject matter of the proposal.)

Program officer turns to Endowment's computerized databank of over 20,000 names of qualified scholars, teachers, administrators, librarians, archivists, curators, media producers, writers, and numerous other professionals in the humanities and members of the public from outside the Federal government. Women and minorities are included in representative numbers in the computerized files, which also reflect institutional and geographic diversity.

From the databank, program officer selects ten scholars specializing in Jack London, American literature, and/or the preparation of annotated editions of literary correspondence.

November. Grant proposal is sent to ten specialists identified by program officer and to three identified by applicant. Reviewers are requested to submit written evaluations, commenting on the project's importance and need for it in the field, on design of work to be undertaken, on qualifications of the staff, and on appropriateness of budget. Reviewers are asked to make an overall assessment of project.

1980

January/February. Outside specialists submit reviews of proposal.

Program staff refers again to reviewers databank to formulate peer review panel. (In the Editions Program two *ad hoc* panels of six members each are formed every year. One panel considers applications dealing with American editions, the other with non-American editions. Panelists are chosen for expertise in the general field of scholarly editing and for knowledge of broad areas of history and literature represented by applications under consideration. Since each panel considers 35 to 45 applications, members are not expected to be specialists in the subject matter of each proposal — that is the role of the individual reviewers.)

Prospective panelists are contacted and asked to serve on American editions panel. Six agree and are sent copies of applications to be reviewed, including *London Letters* proposal. Panelists are asked to bring written comments on each application to the panel meeting.

March. Panel on American editions meets for two days at Endowment offices in Washington, D.C. to consider 35 applications, including *London Letters* proposal. Meeting is chaired by an Endowment staff member, responsible for providing background information on NEH policy and on applications. Panelists are also provided with recommendations of individual reviewers. During meeting, panelists discuss projects and their evaluations of them. In light of discussion, some members change initial assessments of projects.

Panel unanimously endorses Leitz application for full funding. Panel also recommends 10 others for approval, 3 for deferral, and 20 for disapproval. (One applicant withdrew during the process.) Some recommendations for funding were made pending receipt of additional information or with conditions for changes in the project plan, staff, or budget.

April. Information on all NEH applications for the quarterly funding cycle is sent to members of National Council on the Humanities. The council, a 26-member board appointed by the President and approved by the Senate, advises the NEH chairman on policy matters and on funding of proposals.

Information sent to council members contains evaluations of panelists and individual reviewers for each application, including Leitz proposal.

May. The National Council holds quarterly meeting at the Endowment.

On first day of two-day meeting, council divides into small committees to consider in detail the proposals before respective NEH Divisions. Committee reviewing Research Division applications endorses *London Letters* proposal along with vast majority of others recommended for approval by panelists and reviewers.

On second day, full council convenes to discuss funding recommendations of committees. Council recommends some 500 grant awards to NEH chairman, including Leitz proposal.

NEH chairman, who by law has final authority to make awards, considers evaluations of reviewers, panelists, and National Council and endorses council's grant recommendations, including *London Letters* proposal.

Leitz and Labor receive award letter stating that full funding has been approved and outlining conditions under which the grant is being offered.

Grant period will run through 1981. The book, *The Letters of Jack London,* is expected to be published in 1984.

The time frame and review process of the Leitz grant is fairly typical. Applicants should expect a year to pass from first contact to final approval. And like Leitz, applicants should make the first contact well in advance of the program deadline.

Because of the large number of strong proposals received by the NEH, it is seldom possible to provide financial support for all those that are recommended by panelists and reviewers. Many proposals demonstrate a potential for strength but may need further work on critical elements. Submission of a revised proposal is always possible, and failure to gain support in one application round does not prevent a grantee from reapplying. At the applicant's request, Endowment staff will provide information on the comments of reviewers and panelists in order to assist the applicant in determining whether to submit a revised proposal.

The Grant Period

During the period of the grant, usually six months to three years, the grantee receives payment of the awarded funds in installments every one to three months, depending on the amount and length of the grant.

There are four types of NEH grants:

1. Outright grants provide direct support of the project costs and usually require some level of cost-sharing — cash and/or in-kind — by the grantee.

2. Matching grants authorize the grantee to raise gifts for a project up to a level approved by the NEH. The Endowment then matches this money with federal funds.

3. Combined grants are composed of both outright and matching funds.

4. Challenge grants provide humanities institutions with one federal dollar for a minimum of every three dollars raised in the private sector or from state or local revenues. Funds are to be used for activities that help insure financial stability.

Reporting requirements for grantees vary, depending on the type of grant, its size and duration, and on the program which made the award. However, all grantees are required to submit two kinds of reports to the Endowment: performance reports and financial reports.

Interim performance reports are required at least annually and at most quarterly. They are submitted to the NEH Grants Office which forwards a copy to the appropriate program. The reports detail the progress being made on the funded project. A final performance report is required within three months after the end of the grant period.

Interim financial reports are submitted to the NEH Accounting Office every three months. Final expenditure reports are also due three months after the end of the grant period.

NEH GRANT REVIEW PROCESS

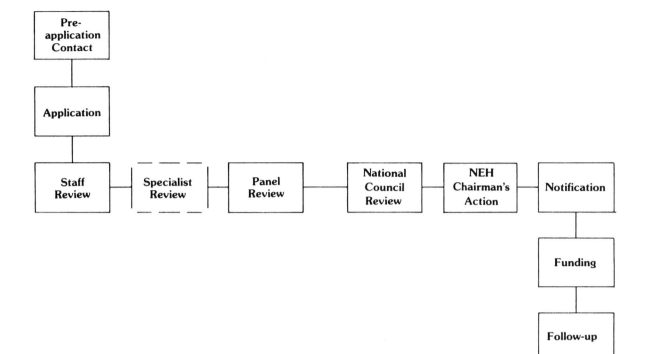

In cases where the product of a grant is published or broadcast, the NEH requests acknowledgment of its support in all printed and promotional materials.

Should a grantee earn income in excess of $50,000 a year from the product of an NEH grant, the Endowment can claim half of the annual net income in excess of $50,000, not to exceed the total amount of the grant.

Through all stages of the application and grant process the NEH staff is most willing to provide information and assistance. The first point of contact should be the Public Affairs Office, which can answer general questions and provide all NEH brochures. The address and phone number are:

Public Affairs Office
M.S. 351
National Endowment for the Humanities
806 15th St. NW
Washington, D.C. 20506
(202) 724-0386

Another good source of information about NEH programs, deadlines, and recent grants, as well as feature articles, is the NEH bimonthly publication *Humanities,* published by the Endowment and available for $7.00 a year from the Superintendent of Documents, U.S. Government Printing Office, Washington, D.C. 20402.

FEDERAL CONTRACTS—REQUEST FOR PROPOSAL (RFP)

Grants are, generally speaking, available only to nonprofit organizations, although the federal government makes exceptions to this rule in some cases.

Grant applications are normally requests for support of work that springs from the original ideas of the applicants. Contracts are a mechanism used by the government for the acquisition of material or services for which the need or the idea arose within the governmental agency.

Announcement of the availability of contracts to fulfill these governmental needs are made in several ways. An organization may have its name placed on an Agency Bidders' List and receive all RFPs issued by that agency; the Commerce Business Daily (CBD) published daily by the Department of Commerce lists available RFPs which may be requested; maintaining communication with a particular agency's technical or contracting office responsible for the issuance of RFPs is another way for an organization to be informed of the availability of RFPs as they are issued; and reading the internal publications of the requirements of a federal agency is another. Obviously these methods are of greatest interest to those organizations with a particular interest in one or two agencies. It would be impossible to keep in communication with more.

If, after receiving and reviewing the RFP the requirements of the project seem to fall within the capability of the institution and to be compatible with the work normally performed there, a contract may serve the same purpose as a grant—that is, provide funds to do something the organization wants to do while it also fulfills a need of the governmental agency. However, it is a mistake for an organization to re-order its own priorities or displace its resources solely to gain a government contract which can in such cases turn out to cost more than is reimbursable and do great damage to morale of personnel in the institution who have made the necessary sacrifices.

The article presented here, written by Dr. Gerald V. Teague, of the University of Maryland describes the proper way to respond to an RFP, and explains in meticulous detail, giving exact examples, the kind of information that is required and the style in which it must be presented. Government contract officers who reviewed this article commented favorably on the presentation and we therefore offer it as a special addendum to this compendium of grant applications. The article appeared in Volume 4, No. 1 of GRANTS MAGAZINE in March 1981.

Federal Contracts—Request for Proposal (RFP)

Bidding on government contracts is a process that is different from the standard grant application

REQUEST FOR A PROPOSAL: SOLICITATION FOR A FEDERAL CONTRACT
by Gerald V. Teague

Federal funding may take one of three forms: the traditional grant, the contract, or, most recently, the cooperative agreement. Recognizing the distinctions, not always clear-cut, among the three types of awards is necessary in understanding the unique characteristics of the Request for Proposal (RFP) and essential to the development of an effective bidding strategy.

The more readily discernible differences between the standard grant and contract are seen in the origin of specifications, announcement vehicle, organization eligibility, number and types of awards, frequency of occurrence, and federal monitoring and control. A brief elaboration of these particulars should help clarify the variations.

Grant programs are the direct result of congressional legislation. The federal agency charged with implementing the provisions of the legislative act develops a broad goal and establishes current priorities. Applicants then respond to a program announcement by designing an approach to satisfy a specific need or resolve a local problem relating to the overall agency goal. In comparison, a contract is initiated by a federal agency for a specific service or product required. Most contract aspects, e.g., objectives, tasks, timetable, and procedure, are determined by the soliciting agency. Grants programs are announced in the *Federal Register* and contract solicitations appear in the *Commerce Business Daily* (*CBD*). As a general rule, nonprofit organizations are eligible for federal grants, whereas contracts may be awarded to profit-making as well as nonprofit organizations. Normally only one contract award is made for a single project. Grants, however, are usually multiple, often dispersed geographically and programmatically. Grant funds are given for support of actual costs regardless of grant type; but contracts, while taking several forms, usually permit a fee in addition to reimbursement for expenses. A contract solicits a service or product on a one-time basis, while a grants program usually invites applications every year. For contracts, agency control and the monitoring of performance are much stricter in terms of reports, deadlines, and specifications and audits than is the case for grants.

Cooperative Agreements are the third mechanism available for award of federal funds. This

Gerald V. Teague, Ph.D., is Director, the Bureau of Educational Research, the College of Education, University of Maryland.

relatively new means of federal support is essentially the same as a grant except for an anticipated "substantial involvement" by the federal agency.[1]

Having grasped the essence of the contract, the questions must be posed: "Is my organization equipped to respond to RFPs?" "Can we handle the stringent record-keeping and report requirements associated with a contract award?" In addition to the traits previously mentioned, one must realize that RFPs are generally announced without advance notice, unlike grants programs, which are described in the *Catalog of Federal Domestic Assistance*. Typically, between 30 and 45 days are allowed for response. That's about half the time normally provided for preparation of a grant proposal. Consider, too, some other facts regarding contract solicitations:[2]

- Approximately 10 percent of RFPs are canceled after being solicited.
- About two-thirds of RFPs are advertised during the summer, the last quarter of the federal fiscal year.
- Contracts restricted to minority and small businesses are increasing.
- Over one-third of RFPs involve management/technical assistance, a study, or evaluation.
- Review time is often twice that allotted for proposal preparation.
- Most projects are for periods of one year or less.
- Vast majority of awards are under $200,000.

If after considering these factors you determine that contracts may be appropriate for your organization, the next step is to locate and understand the sources of information for RFPs.

An RFP can be obtained directly in one of two ways: by requesting an individual RFP after its availability has been announced in the *Commerce Business Daily* (*CBD*) or by being on an agency mailing list. Since not all federal agencies maintain a bidders' mailing list, the former method, albeit time consuming, is also necessary. Procedures for inclusion on bidders' lists vary among agencies and require individual contact to determine if completion of a standard form is necessary. Of course, personal contact with agency personnel and an organizational track record may result in direct contact, perhaps for sole-source contracts. One additional means of obtaining information on contract solicitations is through an independent service agency or professional association publication. An example of the former is *Federal Contracts and Grants Weekly*, published by Capitol Publications, Inc. A complete package deal is available from some firms, including the identification of appropriate solicitations and the preparation and delivery of proposals.

The *CBD*, published every federal working day by the Government Printing Office ($80 per year), must be scrutinized daily. Since each RFP is advertised only once, it is imperative that you be conscientious in reviewing every issue. With such short lead time and, in some cases a limited supply of RFPs for distribution, less than daily review could prove costly.

Once familiar with the *CBD* format, reviewing becomes less taxing. The two major headings of "Services" and "Supplies, Equipment and Materials" are divided into such subcategories as research, expert and consultant services, construction, and communication equipment. Only a portion of the *CBD* will normally be pertinent to your particular organization. A listing of contract awards exceeding $25,000 constitutes the back portion of each issue. This information might provide a lead for subcontracting with the primary contractee as well as keeping track of the competition.

Each *CBD* announcement alerts prospective bidders to the availability of a specific RFP. Announcements generally consist of a solicitation synopsis, often with task specifications and bidder qualifications, an assigned RFP number, in-

[1] Public Law 95-224, Federal Grant and Cooperative Agreement Act of 1977.
[2] *FY 78 Procurement Analysis of U.S. Contract Awards*, Washington Representative Services, Washington, D.C.

formation needed to obtain RFP, and sometimes a numbered note(s) restricting or clarifying the announcement. Because of the conciseness of the product/service description, you cannot always discern what is involved. Information on eligibility, level of effort, duration of project, for example, is often missing from the advertisement. Look for key terms and request any RFPs that the *CBD* indicates are or will be available, including those that seem even remotely relevant. Figure 1 illustrates two *CBD* advertisements with notations on particular points of interest to the prospective bidder.

Once the RFP is obtained, a quick perusal is in order to determine if: (1) your organization is eligible; (2) expertise and resources are available to provide the service or product solicited; and (3) sufficient time is allowed for preparation of a responsive proposal. If this initial skimming of the RFP results in an affirmative response to these three questions, a closer scrutiny of the entire document is warranted to determine if a proposal will be submitted, and if so what procedures must be followed in responding.

The first thorough reading should concentrate on sections of the RFP that contain information bearing on your decision to apply. This is a crucial stage because a great deal of time, money, and effort will be invested in preparation of the proposal. Being eligible, interested, and capable is not sufficient reason to respond. You must conclude that your organization has a reasonably good chance of receiving an award. Unfortunately, this is a most difficult task.

One means helpful in determining your chances is the bidders' conference. Unfortunately, not all solicitations are coupled with such a meeting. The conference is often scheduled in advance and announced in the RFP letter of transmittal. Sometimes a meeting is called after an RFP is issued if a sufficient number of questions are raised. Agencies are hesitant to respond to individual inquiries because their response may provide an unfair advantage. Attending will not only provide a chance to have your questions answered but will allow you to size

up the competition. Determine if possible the number and type of bidders. If all questions and answers are to be mailed to non-attendees this is impossible. Also, find out if the current solicitation piggybacks a previous contract. If so is that contractee bidding on this solicitation? Whoever actually wrote or helped design the RFP can sometimes be ascertained during the course of the meeting. If one of the bidders was involved, as sometimes happens, your chances are greatly decreased. The bidders' conference is similar to a poker game: Learn as much as you can about the other players without divulging the cards in your own hand.

Let's look at portions of the actual RFP one would receive as a result of requesting RFP 79-68, "Curriculum Adaptation and Dissemination for the Handicapped at the Post Secondary Level" (second announcement in Figure 1). Typical questions are posed in various sections that represent the type of analysis a potential bidder must perform to arrive at a decision to respond or not. Also, a few additional items are circled that provide important information bearing on the development and processing of the proposal.

Should you decide to respond after receiving the RFP, the next step is a second thorough reading, pinpointing those items pertinent to the actual writing. Several components of the RFP are particularly helpful and should be used as a guide in framing your response. Although not all RFPs contain the same components or use the same headings, you will likely find sections entitled "Scope of Work," "Proposal Evaluation Criteria," and "Proposal Preparation Requirements." Besides specifying format, sequence, page limits, etc., these sections provide vital information for the content, focus, and emphasis of your proposal. Undoubtedly you will see similarities between the RFP and a grant application. The most striking difference is the amount of detail and structure given in the RFP.

The "Scope of Work" section (Figure 2E) delineates the tasks to be performed or product or service to be provided. Writing this section is often merely a playback of what is described in

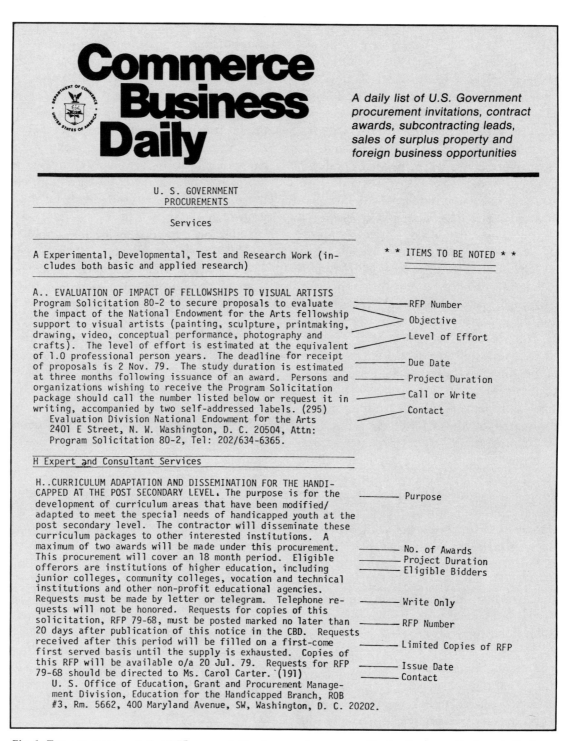

Fig. 1. Two announcements that RFPs are available, shown as they appeared in the *Commerce Business Daily*. Items to be noted are indicated in the margin by the author.

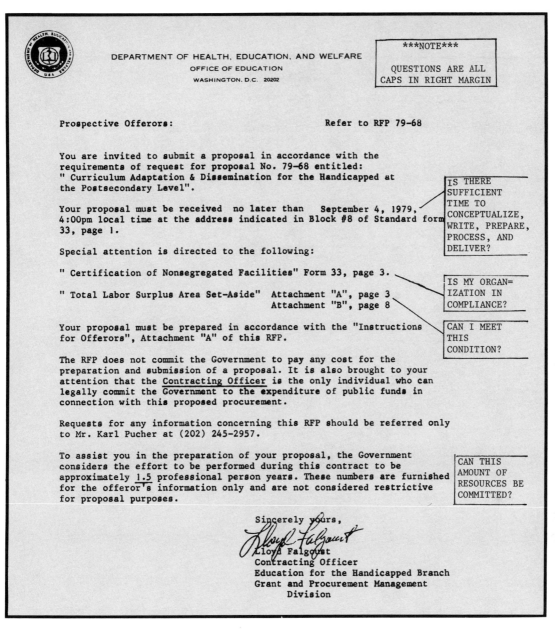

DEPARTMENT OF HEALTH, EDUCATION, AND WELFARE
OFFICE OF EDUCATION
WASHINGTON, D.C. 20202

```
                                              ***NOTE***

                                          QUESTIONS ARE ALL
                                         CAPS IN RIGHT MARGIN
```

Prospective Offerors: Refer to RFP 79-68

You are invited to submit a proposal in accordance with the
requirements of request for proposal No. 79-68 entitled:
" Curriculum Adaptation & Dissemination for the Handicapped at
the Postsecondary Level".

Your proposal must be received no later than   September 4, 1979,
4:00pm local time at the address indicated in Block #8 of Standard form
33, page 1.

IS THERE SUFFICIENT TIME TO CONCEPTUALIZE, WRITE, PREPARE, PROCESS, AND DELIVER?

Special attention is directed to the following:

" Certification of Nonsegregated Facilities" Form 33, page 3.

" Total Labor Surplus Area Set-Aside" Attachment "A", page 3
                                       Attachment "B", page 8

IS MY ORGAN= IZATION IN COMPLIANCE?

Your proposal must be prepared in accordance with the "Instructions
for Offerors", Attachment "A" of this RFP.

CAN I MEET THIS CONDITION?

The RFP does not commit the Government to pay any cost for the
preparation and submission of a proposal. It is also brought to your
attention that the <u>Contracting Officer</u> is the only individual who can
legally commit the Government to the expenditure of public funds in
connection with this proposed procurement.

Requests for any information concerning this RFP should be referred only
to Mr. Karl Pucher at (202) 245-2957.

To assist you in the preparation of your proposal, the Government
considers the effort to be performed during this contract to be
approximately 1.5 professional person years. These numbers are furnished
for the offeror's information only and are not considered restrictive
for proposal purposes.

CAN THIS AMOUNT OF RESOURCES BE COMMITTED?

Sincerely yours,

Lloyd Falgoust
Contracting Officer
Education for the Handicapped Branch
Grant and Procurement Management
Division

Fig. 2A. The letter of invitation to submit a proposal to the Office of Education according to the requirements set forth in RFP 79-68.

the RFP itself, rephrasing and expanding on the activities as seems pertinent. Detail is important. Demonstrate that you have thought through the entire process, anticipated potential barriers, and planned for alternatives. Frequently even the approach and schedule are specified. Whenever possible be creative, for example, in the procedural plan, evaluation technique, or dissemination activity. If a Calendar of Events is already given, perhaps a restructure of tasks and dates into a Program Evaluation and Review Technique (PERT), Ganntt, or Milestone chart will clarify sequence and show relationships not otherwise evident.[3] Whatever procedure, evaluation technique, scheduling method, etc. is selected must

[3] Desmond L. Cook, *Educational Project Management,* Columbus, Ohio: Charles E. Merrill, 1971, pp. 45–53.

SOLICITATION, OFFER AND AWARD	3. CERTIFIED FOR NATIONAL DEFENSE UNDER DPS REG. 1 AND/OR DMS REG. 1 RATING:		4. PAGE 1	OF

| 1. CONTRACT (Proc. Inst. Ident.) NO. 300- | 2. SOLICITATION NO. RFP 79-68 ☐ ADVERTISED (IFB) ☒ NEGOTIATED (RFP) | | 5. DATE ISSUED 7-20-79 | 6. REQUISITION/PURCHASE REQUEST NO. 560AH90008   BEH 9136 |

7. ISSUED BY CODE	8. ADDRESS OFFER TO (If other than block 7) & IF HANDCARRIED
DHEW/Office of Education Grant & Procurement Management Division Application Control Center Washington, D.C. 20202	DHEW/Office of Education Grant & Procurement Management Division Application Control Center 7th & D Sts., SW, GSA Region #3 Bldg., Room 5673 Washington, D.C. 20202

In advertised procurement "offer" and "offeror" shall be construed to mean "bid" and "bidder"

SOLICITATION

9. Sealed offers in original and _____2_____ copies for furnishing the supplies or services in the Schedule will be received at the place specified in block 8, or if handcarried, in the depository located in ___See Block 8 above___ until ___4:00 P.M.___ local time ___9-4-79___

(Hour)   (Date)

If this is an advertised solicitation, offers will be publicly opened at that time. NOTE: SUBMIT 3 COPIES OF BUSINESS PROPOSAL
CAUTION – LATE OFFERS: See pars. 7 and 8 of Solicitation Instructions and Conditions. INCLUDING OPTIONAL FORM 60
All offers are subject to the following: ALSO NOTE: SUBMIT 9 COPIES OF TECHNICAL PROPOSAL

1. The Solicitation Instructions and Conditions, SF 33-A, ___Rev. 1/78___ edition which is attached or incorporated herein by reference.
2. The General Provisions, SF 32, ___315, 315A, 316 Rev. 7/76___ edition, which is attached or incorporated herein by reference.

3. The Schedule included herein and/or attached hereto.
4. Such other provisions, representations, certifications, and specifications as are attached or incorporated herein by reference.

(Attachments are listed in schedule.)

FOR INFORMATION CALL (Name & telephone no.) (No collect calls) ▶ Karl Pucher   Area Code (202) 245-2957

SCHEDULE

10. ITEM NO	11. SUPPLIES-SERVICES	12. QUANTITY	13. UNIT	14. UNIT PRICE	15. AMOUNT
1.	Type of Contract: Cost Reimbursement				
2.	Title: Curriculum Adaptation & Dissemination for the Handicapped at the Postsecondary Level				
3.	Performance Period: 18 months from time of award				
4.	In accordance with Attachments A, B, C and Optional Form 60				

See continuation of schedule on page 4

OFFER *(pages 2 and 3 must also be fully completed by offeror)*

In compliance with the above, the undersigned agrees, if this offer is accepted within _____ calendar days (60 calendar days unless a different period is inserted by the offeror) from the date for receipt of offers specified above, to furnish any or all items upon which prices are offered at the price set opposite each item, delivered at the designated point(s), within the time specified in the schedule.

16. DISCOUNT FOR PROMPT PAYMENT (See par 9. SF 33-A)			
% 10 CALENDAR DAYS.	% 20 CALENDAR DAYS.	% 30 CALENDAR DAYS.	% CALENDAR DAYS

17. OFFEROR CODE	FACILITY CODE	18. NAME AND TITLE OF PERSON AUTHORIZED TO SIGN OFFER (Type or print)
NAME AND ADDRESS (Street, city, county, State and ZIP code) AREA CODE AND TELEPHONE NO ▶ ☐ Check if remittance address is different from above – enter such address in Schedule		19. SIGNATURE 20. OFFER DATE

AWARD *(To be completed by Government)*

21. ACCEPTED AS TO ITEMS NUMBERED	22. AMOUNT	23. ACCOUNTING AND APPROPRIATION DATA

24. SUBMIT INVOICES (4 copies unless otherwise specified) TO ADDRESS SHOWN IN BLOCK _____	25. NEGOTIATED PURSUANT TO	10 U.S.C. 2304(a) ( ) ☒ 41 U.S.C. 252(c) ( )

26. ADMINISTERED BY (If other than block 7) CODE	27. PAYMENT WILL BE MADE BY CODE
	DHEW/Office of Education Finance Division Fiscal Services Branch 400 Maryland Avenue, S.W. Washington, D.C. 20202

28. NAME OF CONTRACTING OFFICER (Type or print)	29. UNITED STATES OF AMERICA	30. AWARD DATE
	BY *(Signature of contracting officer)*	

Award will be made on this form, or on Standard Form 26, or by other official written notice

33-131   Standard Form 33 Page 1 (REV. 3-77)
                                                                                          Prescribed by GSA, FPR (41 CFR) 1-16.101

Fig. 2B. Page 1 of the Solicitation, Offer and Award form for the Office of Education RFP.

RFP 79-68 ATTACHMENT C

REQUEST FOR PROPOSAL

CURRICULUM ADAPTATION AND DISSEMINATION FOR THE HANDICAPPED
AT THE POSTSECONDARY LEVEL

I. INTRODUCTION

A. **Purpose of Procurement**

This procurement is/for the development of curriculum(a) area(s) which
has/have been modified/adapted to meet the special needs of a handicapped
populaton(s) enrolled in a postsecondary educational institution, and for
the packaging and dissemination of this/these modified/adapted curriculum(a)
to other interested postsecondary institutions, agencies, and organizations.
The curriculum(a) shall identify the handicapped population(s) for which it/
they has/have been adapted. In order to allow for maximum student independence
when interacting with the modified curriculum it is expected that instructional
media will be used to the fullest extent feasible.

[IS THIS AN AREA OF INTEREST TO ME?]

[CAN I FULFILL THIS EXPECTATION?]

The expertise required under this procurement will include, but not necessarily
be limited to,:

1. curriculum design, development, and evaluation;
2. knowledge and experience with the general and unique learning characteristics and needs of the participating populations;
3. knowledge of how the teaching process, instructional materials, and instructional equipment must be modified/adapted to meet the special needs of the participating handicapped population(s);
4. product development, packaging, and dissemination;
5. staff development; and
6. instructional media.

[DO CURRENT STAFF HAVE THIS EX= PERTISE OR MUST CON= SULTANTS BE HIRED OR A SUBCONTRACT BE ARRANGED?]

It is expected that 2 or more awards will be made under this procurement.

B. **Authorization**

The authorization for this procurement is contained in Title VI, Part C, section
625, of P. L. 93-380 (Education of the Handicapped Act Amendments of 1974),
Regional Education Program for Deaf and Other Handicapped Persons. This legislation is presented as Appendix A.

[ARE CHANCES FOR AN AWARD IN= CREASED? NOTE THAT CBD INDI= CATED "MAX= IMUM OF 2 AWARDS WILL BE MADE"-- NEED CLAR= IFICATION.]

C. **Eligible Offerors**

Eligible offerors under this procurement are institutions of higher education,
including junior and community colleges, vocational and technical institutions,
and other appropriate nonprofit educational agencies.

[IS MY ORGAN= IZATION ELIGIBLE?]

D. **Background Information**

Historically, the participation of handicapped persons in postsecondary programs

Fig. 2C. Attachment C of the Request for Proposal, along with the author's pinpointing of important sections.

be justified and shown to be the most appropriate.

Proposal writers often fail to use effectively the part of the RFP that specifies the criteria by which the proposal will be evaluated. The *Proposal Evaluation Criteria* section, to some extent, should dictate the proposal framework or format and the emphasis to be placed on certain proposal elements. Although the description of the criteria to be used in the review process may constitute as little as one-half page, its importance should not be underestimated. It is

RFP 79-68

ATTACHMENT C   -3-

handicapped populations. Recipients of awards included baccalaureate and graduate
institutions, two-year institutions, and vocational technical schools. The funding
level for this fiscal year was $2,000,000.

In FY '77 the funding level remained at $2,000,000. Thus, no new projects were added.
In FY '78 and FY '79 the funding levels were $2,400,000. Of the original
13 projects seven are still funded under the Regional Education Program. The
grant period for the other 6 projects expired either at the end of FY 77 or FY '78.

Illustrative of the kinds of services provided under this program were/are counseling,
interpreting, notetaking, tutoring, assistance with mobility, eating, dressing, and
toileting (for the wheelchair bound), test proctoring, housing location, reading,
registration assistance, brailling, and preparatory programs.

F. **Award Period**

This award will extend over an 18 month period.

> AM I INVOLVED IN SERVICES PREVIOUSLY/CURRENTLY SUPPORTED?

> CAN RESOURCES BE COMMITTED FOR THIS LENGTH OF TIME?

G. **Level of Effort**

In order to complete the tasks detailed in this scope of work, it is anticipated
that the contractor would provide no more than 1.5 professional person-years, along
with the necessary support staff time. A professional person-year includes the
services of one professional, necessary support staff, indirect charges, supplies,
and materials.

> IS THIS WITHIN MY PER= IMETERS? NOT TOO SMALL OR TOO LARGE A TASK?

H. **Target Population**

The target population designated to benefit through the awarding of a contract
under this procurement are "handicapped persons", which for purposes of this procurement means persons who are mentally retarded, hard of hearing, deaf, speech
impaired, visually handicapped, learning disabled, emotionally disturbed, crippled
or in other ways health impaired and by reason thereof require special education
programming and related services.

> DO I HAVE ACCESS TO ONE OR MORE OF THESE GROUPS?

I. **Characteristics of Offerors**

It is the purpose of this procurement to fund institutions or agencies which are
characterized by:

1. **Handicapped Students**

> DOES THIS DESCRIBE MY ORGANIZATION?

Institution must have an adequate number of enrolled students with the
handicap(s) for which the curriculum(a) is/are being modified to serve
as a validation group.

2. **Multidisciplinary Effort**

Institution must demonstrate viable cooperation agreement among specific
subject area personnel, special education personnel, regular education

Fig. 2D. Attachment C of the Request for Proposal, continued.

this list of criteria that will guide those who will ultimately judge the worth of the proposal.

The method used to evaluate proposals varies among agencies and among programs within the same agency. Typically (as shown in Figure 2F) a point value will be assigned to each criterion. At times, reviewers may be required to indicate the presence or absence of specific elements, rate the adequacy of the elements on a descriptive scale, and justify the rating in a narrative manner. Relative importance of each criterion, as evidenced by assigned weights, varies among solicitations. The type of activity under consideration for funding will dictate the weighting of

RFP   79-68

ATTACHMENT   C

-4-

personnel (including curriculum specialists), media specialists,
and dissemination resources as participants in activities under this
procurement.

3. **Compliance with Section 504**

> IS MY
> ORGANIZATION
> IN COMPLIANCE?

Institution shall be in substantial compliance with the provisions
of section 504 of the Vocational Rehabilitation Act of 1973, and
be on target with all program compliance deadlines contained in
this section. For each such deadline which has not been met by
the institution there must be presented a reason for the failure
to meet each deadline and a plan for meeting the requirements of
the deadline(s).

II.   SCOPE OF WORK

This section is a statement of the scope of work which shall be performed by the
contractor under this procurement. The details for preparation of a proposal,
the requested format, and suggestions to the offeror for supplementary information
are provided in Sections IV and V.

A. **Tasks to be Accomplished**

> CAN I HANDLE THESE
> SPECIFIC TASKS?

The tasks for which funds shall be utilized under this procurement are the development, validation, and evaluation of no more than two curriculum areas for no more
than two handicapped populations, the compilation of the results of these
activities into a disseminable package, and the dissemination of these packages
to institutions, agencies, and organizations involved in the postsecondary education of handicapped students.

1. **Phase I: Planning and Development.**   (12 months)

> DO I HAVE A REPUTATION/
> PREVIOUS EXPERIENCE WITH
> TYPE OF WORK?
>   (TRACK RECORD)

a. **Curriculum Development**

1) Develop modified curriculum(a) which is designed to meet the particular
educational needs of the handicapped population designated in Part V,
A 3

2) Effect the multidisciplinary coordination designated in Part V, A 5 e.

b. **Curriculum Validation**

1) Validate curriculum on population described in 3, above

2) Assess the results of the validation

Fig. 2E. Attachment C of the Request for Proposal, continued.

the various components. In some cases the funding agency will not indicate the weights assigned
to each criterion but simply list them in order of
importance.

Certain categories are generally addressed in
evaluation criteria: (1) understanding of the purpose and objectives of the solicitation; (2) proposed approach to address the need; (3) adequacy
of the management plan; (4) qualifications and
past experience in related areas of key project
staff; and (5) previous experience of the organization. Various combinations of these elements

RFP   79-68

ATTACHMENT   C   -6-

e. Other Reports

All significant problems and slippages concerning curriculum
design and product development which may occur and are of a
critical nature should be brought immediately to the attention
of the contracting officer and the project officer in writing.

All packages/products shall be submitted to the contracting
officer and the project officer for approval at least 30 days
prior to their dissemination.

III. Technical Review Procedures and Evaluation Criteria

The technical section of each proposal submitted under this procurement will
be evaluated on the basis of the criteria and weighting factors which follow.
The proposals will be reviewed for content, completeness, and conformity to
the specifications of this Request for Proposal.

NOTE: An abstract of the proposal submitted must be provided as part of
       the submission.

A. Evaluation Criteria

    1. Procedural Plan   Maximum points: <u>85</u>

        a) Conceptualization. (15 points)

        b) Appropriateness of curriculum(a) for handicapped populations. (20 points)

        c) Validation plan. (10 points)

        d) Packaging and dissemination plan. (15 points)

        e) Multidisciplinary coordination plan. (5 points)

        f) Plan for use of instructional media. (10 points)

        g) Consumer input. (10 points)

    2. Management Plan   Maximum points: <u>15</u>

        a) Adequacy of qualifications and experience of personnel
           designated to carry out proposed activities. (5 points)

        b) Applicant agency's demonstrated competence and experience
           in developing, evaluating, and adapting curricula and develop-
           ing, evaluating and disseminating curriculum packages.
           (5 points)

        c) Project time frame and scheduling. (5 points)

        TOTAL POINTS ------------------------------- 100

> IS THE EVALUATION CRI=
> TERIA BREAKDOWN FAVOR=
> ABLE TO MY ORGANIZATION,
> E.G., POINTS FOR PRE=
> VIOUS EXPERIENCE?

Fig. 2F. Attachment C of the Request for Proposal, continued.

with associated modifications will be found in RFPs and grant announcements.

An examination of a sample of RFPs and grant announcements will often reveal a trend in weighting certain components. For example, the *technical approach* to the problem, the anticipated procedures for conducting the project, often exceeds all others in importance, sometimes being assigned 25 to 50 points of a possible 100 points. Since the technical approach determines the appropriateness of the proposed activities to the accomplishment of the stated objectives, its importance is readily justified. The success of a project is often determined by the suitability of the methodology. This particular RFP shows the greatest weight on "Appropriateness of curriculum" (20 points) with only 15 points assigned to the entire management plan. (See Figure 2F.)

Writers should carefully consider the specificity of plans and strategies and the potential problems inherent in certain procedures. Linking individual tasks to major activities, personnel, resources, budget, and overall objectives is a practice that should provide the necessary format for acceptability for this criterion. The time and careful review needed to formulate a comprehensive design should receive primary emphasis due to its paramount importance in many solicitations.

The *adequacy of qualifications and experience of proposed personnel*, particularly the principal investigator, often receive high priority in a criteria section. Since the competence of the project staff will ultimately affect the success of any endeavor, potential sponsors are concerned about the key individuals who will be responsible for implementing project activities. Personnel of a high caliber are essential to the completion of a carefully planned project. Expertise and experience must also be related to the proposed activity. National prominence of an individual will not suffice if the area under consideration is a field widely divergent from the person's areas of specialty.

Presentation of relevant aspects of personnel vitae becomes critical in support evidence for proposed project staff. Many reviewers, if they are truly qualified, will recognize individuals of stature in a particular field. However, few will struggle through a 20-page vita to locate presentations, publications, and experience pertinent to the proposed project. It becomes imperative that the proposal writer highlight the relevant expertise and experiences.

Several methods have proved successful in presentation of personnel expertise. Inclusion of only a short version of an individual's full vita with relevant experiences on the condensed version is one possibility. If the full-length vita is used, highlighting selected portions using asterisks or colored pencils is a useful practice. A third option would be to provide a one-half to one-page addition to a vita that describes an individual's qualifications most directly related to the proposed project. By whatever method, attention must be directed to important aspects of personnel choices so that reviewers can accurately assess those individuals selected to conduct the project.

The experience of an organization is considered worthy of points in many evaluation criteria and was assigned five points in this RFP (Figure 2F). Organizations must carefully document their previous projects and experiences to justify their capabilities as a contractee or grantee. Those organizations with limited experiences must be even more diligent in showing appropriate planning for their project to assure reviewers that the organization is capable of conducting the tasks outlined for the project. They must demonstrate how their organization can successfully complete the tasks more expertly, efficiently, and economically than more experienced organizations. Highlighting previous successes in other fields, identifying resources available, and utilizing appropriate consultants will increase a new organization's rating for this criterion.

The evaluation criteria can be a definite aid in writing a proposal. It will help ensure completeness, provide a more responsive plan, and demonstrate to reviewers an awareness of the standards by which proposals will be evaluated.

Proposal Preparation Requirements stipulate the organization and required components of

```
                              RFP   79-68


                        ATTACHMENT    C




                      OUTLINE OF PROPOSAL FOR
        CURRICULUM ADAPTION AND DISSEMINATION FOR THE HANDICAPPED
                        AT THE POSTSECONDARY LEVEL



                                                         Proposal
                                                         Page Limit



     A.  Technical Section

            1.  Abstract . . . . . . . . . . . . . . . . . . . . . . . . . . .  1
            2.  Table of Contents  . . . . . . . . . . . . . . . . . . . . . .  As necessary
            3.  Description of Project Participants  . . . . . . . . . . . . .  As necessary
            4.  Current Contractual Obligations of Offeror . . . . . . . . . .  As necessary
            5.  Procedural Plan  . . . . . . . . . . . . . . . . . . . . . . .  As necessary

                  a. Conceptualization
                  b. Curriculum(a)- Population Match
                  c. Validation
                  d. Packaging and Dissemination
                  e. Multidisciplinary Coordination
                  f. Instructional Media
                  g. Consumer Input

            6.  Management Plan and Schedule . . . · . . . . . . . . . . . . .  10
                                                           (Exclusive of Vitae)

                  a. Personnel
                  b. Agency
                  c. Time Frame and scheduling


            7.  Appendices . . . . . . . . . . . . . . . . . . . . . . . . . .  As necessary

                  a. Subcontract agreements
                  b. Letters of endorsement
                  c. Other relevant information

     B.  Cost Estimate Section

            1.  Contractor Cost Estimate . . . . . . . . . . . . . . . . . . .  As necessary
            2.  Subcontractor Cost Estimate  . . . . . . . . . . . . . . . . .  As necessary
```

Fig. 2G. Page 8 of Attachment C, which gives the outline of elements to be contained in the proposal, submitted in connection with RFP 79-68.

the proposal. When an outline is provided, such as for this RFP (Figure 2G), it is a good idea to adopt it as your own, following it step-by-step in writing and packaging your proposal. This ensures coverage of all areas in the sequence expected by the agency. It may well serve as your table of contents and provide the headings and subheadings for the narrative.

Notice that Section B of this particular outline addresses the cost component. You may recall that Standard Form 33 (Figure 2B) indicates three copies of the business (cost) proposal and nine copies of the technical (narrative) proposal are required. Here is another departure from a grant application — narrative and budget are bound separately. The following note appearing in most RFPs clarifies their relationship:

Award will be made to the offeror whose proposal represents the combination of technical merit and cost most favorable to the government. However, technical consideration will be of paramount importance.

As with a grant budget all items must be explained and justified. Sometimes guidance is given in the form of a maximum, range or person-years. In the case of the RFP example given here, 1.5 person years of effort is estimated. Converted to a dollar figure, your proposed budget might range from $50,000 to $100,000 depending on the agency standard. Although not restrictive, it is best to stay within range of the figure quoted.

Except for two separate sections, a proposal is packaged like a grant application. Be tasteful and novel if possible, but avoid elaborate bindings and covers — federal agencies view this as wasteful. Like a grant application, you may either mail the required number of proposal copies or hand-carry them. Addresses may vary depending on the means of delivery. If mailed, make sure a postmark is placed on the package. Normally registered mail or a delivery service is preferable. Remember, there is no such thing as a late proposal! Provide sufficient time for typing and retyping, editing, binding, routing, and delivery.

If your proposal is one selected for further consideration you will receive a call from the agency's contract officer. Questions will be asked of you regarding various aspects of your proposal. Negotiation of budget items will likely occur, so be prepared to justify everything. Don't accept reduction in budget unless a corresponding reduction in tasks is approved. Sometimes the time schedule, number and type of deliverables, and even type of contract are negotiable. It's better to decline an award than undertake a project that will tax your resources without adequate remuneration.

Should you be awarded the contract, your work has just begun. Understanding the RFP and preparing the proposal and necessary forms will likely prove simpler than managing the project due to the stricter accounting and reporting provisions of most contracts. So be prepared.

FOUNDATIONS AND CORPORATIONS

As federal funds for social programs, the arts, and the humanities are diminishing, there is increasing pressure for more support from the private sector, particularly from foundations and corporations.

Although corporations still give only about 1% of pre-tax profits to charitable causes, many do a great deal more than that, and it behooves non-profit organizations to become acquainted with those businesses that have a stake in the community where the organization operates. In 1981 corporate giving rose to $3 billion, an increase of 11% over 1980. Foundations spent $2.62 billion that year, an increase of 9% over 1980. Most private gifts for charitable and other philanthropic purposes are made by individuals, about 83%. Bequests, usually by individuals, account for 6.5% leaving 10.5% given by corporations (5.6%) and foundations (4.9%).

For years, foundations led corporations in philanthropy, at one time by a factor of two, but in recent years, corporations have taken the lead.

Although it is not as easy to get information about giving patterns and philanthropic interests from the private sector as it is from government agencies, it is essential that grantseekers learn to do it, especially those looking for support for activities that can no longer count on governmental support to the same extent as in the past.

The best sources of information from both corporations and foundations is the annual report. Foundation reports usually give lists of grants made during the past year and serve as a guide to the type of activity they like to support. Corporations may or may not list their awards, but the reports do give clues as to their interests.

Only about 450 foundations out of about 22,000 issues separately published annual reports, and many will not send copies to individuals but distribute only to libraries and other public bodies. Corporation reports may be seen in business libraries, and of course anyone who owns at least one share of stock in a publicly owned corporation receives quarterly and annual reports.

The most promising approach to a foundation or corporation official is an introduction through a mutual acquaintance, preferably a professional colleague. It would be impossible for the officials in large organizations or even in middle-sized ones to talk with anyone who chooses to come and see them. Therefore, an introduction—which may be only a reference ("Mr. So-and-so suggested that I call you.")—indicates that the caller is a serious professional and not a "shopper" or "time waster." Or may not be.

If it is impossible to find a member of your organization's policy-making board or anyone close to the organization who can provide such a reference, the only recourse is to send a preliminary letter. This feature tells what ought to go into such letters and gives an example of one that was first written and also the later, improved version of the same letter.

A model letter, also given here, was prepared by a foundation official using phantom names and details. It includes all the information that official believes should ideally go into a first letter to a foundation official whom the writer has never met. In most cases letters to corporate officials can also follow this model.

Some funding organizations that do not use application forms provide applicants with descriptions of the information their applications should contain. We have included here the instructions issued to potential applicants by a community foundation, The New York Community Trust, and a private foundation, the Jerome Foundation, Inc. These outlines constitute excellent guides for applications to any funding organization that does not require the use of a standard form.

The Initial Approach to Private Foundations and Corporations

"International Dance Foundation of North America, Inc." and other material

in this article were contributed by Granville Meader, a foundation consultant,

Ridgewood, New Jersey

THE PRELIMINARY LETTER
by Paul Hennessey

As most actors, salesmen, and lovers know, first impressions are often the most important. When approaching private foundations or corporations for project funds, the crucial first impression is often created by the preliminary letter. This letter has to be brief and concise, yet sufficiently comprehensive to tell the first program officer who reads it who you are, precisely what you want to do, how much it will cost, and why you believe the addressee will be and should be interested in the proposed activity.

Most potential donors prefer this preliminary letter to be short, one page if possible, but comprehensive enough to contain the following information:

- A brief statement of the proposal
- The reason for approaching this particular funding organization
- The total sum needed; this should include the whole amount of the proposed project, including those portions from other sources
- The specific portion of funding being requested
- The background of the applicant organization, with references and write-ups attached
- A concluding statement asking for an appointment and indicating that the applicant will follow-up with a phone call within a specific time period.

The letter should be typed on your organization's stationery, individually for each grantor you approach. A mechanically reproduced letter should *never* be used in applying for a grant. Your letterhead should list all persons who are officially connected with your organization, the organization's legal address, and phone number.

Paul Hennessey is Vice President of the Public Management Institute, San Francisco, California. (Currently, Program Coordinator, University of California at Berkeley.)

All supporting documents that are included with your preliminary letter should be clear and concise, and if you have a brochure or prospectus, it should clearly reflect the size of your operating budget. Grantmakers will not be impressed with a lavish brochure from an organization that is requesting funds in order to carry on its program.

The accompanying documents should include:

- A statement of what your organization is trying to do, and by what standards it is succeeding
- Assessment of its value to the community
- Its clientele or audience
- A budget for the preceding, current, and succeeding years, together with an audited financial statement if available
- List of board members and salaried officials
- Copies of Internal Revenue Service forms indicating tax exempt status

This preliminary letter should make clear to the funding organization that you are approaching them because you are sure that they will be interested in supporting your work. This means that you will have done your homework and know that they support the kind of project you propose. This letter should also indicate that requested support will result in a very useful contribution to work in your field because your organization does its job well. If there are reasons why the applicant organization presents a clearly novel and significant approach in its field, and thereby is the more effective in its work, it should be clearly stated and documented.

The following letters are examples of preliminary approaches to funders that run the gamut from being totally ineffective, to being excellent. The first two are from the Hospice of the Monterey Peninsula in Carmel, California. You will note that there is a significant improvement in the second of these letters, but even it still has some deficiencies. The third letter, reproduced here, contains all the elements mentioned in the preceding paragraphs, and is written in a brisk and attractive style. It is the one you should strive to emulate.

Letter 1 focuses on the operation of the Hospice project to the exclusion of all else. It does not explain the most important aspect of the Hospice movement, the benefit of the non-hospital setting to those suffering terminal illness. A funder might be approached in this manner if bricks and mortar were being sought (building funds), but in this case the Hospice is seeking operating funds for a facility already in place. The assumption of the grantseeker, in this case, is that the foundation being approached is interested in funding projects that have innovative, positive benefits in the health field, but there is no indication in this letter what those benefits might be. The letter also fails to mention why this particular foundation is being approached, and in the end, has a weak, tentative tone. The use of the word "possibility" in the first sentence is inappropriate. If this foundation gives money for health care, there is a strong likelihood that they are interested in the hospice movement. The question is will they be interested in this particular hospice?

Letter 2 is much better than the first one. It is presented on official letterhead, but, unfortunately, it is mechanically reproduced. It begins with a brief statement of the need for hospices bolstered by hard figures from the area in which this one operates. However, it begins to go wrong in the second paragraph which is devoted to a rather lengthy history of the movement. The last two sentences, giving the precise beginning of this concept in recent times, should be part of the first paragraph. When you are aiming for a one page letter, you cannot waste a paragraph describing what the potential donor is already likely to know as well as you do, and it is unnecessary to include details that will appear in appended documents.

The letter does not request a specific amount of money, although there is a reference in the last paragraph to an enclosed, detailed proposal. It should be kept in mind that the letter's purpose is to give the initial reader enough insight to know if it is worth his time to explore the detailed proposal, including the budget. This letter does not accomplish that. Foundation program

HOSPICE OF THE MONTEREY PENINSULA
Post Office Box 7236
Carmel, California 93921

March 20, 1978

Ms. _____
Grants Administrator
_____ Foundation
San Francisco, California 94104

Dear Ms. _____ :

I am contacting you concerning the possibility of securing grant funds from the_____ Foundation for our hospice programs. We are operating a hospice home care program (similar to Hospice of Marin), and in-hospital volunteer program at Community Hospital of the Monterey Peninsula, and are now in the process of opening a six bed hospice facility in Carmel Valley, California. All these programs are designed to meet the varied needs of the terminally ill in our community.

We anticipate becoming essentially financially self sufficient from adequate third party reimbursement within the next two years. In the meantime, more funds are necessary to keep the Project going. For the year 1978 we have raised approximately $122,000.00 from Monterey County, The American Cancer Society, and private donations. We are in the process of contacting a number of private foundations to raise a total of $40,000.00 needed to meet further expected program costs.

I would stress that our organization is an extremely unique innovative program that is in a position to pioneer the development of hospice services, reimbursement, and licensure by opening the first free standing in-patient hospice facility in California. Our service model stresses continuity of care to patients in the hospital, at home, and in a hospice in-patient facility. We feel it will become a most useful model for other developing hospice programs around the country.

Enclosed is a brief program description. If you have any questions, please feel free to contact me. Otherwise, I will be contacting your office to inquire about a possible preliminary interview.

Sincerely,

Stephen Connor
Executive Director

Enclosures

Letter 1

officers are as swamped with proposals as publishers are with manuscripts, and they have to be extremely selective about which ones they examine lengthily. This letter also fails to mention that essential next step, further contact and the arrangements for a meeting. This, as stated earlier, is the responsibility of the applicant, not the donor.

This letter has some very good features. It does emphasize the most essential rationale for hospices, benefits to the terminally ill, and its style conveys an appropriate sense of urgency. It also tells why the addressee was selected as a potential funder, and in the process, states that the funding is needed only until third-party reimbursement is obtained for continuing operations. This is a vital point because many foundations prefer to provide "seed" or "start-up" money for projects that promise to become self-sufficient in a matter of two or three years.

Letter 3, prepared for this feature by a foundation official, and missing the names of this phantom organization's board and staff members, is, in every other way, the ideal preliminary

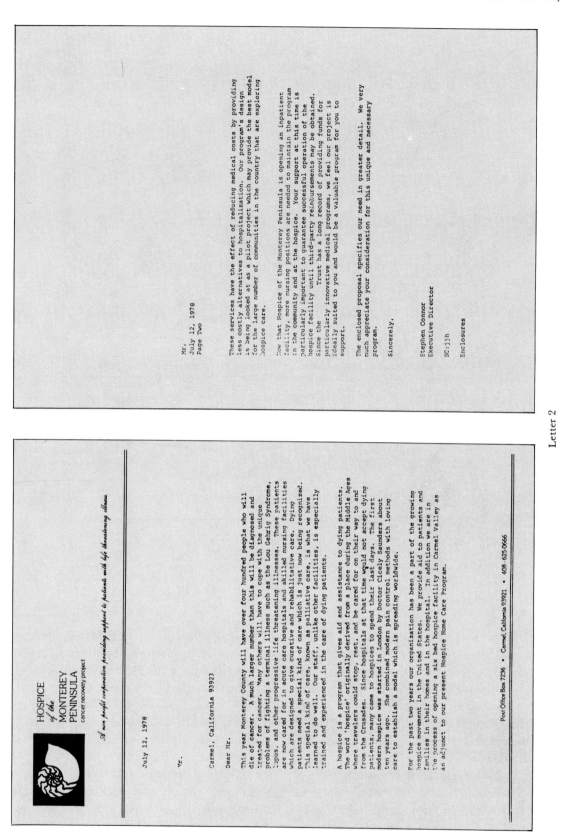

HOSPICE *of the* **MONTEREY PENINSULA**
cancer recovery project

A non-profit corporation providing support to patients with life threatening illness.

July 12, 1978

Mr.

Carmel, California 93923

Dear Mr.

This year Monterey County will have over four hundred people who will die of cancer. A much larger number than this will be diagnosed and treated for cancer. Many others will have to cope with the unique problems of fighting a terminal illness such as the Lou Gehrig Syndrome, Lupus, and other progressive life threatening illnesses. These patients are now cared for in acute care hospitals and skilled nursing facilities which are designed to give curative and rehabilitative care. Dying patients need a special kind of care which is just now being recognized. This special kind of care, known as palliative care, is what we have learned to do well. Our staff, unlike other facilities, is especially trained and experienced in the care of dying patients.

A hospice is a program that gives aid and assistance to dying patients. The word 'hospice' originally derived from a place during the Middle Ages where travelers could stop, rest, and be cared for on their way to and from the Crusades. Since hospitals at that time would not accept dying patients, many came to hospices to spend their last days. The first modern hospice was started in London by Doctor Cicely Saunders about ten years ago. She combined modern pain control methods with loving care to establish a model which is spreading worldwide.

For the past two years our organization has been a part of the growing hospice movement in the United States. We provide aid to patients and families in their homes and in the hospital. In addition we are in the process of opening a six bed hospice facility in Carmel Valley as an adjunct to our present Hospice Home Care Program.

Post Office Box 7236 • Carmel, California 93921 • 408-625-0666

Mr.
July 12, 1978
Page Two

These services have the effect of reducing medical costs by providing less costly alternatives to hospitalization. Our program's design is being looked at as a pilot project which may provide the best model for the large number of communities in the country that are exploring hospice care.

Now that Hospice of the Monterey Peninsula is opening an inpatient facility, more nursing positions are needed to maintain the program in the community and at the hospice. Your support at this time is particularly important to guarantee successful operation of the hospice facility until third-party reimbursements may be obtained. Since the   Trust has a long record of providing funds for particularly innovative medical programs, we feel our project is ideally suited to you and would be a valuable program for you to support.

The enclosed proposal specifies our need in greater detail. We very much appreciate your consideration for this unique and necessary program.

Sincerely,

Stephen Connor
Executive Director

SC:jjh

Enclosures

Letter 2

```
          INTERNATIONAL DANCE FOUNDATION OF NORTH AMERICA, INC.
          642 Prince Street, New York, NY 10012  (212) 555-1212

     Dr. H. S. Wilmont
     The Philanthropic Foundation
     1133 Avenue of the Americas
     New York, NY   10036


     Dear Dr. Wilmont:

          Our research at The Foundation Center and elsewhere indicates
     that The Philanthropic Foundation is interested in assisting the de-
     velopment of innovative dance choreography.  We hope you will consider
     assisting our organization.

          The International Dance Foundation of North America, Inc.
     (IDFNA) respectfully requests a contribution from The Philanthropic
     Foundation of $5,000 toward the expenses of preparing a new dance
     by a choreographer whose work has not yet been widely recognized.
     We are also approaching Exxon, American Telephone and Telegraph, The
     Andrew W. Mellon Foundation, The Ford Foundation and The Rockefeller
     Foundation, requesting similar sums.

          The total cost of the project is estimated at $24,135 (budget
     enclosed).  Of this, $5,000 has been contributed by the National En-
     dowment for the Arts, an estimated $3,000 will be earned at the box
     office, and the remainder must be raised from individuals, corpora-
     tions and foundations.

          The dance will be choreographed by Joseph Smith, a graduate
     of the Martha Graham School and later a student of various ballet
     masters (resume enclosed).  He has successfully prepared works for
     Washington Ballet, Joffrey II and Alvin Ailey (reviews enclosed).
     He plans to use seven dancers and a small live orchestra of six
     instruments.  If the work is successful, it will become a part of
     the IDFNA repertoire.

          IDFNA was started two years ago by Joan Dennison, who studied
     at the School of American Ballet.  A list of works previously pre-
     sented by her group is attached, together with some reviews and her
     resume.   IDFNA is registered with the Internal Revenue Service as
     a non-profit organization (copy of exemption letter enclosed).
     Management is currently handled by PDQ Enterprises.

          We would appreciate an opportunity to discuss the proposal
     with you or an executive you might designate.  I will telephone
     you the week of September 15 to determine your interest and
     availability for a meeting.


                                        Sincerely,

                                        Joan Dennison
                                        Artistic Director
```

Letter 3

letter for approaching a funding source for the first time. It demonstrates that the International Dance Foundation of North America, Inc., has done its research for sources of possible funding, and has a clear idea of what and how it will accomplish its project with the money it is seeking. The budget information, given briefly in the third paragraph, lets the addressee know precisely what the total cost of the project will be, and what other sources are already com-

mitted, and for exactly how much. Since this is a multiple-funder request, this information is essential. The foundation is being asked for a $5,000 contribution, and the remaining funds will be sought from five other foundations known to support innovative choreography. When a funding organization is approached in this manner, the job of dealing with the request is greatly simplified. The program officers at all the foundations being approached can confer

The New York Community Trust
Information for Grant Applicants

Thank you for your interest in The New York Community Trust. The information that follows is intended to assist you in seeking funds from The New York Community Trust.

As the Trust is a community foundation for the greater New York City area, our Distribution Committee gives priority with many of its funds to grant proposals which deal with the problems of this metropolitan region with a particular emphasis on New York City. In addition, program priorities reflect two factors: available dollars (within particular areas) and the Distribution Committee's current assessment of community needs. Preference is given to projects for which specific amounts over a predetermined duration are expected to generate significant benefits.

Currently, a lower priority is given to requests for:

— endowments, capital projects or other building fund campaigns;
— deficit financing;
— general operating support or annual giving;
— religious purposes;
— specific projects in the areas of:

  • environment   • summer youth programs
  • transportation   • tutorial programs
  • vocational training and manpower development   • addiction services and treatment

In addition, we are not able to give financial assistance or scholarships to individuals who apply to us.

We do not use grant application forms. However, we have developed a few guidelines which should help you in the preparation of your application.

Specifically, a complete proposal should contain:

— a cover letter transmitted on the organization's letterhead (please include telephone number) signed by its chief executive officer on behalf of its governing body;
— a one-page summary of the proposal including at least the amount requested, total project budget, specific grant purpose, and anticipated end results of the effort;
— the main body (not to exceed fifteen pages) plus attachments.

Proposals should generally address the following subjects:

1. What the need or problem is that will be met by the actions for which funds are requested.
2. How the need will be met or the problem addressed by the project or program proposed *including a specific statement of program objectives.*
3. A brief timetable for conduct of the program.
4. Names and qualifications of persons who will be responsible for implementation of the program.
5. Why your organization is the logical one to carry out the project.
6. A list of the organization's board.
7. A statement of how and when the success of the program would be measured.
8. A detailed budget of the proposed program.
9. If the Trust is not the only funding source being approached, names of other sources contacted. (This is for informational purposes only and should not be interpreted to mean that aid from other sources is discouraged; in fact, participation of other donors is encouraged.)
10. Plans for financial support of the program after the proposed funding is completed (assuming the program is to be of an ongoing nature).
11. Additional organizational information requested:

    — the most recent audited financial statement;
    — a current operating statement (financial data available for the year to date);
    — current overall organization budget;
    — written evidence of current tax-exempt status.

Conferences with grant applicants or site visits will be arranged by the Trust's staff as appropriate. *These will take place only after we have had the opportunity to study a written grant proposal.* All applicants will receive notification as to whether or not there is a possibility of support; however, it is not always possible to have in-person conferences. The Trust's Distribution Committee meets bimonthly to make final grant decisions in the light of current program priorities, staff recommendations and available funds.

When your proposal arrives, we will acknowledge it with a postcard so that you will know it is here and being studied. You may not hear from us for three or four weeks following the receipt of our postcard. Following that interval, please feel free to call _____ for information as to the status of your application.

Grant Application Outline

(To be used as guide in drafting proposals)

REQUIRED OF ALL APPLICANTS

A. Applicants' status with Internal Revenue Service.

1. Evidence of nonprofit and tax exempt status by an accompanying copy of a letter from the U. S. Internal Revenue Service to this effect, plus a ruling whether or not the organization is a "private foundation."

B. In addition to the above, every application must include:

1. Name and address of institution or organization submitting the proposal. (NOTE: The Foundation does not make grants directly to individuals.)
2. Name(s) of chief administrative officer(s) of applying organization, plus letter from an administrative officer, endorsing the proposal and agreeing that the organization will assume the full responsibilities involved in the proper fiscal management of and accounting for any grant received, and will make certain that any reports required by Jerome Foundation are submitted on time.
3. Statement by administrative official that no part of a grant from the Foundation will be used to support propaganda for or in opposition to legislation, either enacted or proposed, or in campaigning for or against any candidate for public office, or to employ or compensate officials contrary to Section 494(d) of the Internal Revenue Code.
4. Commitment to submit regularly and on time such progress evaluations and financial reports as are requested by the Foundation. (The Foundation usually requests semiannual progress and financial reports and may request semiannual evaluation reports if approriate.)
5. List of Board members with occupations, number of meetings each year and average attendance.

INFORMATION RECOMMENDED FOR ALL APPLICANTS

1. Brief description of proposal, including a summary of background information contributing to an understanding of the reason for and purpose of the project.
2. Brief description of plan of development of the project, including when appropriate, a description of method or methods proposed to be used to test outcomes.
3. Expected outcome or results from the proposal.
4. How and by whom will the expected or anticipated results be used?
5. Information on the key personnel involved in the proposed project.
    a) Qualifications.
    b) Are they replaceable?
    c) Who will provide overall direction and supervision?
    d) Are all these persons now available in the applying institution?
        If so, are they on the institution's regular payroll or a project budget?
        If the latter, what project, and what is the source of funds?
6. Project budget by major headings, i.e., salaries and titles of each of the professionals, total of budgets for each of the following classifications: technicians, clerical services, equipment, expendable supplies, travel, etc.
    a) Show amounts applying instituiton is contributing, either in "kind" or in cash.
    b) Show amounts received from other grant-making agencies.
7. How long will the project run?
8. Has this proposal been submitted to other grant-making organizations, including federal and state agencies? Has it been declined or is it still pending?
9. A statement by grant applicant describing its proposed method(s) of evaluation of the outcomes of the project.
10. Provide a copy of your most recent financial audit.

From the Jerome Foundation, Inc. brochure for grant applications.

and arrive at a consensus on the value of the proposed project. It is also good for the grantee, because if one foundation favors the idea, chances are that the others will want to join the effort. The last paragraph gives the officer at the foundation a clear fix on when he will be contacted by the prospective grantee, and there-

fore a clear idea of how much time he will have to deal with the request and set up a meeting.

The simple principles demonstrated in this letter are adequate for the preliminary letter approach to any source in the private sector, and should be part of any grantwriter's arsenal. The first impression is often the crucial one, and that first letter has to motivate the reader to examine the entire proposal, budget, and addenda, and then act!

Many funding organizations provide applicants with descriptions. Two foundations that do provide detailed outlines for application, including funding priorities and subjects to be addressed are, Jerome Foundation, Inc., a private foundation, and The New York Community Trust, a community foundation. Since these outlines constitute excellent guides for application to *any* funding organization in the private sector, they are reprinted here.

INDEX